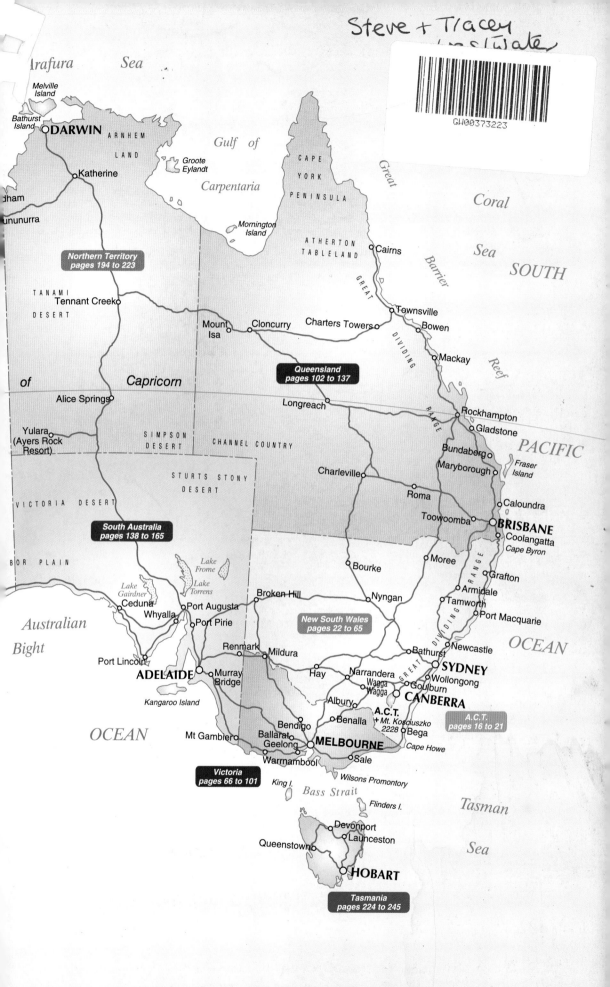

Arafura Sea

Melville
Island
Bathurst
Island
DARWIN
ARNHEM
LAND

Gulf of
Carpentaria

Groote
Eylandt

CAPE
YORK
PENINSULA

Coral

Sea SOUTH

dham
Katherine
ununurra

Mornington
Island

ATHERTON
TABLELAND

Cairns

Great

Barrier

TANAMI
DESERT
Tennant Creek

Mount
Isa
Cloncurry
Charters Towers
Townsville
Bowen

GREAT

DIVIDING

Mackay

Reef

Capricorn

of

Alice Springs

Longreach

Rockhampton
Gladstone

RANGE

PACIFIC

Yulara
(Ayers Rock
Resort)

SIMPSON
DESERT

CHANNEL COUNTRY

Charleville

Bundaberg
Maryborough

Fraser
Island

STURTS STONY
DESERT

Roma

VICTORIA DESERT

Toowoomba

Caloundra

BRISBANE
Coolangatta
Cape Byron

Bourke

Moree

Grafton

BOR PLAIN

Lake
Frome
Lake
Torrens

Broken Hill

Nyngan

Armidale
Tamworth
Port Macquarie

GREAT

Lake
Gairdner

Ceduna
Whyalla
Port Augusta
Port Pirie

DIVIDING

Newcastle

OCEAN

Australian
Bight

Port Lincoln

ADELAIDE
Murray
Bridge

Renmark
Mildura

Hay

Narrandera
Wagga
Wagga
Albury

Bathurst
SYDNEY
Wollongong
Goulburn
CANBERRA

RANGE

GREAT

Kangaroo Island

OCEAN

Mt Gambier

Bendigo
Benalla
Ballarat
Geelong
MELBOURNE
Warrnambool
Sale

A.C.T.
+Mt. Kosciuszko
2228
Bega

Cape Howe

King I.

Bass Strait

Wilsons Promontory

Flinders I.

Tasman

Sea

Devonport
Launceston

Queenstown

HOBART

Published in Australia by Gregory's Publishing Company
(A division of Universal Publishers Pty Ltd)
ABN 83 000 087 132

The Publisher would be pleased to receive additional or updated material, or suggestions for future editions.
Please address these to the Publishing Manager at Universal Publishers Pty Ltd.
If you would like to use any of the maps in this book please contact the CMS Manager at Universal Publishers Pty Ltd.

Marketed and distributed by Universal Publishers Pty Ltd

New South Wales: 1 Waterloo Road,
Macquarie Park 2113
Ph: (02) 9857 3700 Fax: (02) 9888 9850

Queensland: 1 Manning Street,
South Brisbane 4101
Ph: (07) 3844 1051 Fax: (07) 3844 4637

South Australia:
Freecall: 1800 021 987

Victoria: 585 Burwood Road,
Hawthorn 3122
Ph: (03) 9818 4455 Fax: (03) 9818 6123

Western Australia: 38a Walters Drive,
Osborne Park 6017
Ph: (08) 9244 2488 Fax: (08) 9244 2554

International distribution
Ph: (61) 2 9857 3700 Fax: (61) 2 9888 9850

1st edition published 2000

Cover design and internal design by DIZign

Cartography, research and writing, photographic research and DTP, project management and editing by the staff of Universal Publishers Pty Ltd.

PlanBookTravel assisted with the following for this edition: research, photographic research, DTP, copy editing, cartography and indexing.

Printed by: Craft Print Pte Ltd

Disclaimer
The publisher disclaims any responsibility to any person for loss or damage suffered from any use of this atlas for any purpose. While considerable care has been taken by the publisher in researching and compiling this atlas, the publisher accepts no responsibility for errors or omissions. No person should rely upon this atlas for the purpose of making any business, investment or real estate decision.

The representation of any maps of any road or track is not necessarily evidence of public right of way. Third parties who have provided information to the publisher concerning the roads and other matters did not warrant to the publisher that the information was complete, accurate or current or that any of the proposals of any body will eventuate and, accordingly, the publisher provides no such warranty.

Acknowledgments
This atlas was produced with the help of state and regional tourist organisations and local tourist offices throughout Australia, whose kind assistance is gratefully acknowledged.

Photographic Acknowledgements

The publisher would like to gratefully acknowledge the following individuals and organisations for their generosity in supplying photographs and images, and for their permission to reproduce photographic material used in this book.

Bill Bachman p.166-7 Flinders Island Area Marketing & Development Office p.242 (T) Geoff Higgins/Photography E-Biz pp.4-5,9,11,12 Grant Nichol p.10 Jeff Drewitz pp.167 (T),168 (T & B), 186 (BL), 188 (T), 193, 224-225, 226, 240 (T), 244 (BR) Northern Territory Tourist Commission pp.194, 195, 196, 216, 218, 219, 220, 221, 222, 223 Richard Newton p.242 (B) South Australian Tourism Commision pp.138, 139, 140, 156, 158, 159, 160, 161, 162, 164, 165 Steven David Miller pp.225 (T), 240 (BR) Tamsin O'Neill p.244 (T & BL) Tourism New South Wales pp.16, 17, 18, 22, 23, 24, 46, 47, 50, 52, 54, 56, 57, 58, 60, 62, 63, 64 Tourism Queensland pp.7, 102, 103, 104, 122, 124. 126. 128, 130, 132, 133, 134, 136 Tourism Tasmania pp.239, 243 Tourism Victoria pp.8, 66, 67, 68, 86, 87, 90, 91, 92, 94, 96, 98, 99, 100 Western Australian Tourism Commission pp.186 (T & BR), 188 (BL & BR), 191, 192

FRONT COVER & TITLE PAGE
Main Photograph: Australian Scenics
Small Photographs: Photolibrary.com (T & M) Australian Scenics (B)

BACK COVER
Tourism New South Wales, Tourism Victoria, Bill Bachman, Tourism Queensland, Northern Territory Tourist Commission, and South Australian Tourism Commission

ROAD ATLAS OF
AUSTRALIA

SECOND EDITION

Contents

The Pinnacles Desert, Nambung National Park, Western Australia

Explanation of Map Symbols

MOTORWAY	HUME HIGHWAY		Dual Carriageway	✈ Aerodrome
HIGHWAY	PACIFIC HIGHWAY		Metroad	✈ Airport
HIGHWAY	NEPEAN HIGHWAY	Sealed Unsealed	Through Route	✚ Ambulance
MORT ST	VULTURE ST	Sealed Unsealed	Major Road	Beach
LAWSON RD	HONEYPOT RD	Sealed Unsealed	Minor Road	Boat Ramp
LEURA ST		Sealed Unsealed	Street	Wiso Bore — Bore
			Railway line, station	Building
🚲 🚶	🚲 🚶	🚲 🚶	Cycle, Walking Track	▲ Camping Ground
			Ferry Route	Caravan Park

Coolong ⌒ Caves — Cave

◎ SYNDEY
State Capital or Population 1 000 000 plus

12 Cumulative distance

○ Geelong
City - Population 100 000 - 1 000 000

Cumulative distance marker

○ Bendigo
City - Population 50 000 - 99 999

Forest Recreation Reserve

○ Albany
Town - Population 20 000 - 50 000

Golf Course

○ **Ulverstone**
Town - Population 5 000 - 20 000

✚ Hospital

○ Childers
Town - Population 1 000 - 5 000

Cluny — Hydro-Electric Power Station

○ Elliott
Town - Population 200 - 1000

Information Centre

○ Acheron
Locality - Population under 200

5 Intermediate distance

□ Birrimba
Homestead

Lighthouse

♠ Arawerr
Aboriginal Community

Lookout

SYDNEY
Major Centre

① Metroad Route Marker

Frankston
Main Centre

The Granites — Mine, Fossicking Area

Toowong
Suburb

Burke & Wills Memorial — Monument

Aboriginal Land

+ Glebe Hill 135 — Mountain, height in metres

Coral Reef

23 A1 A1 — National Route Marker

Educational Institution

Della Gas Field — Oil/Gas Field

Mall (City Map)

One Way Street

Marine Park

P Parking Area

National Park

Picnic Area

Other Areas

★ ▪ Point of Interest

Prohibited Area

○ Roundabout

Reserve, State Park, Conservation Park

The Granites — Ruins

Sand

Rocket, 1880 — Shipwreck

State Forest

Shopping Centre

20 C3 — State Route Marker

Toilets

○ Alice Well — Well

Winery

Kewarra Beach, Queensland

Touring Australia

It is often difficult for visitors, as well as many Australians, to grasp just how huge Australia is: approximately the same size as the European continent, excluding the former USSR, or the mainland area of the United States of America.

This vast land is the world's flattest and, apart from Antarctica, driest continent, but includes an extraordinary diversity of environments. These range from the tropical rainforests and coral reefs of the north-east to the monsoonal wetlands of the north, the red deserts and salt lakes of the Outback and the more temperate forests, coastal plains, mountain ranges (and winter snowfields) of the south-east. Australia's famous Outback stretches almost the entire way from western Queensland and New South Wales to the coastline of Western Australia. At 2228m above sea-level, Mt Kosciuszko, in the Great Dividing Range, is the highest point in Australia, a mere foothill by international standards. There are more than 700 national parks on the continent and 15 unique sites have been declared World Heritage Areas.

Touring Australia requires time and planning, but the rewards are substantial for travellers with a sense of adventure who are well prepared. Please refer to pages 10 to 13 regarding planning your trip and hints for motorists.

Australia's state capitals are hundreds of kilometres apart, but they are linked by sealed highways which are suitable for all vehicles, including caravans. Rural areas of Australia can be accessed from networks of graded roads, although 4-wheel drive vehicles may be necessary in some areas of the Outback, mountain ranges and certain national parks.

The Gippsland Lakes from the air, Victoria

| Total area = 7,686,291 sq km | Length of coast = 37,000 km | Average elevation = 330 m |

Red desert earth of Uluru-Kata Tjuta National Park, Northern Territory

Australia: The Land Down Under

- Area: 7 686 291 km^2

- World's smallest continent and largest island

- World's lowest and flattest continent; average elevation is only 330m; Lake Eyre is 15m below sea level

- World records: Uluru (largest monolith); Great Barrier Reef (longest coral reef); Nullarbor Plain (largest flat bedrock surface); Simpson Desert (largest sand ridge desert); and Mount Augustus (largest exposed rocky outcrop)

- Sixth largest country in the world after the Russian Federation, Canada, China, USA and Brazil

- Fifth longest coastline in the world with the world's largest Exclusive Economic Marine Zone when offshore territories are included

- The Great Dividing Range is the fourth longest mountain range in the world

- About 39% of Australia lies within the tropical zone and 61% in the temperate zone

- Australia extends across 40° of longitude and almost 33° of latitude

- World's oldest fossilised life forms—cyanobacteria (about 3.8 billion years old) have been found in Western Australia

Planning Your Trip

Before any road trip, either short or long, it is important to be prepared. Following are a few tips to help you have a successful trip.

Passes and Permits

Passes and permits are necessary for travelling through certain parts of Northern Australia and South Australia. If needed, they should be organised before you begin the journey.

If you are planning to visit or travel through Aboriginal land, you must obtain a special permit. There are two types of permit. A transit permit will allow you to drive through Aboriginal land but you cannot stop or leave the designated road. An entry permit will allow you to enter a certain area for a specific reason and period of time. Permits are obtained from the relevant Land Council and you should allow up to 3 weeks for processing your application. The principal Land Councils are:

Central Land Council (for Central Australia permits) ph: (08) 8951 6211; Northern Land Council (for Top End permits) ph: (08) 8920 5100.

You may need a Desert Parks Pass if travelling into the desert parks of northern South Australia. The passes are issued by the Dept for Environment and Heritage and are an alternative to the daily camping permits issued for entering the parks. They include detailed maps, information on first aid and survival skills. Desert Parks Hotline: 1800 816 078.

What to take

As much of your holiday will be spent driving in the car, take lots of comfortable clothes. Even if travelling in summer, take at least one set of warm clothing as nights can still be cool. Also, take more changes of clothes if the area you will be exploring is cold and wet. Soft baggage is ideal for car journeys as they can be squashed into tight spaces in the vehicle.

Commonly forgotten items that you should pack include hats, walking shoes, sunblock, sunglasses, insect repellent and a camera. It is a good idea to keep tissues, extra water and snacks, maps and a compass in the car, within easy reach. The glovebox can be used to keep important papers that you may need during your trip, including vehicle registration, the number of your insurance policy and medical prescriptions.

First aid kit

You must always keep a first aid kit in your car. If you are driving to remote areas it is advisable to do a certified first aid course. Commercially prepared kits are available from chemists and camping equipment shops. Alternatively, you can make up your own kit in a clean, waterproof container.

The following are recommended inclusions for a first aid kit:

- Absorbent gauze
- Antihistamine (for bee stings)
- Aspirin or paracetamol
- Bandaids and assortment of adhesive dressings
- Conforming bandages
- Alcohol swabs
- Antiseptic cream and swabs (e.g. Betadine)
- Car-sickness tablets
- Clinical thermometer
- Cotton wool

Before you leave, don't forget:

- Secure home carefully
- Cancel deliveries — milk/paper
- Ask a neighbour to collect mail
- Turn off water
- Leave a blind open, a light on
- Organise pet care
- Leave contact details and key with neighbour

If you are camping don't forget:

- Tent, tent pegs, groundsheet
- Rope, shovel, axe and hammer
- Mattress and bedding
- Folding table, chairs, lamp
- Camp oven, gas stove and gas bottle
- Matches (preferably waterproof)
- Saucepans, frying pan and billy
- Mixing bowl, crockery, cutlery
- Can opener, knives, cutting board
- Airtight food storage containers
- Washing up gear
- Cooler for food and ice
- Water container
- Torch and pocket knife

- Crepe bandages
- Eye bath
- Pen torch
- Saline eyewash
- Sterile dressings
- Stingose
- Triangular bandages
- Current first aid book
- Latex gloves
- Safety pins
- Scissors
- Sticking plaster
- Tongue depressor
- Tweezers

Car Preparation

Nowadays many of Australia's roads are sealed or well-graded, so most cars can drive on them without any problems. However, if venturing off the beaten track is more to your liking, you should investigate hiring or buying a 4WD. If planning to tow a caravan or trailer, stay on the sealed roads, regardless of whether you are travelling in a 4WD.

Before you leave home

Make sure that your car has been checked by a qualified mechanic. If you are towing a caravan or trailer, get them serviced as well — particularly the tyres, lights, blinkers and general condition of their working parts.

Some things that need checking, both before and during the trip, are:
- Battery and mountings
- Tyre condition and pressure (remember the spare!)
- Wheel balance and alignment
- Wheel bearings
- Windscreen wipers - blades and reservoir
- Brake system
- Exhaust system
- Cooling system - radiator, hoses and thermostat
- Engine drive belts
- Automatic transmission
- Heater and demister
- Air conditioning
- Lights
- Filters - air, oil and fuel
- Suspension
- Oil and coolant

Extras to take

Carry a spare set a keys, set of spanners and screwdrivers, jumper leads, WD lubricant, spare engine drive belt(s), radiator hoses, light globes and fuses, fire extinguisher, a jack and tools for changing tyres.

Off the beaten track — What to carry in your 4WD

Along with the extras you should take on any driving holiday, consider taking:
- Tyre pump — 12 volt
- Extra water & oil
- Towing hooks, heavy rope or tow cable
- Flares for signals
- Breakdown warning reflector
- Cooling system leak sealer
- Super glue
- Insulating tape
- Radiator insect screen
- Service & repair manual
- Plastic sheet
- Water bucket
- Ignition points & condenser (if applicable)
- Fuel filter
- Shovel & axe
- Spark plugs
- Heater hoses & clamps
- Brake fluid
- Tyre or tube repair kit
- Inflatable bull bag

Carry excess fuel in metal jerry cans. Plastic containers often crack as the container constantly rubs against parts of the car.

Store extra fuel on the back of the 4WD or in a trailer.

Do not pack fuel on the roof racks or inside the vehicle in case of fire.

Motoring Hints

This practical information is designed to make your trip more comfortable and enjoyable.

Packing the car

Don't overload your car or 4WD as it will cause suspension problems. Have the suspension strengthened if you think you may have to overload the car.

Pack heavy items in the cabin, boot or trailer. The weight of heavy items on the roof could easily throw the car off balance. When packing lighter items on a roof rack, make the load lower at the front and higher at the back so there is little wind resistance.

If carrying tools and equipment inside the car, make sure they are tightly secured. It is sensible to install a cargo barrier for this purpose. Emergency equipment, such as a fire extinguisher, must be easily accessible. Keep close at hand the things you may want or need during the journey.

Fuel Economy

Fuel consumption is affected by both the condition of the car and where it is driven. Here are some ways to help conserve your petrol:

- Avoid delays (peak hour traffic or scheduled bridge closures)
- Distribute weight through the car evenly
- Service the car regularly
- If held up in traffic, turn off engine if safe to do so
- Drive as smoothly as possible
- Ensure tyres are inflated to ideal pressure and wheel alignment and balance are correct
- Make sure handbrake is fully released when car is mobile, and foot operated brakes are not dragging
- If using roof racks, keep load as low as possible to avoid excess drag
- Avoid driving at high speeds
- Use air conditioner only when absolutely necessary

When covering long distances on remote roads, you must know your car's fuel consumption. Here is a basic formula for working out fuel consumption:

Total litres ÷ $\dfrac{\text{total km}}{100}$ = litres per 100km

or 100 x total litres ÷ total km = litres per 100km

Example 60 litres ÷ $\dfrac{300\text{km}}{100}$ = 20 litres per 100km

Beating fatigue

Today, 7 per cent of all accidents are due to driver fatigue. In country areas it accounts for 30 per cent of fatal accidents.

Here are some tips to help combat driver fatigue:

- Take a break from driving every 2 hours
- Change drivers at this point
- Pull over and stop when drowsiness or discomfort occurs
- Wear comfortable clothes and sit upright with good back support
- Keep the windscreen clean and clear
- Avoid alcohol and eating a heavy meal before driving
- Get a good night's sleep before a long drive

Travelling with children

To prevent boredom and fighting after the novelty of travelling wears off, try the following:

- Bring child's favourite toys
- Play music and sing together
- Play family car games (there are books available on these)
- Stop for frequent breaks

Car sickness is very common in children. To lessen the symptoms you should:

- Drive as smoothly as possible
- Keep windows down
- Don't let children read or write while car is moving.
- Don't let children watch things flashing past — encourage them to watch things in the distance

Motoring Survival

Driving in Northern Australia

When travelling around northern Australia, the climate can dictate when to travel.

There are two distinct seasons experienced in northern Australia: the wet season (November to April) and the dry (May to October). Generally, the dry season has comfortable daytime temperatures and cool nights. It is the best time of year to explore the Northern Territory, far north Queensland and northern Western Australia. The wet season is characterised by monsoonal rainfall and it is not a pleasant time for a driving holiday. It is quite common with the heavy rainfall for roads to become impassable.

Driving in Alpine Regions

When driving through the alpine regions of Australia in winter, problems may occur.

Before leaving home:
- Have tyres and brakes checked, add anti-freeze to radiator
- Renew windscreen wiper blades
- Check heater and demister are working properly
- Take blankets and/or sleeping bags
- A torch, old piece of rug or plastic sheet and small shovel could be useful

Some techniques for driving in snow and ice worth learning are:
- Don't put the handbrake on when parking unless the slope demands it
- Use brakes as little as possible to avoid skidding
- Carefully control speed — on downhill sections use low gear instead of brakes
- Going uphill, use higher gears as over-revving can cause wheel slip
- When changing down gears, do it smoothly with engine speed the same as wheel speed
- Put lights on low beam and chains on tyres when it is snowing

Outback Motoring

When driving on unsealed roads there are special techniques that can be employed to avoid problems such as getting bogged.
- On sand, keep 4WD in a straight line — if you have to make a turn, turn the wheel quickly, then back to the original position
- Drive carefully at a safe speed on dirt roads
- When making a creek crossing, check the underlying surface, depth and flow of water — drive slowly in centre of crossing, keep the wheels straight and do not change gear midstream
- When overtaking, beware of soft or loose verges and the dust caused from road trains — if behind a road train, pull over to the side of the road until the dust has settled.
- If stuck in sand, use floor mats to give support and traction. Use hub caps as jack supports — lowering tyre pressure also assists traction

Driving in fog
- Pull off road and wait for fog to lift if in zero or near-zero visibility
- Put parking and hazard lights on
- Keep seat-belt fastened
- If driving in fog, go slowly and keep fog lights on
- Avoid crossing roads or busy highways when visibility is reduced

Survival Hints
- Don't panic — think of a course of action
- Stay with your vehicle – it provides shelter, increasing chances of survival. Spotting a car is easier than finding a person
- Conserve food and water — always carry enough food and water to keep you supplied for a few days (4 litres of water per person per day)
- Stay in the shade — keep clothes on to help protect against exposure
- Prepare adequate signals — if in a remote area use your flares or light a fire to attract attention

Surviving a Bushfire

If you get caught in a bushfire, it is important that you don't keep driving through the dense smoke. Follow the points below for survival. Also note that there is little risk of the petrol tank exploding in a bushfire.
- Pull to the side of the road away from the leading edge of the fire and stop
- Switch on headlights
- Stay in car
- Wind up windows and close air vents
- Crouch in car and shelter body
- Stay there until fire passes

Distance Chart

Approximate Distance	Adelaide SA	Albany WA	Albury NSW	Alice Springs NT	Ayers Rock/Yulara NT	Bairnsdale VIC	Ballarat VIC	Bathurst NSW	Bega NSW	Bendigo VIC	Bordertown SA	Bourke NSW	Brisbane QLD	Broken Hill NSW	Broome WA	Bunbury WA	Cairns QLD	Canberra ACT	Carnarvon WA	Ceduna SA	Charleville QLD	Coober Pedy SA	Darwin NT	Dubbo NSW	Esperance WA	Eucla WA	Geraldton WA	Grafton NSW
Adelaide SA		2644	946	1526	1570	1008	611	1201	1343	638	267	1302	2049	514	4261	2874	3308	1196	3590	767	1755	837	3018	1197	2168	1256	3117	1910
Albany WA	2644		3538	3560	3604	3652	3255	3658	3799	3251	2911	3541	4357	2753	2632	369	5624	3653	1303	1875	3994	2871	4425	3505	476	1388	830	4218
Albury NSW	946	3644		2420	2464	373	430	437	485	308	679	905	1389	984	5115	3768	2656	339	4484	1663	1358	1731	3912	537	3062	2150	4011	1214
Alice Springs NT	1526	3560	2420		442	2534	2137	2540	2681	2164	1793	2423	3239	1635	2735	3790	2414	2535	4506	1685	2332	689	1492	2387	3084	2172	4033	3095
Ayers Rock/Yulara NT	1570	3604	2464	442		2578	2181	2584	2725	2177	1837	2467	3283	1679	3177	3834	2856	2579	4550	1729	2774	733	1934	2431	3128	2216	4077	3139
Bairnsdale VIC	1008	3652	373	2534	2578		397	737	335	437	741	1308	1744	1134	5269	3882	3059	450	4598	1777	1761	1845	4026	940	3176	2264	4125	1409
Ballarat VIC	611	3255	430	2137	2181	397		953	732	122	344	1303	1779	819	4872	3485	3054	770	4201	1380	1756	1448	3629	935	2779	1867	3728	1643
Bathurst NSW	1201	3658	437	2540	2584	737	953		501	765	1136	571	1047	955	5275	3888	2322	287	4604	1783	1024	1851	4032	203	3182	2270	4131	856
Bega NSW	1343	3799	485	2681	2725	335	732	501		772	1076	1072	1409	1245	5416	4217	3110	214	4745	1924	1525	1992	4173	704	3323	2411	4272	1074
Bendigo VIC	638	3251	308	2164	2177	437	122	765	772		371	1129	1613	697	4899	3512	2880	647	4228	1137	1582	1475	3656	761	2806	1894	3755	1474
Bordertown SA	267	2911	679	1793	1837	741	344	1136	1076	371		1453	1937	689	4528	3141	3204	1018	3857	1036	1906	1104	3285	1085	2436	1523	3384	1798
Bourke NSW	1302	3541	905	2423	2467	1308	1303	571	1072	1129	1453		1220	788	4440	3771	2077	858	4487	1666	453	1734	3197	368	3065	2153	4014	1081
Brisbane QLD	2049	4357	1389	3239	3283	1744	1779	1047	1409	1613	1937	1220		1604	4763	4587	1701	1239	5303	2482	776	2550	3250	852	3881	2969	4830	335
Broken Hill NSW	514	2753	984	1635	1679	1134	819	955	1245	697	689	788	1604		4350	2983	2871	1139	3699	878	1241	946	3127	752	2277	1356	3226	1460
Broome WA	4261	2632	5115	2735	3177	5269	4872	5275	5416	4899	4528	4440	4763	4350		2409	4069	5270	1461	4150	3987	3424	1861	4808	2945	3663	1834	5008
Bunbury WA	2874	369	3768	3790	3834	3882	3485	3888	4217	3512	3141	3771	4587	2983	2409		5854	4070	1080	2105	4224	3101	4270	3735	845	1618	607	4448
Cairns QLD	3308	5624	2656	2414	2856	3059	3054	2322	3110	2880	3204	2077	1701	2871	4069	5854		2609	5496	3749	1624	3103	2826	2119	5148	4236	5861	2036
Canberra ACT	1196	3653	339	2535	2579	450	770	287	214	647	1018	858	1239	1139	5270	4070	2609		4599	1778	1311	1846	4027	490	3177	2265	4126	979
Carnarvon WA	3590	1303	4484	4506	4550	4598	4201	4604	4745	4228	3857	4487	5303	3699	1461	1080	5496	4599		2821	4940	3817	5998	4451	1779	2334	473	5164
Ceduna SA	769	1875	1663	1685	1729	1777	1380	1783	1924	1137	1036	1666	2482	878	4150	2105	3749	1778	2821		2119	996	3177	1630	1399	487	2348	2343
Charleville QLD	1755	3994	1358	2332	2774	1761	1176	1024	1525	1582	1906	453	776	1241	3987	4224	1624	1311	4940	2119		2187	2744	821	3518	2606	4467	1132
Coober Pedy SA	837	2871	1731	689	733	1845	1448	1851	1992	1475	1104	1734	2550	946	3424	3101	3103	1846	3817	996	2187		2181	1698	2395	1483	3344	2411
Darwin NT	3018	4425	3912	1492	1934	4026	3629	4032	4173	3656	3285	3197	3250	3127	1861	4270	2826	4027	5998	3177	2744	2181		3879	4576	3664	3695	3847
Dubbo NSW	1197	3505	537	2387	2431	940	935	203	704	761	1085	368	852	752	4808	3735	2119	490	4451	1630	821	1698	3879		3029	2117	3978	713
Esperance WA	2168	476	3062	3084	3128	3176	2779	3182	3323	2806	2436	3065	3881	2277	2945	845	5148	3177	1779	1399	3518	2395	4576	3029		912	740	3742
Eucla WA	1256	1388	2150	2172	2216	2265	1867	2270	2411	1894	1523	2153	2969	1356	3663	1618	4236	2265	2334	487	2606	1483	3664	2117	912		1861	2830
Geraldton WA	3117	830	4011	4033	4077	4125	3728	4131	4272	3755	3384	4014	4830	3226	1834	607	5861	4126	473	2348	4467	3344	3695	3978	740	1861		4691
Grafton NSW	1910	4218	1214	3095	3139	1409	1643	856	1074	1474	1788	1081	335	1460	5008	4448	2036	979	5164	2343	1132	2411	3847	713	3742	2830	4691	
Horsham VIC	425	3069	521	1951	1995	583	186	978	918	213	158	1342	1826	609	4686	3299	3093	860	4015	1194	1795	1262	3443	974	2593	1681	3542	1687
Kalgoorlie/Boulder WA	2173	885	3067	3089	3133	3181	2784	3187	3328	2811	2440	3070	3886	2282	2824	779	5153	3182	4285	2332	3523	2400	4581	3034	409	917	944	3747
Katherine NT	2709	4116	3603	1183	1625	3717	3320	3723	3864	3347	2976	2888	3211	2818	1552	3961	2517	3718	3013	2868	2435	1872	309	3570	4267	3355	3886	3456
Kununurra WA	3221	3604	4115	1695	2137	4229	3832	4235	4376	3859	3488	3400	3723	3330	1040	3449	3029	4230	2501	3380	2947	2384	821	4082	4779	3867	2874	3968
Longreach QLD	2269	4508	1872	1818	2260	2275	2270	1538	2208	2096	2420	967	1290	1755	3473	4736	1368	1825	4934	2633	514	2507	2230	1335	4364	3452	5307	1535
Mackay QLD	2741	4995	2027	2449	2891	2484	2479	1745	2381	2305	2629	1502	972	2296	4104	5225	729	1980	5565	3120	1049	3138	2861	1490	4519	3607	5468	1307
Meekatharra WA	3453	1166	4347	4133	4575	4461	4064	4467	4608	4091	3720	4369	5166	3562	1466	943	5535	4462	1655	2684	4803	3680	3327	4313	1501	2197	1186	5027
Melbourne VIC	726	3370	316	2252	2296	282	115	838	617	155	459	1188	1672	852	4987	3600	2939	655	4273	1495	1641	1563	3744	820	2894	1982	3843	1533
Mildura VIC	396	2853	685	1735	1779	835	520	805	946	398	390	1087	1903	299	4470	3146	2920	800	3799	1165	1540	1046	3227	801	2377	1652	3326	1514
Moree NSW	1570	3878	910	2760	2804	1313	1308	576	1077	1134	1458	741	479	1125	4739	4108	2871	863	4824	2003	752	1971	4252	373	3402	2490	4351	368
Mt Gambier SA	435	3079	793	1961	2005	729	332	1285	1040	430	183	1604	2067	854	4696	3309	3310	1122	4025	1204	2057	1272	3453	1191	2298	1691	3552	2010
Mt Isa QLD	2911	5150	2514	1176	1618	2917	2912	2180	2681	2730	3062	1609	1932	2397	2831	4966	1238	2467	4292	2861	1156	1865	1588	1977	4260	4094	4665	2177
Newcastle NSW	1554	3868	711	2907	2951	906	1142	353	571	1019	1390	731	838	1308	5171	4291	2320	476	4814	1993	1184	2061	3974	363	3392	2480	4341	503
Perth WA	2692	405	3586	3608	3652	3700	3303	3706	3847	3330	2959	3589	4405	2801	2227	182	5672	3701	898	1923	4042	2919	4088	3553	740	1436	425	4691
Port Augusta SA	305	2339	1199	1221	1265	1313	916	1319	1460	943	572	1202	2018	414	3956	2569	3285	1314	3285	464	1655	532	2713	1166	1863	951	2812	1899
Port Hedland WA	4315	2028	5209	3271	3713	5323	4926	5329	5470	4953	4582	5212	5299	4424	604	1805	4673	5324	857	3546	5665	4542	2465	5176	2363	3059	1330	5612
Port Lincoln SA	642	2295	1536	1558	1602	1650	1253	1656	1797	1280	909	1539	2355	751	4293	2525	3622	1651	3241	420	1992	869	3050	1503	1819	907	2768	2216
Renmark SA	239	2696	842	1578	1622	992	613	962	1103	555	269	1244	2060	456	4313	2926	3077	957	3642	821	1697	889	3070	958	2220	1613	3169	1671
Rockhampton QLD	2354	4662	1694	2499	2941	2097	2092	1360	1861	1918	2242	1303	639	1909	4154	4892	1062	1647	5608	2787	850	2855	2911	1157	4186	3274	5135	974
Sydney NSW	1401	3872	558	2754	2798	753	989	200	418	866	1237	771	991	1155	5211	4138	2473	323	4854	2033	1224	2101	4127	403	3432	2657	4381	656
Tamworth NSW	1532	3840	872	2722	2766	1275	1270	538	2763	1096	1420	703	577	1023	5005	4070	2210	825	4786	1965	1018	2033	3715	335	3364	2452	4313	373
Tennant Creek NT	2040	4074	2934	514	956	3048	2651	3054	3195	2678	2307	2271	2594	2149	2221	4304	1900	3049	3682	2199	1818	1203	978	2901	3598	2686	4055	2839
Toowoomba QLD	1916	4224	1256	3106	3150	1659	1654	922	1423	1480	1804	936	125	1471	4556	4454	1707	1209	5170	2349	651	2417	3395	719	3478	2836	4697	452
Townsville QLD	2969	5377	2309	2067	2509	2712	2707	1975	2763	2533	2857	1730	1354	2525	3722	5507	347	1662	5183	3402	1277	2756	2479	1772	4801	3889	5556	1689
Wagga Wagga NSW	958	3415	123	2297	2341	505	554	411	384	466	837	857	1341	861	5032	3645	2608	238	4361	1727	1310	1608	3789	489	2939	2027	3888	1202
Warrnambool VIC	651	941	577	2177	2221	543	277	1099	878	399	399	1449	1933	876	4912	3525	3200	916	4241	1420	1902	1824	3669	1081	2514	1907	3768	1794
West Wyalong NSW	3295	3398	356	2280	2324	738	679	260	617	505	876	624	1108	844	5012	3629	2375	471	4344	1710	1077	1591	3772	256	2922	2010	3871	969

All distances in this chart have been measured over highways and major roads, not necessarily by the shortest route.

Tasmania has not been included. Refer to page 225 for Tasmania distance chart.

Approximate Distance	Horsham VIC	Kalgoorlie/Boulder WA	Katherine NT	Kununurra WA	Longreach QLD	Mackay QLD	Meekatharra WA	Melbourne VIC	Mildura VIC	Moree NSW	Mt Gambier SA	Mt Isa QLD	Newcastle NSW	Perth WA	Port Augusta SA	Port Hedland WA	Port Lincoln SA	Renmark SA	Rockhampton QLD	Sydney NSW	Tamworth NSW	Tennant Creek NT	Toowoomba QLD	Townsville QLD	Wagga Wagga NSW	Warrnambool VIC	West Wyalong NSW
Adelaide SA	425	2173	2709	3221	2269	2741	3453	726	396	1570	435	2911	1554	2692	305	4315	642	239	2354	1401	1532	2040	1916	2969	958	651	941
Albany WA	3069	885	4116	3604	4508	4995	1166	3370	2853	3878	3079	5150	3868	405	2339	2028	2295	2696	4662	3872	3840	4074	4224	5377	3415	3295	3398
Albury NSW	521	3067	3603	4115	1872	2027	4347	316	685	910	793	2514	711	3586	1199	5209	1536	842	1694	558	872	2934	1256	2309	123	577	356
Alice Springs NT	1951	3089	1183	1695	1818	2449	4133	2252	1735	2760	1961	1176	2907	3608	1221	3271	1558	1578	2499	2754	2722	514	3106	2067	2297	2177	2280
Ayers Rock/Yulara NT	1995	3133	1625	2137	2260	2891	4575	2296	1779	2804	2005	1618	2951	3652	1265	3713	1602	1622	2941	2798	2766	956	3150	2509	2341	2221	2324
Bairnsdale VIC	583	3181	3717	4229	2275	2484	4461	282	835	1313	729	2917	906	3700	1313	5323	1650	992	2097	753	1275	3048	1659	2712	505	543	738
Ballarat VIC	186	2784	3320	3832	2270	2479	4064	115	520	1308	332	2912	1142	3303	916	4926	1253	613	2092	989	1270	2651	1654	2707	554	277	679
Bathurst NSW	978	3187	3723	4235	1538	1745	4467	838	805	576	1285	2180	353	3706	1319	5329	1656	962	1360	200	538	3054	922	1975	411	1099	260
Bega NSW	918	3328	3864	4376	2208	2381	4608	617	946	1077	1040	2681	571	3847	1460	5470	1797	1103	1861	418	2763	3195	1423	2763	384	878	617
Bendigo VIC	213	2811	3347	3859	2096	2305	4091	155	398	1134	430	2738	1019	3330	943	4953	1280	555	1918	866	1096	2678	1480	2533	466	399	505
Bordertown SA	158	2440	2976	3488	2420	2629	3720	459	390	1458	183	3062	1390	2959	572	4582	909	269	2242	1237	1420	2307	1804	2857	837	399	876
Bourke NSW	1342	3070	2888	3400	967	1502	4350	1188	1087	741	1604	1609	731	3589	1202	5212	1539	1244	1303	771	703	2271	936	1730	857	1449	624
Brisbane QLD	1826	3886	3211	3723	1290	972	5166	1672	1903	479	2067	1932	838	4405	2018	5299	2355	2060	639	991	577	2594	125	1354	1341	1933	1108
Broken Hill NSW	609	2282	2818	3330	1755	2296	3562	852	299	1125	854	2397	1308	2801	414	4424	751	456	1909	1155	1023	2149	1471	2525	861	876	844
Broome WA	4686	2824	1552	1040	3473	4104	1466	4987	4470	4739	4696	2831	5171	2227	3956	604	4293	4313	4154	5211	5005	2221	4556	3722	5032	4912	5015
Bunbury WA	3299	779	3961	3449	4736	5225	943	3600	3146	4108	3309	4966	4291	182	2569	1805	2525	2926	4892	4138	4070	4304	4454	5507	3645	3525	3628
Cairns QLD	3093	5153	2517	3029	1368	729	5535	2939	2920	2871	3310	1238	2320	5672	3285	4673	3622	3077	1062	2473	2210	1900	1707	347	2608	3200	2375
Canberra ACT	860	3182	3718	4230	1825	1980	4462	655	800	863	1122	2467	476	3701	1314	5324	1651	957	1647	323	825	3049	1209	1662	238	916	471
Carnarvon WA	4015	4285	3013	2501	4934	5565	1655	4273	3799	4824	4025	4292	4814	898	3285	857	3241	3642	5608	4854	4786	3682	5170	5183	4361	4241	4344
Ceduna SA	1194	2332	2868	3380	2633	3120	2684	1495	1165	2003	1204	2861	1993	1923	464	3546	420	821	2787	2033	1965	2199	2349	3402	1727	1420	1710
Charleville QLD	1795	3523	2435	2947	514	1049	4803	1641	1540	752	2057	1156	1184	4042	1655	5665	1992	1697	850	1224	1018	1818	651	1277	1310	1902	1077
Coober Pedy SA	1262	2400	1872	2384	2507	3138	3680	1563	1046	1971	1272	1865	2061	2919	532	4542	869	889	2855	2101	2033	1203	2417	2756	1608	1824	1591
Darwin NT	3443	4581	309	821	2230	2861	3327	3744	3227	4252	3453	1588	3974	4088	2713	2465	3050	3070	2911	4127	3715	978	3395	2479	3789	3669	3772
Dubbo NSW	974	3034	3570	4082	1335	1490	4313	820	801	373	1191	1977	363	3553	1166	5176	1503	958	1157	403	335	2901	719	1772	489	1053	256
Esperance WA	2593	409	4267	4779	4364	4519	1501	2894	2377	3402	2298	4260	3392	740	1863	2363	1819	2220	4186	3432	3364	3598	3478	4801	2939	2514	2922
Eucla WA	1681	917	3355	3867	3452	3607	2197	1982	1652	2490	1691	4094	2480	1436	951	3059	907	1613	3274	2657	2452	2686	2836	3889	2027	1907	2010
Geraldton WA	3542	944	3386	2874	5307	5468	1186	3843	3326	4351	3552	4665	4341	425	2812	1330	2768	3169	5135	4381	4313	4055	4697	5556	3888	3768	3871
Grafton NSW	1687	3747	3456	3968	1535	1307	5027	1514	1514	368	2010	2177	503	4266	1879	5612	2216	1671	974	656	373	2839	452	1689	1202	1794	769
Horsham VIC		2598	3134	3646	2143	2309	3878	301	310	1347	245	2951	1337	3117	730	4740	1067	427	2131	1079	1309	2465	1693	2146	679	313	718
Kalgoorlie/Boulder WA	2598		4272	3864	4369	3358	1358	2899	2382	3407	2608	5011	3397	597	1868	2220	1824	2225	4191	3437	3369	3603	3753	4806	2944	2824	2927
Katherine NT	3134	4272		512	1921	2552	3018	3435	2918	3105	3144	1279	3579	3779	2404	2156	2741	2761	2602	3732	3371	669	3004	2170	3116	3360	3099
Kununurra WA	3646	3864	512		2433	3064	2506	3947	3430	3617	3656	1791	4091	3267	2916	1644	3253	3273	3114	4244	3883	1181	3516	2682	3628	3872	3611
Longreach QLD	2143	4369	1921	2433		793	4289	2155	2054	1184	1670	642	1698	4556	2169	5151	2506	2211	681	1738	1450	1304	1083	1021	1824	2416	1591
Mackay QLD	2309	3358	2552	3064	793		5570	2310	2291	1117	2680	1273	1591	5043	2656	4708	2993	2448	333	1948	1519	1935	1016	382	1979	2571	1746
Meekatharra WA	3878	1358	3018	2506	4289	5570		4179	3662	4687	3583	4297	4677	761	3148	862	3104	3505	5471	4717	4649	3687	6022	4578	4224	3799	4207
Melbourne VIC	301	2899	3435	3947	2155	2310	4179		553	1193	477	2797	1027	3418	1031	5041	1368	710	1977	874	1155	2766	1539	2592	525	261	564
Mildura VIC	310	2382	2918	3430	2054	2291	3662	553		1174	573	2778	1164	2901	514	4524	851	357	1958	1204	1136	2249	1520	2573	562	522	545
Moree NSW	1347	3407	3105	3617	1184	1117	4687	1193	1174		1564	1826	474	3926	1539	5549	1876	1331	784	627	266	2488	1885	1499	862	1454	629
Mt Gambier SA	245	2608	3144	3656	1670	2680	3583	477	573	1564		3168	1554	3127	740	4750	1077	452	2348	1395	1526	2475	1910	2963	896	216	935
Mt Isa QLD	2951	5011	1279	1791	642	1273	4297	2797	2778	1826	3168		2300	4784	2397	3435	2734	2754	1323	2453	2092	662	1725	891	2466	3058	2233
Newcastle NSW	1337	3397	3579	4091	1698	1591	4677	1027	1164	474	1554	2300		3916	1529	5539	1866	1315	1258	153	259	3149	762	1591	610	1288	613
Perth WA	3117	597	3779	3267	4556	5043	761	3418	2901	3926	3127	4784	3916		2387	1623	2343	2744	4710	3956	3888	4122	4272	5325	3463	3343	3446
Port Augusta SA	730	1868	2404	2916	2169	2656	3148	1031	514	1539	740	2397	1529	2387		4010	337	357	2323	1533	1501	1735	1885	2938	1076	956	1059
Port Hedland WA	4759	2220	2156	1644	5151	4708	862	5041	4524	5549	4750	3435	5539	1623	4010		3966	4367	4758	5543	5511	2825	5160	4326	5086	4966	5069
Port Lincoln SA	1067	1824	2741	3253	2506	2993	3104	1368	851	1876	1077	2734	1866	2343	337	3966		694	2660	1870	1838	2072	2222	3275	1413	1293	1396
Renmark SA	427	2225	2761	3273	2211	2448	3505	710	357	1331	452	2754	1315	2744	357	4367	694		2115	1176	1144	2092	1528	2581	719	599	702
Rockhampton QLD	2131	4191	2602	3114	681	333	5471	1977	1958	784	2348	1323	1258	4710	2323	4758	2660	2115		1411	1050	1985	683	715	1646	2238	1411
Sydney NSW	1079	3437	3732	4244	1738	1948	4717	874	1204	627	1395	2453	153	3956	1533	5543	1870	1176	1411		412	3302	915	1744	457	1135	460
Tamworth NSW	1309	3369	3371	3883	1450	1519	4649	1155	1136	266	1526	2092	259	3888	1501	5511	1838	1144	1050	412		2754	503	1765	824	1416	591
Tennant Creek NT	2465	3603	669	1181	1304	1935	3687	2766	2249	3274	2475	662	3149	4122	1735	2825	2072	2092	1985	3302	2754		2387	1553	2811	2691	2794
Toowoomba QLD	1693	3753	3004	3516	1083	1016	6022	1539	1520	1885	1910	1725	762	4272	1885	5160	2222	1528	683	915	503	2387		1398	1208	1800	975
Townsville QLD	2146	4806	2170	2682	1021	382	4578	2592	2573	1499	2963	891	1591	5325	2938	4326	3275	2581	715	1744	1765	1553	1398		2261	2853	2028
Wagga Wagga NSW	679	2944	3116	3628	1824	1979	4224	525	562	862	896	2466	610	3463	1076	5086	1413	719	1646	457	824	2811	1208	2261		786	233
Warrnambool VIC	313	2824	3360	3872	2416	2571	3799	261	522	1454	216	3058	1288	3343	956	4966	1293	599	2238	1135	1416	2691	1800	2853	786		825
West Wyalong NSW	718	2927	3099	3611	1591	1746	4289	564	545	629	935	2233	613	3446	1059	5069	1396	702	1411	460	591	2794	975	2028	233	825	

Australian Capital Territory
The Federal State

The ACT is situated in the Southern Highlands, surrounded by the State of New South Wales. Canberra, the capital city of the ACT, is also the capital city of Australia. Bordered by the Boboyan, Tidbinbilla and Booth mountain ranges, the ACT is close to many national parks including Kosciuszko National Park in New South Wales.

Overlooking the city is the futuristic telecommunications tower on Black Mountain, situated north-west of Canberra. There are panoramic views of the capital from the public galleries on the tower.

Although small in size, the ACT has much for visitors to see when they have exhausted the sight-seeing opportunities in Canberra itself. The mountainous Namadgi National Park covers 48% of the ACT and is the most northern alpine environment in Australia. With amazing views, Aboriginal rock art, rare sub-alpine species of flora and fauna, extensive walking tracks, Namadgi NP is ideal for bushwalking, picnicking and camping.

Another ACT attraction is The Tidbinbilla Nature Reserve. Within easy reach of Canberra, the Reserve is rapidly regenerating after the devastating bushfires of January 2003. Re-opened walks include the Hanging Rock Trail, Church Rock Heritage Loop and the Turkey Hill Geology Trail.

Tourist information

 Canberra and Region
Visitors Centre

330 Northbourne Ave,
Dickson ACT 2602
Ph: (02) 6205 0044
Tollfree: 1300 554 114

Area = 2583 sq km	Covers 0.03% of Australia	Canberra occupies 15 % of the ACT

Australian Capital Territory Key Map

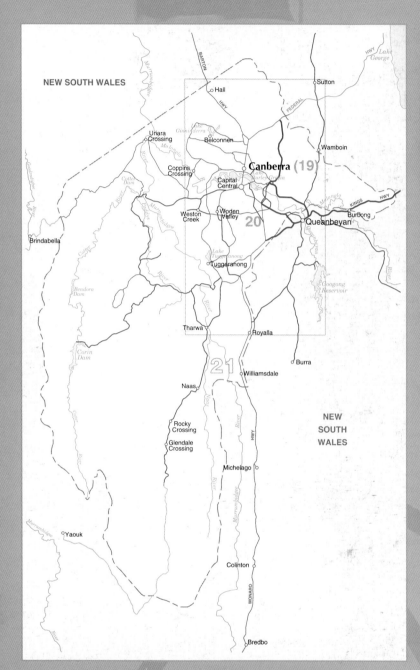

NEW SOUTH WALES

Hall

Sutton

Uriara
Crossing

Lake
Ginninderra

Belconnen

Wamboin

Coppins
Crossing

Canberra (19)

Capital
Central

Lake
Burley Griffin

Brindabella

Weston
Creek

Woden
Valley

20

Queanbeyan

Burbong

KINGS HWY

Cotter
Dam

Bendora
Dam

Lake
Tuggeranong

Tuggeranong

Googong
Reservoir

Corin
Dam

Tharwa

Royalla

Burra

21

Williamsdale

Naas

NEW
SOUTH
WALES

Rocky
Crossing

Glendale
Crossing

Michelago

Yaouk

MONARO HWY

Colinton

Bredbo

Namadgi National Park

Canberra

Parliament House and indigenous mosaic.

Canberra, both the national and the ACT capital, is a planned city built on land acquired by the Commonwealth Government in 1911 after Sydney and Melbourne competed unsuccessfully to be chosen as Australia's premier city. Canberra was designed by American architect Walter Burley Griffin and construction of the first public buildings started in 1913. The original Parliament House building was completed in 1927: although it was only ever intended as a temporary home for the parliament, it was used for the following 60 years.

Canberra occupies approximately 15% of the ACT's land area. The climate is quite severe, ranging from very hot and dry in summer to cold and frosty in winter. The distinct seasons add to the city's charm, especially in autumn, when deciduous trees and shrubs provide a colourful display in the streets, parks and gardens. Floriade, the annual spring flower festival, is celebrated between mid-September and mid-October in Commonwealth Park on the shores of Lake Burley Griffin.

Tourist information

i Canberra and Region
Visitors Centre

330 Northbourne Ave,
Dickson ACT 2602
Ph: (02) 6205 0044
Tollfree: 1300 554 114

Main Attractions

◈ **Australian War Memorial**
This shrine is the most visited building in Canberra. It honours all Australians who fought and died for their country.

◈ **Diplomatic Missions** Most of these are located in the suburban streets of Yarralumla and Red Hill and showcase a variety of international architecture.

◈ **Lake Burley Griffin** Named after the American architect who won the international competition to design the capital.

◈ **National Gallery of Australia** Displays a fine collection of Australian and international art.

◈ **National Museum of Australia** This spectacular new museum opened in 2001 as part of Australia's Centenary of Federation celebrations.

◈ **Parliament House** A focal point for the city, it was designed to merge with and form part of Capital Hill. There are magnificent views of Canberra's cityscape from its grassed roof.

Places of Interest

Ⓐ Anzac Parade **D3**
Ⓑ Australian National Botanic Gardens **A2**
Ⓒ Australian National University **A2**
Ⓓ Australian War Memorial **D2**
Ⓔ Blundell's Cottage **D3**
Ⓕ Canberra Theatre Centre **C2**
Ⓖ Captain Cook Memorial Water Jet **B3**

Ⓗ Casino Canberra **C2**
Ⓘ City Hill Lookout **B2**
Ⓙ Commonwealth Park **C3**
Ⓚ Gorman House Arts Centre **C2**
Ⓛ High Court of Australia **C4**
Ⓜ National Capital Exhibition **C3**
Ⓝ National Carillon **D4**
Ⓞ National Gallery of Australia **C4**

Ⓟ National Library of Australia **B4**
Ⓠ National Museum of Australia **A3**
Ⓡ Old Parliament House and National Portrait Gallery **B4**
Ⓢ Parliament House **B5**
Ⓣ Prime Minister's Lodge **A5**
Ⓤ Questacon – The National Science and Technology Centre **C4**
Ⓥ ScreenSound Australia **B2**

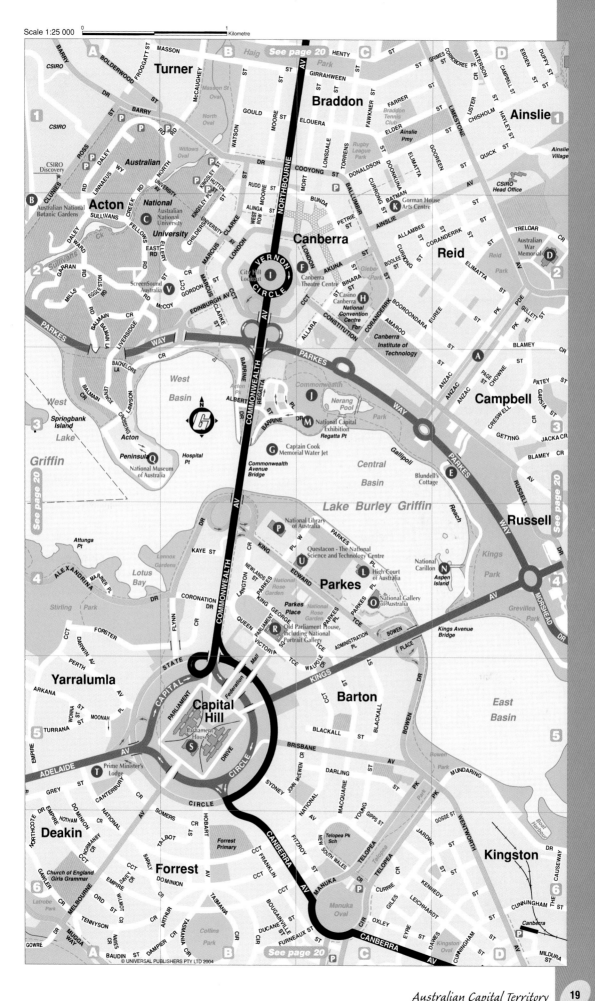

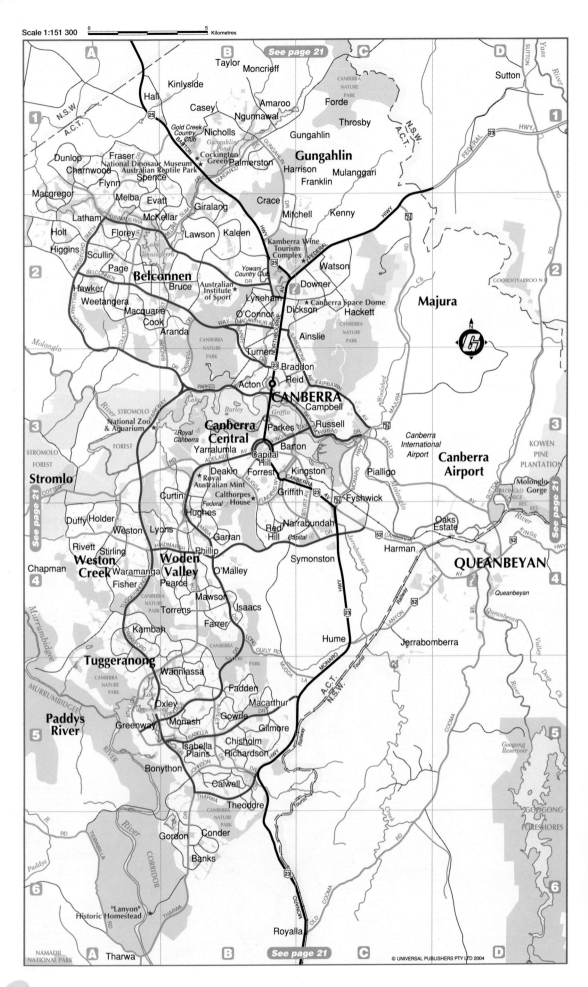

Scale 1:151 300

© UNIVERSAL PUBLISHERS PTY LTD 2004

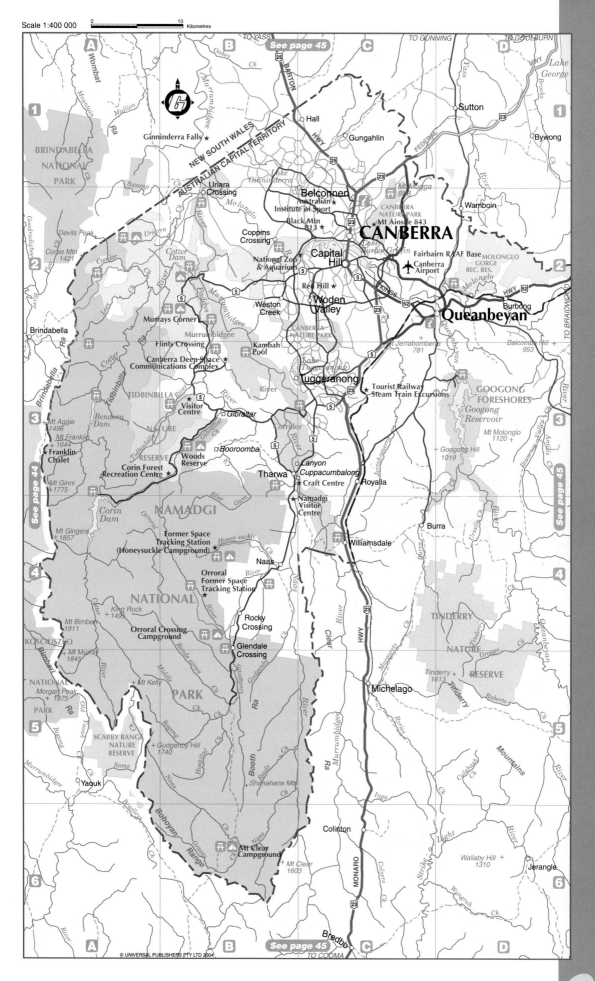

New South Wales
The Premier State

The State of New South Wales was named by Captain James Cook when he landed at Botany Bay in 1770. Seven times the size of England, it is a vast area with a diverse climate ranging from the sub-tropical northern rivers region, to desert-like conditions in the far west, and the ice and snowfalls of the Snowy Mountains in the south.

New South Wales has the largest population of any Australian state or territory and its capital, Sydney, has the largest population of any capital city in Australia.

The range of environments in New South Wales show the country in microcosm: rainforests abound in the north; the romance of the past is preserved along the historic Murray River, which forms the southern boundary of the state; and sparkling surf beaches dot the coast all the way to the Queensland border. New South Wales is also home to the popular alpine region of the Snowy Mountains and Kosciuszko National Park. Completing the picture is the beauty of the rugged outback.

Major highways, all within easy reach of Sydney, will lead tourists to these diverse regions. The Pacific Highway goes north from Sydney, along the coast, all the way to Queensland. The New England Highway follows an inland route north from Newcastle through prime wine country in the Hunter Valley, and the regional centres of Tamworth, Armidale and Tenterfield. The Great Western Highway goes inland from Sydney and follows the dramatic landscape of wild cliffs and valleys that form the Blue Mountains. A couple of hours driving south-west along the Hume Highway reveals the charming Southern Highlands, characterised by historic towns and national parks. The Princes Highway is a coastal road going south from Sydney through the towns of Wollongong, Nowra, Batemans Bay and Bega.

Tourist information

i Sydney Visitor Centre
106 George St, The Rocks
Sydney NSW 2000
Ph: 132 077
www.visitnsw.com.au

| Total area = 801,431 sq km | Occupies 10.4% of Australia | Length of coast = 1099km | Length of seaboard = 1459km |

New South Wales Key Map & Distance Chart

All distances shown in the chart below have been measured over highways and major roads, not necessarily by the shortest route.

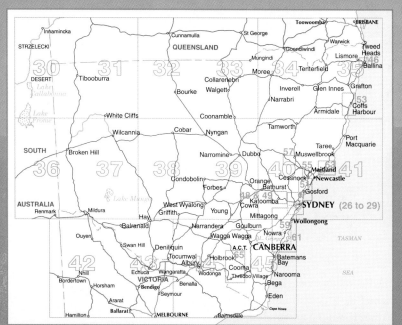

Jervis Bay National Park

Approximate Distance	Albany	Bathurst	Bega	Bourke	Broken Hill	Canberra	Cooma	Dubbo	Goulburn	Grafton	Mildura VIC	Moree	Newcastle	Port Macquarie	Sydney	Tamworth	Tweed Heads	Wagga Wagga	West Wyalong	Wollongong
Albury		443	419	843	884	340	317	588	366	1159	621	963	713	941	563	926	1411	125	273	506
Bathurst	443		508	569	953	291	406	201	196	751	815	576	329	557	196	445	982	318	268	228
Bega	419	508		957	1243	217	102	609	283	1028	944	984	561	799	411	805	1259	479	481	333
Bourke	843	569	957		615	740	855	368	766	946	875	445	745	916	765	640	1177	718	570	797
Broken Hill	884	953	1243	615		1098	1213	752	1124	1328	299	1061	1129	1298	1149	1022	1559	859	846	1181
Canberra	340	291	217	740	1098		115	392	86	879	799	767	412	650	283	656	1110	239	264	226
Cooma	317	406	102	855	1213	115		507	201	994	914	882	809	765	398	771	1225	282	379	341
Dubbo	588	201	609	368	752	392	507		418	644	801	375	377	598	397	338	875	419	254	429
Goulburn	366	196	283	766	1124	86	201	418		793	825	793	326	564	197	570	1024	265	290	140
Grafton	1159	751	1028	946	1328	879	994	644	793		1445	366	469	249	627	306	231	1046	898	709
Mildura VIC	621	815	944	875	299	799	914	801	825	1445		1176	1144	1399	1011	1139	1676	560	547	965
Moree	963	576	984	445	1061	767	882	375	793	366	1176		494	442	623	266	560	794	629	692
Newcastle	713	329	561	745	1129	412	809	377	326	469	1144	494		259	150	278	719	591	587	232
Port Macquarie	941	557	799	916	1298	650	765	598	564	249	1399	442	259		388	276	480	829	825	466
Sydney	563	196	411	765	1149	283	398	397	197	627	1011	623	150	388		407	848	462	464	78
Tamworth	926	445	805	640	1022	656	771	338	570	306	1139	266	278	276	407		617	740	592	476
Tweed Heads	1411	982	1259	1177	1559	1110	1225	875	1024	231	1676	560	719	480	848	617		1289	1129	930
Wagga Wagga	125	318	479	718	859	239	282	419	265	1046	560	794	591	829	462	740	1289		148	405
West Wyalong	273	268	481	570	846	264	379	254	290	898	547	629	587	825	464	592	1129	148		430
Wollongong	506	228	333	797	1181	226	341	429	140	709	965	692	232	466	78	476	930	405	430	

Sydney

Harbour Bridge and Opera House

Main Attractions

◈ **Bondi Beach** Australia's most famous beach offers surf, sand, cafes and coastal walks.

◈ **Chinatown** A district with numerous Chinese restaurants including Kam Fook, the biggest in the Southern Hemisphere.

◈ **Darling Harbour** A waterside plaza with parks, shops, restaurants and nightclubs.

◈ **Macquarie St** This elegant street is lined with many historic sandstone buildings.

◈ **Queen Victoria Building** Once the home of the city markets, this is now a stunning shopping centre.

◈ **The Rocks** This historic seaport now has galleries, shops, restaurants and Sydney's oldest pubs

◈ **Royal Botanic Gardens** Covering 30ha, these gardens include rare and exotic plant life.

◈ **Sydney Harbour Bridge** The world's widest single span arch bridge links the city to the North Shore.

◈ **Sydney Opera House** Regarded as one of the architectural wonders of the world since it opened in 1973.

Considered by many to be Australia's most vibrant and dynamic city, Sydney has flourished as a cosmopolitan cultural and financial centre. Although Sydney is not the national capital, it is the nation's oldest and largest city, occupying 3700 square kilometres.

Sydney's urban sprawl encompasses an immense natural playground made up of Sydney Harbour and the bush parks that hug its coves and bays, the sparkling Pacific Ocean surf beaches in the east, the Blue Mountains to the west, and stunning national parks to the north and south. With Sydney's temperate climate, it is possible to make the most of the city's striking environment in any season.

The major gateway to Australia, Sydney is a prime tourist destination in its own right and boasts many impressive attractions. Sightseeing is easy: the city centre is a manageable size and many visitors prefer to soak up the atmosphere of the city on foot. Alternatively, the bright red Sydney Explorer bus takes in almost all of the major tourist attractions on its 20km route. No one should visit Sydney without taking a ferry ride or cruise on the magnificent harbour. Cruises and regular harbour ferries all depart from Circular Quay.

Places of Interest

Ⓐ Art Gallery of NSW **D3**
Ⓑ Australian Museum of Natural History **D4**
Ⓒ Cadman's Cottage **C2**
Ⓓ Chinatown **B5**
Ⓔ Chinese Garden **B5**
Ⓕ Circular Quay **C2**
Ⓖ Customs House **C2**
Ⓗ Darling Harbour **B5**

Ⓘ Hyde Park **C4**
Ⓙ Martin Place **C3**
Ⓚ Museum of Contemporary Art **C2**
Ⓛ Museum of Sydney **C2**
Ⓜ National Maritime Museum **A4**
Ⓝ Powerhouse Museum **A5**
Ⓞ Queen Victoria Building **B4**
Ⓟ Royal Botanic Gardens **D3**
Ⓠ Star City Casino **A3**

Ⓡ State Library of NSW **D3**
Ⓢ Sydney Aquarium **B4**
Ⓣ Sydney Harbour Bridge **C1**
Ⓤ Sydney Observatory **B2**
Ⓥ Sydney Opera House **D1**
Ⓦ Sydney Tower **C4**
Ⓧ Sydney Town Hall **B4**
Ⓨ The Rocks **C1**

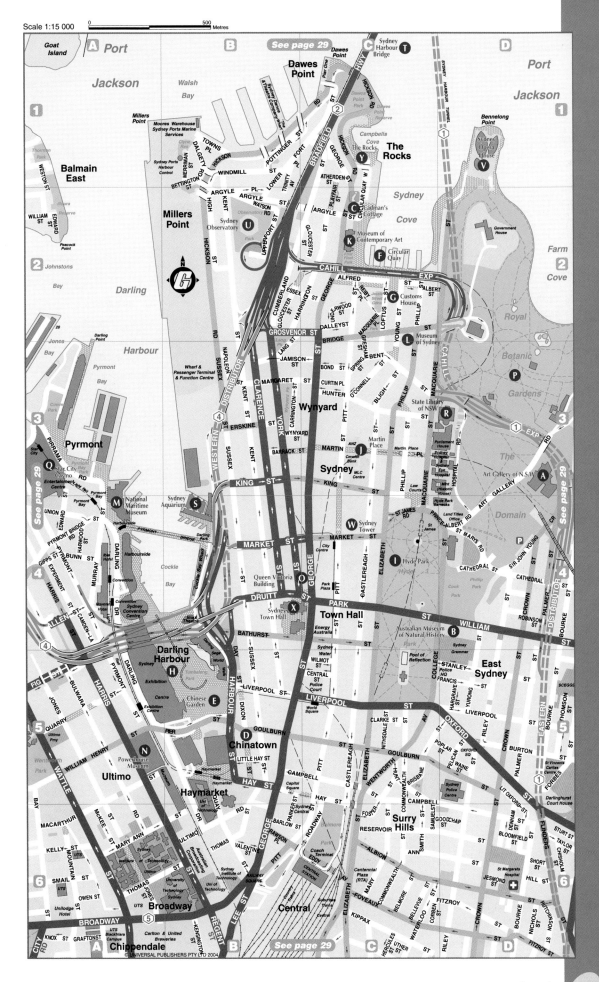

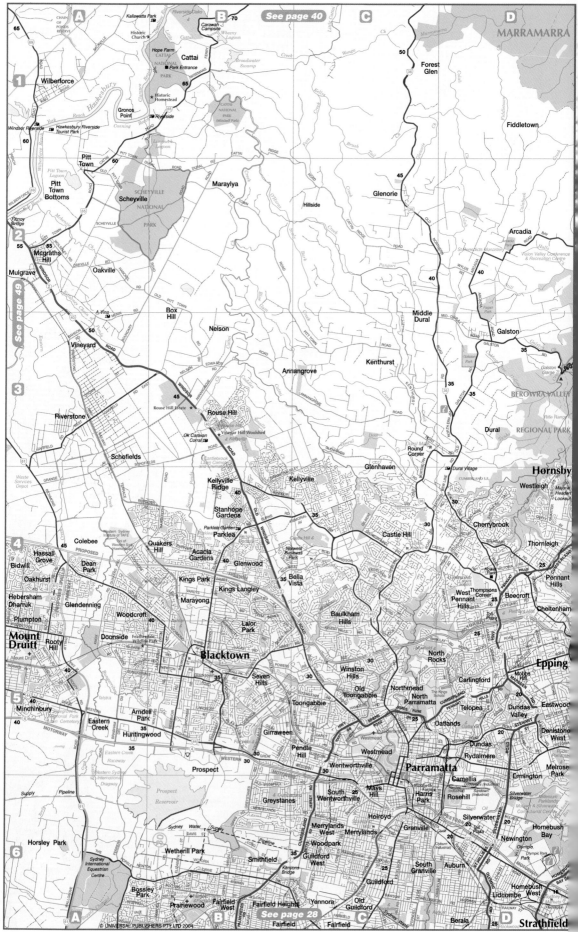

See page 40

MARRAMARRA

See page 49

See page 28

© UNIVERSAL PUBLISHERS PTY LTD 2004

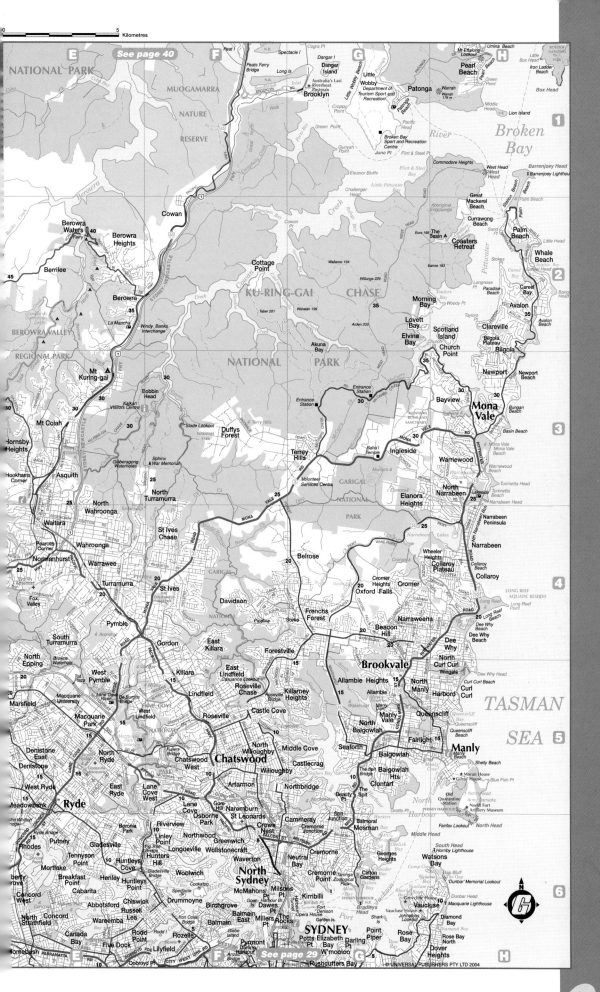

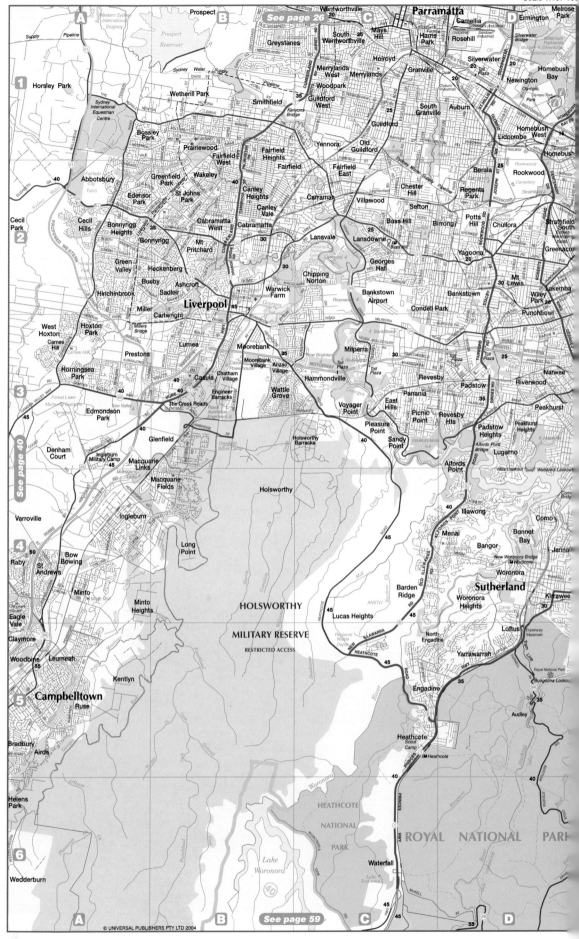

See page 27

See page 59

TASMAN

SEA

Botany

Bay

© UNIVERSAL PUBLISHERS PTY LTD 2004

A B See page 118 C D

1

Nappa Merrie
Dig Tree ★
44

Gidgealpa Innamincka

Cooper

Creek

Orientos

Bransby Cr.

142

Gidgealpa Gas Field

Moomba Oil & Gas Field

Burke-Dullingan Oil & Gas Field

Bransby

141

Della Gas Field

51

Moomba
(Private)

Epsilon

Santos

25

SOUTH AUSTRALIA

QUEENSLAND

Naryilco

43

2

Toolachee Gas Field

52

38

TRACK

Strzelecki

Ck.

45

59

Warry

Merty Merty

57

23 4

10

36

140°

Omicron

S T R Z E L E C K I   D E S E R T

34

40

Warri
Gate

3

Bollards
Lagoon

Tooma
Gate

89

Strzelecki
Crossing

Bollards Lagoon

105

Cameron Corner

Olive Downs

5

28

29°

Corner
Store

STURT NATIONAL PARK

41

125

Fort Grey ★

10

Waka

34

STRZELECKI

Lake
Blanche

Lake Stewart

40

30

19

Tibooburra

Petermarra

318

Ck.

Ck.

47

12 Mile

11 12

Gum Vale

HWY

39

46

Mt Hopeless

Lake
Callabonna

Mt Poole
1250

21

Mt Sturt

17

Milparinka

4

Callabonna (Ruin)

Theldarpa

25

5

Callabonna

Boolkaree

Yandama

103

Mt Brown
274

31

Peak
Hill

Moolawatana

49

Hamilton

Hawker
Gate

Mt Shannon
332

12

Mount
Shannon

63

19

Ck.

36

North Mulga

27

96

Old Moolawatana

21 4

Cooney

SOUTH AUSTRALIA

NEW SOUTH WALES

22

Mount
Arrowsmith

Lake Wallace

14

37

10

Bullea

Lake
Cootabarlow

15

40

21

Border Downs

Pimpara
Lake

Wooltana

Lake Pundalpa

Starvation L.

Packsaddle

52

Ck.

50 Sanpah

Packsaddle Roadhouse

6

Lake Elder

51

Lake
Frome

24

18

16

Wertaloona

Quinyambie

Mount
Westwood

Balcannia

A B See page 36 C Tielta 24 Tielta D 41

© UNIVERSAL PUBLISHERS PTY LTD 2004

See page 149

See page 153

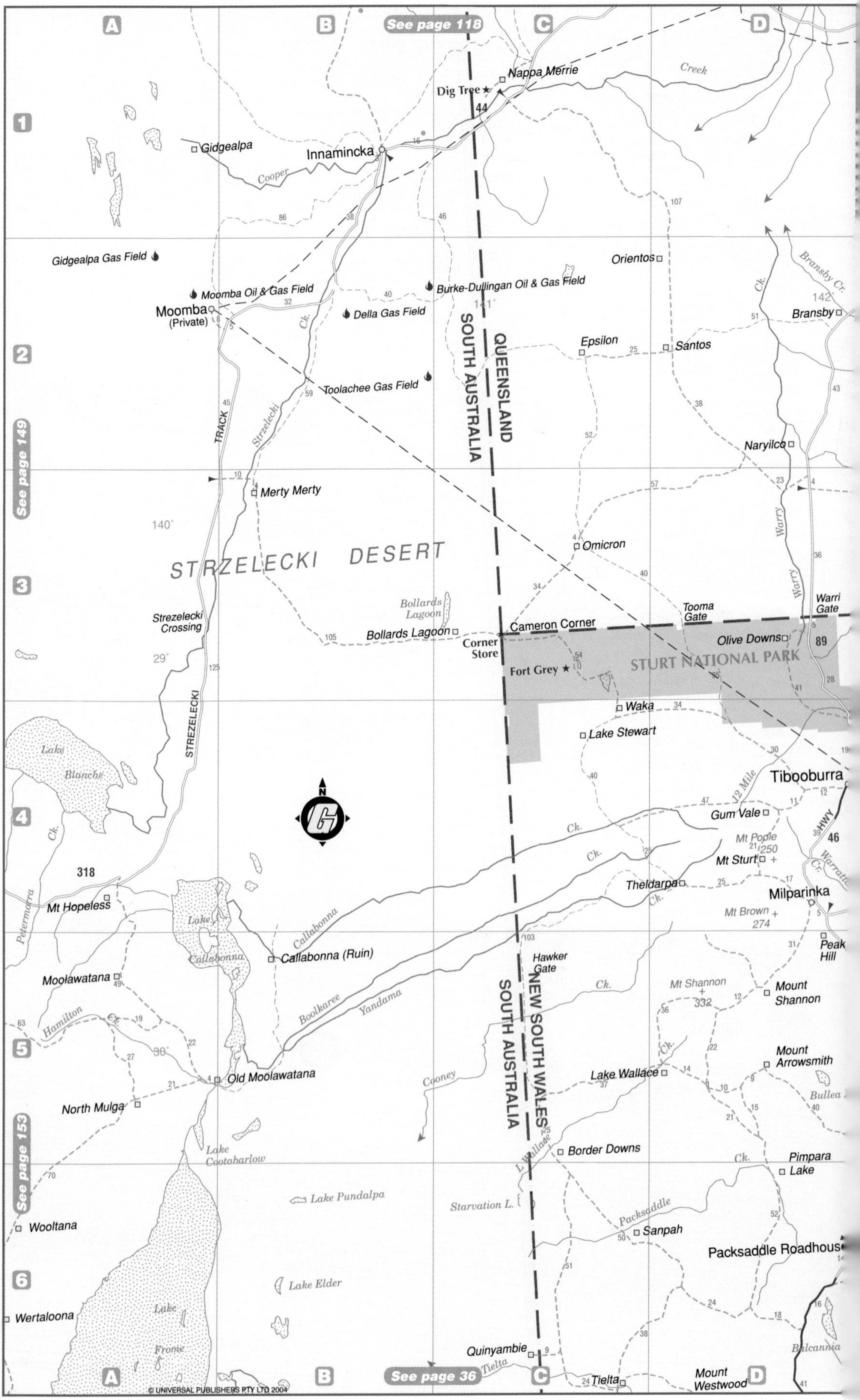

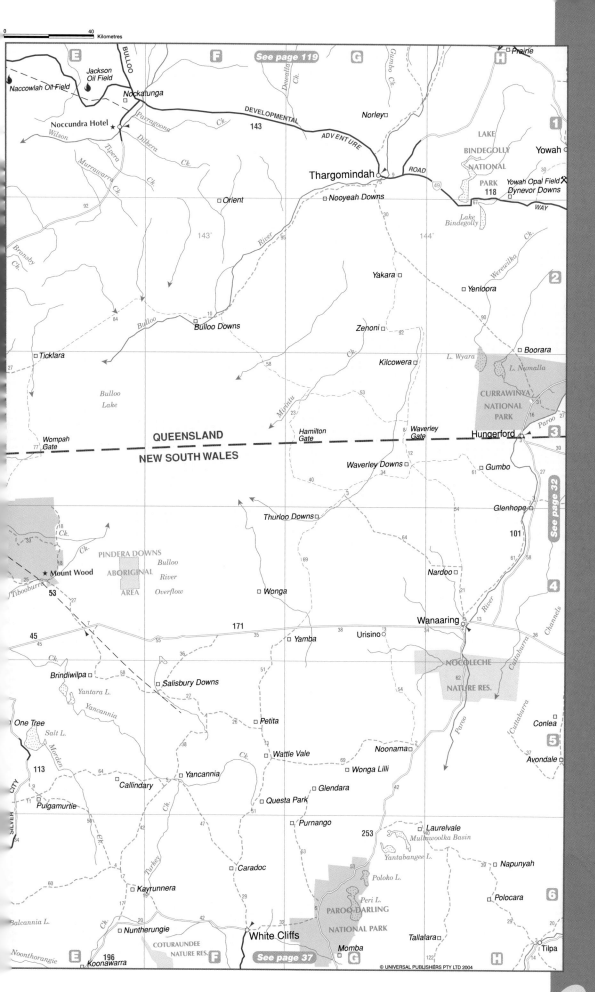

See page 119

0   40 Kilometres

Naccowlah Oil Field

Jackson Oil Field

BULLOO

Nockatunga

Noccundra Hotel

Parragoona   Ck.

Wilson

Dilbera   Ck.

Tipera   Ck.

Murrawarra   Ck.

DEVELOPMENTAL

143

ADVENTURE

Norley

ROAD

Thargomindah   9

WAY

49

67

LAKE
BINDEGOLLY
NATIONAL
PARK
118

Yowah

30

Yowah Opal Field
Dynevor Downs

Orient

Nooyeah Downs

30

River   95

143°

Branshy Ck.

92

84

10

Bulloo

Bulloo Downs

144°

Yakara

Yenloora

Zenoni   92

Werewilka   Ck.

90

Ticklara

27

58

Ck.

Kilcowera

L. Wyara

Boorara

L. Numalla

CURRAWINYA
NATIONAL
PARK

31

16

27

Paroo

Bulloo
Lake

Mirintu

23

53

QUEENSLAND

NEW SOUTH WALES

Wompah
Gate   77

Hamilton
Gate

40

Waverley
Gate

8

Hungerford

30

3

Waverley Downs

34

12

Gumbo

61

27

See page 32

18
Ck.

33

18
Ck.

Thurloo Downs

3

54

Glenhope

101

69

64

Nardoo

61   58

21

PINDERA DOWNS
ABORIGINAL
AREA

Bulloo
River
Overflow

Mount Wood

Tibooburra

25

53

27

7

Wonga

Wanaaring   13

Channels

45
45

171

55

36

35

38

Yamba

Urisino   3

34

36

NOCCOLECHE

NATURE RES.

62

54

Paroo

Cuttaburra

Cuttaburra

Brindiwilpa

Yantara L.

Yancannia

58

Salisbury Downs

27

51

26

Petita

Conlea

37

Avondale

One Tree

Salt L.

Morden

113

64

Yancannia

38

Ck.

Wattle Vale

13

Noonama

Wonga Lilli

69

2

42

SILVER CITY

9

Callindary

5

Pulgamurtie

54

50

42

47

Glendara

Questa Park

51

Purnango

253

Laurelvale

Mulhawoolka Basin

Yantabangee L.

Napunyah

39

Caradoc

63

53

Poloko L.

Polocara

60

Kayrunnera

17

19

29

Peri L.

PAROO-DARLING
NATIONAL
PARK

Tallalara

Balcannia L.

Ck.

20

42

32

6

Nuntherungie

196

Koonawarra

COTURAUNDEE
NATURE RES.

White Cliffs

See page 37

Momba

29

20

Tilpa

14

Noonthorangie

© UNIVERSAL PUBLISHERS PTY LTD 2004

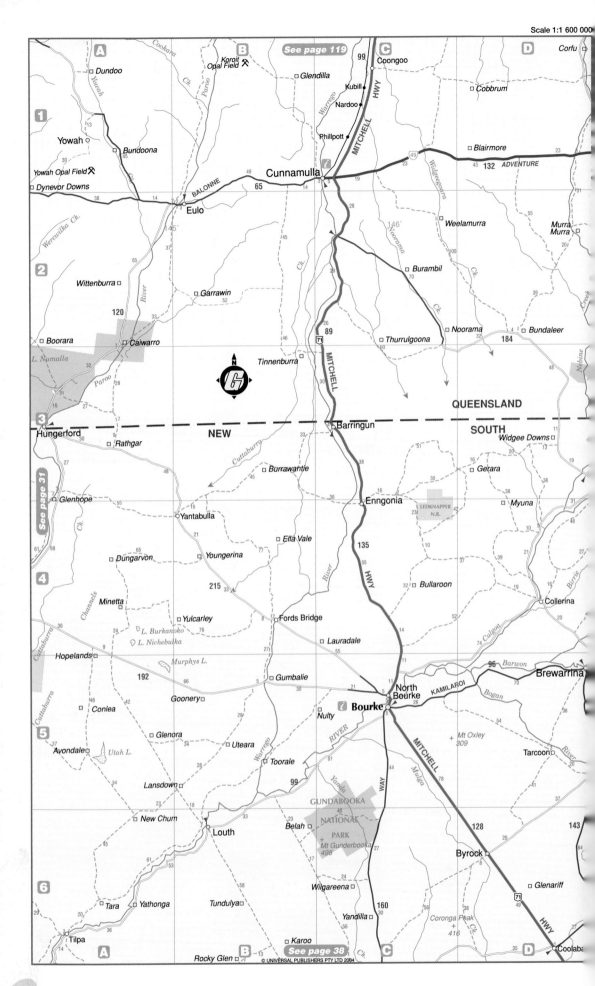

Scale 1:1 600 000

See page 119

A B C D

A1 Dundoo
Koroit Opal Field
Glendilla
99 Coongoo
Kubill
Nardoo
Cobbrum

1 Yowah
13
Bundoona
45
30
Phillpott
Blairmore 23

Yowah Opal Field
Dynevor Downs
BALONNE
49 Cunnamulla
65 14 3 5 19
23
43 132 ADVENTURE
31

38 14 Eulo
2.5
28
Weelamurra
55
Murra Murra

2 Wittenburra
145
145
Burambil
146
100
39

Garrawin
52
29
Noorama
4
Bundaleer

120
33
26
89
71
Thurrulgoona
32
184

Boorara
Caiwarro
146
60

L. Numalla
32
Paroo
28
Tinnenburra
MITCHELL
48
QUEENSLAND

16
31
17
30

3 Hungerford
30
Rathgar
9
33
Barringun
SOUTH
Widgee Downs
11

27
Cuttaburra
38
51
Getara
16
20
13
19

Glenhope
55
45
Burrawantie
36
30
42
1
36

Yantabulla
15
Enngonia
23
LEDKNAPPER N.R.
Myuna
31

21
Ella Vale
16
10
10
1
27

4 Dungarvon
65
Youngerina
77
135
37
39
21
16

215
33
55
Bullaroon
32
19
Collerina
20

Minetta
24
Yulcarley
76
Fords Bridge
14
74
20

L. Burkanko
Murphys L.
271
Lauradale
11
96 Barwon
Brewarrina

Hopelands
9
192
66
5
Gumbalie
21
11
North Bourke
KAMILAROI
70

Goonery
30
Bourke
26
Bogan

5 Conlea
42
29
Nulty
Mt Oxley 309
54

Glenora
34
Uteara
Toorale
44
Tarcoon

Avondale
37
Utah L.
28
Warrego
99
RIVER
WAY
MITCHELL
78

Lansdown
23
18
GUNDABOOKA
40
NATIONAL
37

New Churn
33
Belah
23
PARK
128
143

Louth
Mt Gunderbooka 498
20
Byrock

45
61
53
24

6 Tara
Yathonga
58
Wilgareena
Glenariff

29
20
Tundulya
160
30
Yandilla
49
HWY

Tilpa
36
Karoo
56
Coronga Peak 416
35

Rocky Glen
See page 38
Coolab

© UNIVERSAL PUBLISHERS PTY LTD 2004

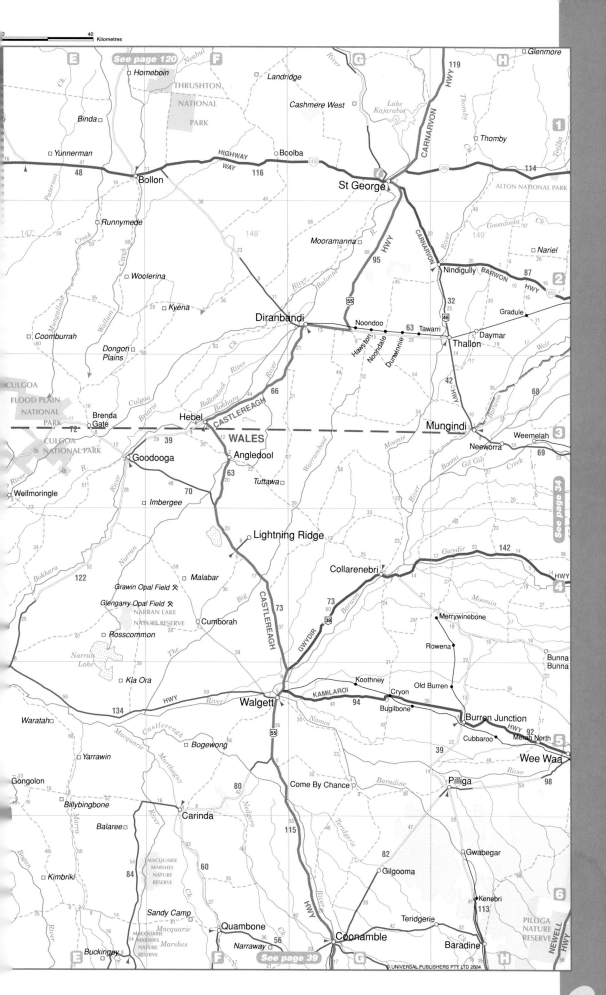

See page 120

□ Homeboin

□ Landridge

THRUSHTON

□ Cashmere West

□ Glenmore

NATIONAL

Lake
Kajarabia

119

CARNARVON HWY

□ Binda

□ Thomby

PARK

□ Yunnerman

HIGHWAY

□ Boolba

WAY

48

47

116

49

114

Bollon

St George

ALTON NATIONAL PARK

□ Runnymede

148°

149°

□ Nariel

Mooramanna □

95

Nindigully

87

BARWON HWY

□ Woolerina

Gradule

□ Kyena

Diranbandi

Noondoo

63

Tawarri

32

Daymar

□ Coomburrah

Hawston

Noondale

Dunninnie

Thallon

42 HWY

Dongon
Plains

66

68

CULGOA

Hebel

CASTLEREAGH

FLOOD PLAIN

Brenda

WALES

Mungindi

Weemelah

NATIONAL

Gate

72

39

Angledool

Neeworra

69

PARK

CULGOA

Goodooga

63

Tuttawa □

NATIONAL PARK

70

See page 34

□ Weilmoringle

□ Imbergee

Lightning Ridge

142 HWY

Collarenebri

122

□ Malabar

Grawin Opal Field

73

73

Merrywinebone

Glengarry Opal Field

38

NARRAN LAKE

Cumborah

GWYDIR

Rowena

Bunna
Bunna

NATURE RESERVE

□ Rosscommon

CASTLEREAGH

Koothney

Old Burren

Narran
Lake

□ Kia Ora

HWY

Cryon

Bugilbone

Burren Junction

134

Walgett

KAMILAROI

94

92

□ Waratah

55

Cubbaroo

Merah North

□ Yarrawin

□ Bogewong

39

Wee Waa

Gongolon

Come By Chance

Pilliga

98

□ Billybingbone

80

□ Gwabegar

Carinda

115

82

□ Balaree

Gilgooma

□ Kimbriki

84

60

Kenebri

113

PILLIGA

Sandy Camp

NATURE

NEWELL HWY

MACQUARIE
MARSHES
NATURE
RESERVE

Teridgerie

RESERVE

Quambone

56

See page 39

Coonamble

Baradine

□ Buckinguy

Narraway

UNIVERSAL PUBLISHERS PTY LTD 2004

New South Wales

33

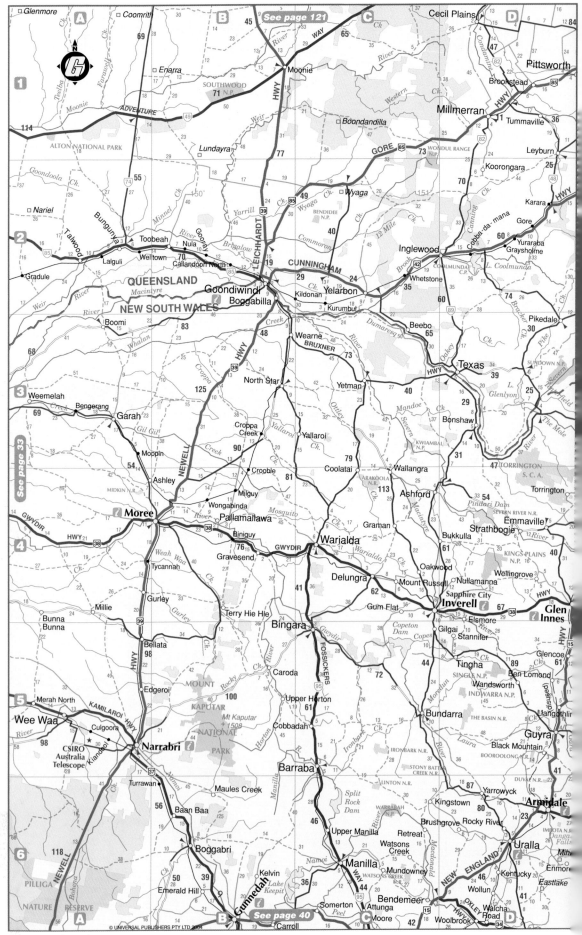

© UNIVERSAL PUBLISHERS PTY LTD 2004

See page 121

See page 40

See page 33

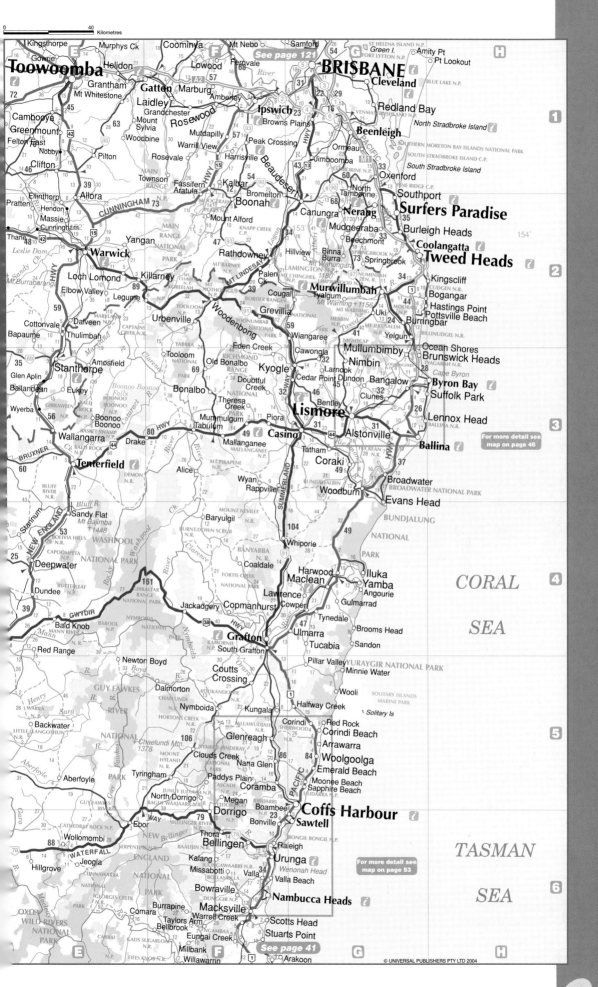

See page 30

SOUTH AUSTRALIA

NEW SOUTH WALES

Lake Frome

Pauls Bore

Frome Downs

Woolshed

Erudina

Curnamona

Glenorchy

Koonamore
Mt Victor

Bindyi

Oopina

Waukaringa

Melton

Old Wabricoola

Yunta

Paratoo

Nackara

Hillgrange

Plumbago

Four Brothers

Morialpa

Bonnie Brae

Winnininnie

Mannahill

Oulina Park

Tiverton

Manunda

Lilydale

Faraway Hill

Bendigo

Pulpara

Willara

Kia Ora

Hog Back

Caroona

Glenora

Muckaby

Chalk Cliffs

Thistlebeds

Redcliffe

Balah

Florieton

Robertstown

Mount Mary

Eudunda

Bower

Sutherlands

Morgan

Cadell

Qualco

Murbko

Ramco

Taylorville

Waikerie

Kingston-On-Murray

Moorook

Mooleulooloo

Yarramba

Kalkaroo

Kalabity

Boolcoomta

Bimbowrie

Bulloo Creek

Outalpa

Olary

Eringa Park

Maldorkey

Wadnaminga

Benda Park

Olorah Downs

Sturt Vale

Pine Valley

Fords Lagoon

Canegrass

Canopus

DANGGALI
Zone
CONSERVATION PARK

Morgan Vale

Hypurna

CHOWILLA
REGIONAL
RESERVE

CHOWILLA
GAME RESERVE

POOGINOOK C.P.

Cobdogla

Barmera

Glossop

Renmark North

Chaffey

Murray River

Renmark

Paringa

Berri

Yamba

See page 42

See page 155

Mulyungarie

Wompinie

Mingary

Cultana

Tepco

Aroona

Corella

Burta

Mutooloo

Wonga

Devonborough Downs

Kimberley

Mazar

Budgeree

Oakvale

Oakbank

COOTONG CONS. PARK

Cal Lal

Meringur North

Cullulleraine

BARRIER HWY
150

Cockburn

STURT HWY
97

Quinyambie

Tielta

Mount Westwood

Fowlers Gap
121

McDougalls Well

Mount Woowoolahra

Kantappa

Corona

Bijerkerno

Wilangee

Paringa

Acacia Downs

Mount Gipps

Purnamoota

Yanco Glen
53

Stephens Creek

Silverton

Living Desert Sculptures

Broken Hill

Huonville

White Leeds

Ascot Vale

Enmore

Pine Point

Langwell

125

Netley

Blackwell

Middle Camp

Kudgee

South Ita

Terrananya

Nagaela

Coombah Roadhouse

Twin Wells

Popiltah

SILVER CITY HWY
79

Nialia Lake

Windamingle

Warrawenia Lake

141

Bunneringee

Huntingfield

Pine Camp

Lake Victoria

Warranangra

Lake Victoria

Rufus River

Moorna

Lake Wallawalla

Stephen Ck. Resvr.

Umberumberka Resvr.

Mount Gipps

Barrier Range

Darling R. Anabranch

MURRAY RIVER

© UNIVERSAL PUBLISHERS PTY LTD 2004

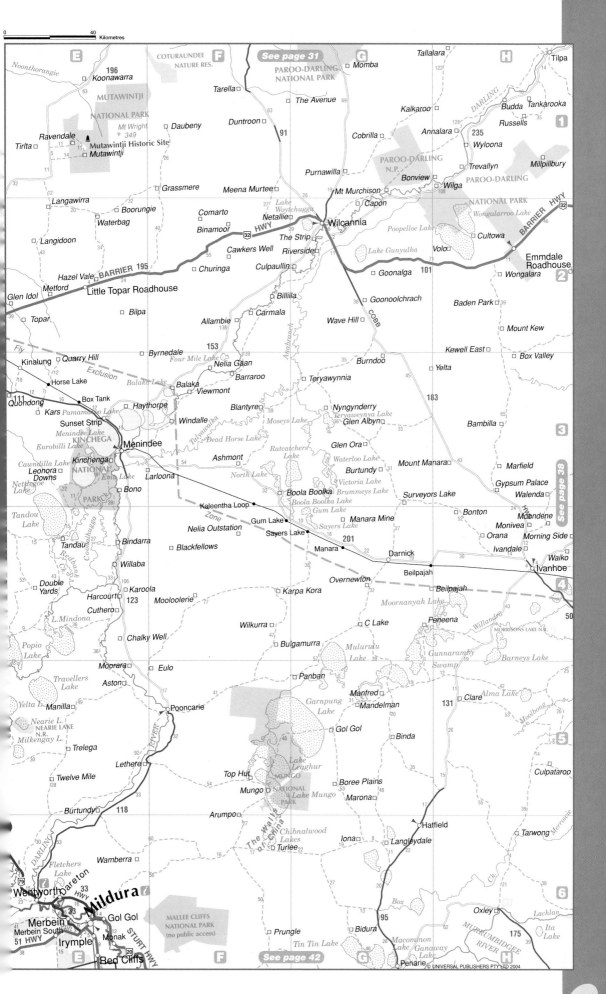

See page 31

See page 38

See page 42

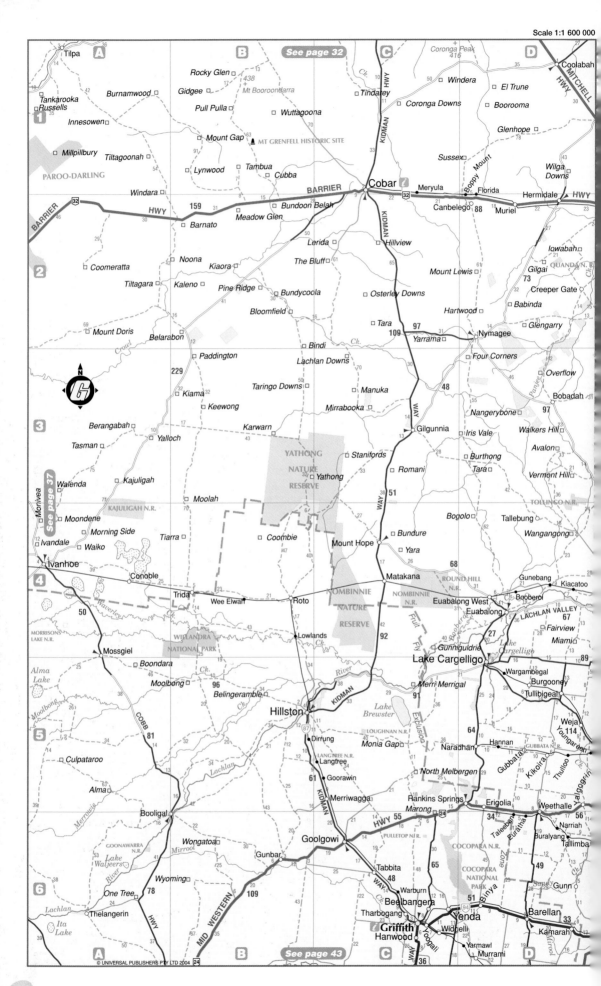

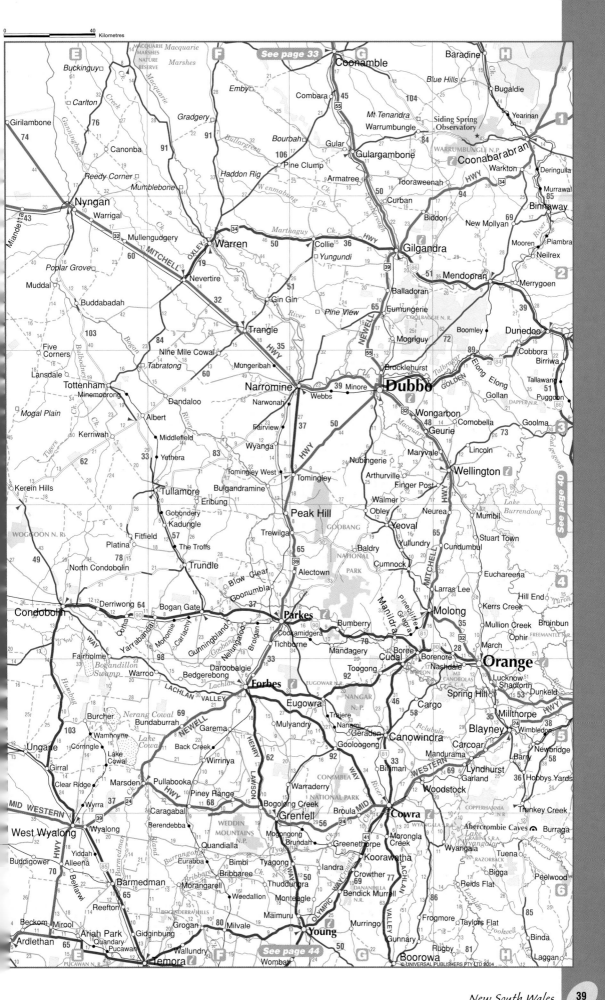

See page 33

See page 40

See page 44

New South Wales

© UNIVERSAL PUBLISHERS PTY LTD 2004

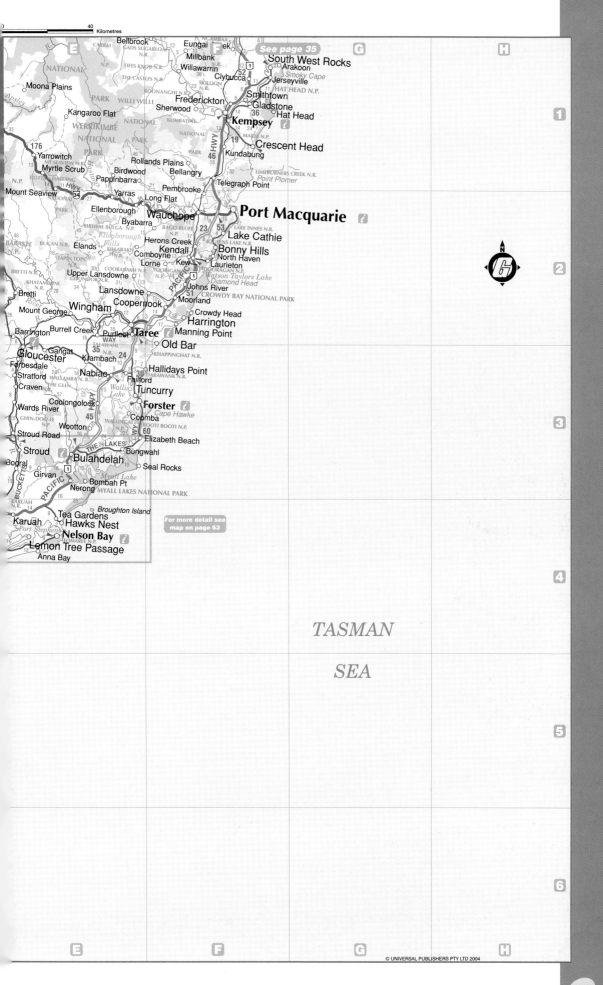

See page 35

TASMAN

SEA

For more detail see
map on page 63

© UNIVERSAL PUBLISHERS PTY LTD 2004

See page 37

See page 155

See page 82

See page 83

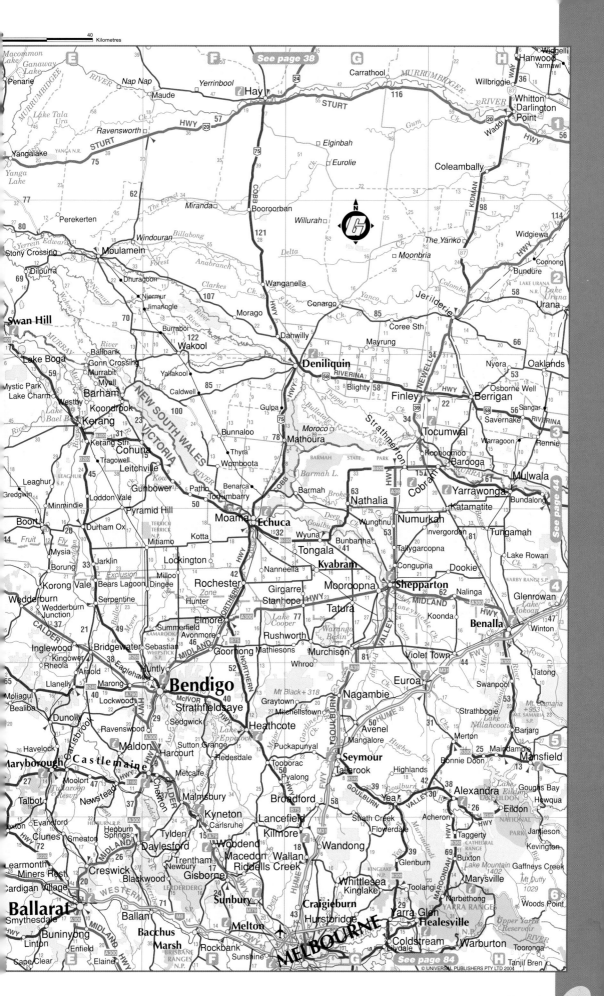

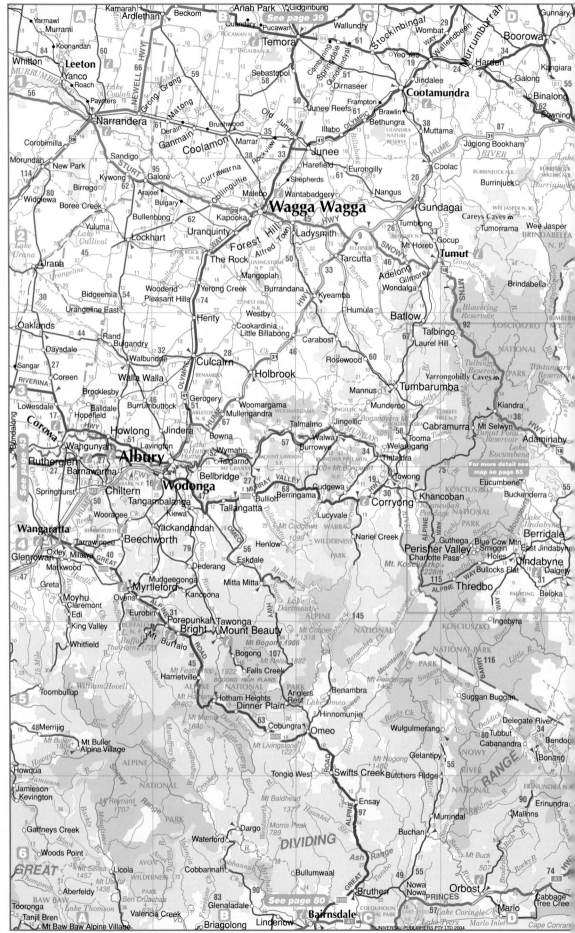

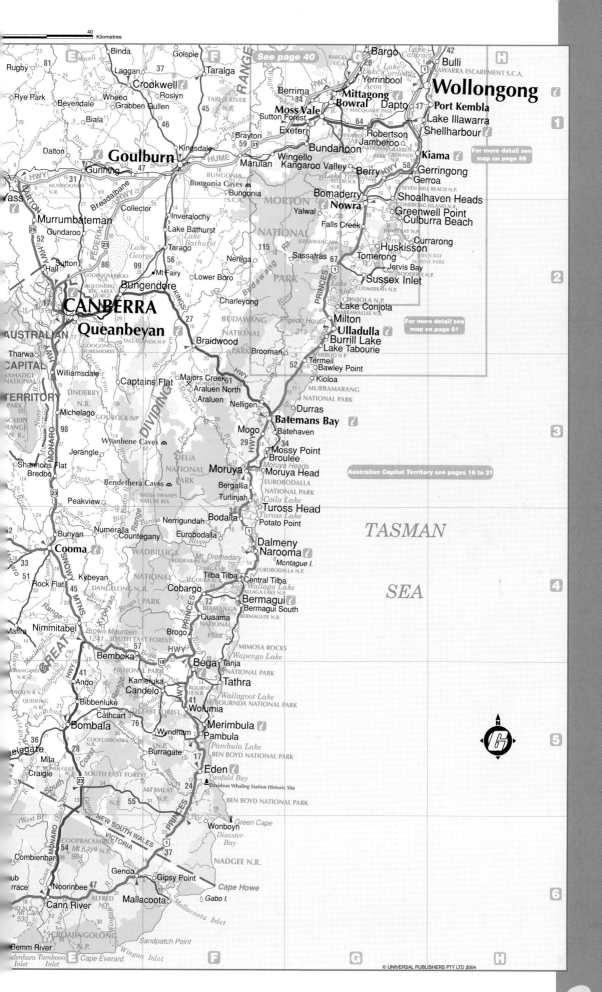

© UNIVERSAL PUBLISHERS PTY LTD 2004

Ballina to Byron Bay

Whale off Cape Byron

S ituated on the far north coast of New South Wales, the stunning stretch of coastline between Ballina and Byron Bay boasts an array of beaches framed by lush sub-tropical forest.

Although the two townships share a sunny climate and are increasingly popular as holiday destinations, their histories reveal very different pasts. Ballina was the site of a short-lived gold rush in the 1880s while Byron Bay, once known for its abattoir, became a centre for alternative lifestyles in the 1970s.

The charm of the area's beaches and secluded hinterland towns now attracts so many visitors that locals are outnumbered by tourists in the summer months; nevertheless it is still possible to find a private spot to enjoy the sun in this idyllic coastal retreat.

Tourist information

 Ballina Visitor
Information Centre

Cnr River St & Las Balsas Plaza,
Ballina NSW 2478
Ph: (02) 6686 3484
www.discoverballina.com

 Byron Bay Visitor
Information Centre

80 Jonson St, Byron Bay
NSW 2481
Ph: (02) 6680 8558
www.byronbay.com

Must Visit

- Ballina Naval & Maritime Museum
- Cape Byron Lighthouse
- Brunswick Heads
- Nightcap National Park
- Nimbin

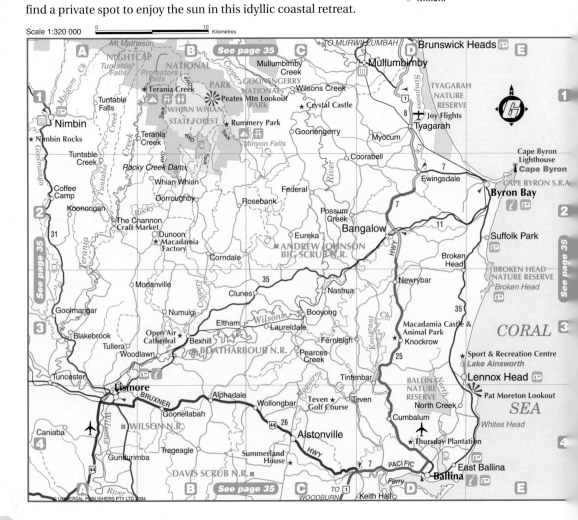

Blue Mountains

Looking out at the Grose Valley

The Blue Mountains received their name from the bluish haze created when light interacts with the mist released from millions of eucalypt trees. This rugged region features cliffs, rock formations, waterfalls and caves. Once seen as a barrier to the infant NSW colony's expansion westwards, the Blue Mountains are now a popular holiday or weekend destination due to their easy access from Sydney, 105km away.

This spectacular mountain range can be enjoyed all year round, although seasonal changes are more marked than in Sydney and temperatures can plummet, especially in winter, so it is always wise to be prepared for the cold. This climate makes the Blue Mountains an ideal location for Yulefest: a series of mid-winter events celebrating Christmas traditions, held annually between June and August. Many quaint villages dot the landscape, offering excellent restaurants, cafes, pubs, gardens, antique stores and other shops to entertain less energetic visitors.

The Three Sisters' Legend

To protect them from the bunyip, the three sisters' witchdoctor father used his magic bone to turn them into stone, and himself into a lyrebird. He lost the bone and is still searching for it today, while the sisters silently wait.

Tourist information

i Echo Point Visitor Information Centre

Echo Point Rd, Echo Point, Katoomba NSW 2780
Tollfree: 1300 653 408
www.bluemountainstourism.org.au

Main Attractions

◈ **Blue Mountains National Park** This popular park offers many walks.

◈ **Echo Point** The Echo Point lookout provides breathtaking views from the Jamison Valley to the Three Sisters.

◈ **Hydro Majestic (Mercure Grand)** Built last century, this hotel remains a popular retreat.

◈ **Jenolan Caves** Limestone caverns lie underground, with icy rivers and impressive limestone formations.

◈ **Leura** A picturesque town classified by the National Trust.

◈ **Megalong Valley** This valley is the horseriding centre of the mountains.

◈ **Norman Lindsay Gallery and Museum** The former home of the renegade Australian artist is now a gallery of his works.

◈ **Scenic World** Features cable car rides, a scenic railway and rainforest boardwalks.

◈ **Zig Zag Railway** This was named in 1886 after a series of zig zags were constructed in the track to enable coal trains to descend into the valley.

The Zig Zag railway

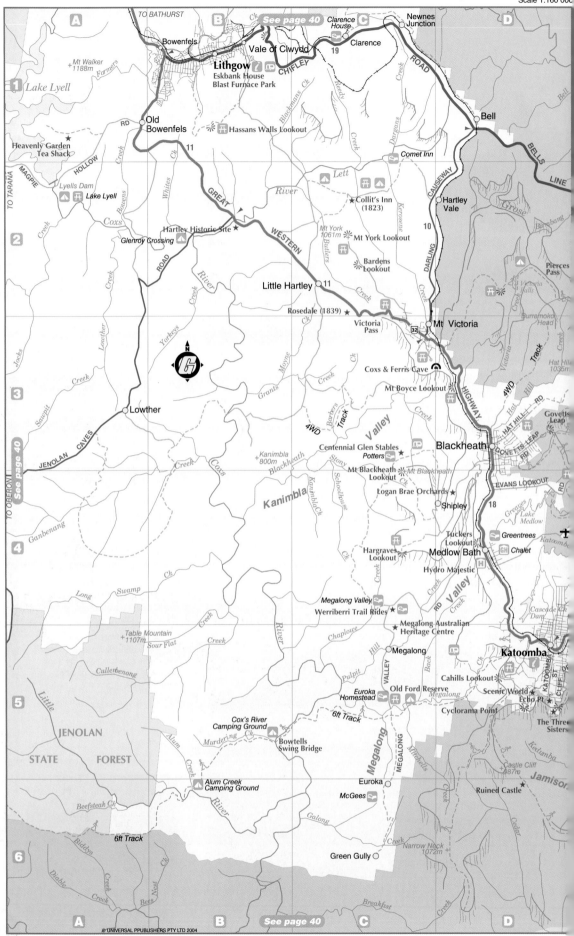

Scale 1:160 000

See page 40

TO BATHURST

Bowenfels

Mt Walker
+1188m
Farmers

Lake Lyell

Lithgow

Eskbank House
Blast Furnace Park

Vale of Clwydd

CHIFLEY

Clarence
House

Clarence

19

Newnes
Junction

ROAD

Bell

Old
Bowenfels

RD

11

Hassans Walls Lookout

Heavenly Garden
Tea Shack

HOLLOW

MAGPIE

TO TARANA

Lyells Dam

Lake Lyell

GREAT

Creek

Whites

Coxs

Bowens

Creek

Ck

RD

GREAT

WESTERN

ROAD

Dargans

Ck

Blackmans Ck

Reedy

Creek

Comet Inn

Lett

River

Collit's Inn
(1823)

Mt York
1061m

Mt York Lookout

Bardens
Lookout

CAUSEWAY

DARLING

Hartley
Vale

10

Grose

River

Victoria Falls

Pierces
Pass

Burramoko
Head

Hartley Historic Site

Glenroy Crossing

ROAD

River

Creek

Little Hartley

11

Creek

Rosedale (1839)

Ck

Victoria
Pass

32

Mt Victoria

BELLS

LINE

Hat Hill
1035m

Yorkeys

N
G

Lowther

Coxs & Ferris Cave

Mt Boyce Lookout

Valley

4WD

Track

HIGHWAY

4WD

HAT HILL

Govetts
Leap

JENOLAN

CAVES

TO OBERON

See page 40

Lower

Creek

Jocks

Creek

Sawpit

Ck

Grants

Barbers

Stony

Ck

Creek

Kanimbla
+800m

Creek

Coxs

Creek

4WD

Blackheath

Ck

Movie

Creek

Kanimbla

Valley

Blackheath

Ck

Kanimbla Ck

Schoolhouse

Centennial Glen Stables
Potters

Mt Blackheath
Lookout

Mt Blackheath

Logan Brae Orchards

Shipley

18

GOVETTS LEAP

EVANS LOOKOUT

RD

Greaves

Creek

Lake
Medlow

Greentrees

Chalet

Katoomba

Ganbenang

Cascade
Dam

Creek

Ck

Long

Swamp

Creek

Table Mountain
+1107m

Sour Flat

Creek

Cullenbenong

JENOLAN

STATE

FOREST

Little

Ck

Beefsteak Ch

Murdering

Cox's River
Camping Ground

Bowtells
Swing Bridge

Alum Creek
Camping Ground

Alum

Creek

6ft Track

River

Creek

Hargraves
Lookout

Megalong Valley
Werriberri Trail Rides

Megalong Australian
Heritage Centre

Megalong

Euroka
Homestead

Old Ford Reserve

6ft Track

Euroka

McGees

Green Gully

Chaplows

Hill

Pulpit

VALLEY

Megalong

Back

Creek

Megalong

Mitchells

Creek

Galong

Ck

RD

Valley

Hydro Majestic

Tuckers
Lookout

Medlow Bath

GH

Cahills Lookout

Scenic World

Echo Pt

Cyclorama Point

The Three
Sisters

Katoomba

KATOOMBA ST

CLIFF

Castle Cliff
+987m

Ruined Castle

Jamison

Kedumba

Cedar

Ck

Narrow Neck
1072m

Breakfast

Ck

See page 40

© UNIVERSAL PUBLISHERS PTY LTD 2004

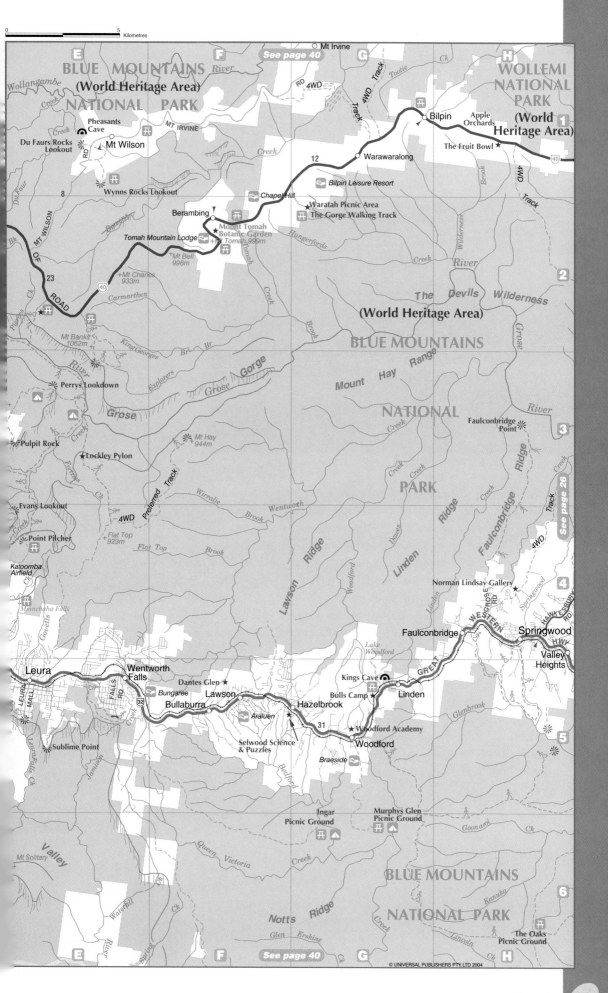

Central Coast

View over Avoca Beach

Located barely an hour from Sydney, the Central Coast is a water playground on the city's northern fringe. Its close proximity to Sydney and easy accessibility via freeways has ensured the region's development as a prime holiday destination. Large saltwater lagoons connected to the ocean via small waterways, and excellent beaches, make this area a haven for water sports. Fishing and surfing opportunities abound, charter cruises and hire boats are available on all major bodies of water, and it is also possible to rent a houseboat on Lake Macquarie, the region's largest lake.

Much of the Central Coast is covered by national parks, where bushwalking, camping and picnicking are popular pastimes. Gosford, the hub of the Central Coast, is about 80 minutes' drive from Sydney, while a number of smaller townships such as Patonga and Umina offer seaside retreats with a village-like atmosphere. At Ettalong Beach the weekend undercover markets attract crowds of bargain hunters who come to explore the colourful stalls.

Tourist information

i Central Coast Tourism
Marine Pde, The Entrance
NSW 2261
Ph: (02) 4385 4430
Freecall: 1800 806 258
www.cctourism.com.au

Main Attractions

◈ **Australian Rainforest Sanctuary** Contains a pristine pocket of original rainforest.

◈ **Australian Reptile Park** Watching venomous snakes being milked of their poison is a highlight here.

◈ **Avoca** This tiny seaside village is a relaxing holiday spot.

◈ **Bouddi National Park** See a diversity of habitats, birds and animal life.

◈ **Gosford-Edogawa Commemorative Garden** This traditional Japanese garden is close to the Gosford Regional Gallery.

◈ **The Entrance** Pelicans are fed at Memorial Park at 3.30pm daily.

◈ **Terrigal** Home to the Central Coast's most impressive hotel development, Terrigal is a top surfing spot.

◈ **Watagan State Forest** Walking tracks lead past giant cedar and turpentine trees to waterfalls and lookouts.

Fishing on the Central Coast

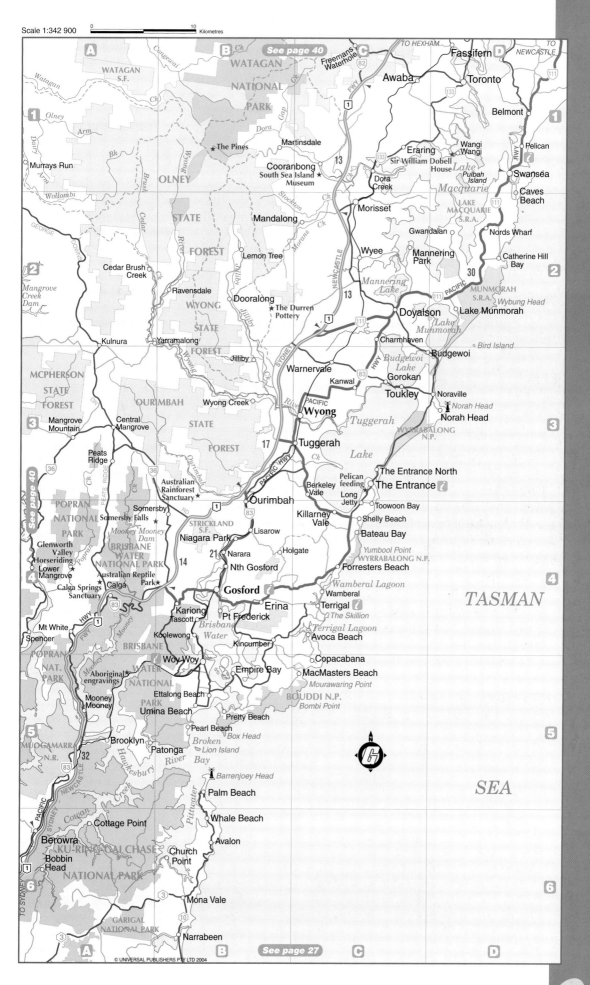

Coffs Harbour

Popular beach at the rivermouth

Between the two popular coastal resort towns of Port Macquarie and Coffs Harbour on the New South Wales mid-north coast lies a scenic sub-tropical retreat. From secluded beaches, tourist towns and luxury resorts to tranquil forests, fishing villages and sleepy townships, this stretch of coast offers many holiday options.

The protected inlets, picturesque bays, rocky promontories and long, sandy beaches along the coastline are backed by the rainforest-clad mountains of the Great Dividing Range. Its lush, thickly wooded areas are protected as national parks or state forests. Fertile river valleys support sub-tropical agricultural ventures such as banana plantations.

The region's moderate climate and relaxed lifestyle have attracted retirees from the cooler southern climes, while holidaymakers of all ages can find many activities to entertain them.

Tourist information

i Coffs Coast Visitor Information Centre

Cnr Pacific Hwy & McLean St, Coffs Harbour NSW 2450
Ph: (02) 6652 1522
Tollfree: 1300 369 070
www.coffscoast.com.au

Main Attractions

◈ **Big Banana** A Coffs Harbour icon, the Big Banana celebrates the banana: the mainstay of the local economy.

◈ **Butterfly House** Walk among native and exotic butterflies in an enclosed sub-tropical garden.

◈ **Coffs Harbour** Water sports can be enjoyed here at a myriad of beaches.

◈ **George's Gold Mine** Facilities include BBQs, picnic grounds and walking trails through the surrounding ancient forest.

◈ **North Coast Regional Botanic Gardens** The sub-tropical gardens include a rainforest patch, a number of endangered plant species, and a mangrove boardwalk.

◈ **Pet Porpoise Pool** Dolphins, seals and penguins are the star attractions of daily shows at this oceanarium.

◈ **Woolgoolga** This town offers an excellent surfing beach, and swimming and boating on Woolgoolga Lake.

Muttonbird Island

Spectacular coastal views abound from this nature reserve, which features Australia's migratory muttonbirds. The birds return to the island in August after travelling thousands of kilometres from south-east Asia. The tiny island is reached by walking along Coffs Harbour's northern sea wall.

Junior lifesavers at Park Beach

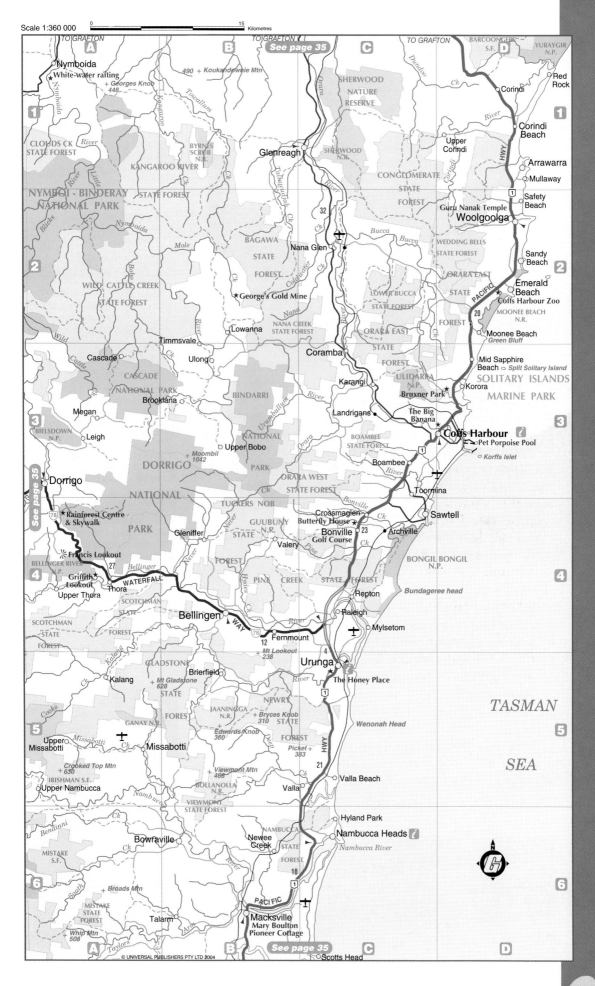

Scale 1:360 000

0   15

Kilometres

See page 35

New South Wales   **53**

© UNIVERSAL PUBLISHERS PTY LTD 2004

Vineyard

Tourist information

i Wine Country Visitors
Information Centre

111 Main Rd
Pokolbin NSW 2325
Ph: (02) 4990 4477
www.winecountry.com.au

Main Attractions

◈ **Hunter Valley Gardens** 25ha of spectacular display gardens next to a village with boutique shops, restaurants and a resort.

◈ **Koolang Observatory** Nestled in bushland, the observatory offers guided tours of the night sky.

◈ **Morpeth** One of the most unspoilt heritage towns in NSW, the entire village of Morpeth has been classified by the National Trust.

◈ **Pokolbin** Home to wineries, galleries, produce shops and the Hunter Valley Wine Society. A good starting point for a tour of the region's vineyards.

◈ **Richmond Vale Railway and Mining Museum** This museum brings the era of steam locomotives to life.

◈ **Rusa Park Zoo** Here you will see the white euro kangaroos, the only albino kangaroos in captivity.

◈ **Wollombi** Endeavour Museum showcases Wollombi's strong links to its colonial past.

A scenic 90-minute drive from Sydney, the Hunter Valley is one of Australia's premier wine-producing regions. The first vines were planted as far back as 1832 and the fertile flats of the Hunter River continue to nourish some of the nation's finest vineyards.

A fabulous place for wine and food lovers, there are close to 100 wineries – large and boutique – and dozens of restaurants. Although only about five per cent of Australia's wine comes from here, the Hunter is home to some of the most respected wineries, including Drayton, Lindemans, Tyrrells, and Tulloch.

Wine lovers' needs are catered for with cellar door sales, winery tours, restaurants, picnic areas and a diverse range of accommodation.

While the region is bursting with natural beauty, seams of high quality coal are also found throughout the valley, and coal mining remains an important part of the local economy. Mining activity is localised, however, and does not disturb the tranquillity of the valley. Cessnock is the region's main coal-mining town; Maitland is another centre for the coal industry and has a rich heritage as one of colonial Australia's most important towns. It also hosts the annual Hunter Valley Steamfest, a premier event for train buffs.

The lush river flats are home to dairy and beef cattle, fruit and vegetable crops, and thoroughbred horses.

There is much to see and do in the valley and many day trippers who come to sample the fruits of the vine return for longer tours of the region.

Harvest Festival

This is a perfect opportunity to experience wine country culture and tradition. After harvesting the grapes (March to April), leading wineries toast their crop with a variety of banquets, lunches and dinners, and more traditional activities such as barrel tastings.

Pepper Tree Wines cellar door

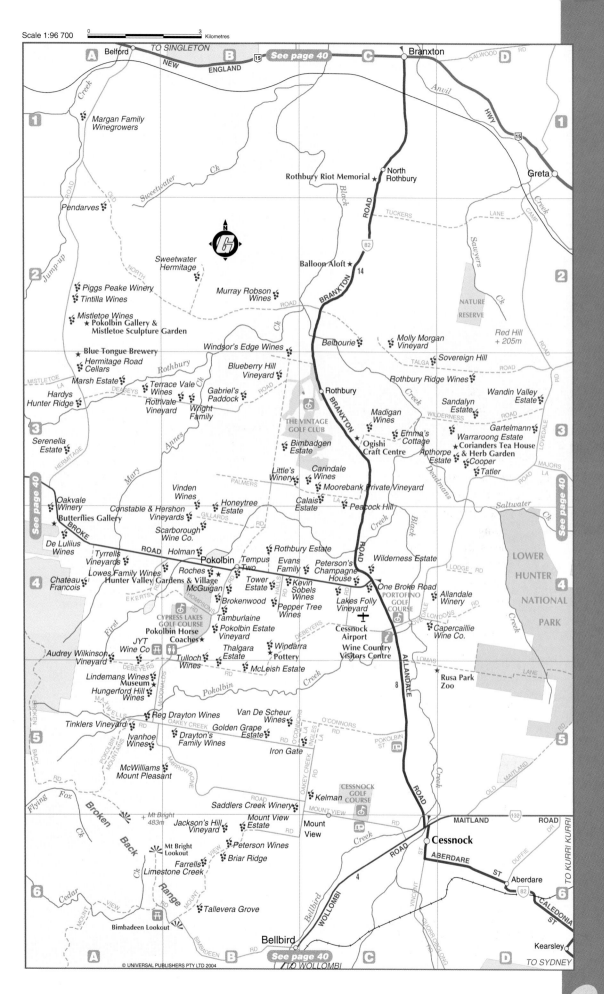

Scale 1:96 700

0 ___ 3 Kilometres

TO SINGLETON

Belford

Branxton

Greta

Margan Family Winegrowers

Rothbury Riot Memorial ★   North Rothbury

Pendarves

Sweetwater Hermitage

Balloon Aloft ★   14

Piggs Peake Winery
Tintilla Wines

Murray Robson Wines

Molly Morgan Vineyard

NATURE RESERVE

Red Hill + 205m

Mistletoe Wines
★ Pokolbin Gallery & Mistletoe Sculpture Garden

Windsor's Edge Wines

Belbourie

Sovereign Hill

★ Blue Tongue Brewery
Hermitage Road Cellars

Blueberry Hill Vineyard

Rothbury Ridge Wines

Wandin Valley Estate

Marsh Estate

Terrace Vale Wines

Gabriel's Paddock

Rothbury

Madigan Wines

Sandalyn Estate

Gartelmann

Hardys Hunter Ridge

Rothvale Vineyard

Wright Family

THE VINTAGE GOLF CLUB

Emma's Cottage

Warraroong Estate

★ Corianders Tea House & Herb Garden

Serenella Estate

Bimbadgen Estate

Ogishi Craft Centre

Apthorpe Estate

Cooper

Tatler

Oakvale Winery

Vinden Wines

Little's Winery

Carindale Wines

Moorebank Private Vineyard

Calais Estate

Peacock Hill

Butterflies Gallery

Constable & Hershon Vineyards

Honeytree Estate

Scarborough Wine Co.

De Luliius Wines

Tyrrells Vineyards

Holman

Rothbury Estate

Wilderness Estate

LOWER

Lowes Family Wines

Roches

Pokolbin

Tempus Two

Evans Family

Peterson's Champagne House

HUNTER

Hunter Valley Gardens & Village

McGuigan

Tower Estate

Kevin Sobels Wines

One Broke Road

Allandale Winery

NATIONAL

Chateau Francois

Brokenwood

Pepper Tree Wines

Lakes Folly Vineyard

PORTOFINO GOLF COURSE

Capercaillie Wine Co.

PARK

CYPRESS LAKES GOLF COURSE

Tamburlaine

JYT Wine Co

Pokolbin Horse Coaches ★

Pokolbin Estate Vineyard

Thalgara Estate

Wipdarra Pottery

Cessnock Airport

Wine Country Visitors Centre

Audrey Wilkinson Vineyard

Tulloch Wines

McLeish Estate

Rusa Park Zoo

Lindemans Wines Museum
Hungerford Hill Wines

Reg Drayton Wines

Van De Scheur Wines

Tinklers Vineyard

Ivanhoe Wines

Drayton's Family Wines

Golden Grape Estate

Iron Gate

POKOLBIN ST

McWilliams Mount Pleasant

Saddlers Creek Winery

Kelman

CESSNOCK GOLF COURSE

Mt Bright 483m

Jackson's Hill Vineyard

Mount View Estate

Mount View

MAITLAND

ROAD

Mt Bright Lookout

Peterson Wines

Briar Ridge

Cessnock

Farrells Limestone Creek

ABERDARE

Aberdare

TO KURRI KURRI

Tallevera Grove

Bimbadeen Lookout

Bellbird

Kearsley

TO SYDNEY

TO WOLLOMBI

© UNIVERSAL PUBLISHERS PTY LTD 2004

See page 40

Hunter Valley – Upper

Segenhoe stud farm

The upper side of the Hunter Valley, surrounding the pretty town of Scone, is widely regarded as Australia's premier thoroughbred and horse-breeding district. There are more than 80 thoroughbred studs located in this part of the Hunter, some offering personalised tours for those who book. The Scone Horse Week in May (complete with rodeos) is a must for equestrian types, while the Merriwa Festival of the Fleeces in June focuses on sheep and wool, with sheep dog trials and spinning exhibitions.

Wineries also characterise the Upper Hunter and the region has been influential in the development of the Australian wine industry. In the 19th century the region's wine growers stopped planting Cabernet Sauvignon vines; in the 1960s these grapes were reintroduced by Max Lake of Lake's Folly, and now 'Cab Sauv' is one of Australia's most popular red wines. Many wineries, including Rosemount Estate and Arrowfield Wines, offer wine tasting and sales at the cellar door.

Prospering from vineyards, horse studs and coal mining, the Upper Hunter is also the site of some of Australia's oldest towns.

Tourist information

i Muswellbrook Tourist Information Centre

87 Hill St, Muswellbrook NSW 2333
Ph: (02) 6541 4050
www.upperhuntercountry.com

Main Attractions

◈ **Barrington Tops National Park** About 85% of the park is declared wilderness. It is part of eastern Australia's World Heritage-listed rainforest.

◈ **Denman** This quaint township, traditionally known for its horse and cattle studs, is the centre for established vineyards such as Rosemount Estate and Arrowfield.

◈ **Lake Glenbawn State Park** This park offers a wonderful diversity of wildlife, bushwalks and fishing.

◈ **Muswellbrook** Originally a government-planned village, it has become a regional centre with vineyards clustered to the south-west of town.

◈ **Singleton** Gateway to the Upper Hunter Valley, Singleton boasts the largest sundial in the southern hemisphere.

◈ **Upper Hunter Wine Centre** This one-stop shop in Muswellbrook showcases the region's wines.

Dog at cellar door

Upper Hunter Wineries

Name	Map	Address	Phone	Open
Arrowfield Wines	E4	Denman Rd, Jerry's Plains	(02) 6576 4041	10am–5pm daily
Bell's Lane Wines	C2	Mangoola Rd, Denman	(02) 6547 1191	Phone for appointment
Cruickshank Callatoota Estate	C1	2656 Wybong Rd, Wybong	(02) 6547 8149	9am–5pm daily
Horseshoe Vineyard	B4	Horseshoe Valley, Denman	(02) 6547 3528	Phone for appointment
Inglewood Vineyard	C3	Yarrawa Rd, Denman	(02) 6547 2556	Phone for appointment
James Estate Wines	A3	951 Rylstone Rd, Baerami	(02) 6547 5168	10am–4pm daily
Rosemount Estate	B3	Rosemount Rd, Denman	(02) 6549 6400	10am–4pm daily
Verona Vineyard	E1	New England Hwy, Muswellbrook	(02) 6541 4777	9am–5pm daily
Yarraman Road Estate	B1	700 Yarraman Rd, Wybong	(02) 6547 8118	10am–5pm daily

Scale 1:295 200

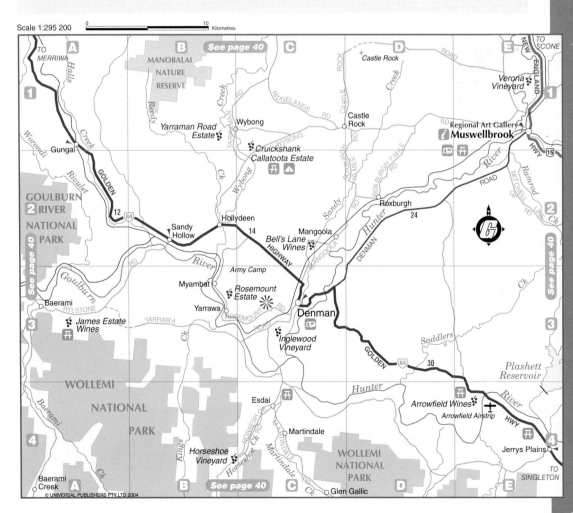

Illawarra and Southern Highlands

View of Bowral from Jellore lookout

The Illawarra and Southern Highlands are both located on Sydney's southwest fringes, but they have distinct identities. Flanked by the Tasman Sea shores and mountainous terrain inland, their landscapes bring together the mountains and ocean in spectacular contrast.

The Illawarra – the name is a corruption of an Aboriginal word meaning 'between the high place and the sea' – has Wollongong as its centre. It is a coastal haven for sun-worshippers and fans of water sports.

The neighbouring Southern Highlands have their own unique character, and the cooler climate and picturesque villages dotting the landscape suggest comparisons with rural England. In summer it is possible to experience all four seasons in a single day while touring the many attractions offered in this diverse region.

Best-kept secret

Kiama's best-kept secret is the Harbour Rock Pool at Blowhole Point: a fantastic place for a refreshing swim. The harbour is also a great spot for family fishing and has a boat ramp.

Tourist information

Southern Highlands Visitor Information Centre

62-70 Main St, Mittagong
NSW 2575
Tollfree: 1300 657 559
www.southern-highlands.com.au

Wollongong Visitor Information Centre

93 Crown St, Wollongong
NSW 2500
Freecall: 1800 240 737
www.tourismwollongong.com

Main Attractions

◈ **Berrima** Several buildings in this town, founded in 1831, are listed on the National Estate. Visit the Surveyor-General Inn, Australia's oldest continuously licensed pub.

◈ **Bowral** Well known for its annual Tulip Time Festival held each spring, Bowral is an idyllic country retreat. The Bradman museum pays tribute to Bowral's most famous son, cricketer Sir Donald Bradman.

◈ **Bundanoon** Visit the Glow Worm Glen between September and May. After dark it becomes a fairy world.

◈ **Kiama** The Kiama Blowhole sprays water 60m into the air.

◈ **Minnamurra Rainforest** The region's finest attraction has won many tourist awards.

◈ **Nan Tien Temple** This is the biggest Buddhist temple in the southern hemisphere.

◈ **Stanwell Park** A great spot for hang-gliding, with sheer cliffs and panoramic vistas.

Paragliding from Bald Hill

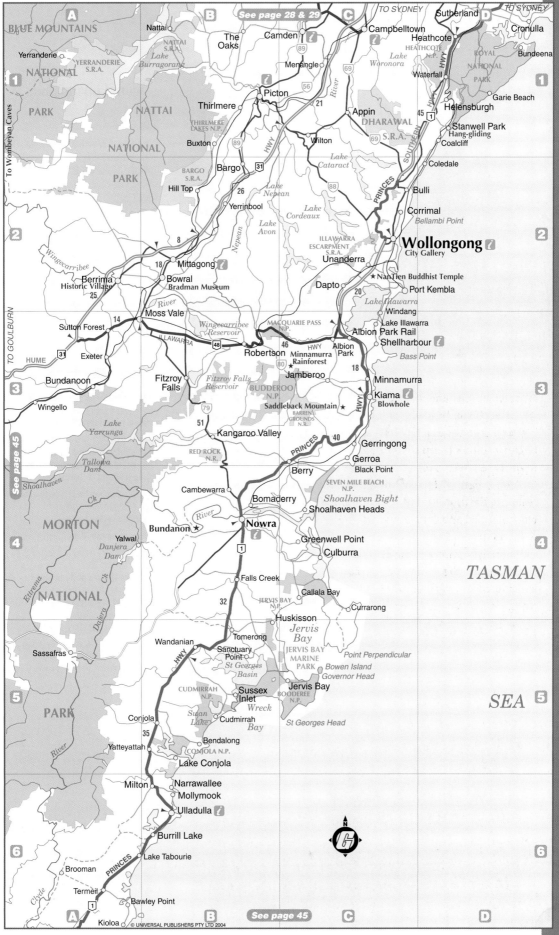

Scale 1:685 700

See page 28 & 29
See page 45
See page 45

TO SYDNEY
TO SYDNEY

BLUE MOUNTAINS

Yerranderie
Nattai
The Oaks
Camden
Campbelltown
Sutherland
Cronulla
Bundeena
Heathcote
Menangle
Picton
Thirlmere
Appin
Waterfall
Helensburgh
Garie Beach
Buxton
Wilton
Stanwell Park
Hang-gliding
Coalcliff
Bargo
Hill Top
Coledale
Yerrinbool
Bulli
Corrimal
Bellambi Point
Mittagong
Wollongong
City Gallery
Berrima
Historic Village
Bowral
Bradman Museum
Unanderra
NanTien Buddhist Temple
Sutton Forest
Moss Vale
Dapto
Port Kembla
Windang
Lake Illawarra
Exeter
Robertson
Albion Park Rail
Shellharbour
Bundanoon
Fitzroy Falls
Minnamurra Rainforest
Albion Park
Bass Point
Wingello
Saddleback Mountain
Jamberoo
Minnamurra
Kiama
Blowhole
Kangaroo Valley
Gerringong
Gerroa
Black Point
Berry
Cambewarra
Bomaderry
Shoalhaven Heads
Bundanon
Nowra
Greenwell Point
Culburra
Yalwal
Falls Creek
Callala Bay
Currarong
Huskisson
Jervis Bay
Sassafras
Wandanian
Tomerong
Sanctuary Point
Jervis Bay
Point Perpendicular
Bowen Island
Governor Head
Sussex Inlet
Jervis Bay
Conjola
Cudmirrah
St Georges Head
Bendalong
Lake Conjola
Yatteyattah
Milton
Narrawallee
Mollymook
Ulladulla
Burrill Lake
Brooman
Lake Tabourie
Termeil
Bawley Point
Kioloa

TASMAN
SEA

Jervis Bay

© UNIVERSAL PUBLISHERS PTY LTD 2004

Nowra and Jervis Bay

Berry township

Located approximately 163km south of Sydney's southern fringe, the area between Nowra and Jervis Bay is a study in contrasts.

The picturesque rolling hills surrounding the south-coast town of Nowra support a thriving dairy industry, and regular produce markets sell fresh, seasonal produce from the region. Heading to the coast, you will pass through quaint rural villages featuring teahouses, antique shops, cosy bed-and-breakfast cottages, and old-fashioned pubs.

Once at Jervis Bay, there is a wonderful ocean playground along the shores of this stunning sheltered inlet. Not surprisingly, fishing is one of the region's key industries and a pleasant pastime for amateurs.

A safe haven

Abraham's Bosom Beach, Jervis Bay, was the site where the shipwrecked passengers of the *SS Merimbula* found safety. Its unusual name refers to the Old Testament story where children found shelter in "the bosom of Abraham"

Tourist information

i Shoalhaven Visitors Centre

Cnr Princes Hwy & Pleasant Way, Nowra NSW 2541
Tollfree: 1300 662 808
www.southcoast.com.au/ shoalhaven

Main Attractions

◈ **Berry** This pretty hamlet boasts many charming buildings classified by the National Trust.

◈ **Bundanon** Here you can visit painter Arthur Boyd's scenic property, now a gallery.

◈ **Coolangatta Historic Village** This historic village was the first European south-coast settlement.

◈ **Jervis Bay & Jervis Bay National Park** The bay has 50km of protected shoreline, while the national park boasts an array of pristine beaches.

◈ **Kangaroo Valley** A National Trust-listed village, surrounded by rolling hills and orchards.

◈ *Lady Denman* Once a ferry, the *Lady Denman* now houses a maritime museum.

◈ **Nowra Animal Park** This features native fauna on show in a rainforest setting.

◈ **Nowra Historical Buildings** St Andrews church, the old police station, and Meroogal House are all historical buildings in Nowra.

◈ **Seven Mile Beach National Park** This park has a long expanse of white sandy beach flanked by sand dunes.

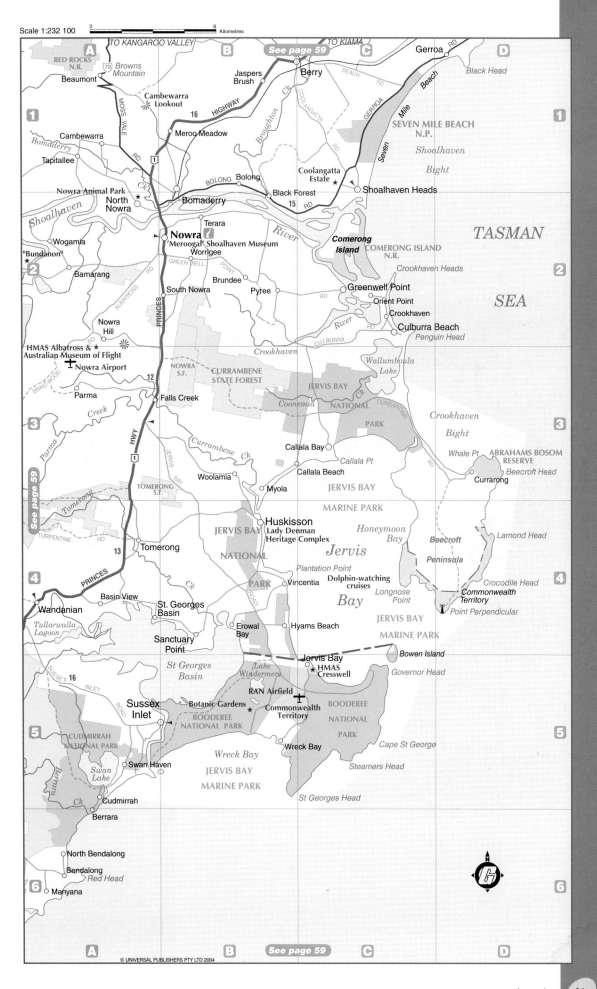

TO KANGAROO VALLEY

A RED ROCKS N.R.
Browns Mountain
Beaumont
Cambewarra Lookout
79
MOSS VALE RD
HIGHWAY
16
Meroo Meadow
Cambewarra
Tapitallee
Bomaderry
Ck
BOLONG
Bolong
Nowra Animal Park
North Nowra
Shoalhaven
Bomaderry
Terara
Wogamia
Nowra i
'Meroogal' Shoalhaven Museum
"Bundanon"
Worrigee
Bamarang
Brundee
South Nowra
GREEN WELL
POINT
ALBATROSS RD
PRINCES
Nowra Hill
HMAS Albatross & ★
Australian Museum of Flight
Nowra Airport
BRAIDWOOD
12
Parma
Falls Creek
NOWRA S.F.
Creek
Parma Creek
Currambene Ck
3
TURPENTINE RD
Tomerong
Woolamia
JERVIS BAY
TOMERONG S.F.
Coonemia
CURRAMBENE STATE FOREST
Callala Bay
Callala Beach
Myola
4
PRINCES
HWY
1
Wandanian
Tullarwalla Lagoon
Basin View
St. Georges Basin
Sanctuary Point
Erowal Bay
JERVIS BAY NATIONAL PARK
Huskisson
Lady Denman Heritage Complex
Vincentia
Hyams Beach
ROAD
5
SUSSEX INLET
16
Sussex Inlet
CUDMIRRAH NATIONAL PARK
Botanic Gardens
BOODEREE NATIONAL PARK
RAN Airfield
Commonwealth Territory
Lake Windermere
Jervis Bay
★ HMAS Cresswell
Swan Lake
Swan Haven
Wreck Bay
St Georges Basin
Wreck Bay
Berrara
Ck
JERVIS BAY MARINE PARK
6
North Bendalong
Bendalong
Manyana
Red Head

TO KIAMA
See page 59
Berry
Jaspers Brush
Gerroa
Black Head
B
C
D
BEACH RD
GERROA
COOLANGATTA
Broughton Ck
Seven Mile Beach
SEVEN MILE BEACH N.P.
Shoalhaven Bight
15
Black Forest
Coolangatta Estate ★
Shoalhaven Heads
Comerong Island
COMERONG ISLAND N.R.
River
Shoalhaven
Crookhaven Heads
Greenwell Point
Orient Point
Crookhaven
Culburra Beach
Penguin Head
River
CULBURRA
Crookhaven
Wallumboula Lake
JERVIS BAY
CURRARONG RD
Crookhaven Bight
Whale Pt
ABRAHAMS BOSOM RESERVE
Beecroft Head
Currarong
PARK
JERVIS BAY
MARINE PARK
Honeymoon Bay
Beecroft Peninsula
Lamond Head
Jervis
Dolphin-watching cruises
Longnose Point
Bay
Crocodile Head
Commonwealth Territory
Point Perpendicular
JERVIS BAY
MARINE PARK
Bowen Island
Governor Head
BOODEREE NATIONAL PARK
Cape St George
Steamers Head
St Georges Head

TASMAN
SEA

New South Wales

Port Stephens and Myall Lakes

Dolphin watching at Port Stephens

The Great Lakes are a system of shallow waterways stretching along the coast of the Tasman Sea, 236km north of Sydney. The tranquillity of this unique area is preserved in a popular national park scattered with camping retreats.

The eastern edges of the lakes can be accessed via numerous roads and trails leading through the forests from the Pacific Highway.

The lakes are ideal for water sports and boating. Their banks are dotted with launching ramps, and boats and canoes can be hired from Myall Shores, Smiths Lake boatshed, and the town of Tea Gardens. For a different sort of adventure, hire a houseboat from the nearby town of Bulahdelah, whose name originates from an Aboriginal word for 'meeting of two streams'. The Myall River forms the town's southern boundary.

Wang Wauk State Forest has a creek-side walk past giant gum trees with opportunities to sight bandicoots, goannas, koalas, gliders and many bird species. For those feeling more active, the entire river system and Great Dividing Range can be viewed from the Alum Mountain lookout.

On the other side of the narrow strip of sand dunes separating the lakes from the ocean, there are surf beaches.

Nelson Bay is the main town on the Tomaree Peninsula. This resort town boasts galleries, gardens, and ocean fish to catch or buy. Nearby Nelson Head houses the Inner Lighthouse, carefully restored by the National Trust. It includes a teahouse, cottage, maritime museum and a coastal patrol base. Nelson Bay is a good starting point for whale watching and dolphin spotting cruises. Game fishing is popular and boats of various sizes can be chartered.

Nelson Bay and its nearby townships, including Shoal Bay, Fingal Bay and Salamander Bay, offer a wide range of accommodation and activities year round. The Tomaree National Park is also worth visiting for its koala colonies.

Tourist information

 Port Stephens Visitor Information Centre

Victoria Pde, Nelson Bay
NSW 2315
Freecall: 1800 808 900
www.portstephens.org.au

 Bulahdelah Visitor Information Centre

Cnr Pacific Hwy & Crawford St
Bulahdelah NSW 2423
Freecall: 1800 802 692
www.greatlakes.org.au

Main Attractions

◈ **Bulahdelah** This tiny township is a convenient base for exploring the region.

◈ **Myall Lakes National Park** A unique and very popular national park with lakes that are ideal for water sports and house-boating. Wildlife in the park includes kangaroos, swamp and red-necked wallabies, bandicoots, gliders, spiny anteaters, and marsupial mice.

◈ **Nelson Bay** Located on a protected inlet surrounded by towering headlands, it is a great place for spotting dolphins.

◈ **Seal Rocks** This small and remote fishing village, popular with surfers and campers, is a secluded spot with excellent surfing opportunities. There is a blowhole, and the lighthouse gives sweeping views of the coast.

◈ **Tea Gardens and Hawks Nest** These twin towns are connected by a single bridge. Hawks Nest boasts a 40km surf beach; at Tea Gardens, houseboats and adventure cruises are available.

Scuba diving, Nelson Bay

Dolphin and Whale Watching

Pods of friendly bottlenose dolphins are one of this region's noted attractions, and during winter and spring Tomaree Heads provides an excellent vantage point for sighting migrating whales from a number of lookouts dotting the headlands. Approximately 10 operators offer cruises from Port Stephens or Nelson Bay, providing opportunities for visitors to enjoy dolphin and whale watching; cruises to Broughton Island, Myall River and Lakes, and Tea Gardens; and viewing the area's dramatic sunsets.

MV Surprise conducts a range of cruise options for exploring Port Stephens, with booking recommended for the dolphin cruises which operate daily.

The *Tamboi Queen* runs daily dolphin-watching cruises from Port Stephens and bookings are recommended. A boom net allows observers to have closer encounters with the dolphins.

Advance II, a sleek 18m yacht, runs private charters for dolphin and whale watching and live-on-board getaways between November and May.

Moonshadow Cruises offers whale-watching cruises in season and dolphin-watching cruises daily, plus dinner cruises and Broughton Island cruises.

Features of Myall Lakes National Park

Containing the largest coastal lake system in NSW, this national park is an important waterbird habitat. Walk through rainforest, hire a houseboat, or go four-wheel-driving along permitted beaches. With an area of just over 44ha, this popular park has something to offer everyone.

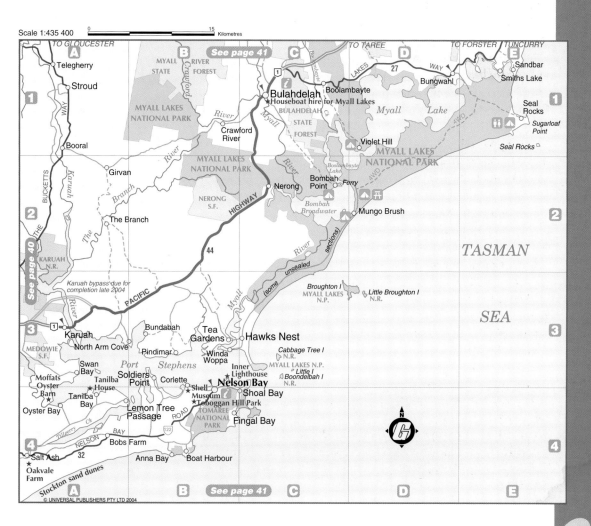

Scale 1:435 400

Snowy Mountains

Trout fishing in the Snowy Mountains

Part of the New South Wales section of the Great Dividing Range, the Snowy Mountains are approximately 160 km long and 80 km wide. Much of the rugged terrain is 900m or more above sea level, with the mountainous ridge rising to 2228m at Mt Kosciuszko, Australia's highest point. Although the Snowy Mountains are located in New South Wales, they are close to the ACT, and their southern boundary extends to the Victorian border.

Lake Jindabyne was created as part of the Snowy Mountains Hydro Electric Scheme when the old township of Jindabyne was flooded. Jindabyne now provides the venues for many summer activities, including bushwalking, trout fishing, sailing, sailboarding, water-skiing, canoeing and swimming.

Kosciuszko National Park, the largest national park in New South Wales, occupies most of this region. The park offers year-round activities including golf, horseriding, mountain bike riding, trout fishing and white-water rafting.

Despite their name, the Snowy Mountains actually lie beneath the line of permanent snow and heavy snowfalls only occur between June and October. During the winter months, both local and international skiers flock to the many ski resorts dotting the mountains.

Summer also has much to offer visitors to the region. Lower prices and fewer visitors make the area a perfect destination for bushwalking, trout fishing, or a cycling holiday. The wildflowers and bird life are particularly impressive during the summer months.

Snowfields

Thredbo is a popular ski resort town, sandwiched in a small valley between the Thredbo River and the road. Charlotte Pass, Perisher Valley and Smiggin Holes lie within the Kosciuszko National Park's borders: all offer great skiing, and visitors can easily travel between some of the resorts in winter on the Skitube.

Tourist information

ℹ️ **Snowy Region Visitor Centre**

Kosciuszko Rd, Jindabyne
NSW 2627
Ph: (02) 6450 5600
www.snowymountains.com.au
www.nationalparks.nsw.gov.au

Main Attractions

◈ **Jindabyne** The gateway to the alpine ski resorts.

◈ **Kosciuszko National Park** This park occupies most of the Snowy Mountains region. Due to the heavy snowfall, vehicles inside the park must carry chains between 1 June and 10 October.

◈ **Mt Kosciuszko** At 2228m above sea level, Mt Kosciuszko is Australia's highest point. An accessible walking trail crosses the flattened top of the mountain, providing breathtaking views.

◈ **Thredbo Alpine Village** Sandwiched in a small valley, this most popular resort village is dotted with Alpine-style chalets. The area offers some of the best skiing.

◈ **Yarrangobilly Caves** Surrounded by virgin bush, this is a system of about 60 limestone caves. Walking trails next to the caves offer panoramic views of Yarrangobilly Gorge.

Skiing in the Snowy Mountains

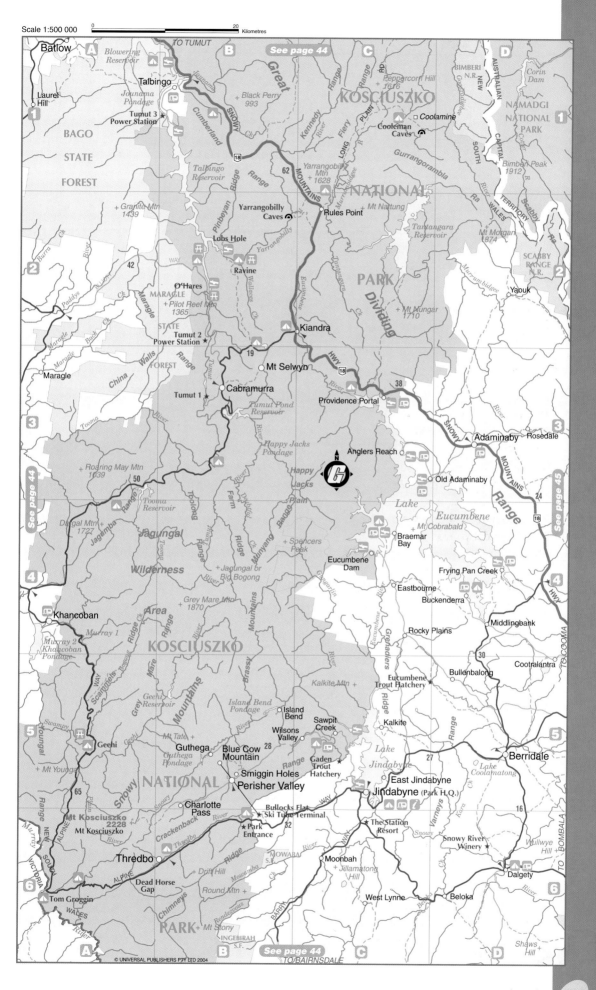

Victoria

The Place To Be

Occupying the south-eastern corner of the continent, Victoria is Australia's second smallest state after Tasmania. Its manageable size and efficient highway system make touring the state's attractions relatively easy, with most places within a five-hour drive of the state's cultured and cosmopolitan capital city, Melbourne.

Victoria packs a lot within its boundaries and there is a diversity of natural, cultural, and historic areas to be explored. The southern coastline is spectacular and varied, taking in the Great Ocean Road to the west, and the wilderness of Wilsons Promontory and the Gippsland Lakes area to the east. Victoria's magnificent Alpine region has much to explore and the Murray River, which stretches along the state's northern border with New South Wales, is a delightful destination in itself.

Victoria's goldfields exhibit the history of a dynamic period. Aboriginal history is also evident, with rock paintings and a cultural centre in the Grampians region.

Victoria caters well for the discerning traveller. Fresh produce is a specialty of the state, with gourmet focal points in the Milawa Gourmet Region near Wangaratta, and the Gourmet Deli Trail in West Gippsland. Wine lovers can tour 22 regions with more than 350 wineries, stretching from the Grampians in the south-west to Rutherglen in the north-east.

Tourist information

i Melbourne Visitor Information Centre

Federation Square
Cnr Swanston St and Flinders St,
Melbourne Vic.3000
Ph: 9658 9658
www.visitvictoria.com
Victorian Tourism
Information Service
Ph: 132 842

| Area = 220,620 sq km | Occupies 2.9% of Australia | Length of coast = 1,577 km | Length from east to west = 793km |

Victoria Key Map & Distance Chart

All distances shown in the chart below have been measured over highways and major roads, not necessarily by the shortest route.

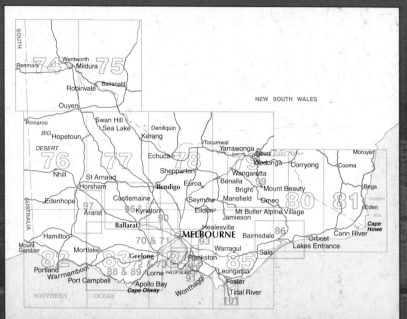

Melbourne skyline

Approximate Distance	Albury NSW	Bairnsdale	Ballarat	Bega NSW	Bendigo	Bordertown SA	Cooma NSW	Geelong	Hamilton	Horsham	Melbourne	Mildura	Mount Gambier SA	Portland	Renmark SA	Shepparton	Swan Hill	Traralgon	Wangaratta	Warrnambool
Albury NSW		377	431	424	308	679	312	388	591	521	316	619	723	678	764	188	403	480	79	577
Bairnsdale	377		397	326	437	741	341	354	586	583	282	827	759	644	966	457	626	118	308	543
Ballarat	431	397		723	122	344	738	88	176	186	115	546	308	261	595	242	311	279	357	179
Bega NSW	424	326	723		726	1067	112	680	899	908	608	1031	1031	970	1176	600	815	444	491	869
Bendigo	308	437	122	726		371	608	210	298	213	155	399	430	383	538	120	189	319	234	301
Bordertown SA	679	741	344	1067	371		979	432	288	158	459	373	183	298	279	491	411	623	605	399
Cooma NSW	312	341	738	112	608	979		695	891	821	623	919	1023	985	1064	488	703	459	374	884
Geelong	388	354	88	680	210	432	695		232	274	72	544	364	290	683	247	399	236	314	189
Hamilton	591	586	176	899	298	288	891	232		130	291	442	132	85	581	418	371	455	532	103
Horsham	521	583	186	908	213	158	821	274	130		301	312	262	215	451	333	246	465	447	267
Melbourne	316	282	115	608	155	459	623	72	291	301		545	423	362	684	175	344	164	242	261
Mildura	619	827	456	1031	399	373	919	544	442	312	545		574	527	139	444	216	709	558	557
Mount Gambier SA	723	759	308	1031	430	183	1023	364	132	262	423	574		105	478	550	528	587	664	185
Portland	678	644	261	970	383	298	985	290	85	215	362	527	105		593	503	456	526	609	101
Renmark SA	764	966	595	1176	538	279	1064	683	581	451	684	139	478	593		589	361	848	708	694
Shepparton	188	657	242	600	120	491	488	247	418	333	175	444	550	503	589		228	339	114	436
Swan Hill	403	626	311	815	189	411	703	399	371	246	344	216	528	456	361	228		508	342	526
Traralgon	480	118	279	444	319	623	459	236	455	465	164	709	587	526	848	339	508		406	425
Wangaratta	79	308	357	491	234	605	374	314	532	447	242	558	664	609	708	114	342	406		503
Warrnambool	577	543	179	869	301	399	884	189	103	267	261	557	185	101	694	436	526	425	503	

Melbourne

Federation Square

The capital of the 'Garden State', Melbourne sits on the shores of Port Phillip, with the picturesque Yarra River meandering through the city and its suburbs.

Melbourne is a sophisticated and vibrant city. Its grand-scale architecture, wide boulevards, and landscaped parks and gardens are legacies of the late-nineteenth century gold rushes in nearby Ballarat and Bendigo.

Melbourne's trams give the city an old-world charm: quiet and pollution free, they are a gracious means of transport and efficiently carry passengers along the main thoroughfares. The free city circle tram transports visitors on a loop that takes in all the major CBD sights.

Melbourne's changeable climate is renowned and its four distinct seasons give the city a European feel. Large-scale immigration from Europe also adds to this atmosphere and, along with more recent immigration from South-East Asia, contributes to the diverse mix of cultures, foods and people which make Melbourne the cosmopolitan city that it is today.

Melbourne's contrasts are reflected in its reputation as both a cultured and sports-mad city. Major events include the Australian Open Tennis Championship in January, the Australian Grand Prix in March, the Melbourne International Comedy Festival in March and the Melbourne International Arts Festival in October.

Tourist information

 Melbourne Visitor Information Centre

Federation Square
Cnr Swanston St and Flinders St,
Melbourne 3000
Ph: (03) 9658 9658
www.tourism.vic.gov.au

 Victorian Tourism Information Service

Ph: 132 842
www.visitvictoria.com

Main Attractions

◈ **AFL** 'Aussie Rules' football is a Melbourne obsession during winter.

◈ **Chapel St** Sample Melbourne food and fashion in one of the city's most vibrant strips.

◈ **Federation Square** The city's new public space brings together striking architecture, restaurants, and arts venues. The NGV Australia at Federation Square is the spectacular new home of the gallery's Australian art collection.

◈ **Lygon St** One of the city's premier eat streets.

◈ **National Gallery of Victoria (NGV)** The oldest and most visited public art gallery in Australia.

◈ **Old Melbourne Gaol** This historic gaol houses a museum and the gallows on which bushranger Ned Kelly was hanged.

◈ **Royal Botanical Gardens** See over 10,000 different plant species in this haven close to the CBD.

◈ **Shopping in Melbourne** Wander along Collins St and the streets running west off Swanston St for major department stores, boutiques and designer labels.

Places of Interest

Ⓐ Albert Park **C6**
Ⓑ Australian Grand Prix **C6**
Ⓒ Chinatown **C2**
Ⓓ Crown Casino **A4**
Ⓔ Federation Square **C3**
Ⓕ Gold Treasury Museum **D2**
Ⓖ Immigration Museum **B3**
Ⓗ Melbourne Aquarium **B3**
Ⓘ Melbourne Central Shopping Centre **B2**

Ⓙ Melbourne Cricket Ground **D3**
Ⓚ Melbourne Museum **C1**
Ⓛ Melbourne Park **D3**
Ⓜ Melbourne Observation Deck **A3**
Ⓝ Myer Music Bowl **C4**
Ⓞ National Gallery of Victoria **C4**
Ⓟ Old Melbourne Gaol **B2**
Ⓠ Parliament House **C2**
Ⓡ Polly Woodside Maritime Museum **A4**

Ⓢ Queen Victoria Market **A2**
Ⓣ Royal Botanic Gardens **D5**
Ⓤ Royal Exhibition Buildings **C1**
Ⓥ Shrine of Remembrance **C5**
Ⓦ Southgate Sheraton Towers **B3**
Ⓧ State Library of Victoria **B2**
Ⓨ Victorian Arts Centre **C4**

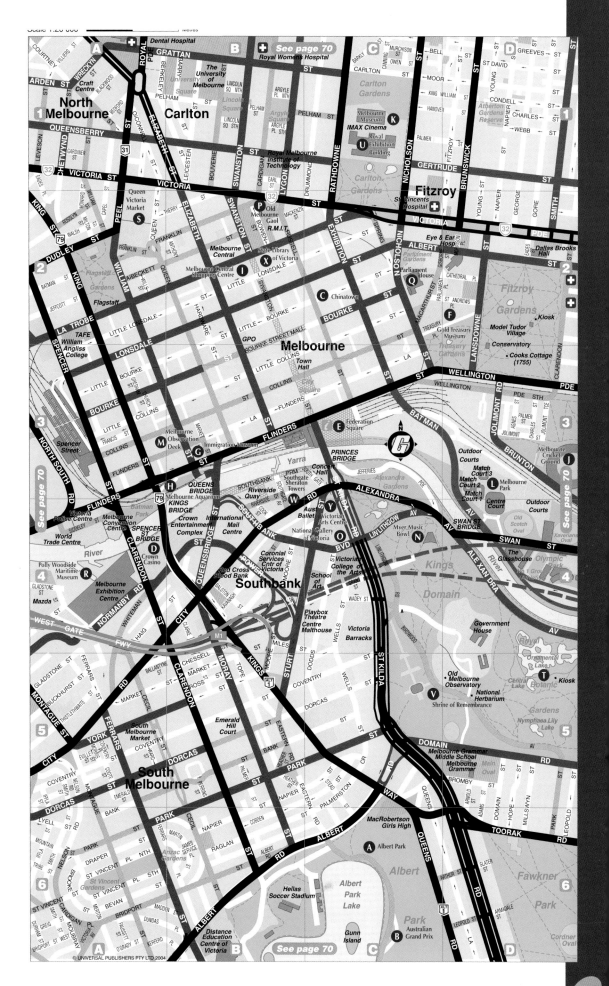

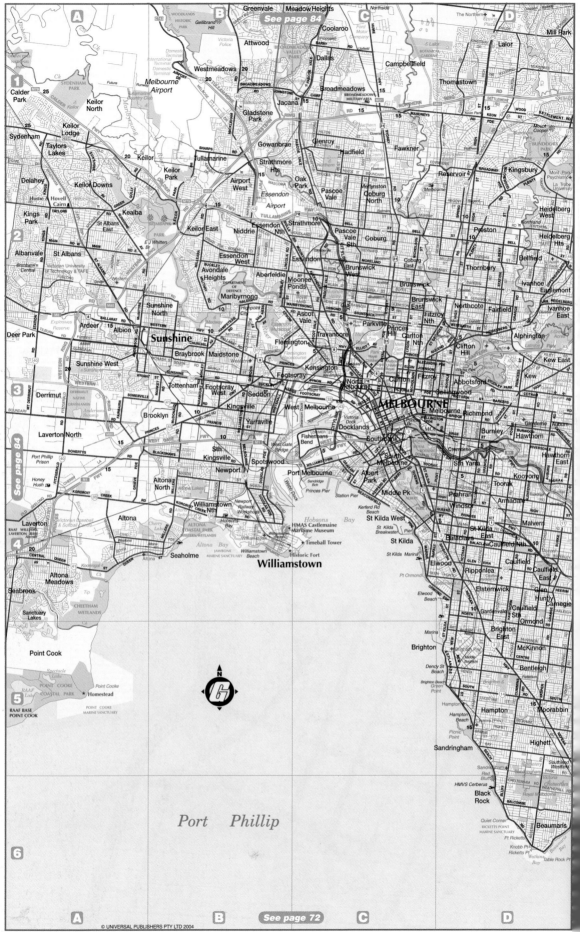

Port Phillip

See page 84
See page 72

See page 84

Yarra Glen

0   5   Kilometres

Plenty

Wattle Glen

Diamond Creek

Kangaroo Ground

Bend Of Islands

Sugarloaf Reservoir Park

Sugarloaf Reservoir

RMIT (Bundoora East)

Janefield Training Centre

Bundoora

St Helena

Eltham North

Research

Watsonia North

Greensborough

Briar Hill

Eltham

Coldstream

Watsonia

Montmorency

North Warrandyte

Wonga Park

Macleod

Yallambie

Chirnside Park

Rosanna

View Bank

Lower Plenty

Warrandyte

Lilydale

Heidelberg

Templestowe

Warrandyte South

Warranwood

Bulleen

Templestowe Lower

Park Orchards

Croydon Hills

Croydon North

Doncaster

Doncaster East

Donvale

Croydon

Mooroolbark

Balwyn North

Blackburn North

Ringwood North

Croydon Sth

Kilsyth

Montrose

Doncaster

Box Hill North

Nunawading

Ringwood East

Bayswater North

Kilsyth South

Balwyn

Mont Albert North

Mitcham

Ringwood

Deepdene

Mont Albert

Box Hill

Blackburn

Heathmont

Canterbury

Surrey Hills

Box Hill South

Blackburn South

Vermont

Bayswater

The Basin

Olinda

Camberwell

Riversdale

Forest Hill

Wantirna

Boronia

Sassafras

Glen Iris

Burwood

Vermont South

Wantirna South

Ferny Creek

Ashburton

Ashwood

Burwood East

Ferntree Gully

Tremont

Sherbrooke

Malvern East

Holmesglen

Mount Waverley

Glen Waverley

Knoxfield

Upper Ferntree Gully

Tecoma

Murrumbeena

Chadstone

Scoresby

Upwey

Hughesdale

Oakleigh East

Notting Hill

Wheelers Hill

Rowville

Belgrave

Bentleigh East

Oakleigh

Huntingdale

Lysterfield

Belgrave Heights

Clayton

Mulgrave

Lysterfield South

Belgrave South

Oakleigh South

Clarinda

Springvale

Narre Warren East

Heatherton

Clayton South

Sandown Park

Noble Park

Dandenong North

Endeavour Hills

Cheltenham

Springvale South

Narre Warren North

Harkaway

Mentone

Moorabbin Airport

Dingley Village

Doveton

Narre Warren

Parkdale

Braeside

Keysborough

Dandenong

Eumemmerring

Hallam

Mordialloc

Aspendale Gardens

Dandenong South

See page 73

Aspendale

© UNIVERSAL PUBLISHERS PTY LTD 2004

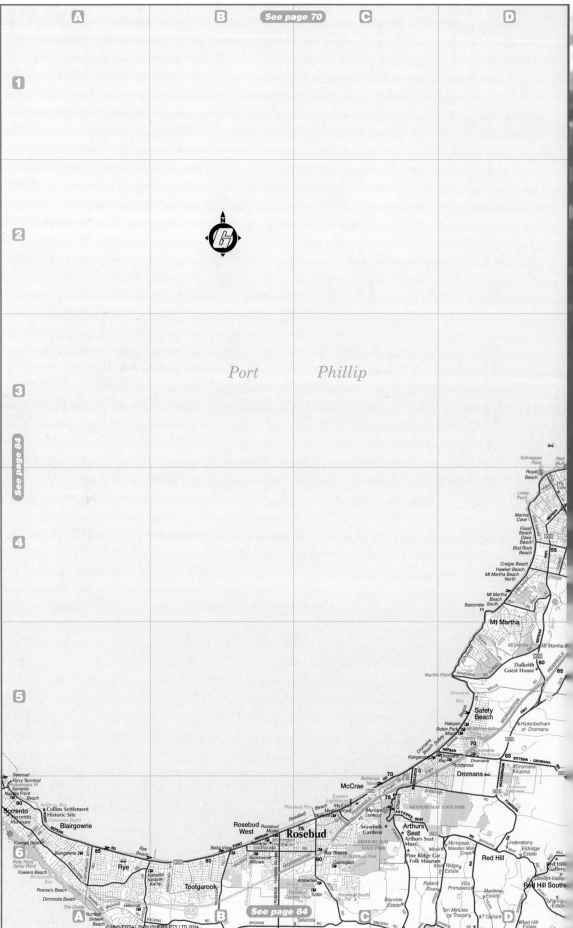

Port Phillip

See page 70

See page 84

See page 84

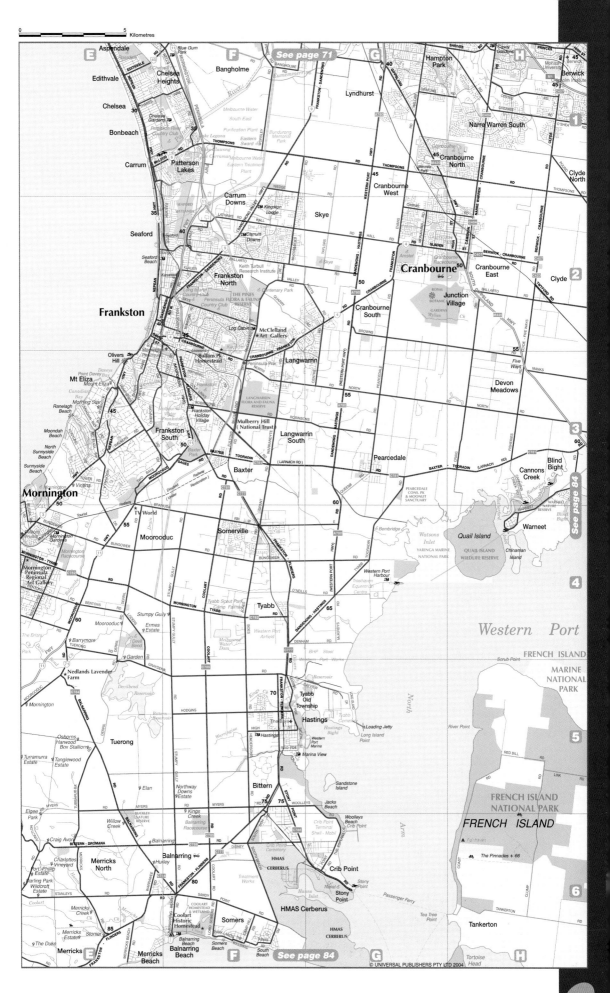

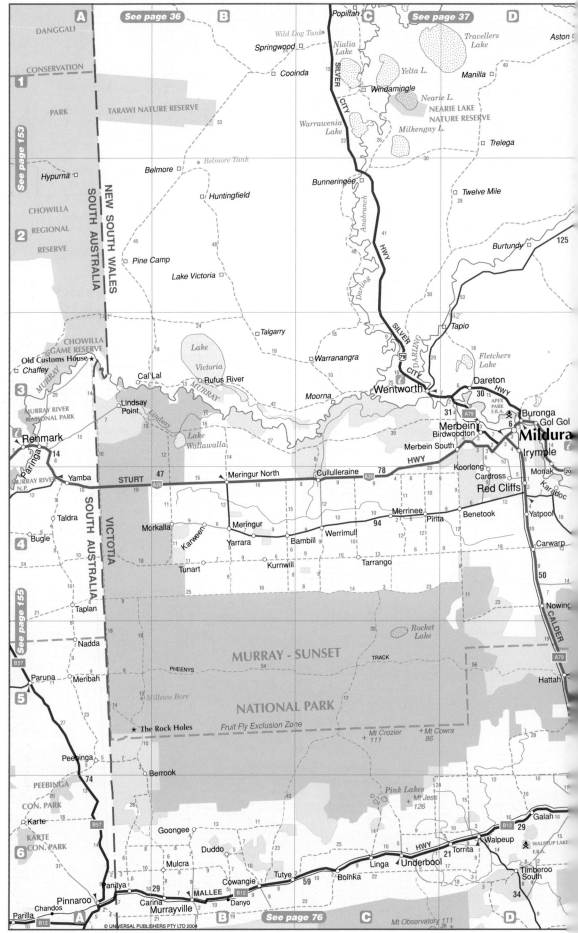

Scale 1:950 00

DANGGALI

CONSERVATION

PARK

TARAWI NATURE RESERVE

See page 36

See page 37

Popiltah

Wild Dog Tank

Springwood

Cooinda

Nialia Lake

Yelta L.

Windamingle

Warrawenia Lake

Milkengay L.

NEARIE LAKE NATURE RESERVE

Travellers Lake

Manilla

Trelega

CHOWILLA

REGIONAL

RESERVE

Hypurna

Belmore

Belmore Tank

Huntingfield

Pine Camp

Lake Victoria

Bunneringee

Warranangra

Twelve Mile

Burtundy

Tapio

Fletchers Lake

CHOWILLA GAME RESERVE

Old Customs House ★

Chaffey

MURRAY

Cal Lal

Rufus River

Lake Victoria

MURRAY

Talgarry

Moorna

Wentworth

Dareton

APEX PARK F.R.A.

Buronga

Gol Gol

Mildura

MURRAY RIVER NATIONAL PARK

Renmark

Paringa

Lindsay Point

Lindsay

Lake Wallawalla

Merbein

Birdwoodton

Merbein South

Koorlong

Irymple

MURRAY RIVER N.P.

Yamba

STURT

Meringur North

Cullulleraine

HWY

Cardross

Red Cliffs

Monak

Karadoc

Taldra

Bugle

Morkalla

Karween

Yarrara

Meringur

Bambill

Werrimull

Merrinee

Pirita

Benetook

Yatpool

Carwarp

Tunart

Kurnwill

Tarrango

Taplan

CALDER

Nowing

VICTORIA

SOUTH AUSTRALIA

Nadda

Rocket Lake

MURRAY - SUNSET

TRACK

Paruna

Meribah

Millewa Bore

PHEENYS

NATIONAL PARK

Hattah

★ The Rock Holes

Fruit Fly Exclusion Zone

Mt Crozier
+ 111

+ Mt Cowra
86

Peebinga

Berrook

Pink Lakes

+ Mt Jess
126

Galah

PEEBINGA CON. PARK

Karte

Goongee

Duddo

Mulcra

Cowangie

Tutye

Linga

Bolnka

Underbool

Torrita

Walpeup

WALPEUP LAKE F.R.A.

Timberoo South

KARTE CON. PARK

MALLEE

Pinnaroo

Chandos

Parilla

Panitya

Carina

Murrayville

Danyo

HWY

Mt Observatory 111

See page 76

© UNIVERSAL PUBLISHERS PTY LTD 2004

Kilometres 30

Toorara □ Eulo E

See page 37

F □ Panban G Mulurulu Lake H

□ Manfred 31 □ Mandelman Clare □

17 Pooncarie Garnpung Lake □ Gol Gol □ Binda

RIVER 32 Lake Leaghur Lake Leaghur 35 15

92 Lethere MUNGO NATIONAL Lake 53 Marona Hatfield

33 Top Hut □ Mungo PARK Boree Plains □ 48

Arumpo □ The Walls of China Iona Langleydale

□ Wamberra 143 Chinbalwood Lakes □ Turlee 22

52 N (G) Box

MALLEE CLIFFS 97 □ Bidura

Rio Vista, NATIONAL PARK
Old Mildura Homestead,
Murray River Cruises □ Prungle Tin Tin Lake Macommon Lake

Ganaway Lake RIVER

STURT RIVER 27 Penarie

Nangiloc L. Benanee Pitarpunga Lake Lake Tala

Colignan Benanee L. Caringay 20 78 HWY Balranald

Euston □ Robinvale McWilliams Winery, Yangalake YANGA N.R.

ATTAH- Rural Life Museum NEW 20 76

KULKYNE 16 20 MURRUMBIDGEE Yanga Lake

KULKYNE B400 Bannerton 7 MURRAY VALLEY SOUTH Perekerten

NATIONAL PARK Wemen Boundary Bend WALES

Cramenton 45 Yungera Koorkab Piamble 80

ANNUELLO Annuello Kooloonong Kenley

FLORA & FAUNA Haysdale Kyalite

RESERVE Winnambool Bolton Natya Goodnight 78 Edward

Prooinga VICTORIA Yerrein River

MALLEE 56 Kulwin Kulwyne Manangatang 41 HWY B12 Tooleybuc Stony Crossing

Ouyen Wagant Piangil Wood Wood Koraleigh Dilpurra 69

Nunga 43 Cocamba Miralie 15 Nyah

Bronzewing A79 Mittyack 24 Chinkapook Yarraby Nyah West Vinifera Speewa

Pier Millan Chillingollah Nowie Nth 40 Beverford 26 Tyntynder Central

Nandaly Lake Tyrrell L. Wahpool L. Timboram Tyntyndyer Homestead Tyntynder South

Tempy See page 77 Waitchie Woorinen Swan Hill Pioneer Settlement, Murray River Cruises

E F G H

© UNIVERSAL PUBLISHERS PTY LTD 2004

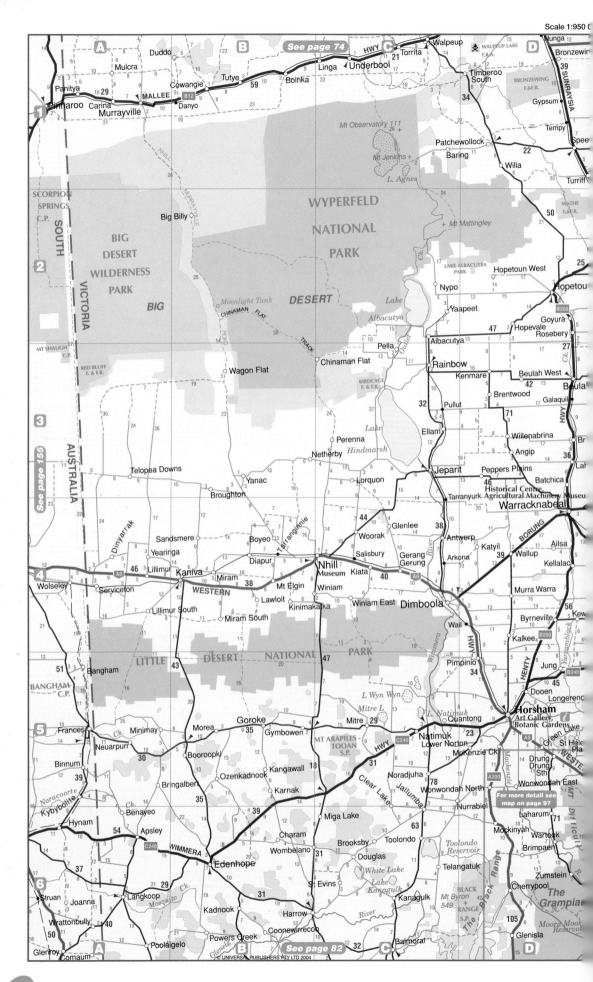

© UNIVERSAL PUBLISHERS PTY LTD 2004

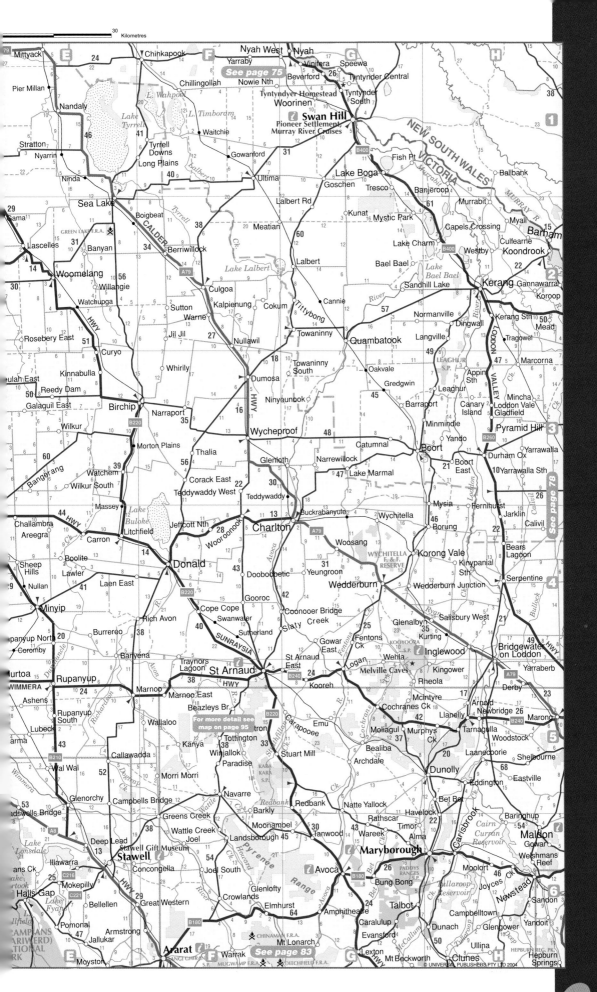

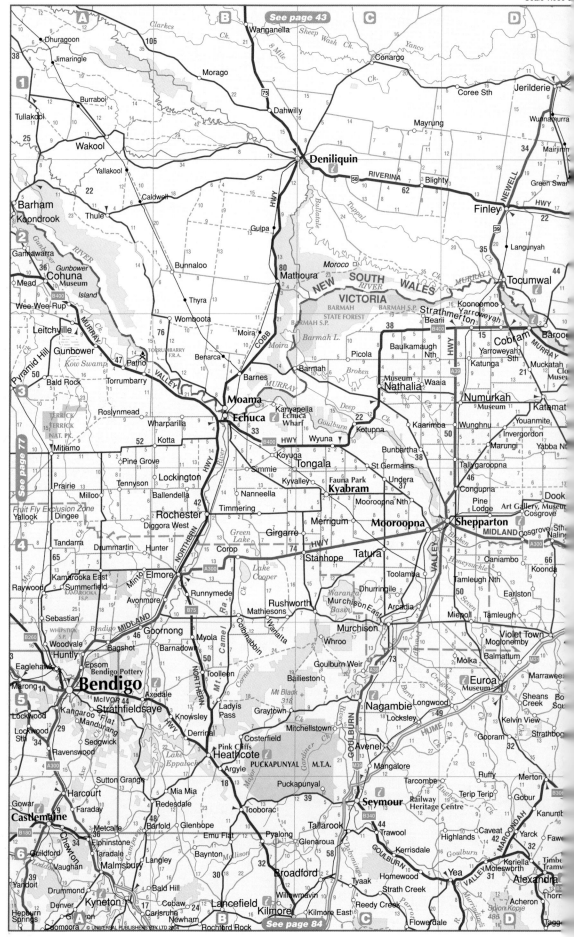

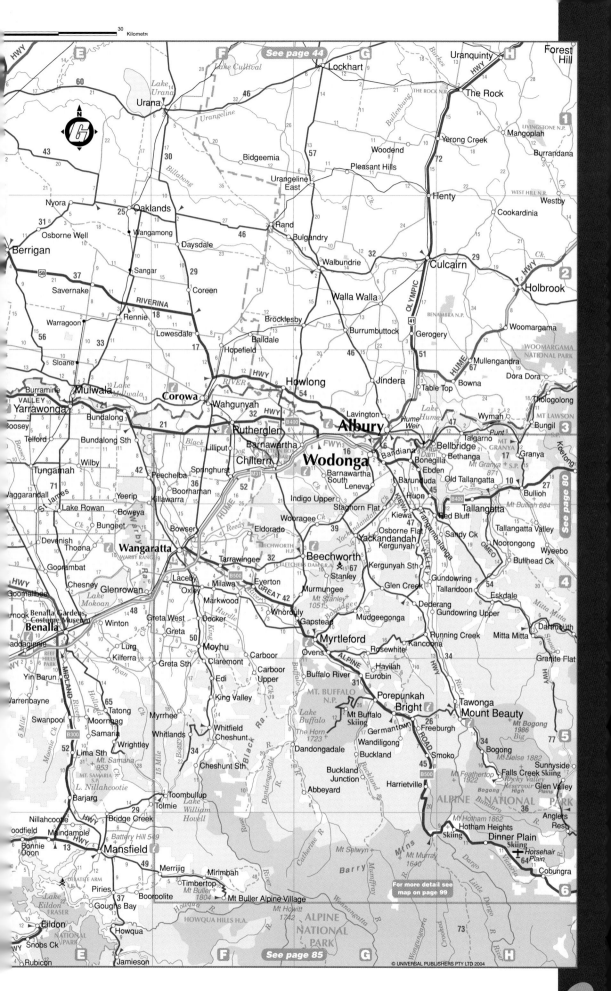

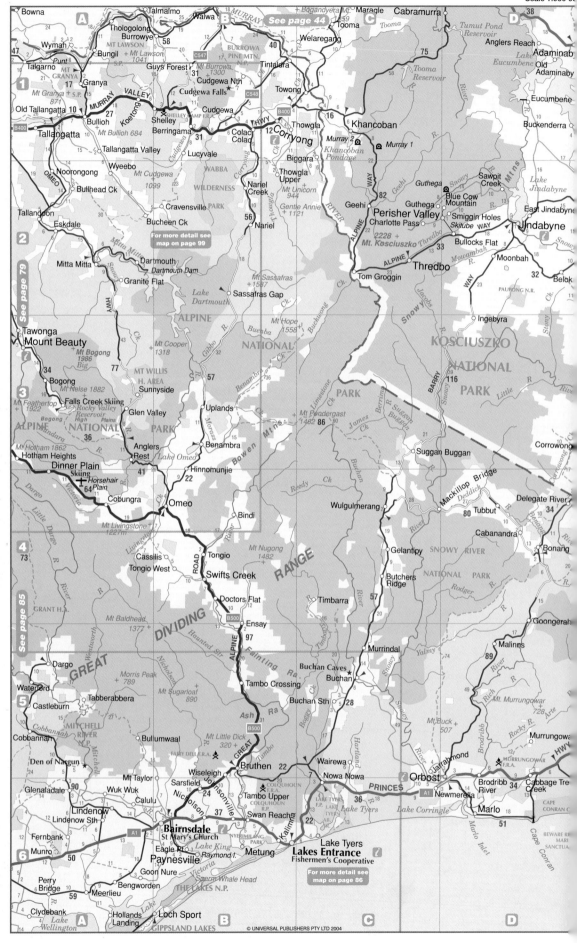

Scale 1:950 000

See page 44

For more detail see map on page 99

See page 79

See page 85

For more detail see map on page 86

© UNIVERSAL PUBLISHERS PTY LTD 2004

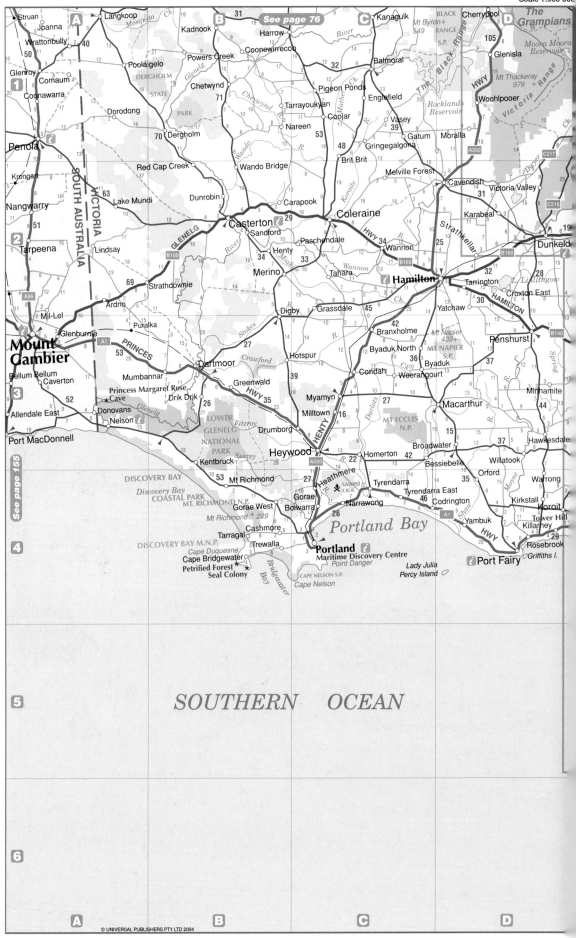

Scale 1:950 000

SOUTHERN OCEAN

© UNIVERSAL PUBLISHERS PTY LTD 2004

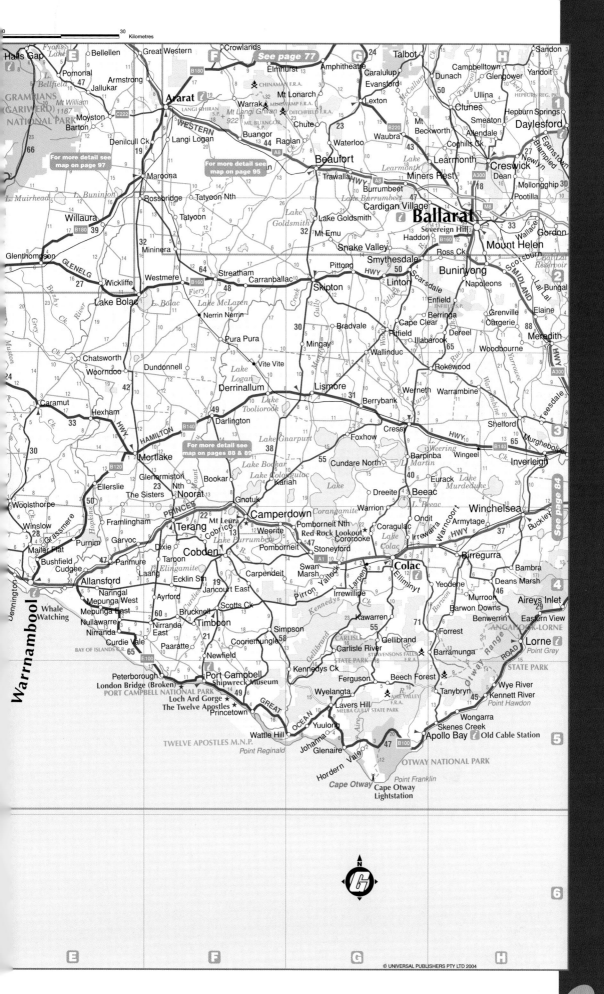

© UNIVERSAL PUBLISHERS PTY LTD 2004

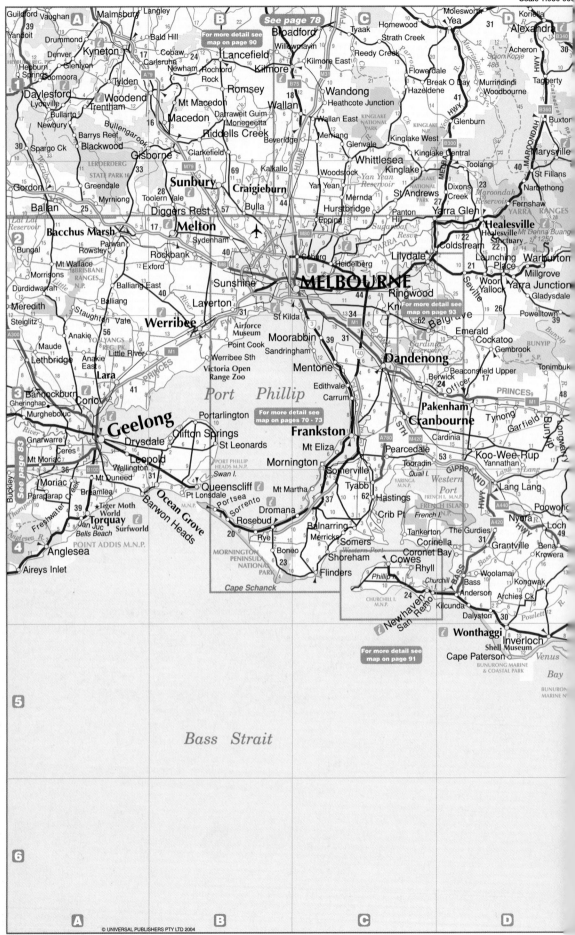

Scale 1:950 000

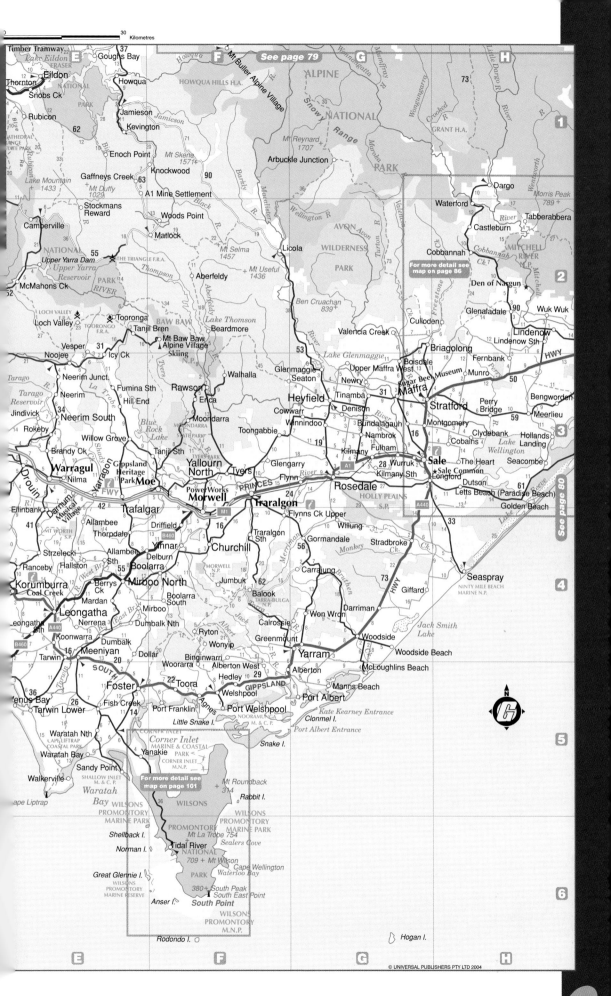

Gippsland Lakes

Gippsland Lakes

Lying parallel to Bass Strait, separated from the ocean by Ninety Mile Beach, the Gippsland Lakes is Australia's largest system of inland waterways. Stretching from Yarram in the west to Lakes Entrance in the east, and the foothills of Victoria's high country to the north, this rich water playground has five lakes covering around 400 square kilometres – King, Coleman, Wellington, Reeve and Victoria. These create a unique natural environment protected by The Lakes National Park and Gippsland Lakes Coastal Park.

In this Victorian riviera, temperatures can be up to 6°C warmer than in Melbourne, and holiday villages, opportunities for fishing, and every imaginable form of water sport abound.

Tourist information

i Central Gippsland
Visitor Information Centre

8 Foster St, Sale 3850
Ph: (03) 5144 1108
Freecall: 1800 677 520
www.gippslandinfo.com.au

Must Visit

- Bairnsdale
- Dargo
- The Lakes National Park
- Metung
- Ninety Mile Beach
- Paynesville

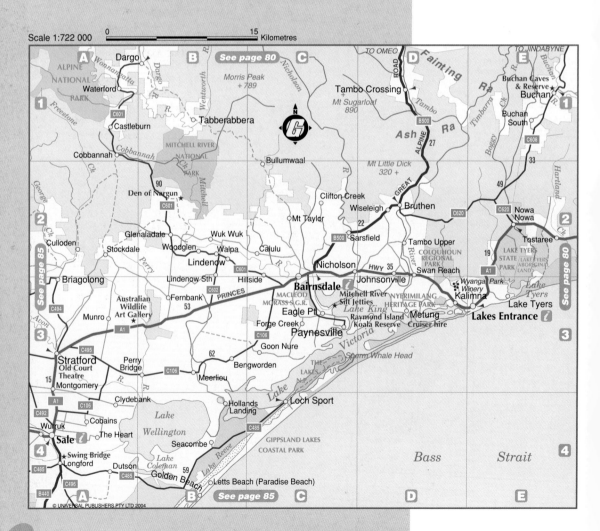

Scale 1:722 000

Great Ocean Road

Surfing at Bells Beach

This legendary coastal route, starting at Torquay and extending 285km west to Warrnambool, is a journey along a stretch of spectacular coastline via seaside holiday towns, surf beaches, rugged cliffs, expansive ocean, lush rainforest and woodlands.

Built between 1919 and 1932 as a memorial to soldiers who died in World War One and as employment for returned servicemen, the road was designed to be a tourist route through this wild, forested terrain.

Also known as the 'Shipwreck Coast' due to the hundreds of ships sunk by reefs, foul weather and the treacherous Southern Ocean, the stretch to Peterborough is a stark reminder of the perils of this jagged coastline.

Historic seaside towns offer safe, sandy beaches for swimming, while waves pound the shores of some of Australia's best surf beaches including Bells Beach, which hosts the Rip Curl Pro contest during Easter.

For a change of pace visitors can explore the waterfalls, lakes, and glades of massive tree ferns in the magnificent Otway Ranges. A 120-km waterfalls-and-rainforest drive takes in Triplet, Beauchamp and Hopetoun falls, and the Otway National Park's rainforest.

Tourist information

i Geelong and Great Ocean Rd Visitor Information Centre

Stead Park, Princes Hwy,
Geelong 3214
Ph: (03) 5275 5797
Freecall: 1800 620 888
www.greatoceanroad.org

i Great Ocean Rd Visitor Information Centre

Great Ocean Rd,
Apollo Bay 3233
Ph: (03) 5237 6529

Main Attractions

◈ **Anglesea** This holiday town is renowned for the large population of grey kangaroos at Anglesea Golf Course.

◈ **Cape Otway Lightstation** Built in 1848, this is Australia's oldest standing lighthouse.

◈ **Flagstaff Hill Maritime Museum** Explore the stories of the Shipwreck Coast at this interactive museum in Warrnambool.

◈ **Little Penguins** To observe a colony of little penguins, cross at low tide to Middle Island from the breakwater in Warrnambool.

◈ **Lorne** A prime coastal holiday location surrounded by densely forested bushland and plunging waterfalls.

◈ **Otway Fly** This new rainforest treetop walk in the heart of the beautiful Otway State Forest is the highest and longest of its kind in the world.

◈ **Torquay** Visit the Surfworld Museum and nearby Bells Beach for a taste of surf culture.

◈ **Whale watching** From June to late September see southern right whales at Logans Beach, Warrnambool.

The 12 Apostles

Within the Port Campbell National Park, these majestic rock formations, seen from the Great Ocean Road, were once part of the mainland's limestone cliffs, demonstrating the power of the coastline's waves. Rising 65m from the ocean and stretching along the coastline, they are an impressive sight. Other attractions of the national park include London Bridge, Loch Ard Gorge and The Grotto.

Scale 1:588 387

See page 83

© UNIVERSAL PUBLISHERS PTY LTD 2004

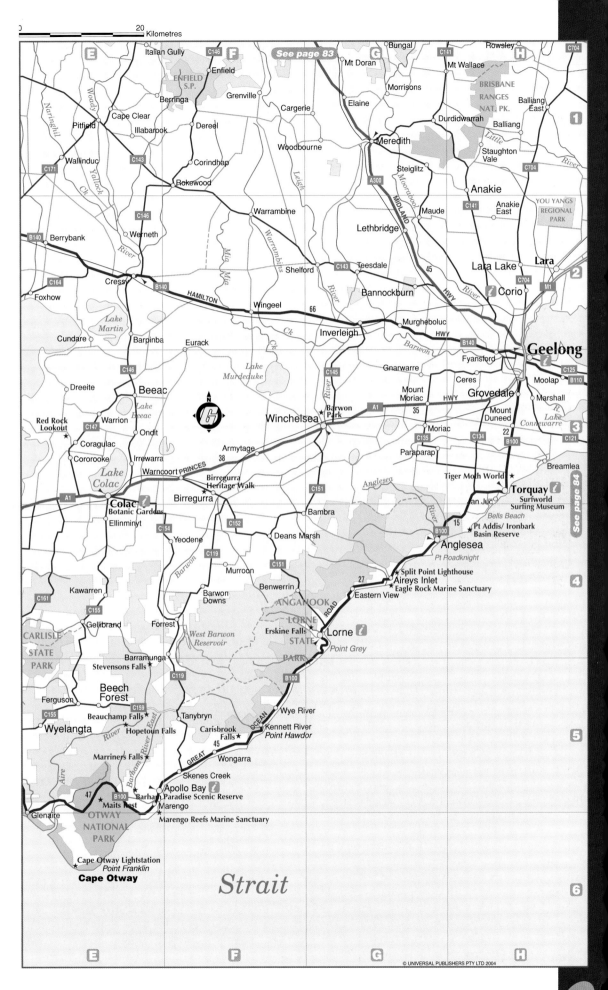

20
Kilometres

E | **F** | **G** | **H**

Italian Gully
Enfield
ENFIELD S.P.
Berringa
Grenville
Cape Clear
Pitfield
Illabarook
Dereel
Cargerie
Woodbourne
Mt Doran
Bungal
Rowsley
Mt Wallace
Morrisons
Elaine
Durdidwarrah
BRISBANE RANGES NAT. PK.
Balliang East
Balliang
Staughton Vale
Anakie
Anakie East
YOU YANGS REGIONAL PARK

Meredith
Steiglitz
Maude
Lethbridge

Wallinduc
Corindhap
Rokewood
Warrambine
Shelford
Teesdale
Bannockburn
Lara Lake
Lara
Corio
Berrybank
Werneth
Cress
Wingeel
Inverleigh
Murgheboluc
Fyansford
Geelong

Foxhow
Cundare
Barpinba
Eurack
Lake Murdeduke
Gnarwarre
Ceres
Grovedale
Moolap
Marshall

Dreeite
Beeac
Lake Beeac
Warrion
Ondit
Winchelsea
Barwon Park
Mount Moriac
Mount Duneed
Lake Connewarre
Red Rock Lookout
Coragulac
Cororooke
Irrewarra
Armytage
Moriac
Paraparap
Breamlea

Lake Colac
Warncoort PRINCES
Birregurra Heritage Walk
Birregurra
Bambra
Tiger Moth World
Torquay
Surfworld Surfing Museum
Colac
Botanic Gardens
Ellinminyt
Yeodene
Deans Marsh
Anglesea
Pt Roadknight
Bells Beach
Pt Addis/ Ironbark Basin Reserve

Murroon
Benwerrin
ANGAHOOK LORNE STATE PARK
Eastern View
Split Point Lighthouse
Aireys Inlet
Eagle Rock Marine Sanctuary

Kawarren
Barwon Downs
Gellibrand
Forrest
West Barwon Reservoir
Erskine Falls
Lorne
Point Grey

CARLISLE STATE PARK
Barramunga
Stevensons Falls
Beech Forest
Ferguson
Beauchamp Falls
Tanybryn
Carisbrook Falls
Wye River
Kennett River
Point Hawdor

Wyelangta
Hopetoun Falls
Wongarra
Marriners Falls
Skenes Creek
Apollo Bay
Barham Paradise Scenic Reserve
Marengo
Marengo Reefs Marine Sanctuary
Glenaire
Maits Rest
OTWAY NATIONAL PARK

Cape Otway Lightstation
Point Franklin
Cape Otway

Strait

E | **F** | **G** | **H**

© UNIVERSAL PUBLISHERS PTY LTD 2004

Victoria 89

Macedon Ranges and Sunbury Wineries

Convent Gallery, Daylesford

Boasting more than 98 mineral springs, this region is recognised as a premier boutique holiday destination. Located only a short distance from Melbourne, the Macedon Ranges and nearby spa country offer a unique opportunity for 'taking the waters'.

This European tradition dates from the 1840s, when the large Swiss-Italian community realised the potential of the region's natural springs. Mineral water has been bottled here since 1850 and the towns of Hepburn Springs and Daylesford have been spa resorts since the 1880s. Natural therapies including herbal baths and massages are also offered, making the region a great place to relax and revitalise.

The district also offers wineries, galleries, antique shopping and local markets. Local reserves such as Lerderderg State Park and the Macedon Ranges are ideal for horseriding, fishing and picnicking, and the Tipperary Walking Track between Hepburn Springs and Daylesford passes through old gold-mining areas.

Tourist information

i Daylesford Regional Visitor Information Centre

98 Vincent St, Daylesford Vic. 3460
Ph: (03) 5321 6123
www.visitdaylesford.com

i Kyneton Visitor Information Centre

Jean Hayes Reserve
High St, Kyneton Vic. 3444
Ph: (03) 5422 6110

Must Visit

◈ Convent Gallery, Daylesford
◈ Hanging Rock
◈ Hepburn Springs Spa Resort
◈ Lake Daylesford
◈ Lavandula Lavender Farm (outside Hepburn Springs)

Scale 1:493 714   0   20 Kilometres

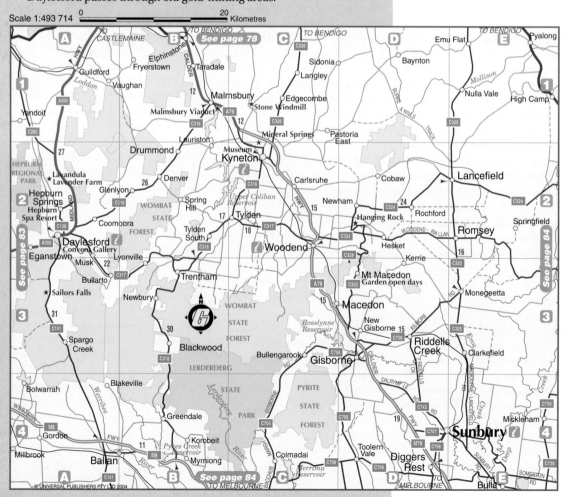

Phillip Island

Seal watching

Located in the calm waters of Western Port, only a ninety-minute drive from Melbourne, Phillip Island is accessed by a bridge from the mainland at San Remo.

It has been a popular destination for summer holidays since ferries began running from Stoney Point in the 1890s. Now many international visitors come to experience the nightly parade of little penguins at Summerland Beach. The island boasts koalas in their natural habitat, and one of Australia's largest colonies of fur seals at Seal Rocks. Unspoilt beaches provide excellent surfing conditions.

Phillip Island also has geological formations, including The Pinnacles (ancient columns of basalt), the Forest Caves (large sea-eroded caverns), and Pyramid Rock (a column of basalt in the shape of a pyramid). The Australian leg of the 500cc world motorcycle championship is held on the island in October.

Tourist information

i Phillip Island Visitor Information Centre

Phillip Island Tourist Rd, Newhaven Vic. 3925
Ph: (03) 5956 7447
Tollfree: 1300 366 422
www.phillipislandgippsland.com.au

Must Visit

◈ Cape Woolamai Trail
◈ Koala Conservation Centre
◈ Penguin Parade
◈ Seal Rocks and the Nobbies

Scale 1:222 222

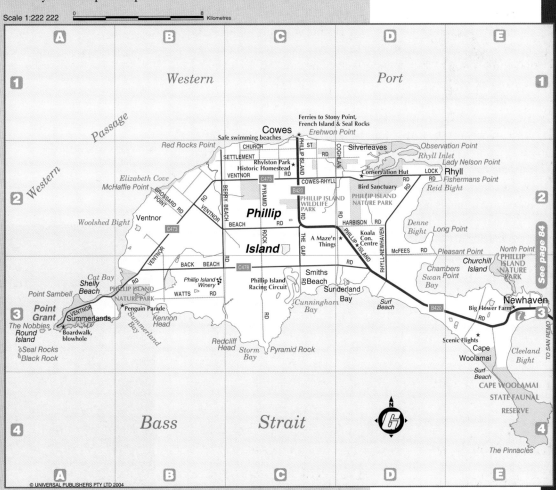

The Dandenongs

Puffing Billy, Dandenong Ranges

Only an hour's drive from Melbourne, the beautiful Dandenong Ranges form a natural backdrop to Victoria's capital city, attracting hordes of city visitors annually to this green haven of hills and forests. Rising to an average elevation between 500 and 600m, the Dandenong Ranges peak at Mt Dandenong, 633m above sea level.

Colourful, inviting and cool, especially in spring and summer, the Dandenongs are popular for day trips, not only for their intrinsic beauty but also for the many gorgeous landscaped gardens and a great variety of European trees and shrubs. The rich, volcanic soil and plentiful rain ensures that plants flourish: the Dandenongs are home to six of the Great Gardens of Melbourne and to many nurseries.

A smattering of art galleries, antique shops, restaurants and tearooms in the townships provides some excellent detours when exploring the region's stunning scenery.

Tourist information

 Dandenong Ranges and Knox Visitor Information Centre

1211 Burwood Hwy,
Upper Ferntree Gully Vic. 3156
Ph: (03) 9758 7522
www.yarrarangestourism.com.au

Main Attractions

◈ **Belgrave** Home to the beloved vintage steam train Puffing Billy.

◈ **Dandenong Ranges National Park** See the world's tallest flowering plant: the mountain ash tree.

◈ **Mt Dandenong Lookout** This lookout offers panoramic views over Melbourne, Port Phillip and Western Port.

◈ **Olinda** Spring is the ideal time to visit Olinda, when the flower gardens are in full bloom.

◈ **Sassafras** Picturesque Sassafras offers charming stores and galleries.

◈ **William Ricketts Sanctuary** The artist William Ricketts created this magnificent sanctuary in the gardens of his home after spending much time with the Aboriginal people of Central Australia. The setting of fern gardens and rock waterfalls provide a natural gallery for his kiln-fired sculptures of Aboriginal people.

Puffing Billy

This vintage steam train has run almost continuously since 1900 (replaced with a diesel locomotive on days of total fire ban). With its open carriages and restaurant car, it is one of Victoria's most charming attractions. The 48km return trip between Belgrave and Gembrook is beautiful and includes travelling over timber trestle bridges, through forests, and past vast stands of tree ferns.

William Ricketts Sanctuary

Scale 1:109 000

0 — 4 Kilometres

See page 84

A **B** **C** **D**

Chirnside Park

Museum at Lillydale

Warburton

Boundary RD

Gruyere RD

Lilydale
Swinburne
Uni of Tech.
Lillydale Lake

Hereford RD

Mount Evelyn

Wandin North

1

Croydon North

Mooroolbark

Swinburne Uni
Eastern Campus

York

Mont De Lancey ★
Home & Museum

Gumnut Village

Kilsyth

Montrose

Mt Dandenong Arboretum

Kalorama

Melbourne Water

DANDENONG RANGES NATIONAL PARK

Silvan Reservoir Park

Silvan

2

Croydon Sth

Bayswater North

Kilsyth South

Mt Dandenong 633
GTV9 Tower

WILLIAM RICKETTS SANCTUARY

DOONGALLA RESERVE

Burkes 630
ATV10 Tower

Mount Dandenong

DANDENONG RANGES

Olinda Falls
Eagle Nest

DANDENONG RANGES NATIONAL PARK

Melbourne Water

Silvan

Tesselaar Tulip Farm

Melbourne Water Reservoir

3

The Basin

Olinda

National Rhododendron Gardens

R.J. Hamer Forest Arboretum

Monbulk MACCLESFIELD RD

Boronia

Olinda

Edward Henty Cottage

Woolrich

DANDENONG RANGES NATIONAL PARK

Sassafras

Monbulk

Ferntree Gully

Tremont

Ferny Creek

ONE TREE HILL

Acadia

Sherbrooke Falls

Sherbrooke

Grants Picnic Ground

The Patch

Kallista

4

Upper Ferntree Gully

Tecoma

Upwey

Micawber Park

DANDENONG RANGES NATIONAL PARK

Puffing

Belgrave

Menzies Creek

Lysterfield

Belgrave Heights

Selby Stn

Selby

Menzies Ck
Railway

Clematis

Emerald

5

Lysterfield South

LYSTERFIELD LAKE PARK

Lysterfield Lake

Belgrave South

BAŁUK WILLAM FLORA RESERVE

275

Aura Vale Lake

Cardinia Reservoir

Cardinia Park

Cardinia Reservoir

6

Endeavour Hills

Narre Warren North

Campbelltown Miniature Rly Park

Narre Warren East

Harkaway Scout Camping Area

Beaconhills Country Club

See page 71

Victoria

93

The Goldfields

Sovereign Hill, Ballarat

Situated, just over 100km north-west of Melbourne, the Goldfields region is filled with opportunities to experience the heady days of the gold rush era.

In 1851, news of the discovery of gold spread like wildfire through the colonies of Victoria and New South Wales and as far away as China, England and the USA. A population explosion occurred: 8,000 hopeful prospectors had arrived by October 1851; the number swelled to 30,000 a year later; and by 1856 a record 100,000 people were trying their luck.

Tiny settlements became boomtowns virtually overnight, while Melbourne was deserted – during 1851, 20,000 of its population of 25,000 abandoned the capital for the Mt Alexander diggings.

As prosperity spread to the industries that supported the miners and developing mining companies, the Goldfields towns became thriving regional centres.

The rich history of the Goldfields and its Victorian architecture is evident everywhere in the region and visitors can explore this through activities such as prospecting, fossicking, camping and bushwalking. Other attractions include the area's established wineries, art galleries, antiques, gardens and intriguing wildlife.

The Gold Rush

The wealth from the gold diggings made Melbourne the largest city in Australia at that time. The status of the country was transformed from a colonial settlement with a dubious reputation to a respectable place for migration and investment.

Tourist information

 Ballarat Visitor Information Centre

39 Sturt St, Ballarat Vic. 3350
Ph: (03) 5320 5741
Freecall: 1800 446 633
www.ballarat.com

 Bendigo Visitor Information Centre

51-67 Pall Mall, Bendigo Vic. 3350
Ph: (03) 5444 4445
Freecall: 1800 813 153
www.bendigotourism.com

Main Attractions

◈ **Ararat** Visit Gum San Chinese Heritage Centre, commemorating the Chinese miners who discovered alluvial gold in 1857.

◈ **Ballarat** Visit the Eureka Centre located near the site of the infamous Eureka Stockade uprising.

◈ **Ballarat Wildlife Park** Meet emus, koalas, wallabies, wombats and other Australian animals at Ballarat Wildlife Park.

◈ **Bendigo** Built on its gold rush prosperity, Bendigo is still a thriving regional centre.

◈ **Buda Historic Home and Gardens** Visit this colonial home and see the best of 19th and 20th-century landscaping.

◈ **Castlemaine** Noted as much for its art as for its gold rush history, Castlemaine Art Gallery and Historical Museum boasts a fine collection of Australian art.

◈ **Clunes** This was Victoria's first gold town.

◈ **Golden Dragon Museum, Bendigo** A tribute to Chinese miners who flocked to the goldfields.

◈ **Sovereign Hill** Built on a gold mining site, Sovereign Hill recreates Ballarat during its gold rush years. Visit mines, pan for gold and watch craftspeople at work.

The Goldfields Wineries

Although the Goldfields are known mostly for their gold rush heritage, the region also offers an array of impressive wineries that are well worth visiting. The foothills of the ranges boast many vineyards, some of which are listed below.

The best known of these is Seppelt Great Western Winery, a household name throughout Australia.

The French game petanque (similar to Italian bocce) is played at many of the local wineries. In late November, the region pays tribute to the game by hosting the Pyrenees Vignerons Petanque Festival in the main street of Avoca. Australian petanque champions teach the finer details of the game in a festive environment of fine regional food and wine.

Name	Address	Phone	Open
Blue Pyrenees Estate	Vinoca Rd, Avoca	(03) 5465 3202	10am–4:30pm Mon–Fri, 10am–5pm weekends
Dalwhinnie Vineyard	Taltarni Rd, Moonambel	(03) 5467 2388	10am–5pm daily
Kara Kara Winery	Sunraysia Hwy, 10km south of St Arnaud	(03) 5496 3294	10am–6pm daily
Mt Avoca	Moates Lane, Avoca	(03) 5465 3282	10am–5pm daily
Redbank Winery	Sally's Lane, Redbank	(03) 5467 7255	9am–5pm Mon–Sat, 10am–5pm Sun
Seppelt Great Western Winery	Moyston Rd, Great Western	(03) 5361 2222	10am–5pm daily
Summerfield Wines	5967 Stawell-Avoca Rd, Moonambel	(03) 5459 7900	9am–5:30pm Mon–Sat, 10am–5:30pm Sun
Taltarni Vineyards	339 Taltarni Rd, off Stawell-Avoca Rd, Moonambel	(03) 5467 2218	10am–5pm daily
Warrenmang Vineyard Resort	Mountain Creek Rd, Moonambel	(03) 5467 2233	10am–5pm daily
Yellowglen Winery	Whites Rd, Smythesdale	(03) 5342 8617	10am-5pm Mon-Fri, 11am-5pm weekends

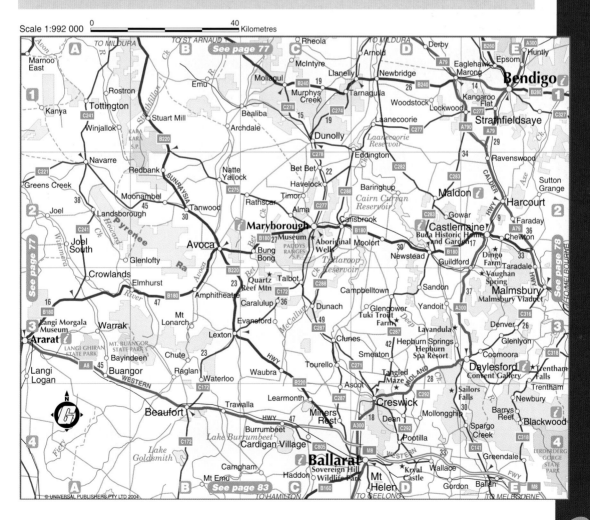

The Grampians National Park

Lake Bellfield, The Grampians

This dramatic landscape of stark ridges and strangely-shaped rocky outcrops rises spectacularly from western Victoria's flat wheat plains and grazing fields.

Known to Aboriginal people as Gariwerd, the area is renowned for its rock art and heritage and the majority of south-east Australia's Aboriginal art sites are located within this impressive region.

Archaeologists have carbon-dated campfire charcoal to 5000 years ago, although the earliest rock art suggests Aboriginal activity in the area as far back as 22,000 years ago.

The landscape is punctuated by four main ranges: Mt Difficult to the north, Mt William to the east, Serra to the south and Victoria to the west.

Protected by one of Victoria's largest national parks, the Grampians covers 1671 square kilometres of stunning scenery featuring wildflowers, panoramic mountain views and intricate ecosystems.

The national park's unique habitat is home to 800 indigenous plant species (20 of which are found nowhere else in the world), 40 species of native mammal, 200 bird species and 27 reptile species.

To preserve this natural wonderland, visitors are asked not to bring in pets or remove any plants, to stay on walking trails and to observe fire restrictions.

Activities in the region include rock climbing and abseiling, horseriding through rugged wilderness, hot air balloon rides, bushwalking, fishing and camping.

Tourist information

 Brambuk the National Park and Cultural Centre

Grampians Tourist Rd,
Halls Gap Vic. 3381
Ph: (03) 5356 4381
www.parkweb.vic.gov.au

i Halls Gap and Grampians Visitor Information Centre

Centenary Hall, Grampians Tourist Rd, Halls Gap Vic. 3381
Ph: (03) 5356 4616
Freecall: 1800 246 880
www.visitgrampians.com.au

Main Attractions

◈ **Aboriginal Art Tours** Run by the Brambuk Aboriginal Cultural Centre, these tours visit the region's main art sites.

◈ **Dunkeld** This town is a convenient southern departure point for a tour of The Grampians.

◈ **Halls Gap Wildlife Park and Zoo** See a range of animals including monkeys, red deer and kangaroos.

◈ **MacKenzie Falls** This spectacular waterfall is a worthwhile detour from a visit to the Wonderland Range.

◈ **Mount William** A steep walk takes you to the highest point of the Grampians for breathtaking views.

◈ **The Balconies Lookout** An easy walk from Reed Lookout car park to spectacular rock formations.

Aboriginal Art Sites

The Grampians National Park is an important area for studying the history of Aboriginal rock art. Rock paintings are believed to serve many functions, such as recording days or visits, retelling stories, communicating laws and teaching spiritual principles.

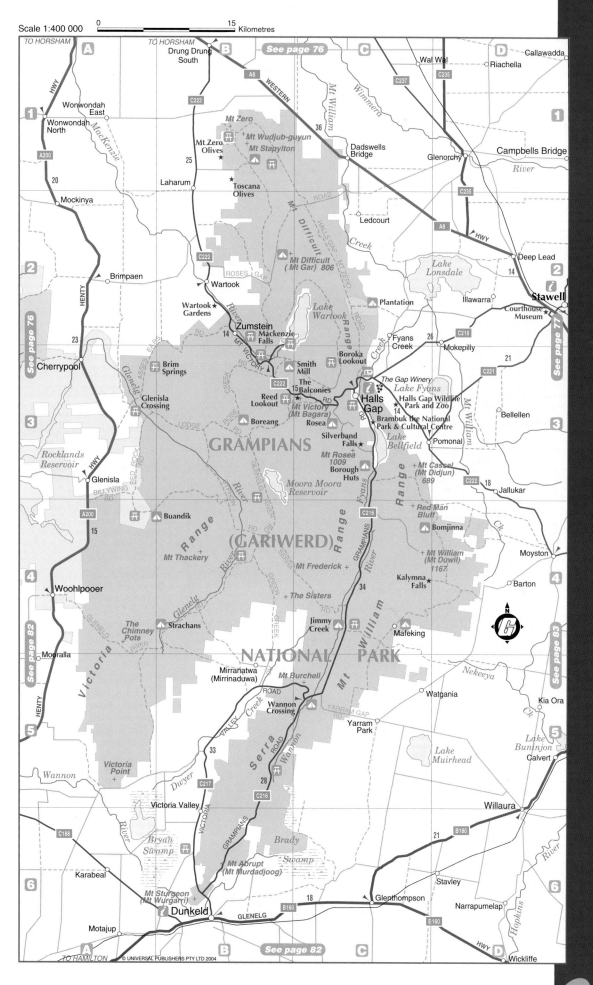

TO HORSHAM

A   B   See page 76   C   D

TO HORSHAM
Drung Drung
South

Callawadda

Wal Wal   Riachella

WESTERN

A8

C222

C237

C235

1

Wonwondah
East

Wonwondah
North

HWY

A200

Mt Zero

Mt Wudjub-guyun
Mt Stapylton

Mt Zero
Olives

36

Dadswells
Bridge

Glenorchy

Campbells Bridge

River

20

Mockinya

25

Laharum

Toscana
Olives

ROAD

HALLS GAP ROAD

Ledcourt

A8   HWY

Deep Lead

2

Mackenzie

HENTY

23

Brimpaen

Wartook

Mt Difficult
(Mt Gar) 806

ROSES GAP

Lake
Wartook

Plantation

Lake
Lonsdale

Illawarra

14

Stawell

i

Cherrypool

Wartook
Gardens

Zumstein
Mackenzie
Falls

Smith
Mill

River

Mt Victory

Mt Zero

Range

Boroka
Lookout

Fyans
Creek

Mokepilly

Courthouse
Museum

26

C216

C235

C221

2

See page 76

Glenelg

3

Brim
Springs

Glenisla
Crossing

C222

14

RD

Reed
Lookout

The
15 Balconies

C222

Boreang

Mt Victory
(Mt Bagara)

Rosea

Silverband
Falls

Mt Rosea
1009

RD

Halls
Gap

14

The Gap Winery
Lake Fyans

Halls Gap Wildlife
Park and Zoo

Brambuk the National
Park & Cultural Centre

Lake
Bellfield

Pomonal

Bellellen

Mt William

C216

See page 77

3

ASSES

EARS

Rocklands
Reservoir

Glenisla

A200

15

RED ROCK RD

LODGE

RD

ROSE

CREEK

GLENELG RIVER

BILLYWING
RD

GRAMPIANS

(GARIWERD)

Moora Moora
Reservoir

Borough
Huts

Mt Cassel
(Mt Didjun)
689

C222

18

Jallukar

4

Woohlpooer

HENTY

HWY

Range

Buandik

Mt Thackery

River

SERRA

GREEN

Range

C216

Mt Frederick

The Sisters

Range

Red Man
Bluff

Bomjinna

Mt William
(Mt Duwil)
1167

Kalymna
Falls

34

Fyans
River

Moyston

Barton

G

4

See page 83

5

HENTY

Glenelg

River

The
Chimney
Pots

Strachans

Mooralla

NATIONAL

Jimmy
Creek

PARK

Mafeking

Mt William

Nekeeya

Watgania

Ck

Kia Ora

5

See page 82

Victoria

33

VALLEY

Creek

Duyer

Victoria
Point

Mirranatwa
(Mirrinaduwa)

Mt Burchell

ROAD

Wannon
Crossing

C217

28

C216

VICTORIA

Wannon

ROAD

YARRAM GAP
RD

Yarram
Park

Lake
Muirhead

Lake
Buninjon

Calvert

21

B180

Willaura

River

6

C188

River

Bryan
Swamp

Victoria Valley

GRAMPIANS

Brady

Swamp

Mt Abrupt
(Mt Murdadjoog)

18

B160

Glenthompson

Stavley

Narrapumelap

Hopkins

River

6

Karabeal

Mt Sturgeon
(Mt Wurgarri)

i   Dunkeld

Motajup

GLENELG

E160

HWY

Wickliffe

A   B   See page 82   C   D

TO HAMILTON   © UNIVERSAL PUBLISHERS PTY LTD 2004

Victorian Alps

Howqua River

The Victorian Alps are the southern-most part of the Great Dividing Range. These dramatic, rounded mountains are less challenging for skiers than the jagged peaks of their northern hemisphere counterparts.

Located south-east of Wangaratta, the Victorian Alps cover a vast and rugged terrain, much of which is protected inside national parks. The ski resort towns dotting the mountains are within an hour's radius of each other, offering many opportunities for downhill and cross-country skiing.

The snow season usually starts in June, lasting at least until September, although in some years it has extended as late as November. Bushwalking, horseriding, paragliding, hanggliding and trout fishing are some of the many recreational activities that attract visitors during the warmer months.

Where to ski

Resorts cater for different skill levels of skiers: Mt Hotham, Falls Creek and Mount Buller have ski runs for beginners, intermediate and advanced skiers; Mt Baw Baw is more suited to beginners; while Lake Mountain is the place to go for cross-country runs.

Tourist information

i Bright Visitors Centre

119 Gavan St (Great Alpine Rd),
Bright Vic. 3741
Ph: (03) 5755 2275
Freecall: 1800 500 117
www.visitalpine.com

i Wangaratta and Region Visitor Information Centre

Murphy St,
Wangaratta Vic. 3677
Freecall: 1800 801 065
www.wangaratta.vic.gov.au

Main Attractions

◈ **Alpine National Park** This national park encompasses a large part of the Victorian Alps and many of the region's ski resorts.

◈ **Beechworth** This magnificently preserved gold town is rich in history.

◈ **Bright** A picturesque alpine township that began as a gold town in the 1850s, today Bright is the centre of the local tourism and agricultural industries.

◈ **Falls Creek** Falls Creek has what are considered Victoria's best ski runs, and spectacular views from Roper's Lookout. The walk to Mt Nelse traverses slopes covered with Alpine wildflowers in summer.

◈ **Mt Beauty** A popular base for bushwalking, horseriding and skiing, nestled at the foot of Mt Bogong.

◈ **Mt Buffalo National Park** This stunning national park covers the huge plateau surrounding Mt Buffalo.

◈ **Mt Hotham** The spectacular alpine country at Mt Hotham and nearby Dinner Plain offers both skiing and summer activities.

Milawa Gourmet Region

Lying east of Wangaratta, the townships of Milawa and Oxley are renowned for their regional produce, particularly wines and cheeses. The temperate climate is ideal for viniculture and dairying, and many of the local restaurants and cafés showcase the region's produce. Orchards and vineyards are located throughout this charming region and attractions such as Wabonga Plateau and the impressive amphitheatre at Paradise Falls create ideal picnic spots where one can indulge in local gourmet offerings. Many of the region's wineries are found in King Valley's northern end, where visitors can enjoy a stunning combination of excellent food and wine.

One of Australia's leading wine exporters, Brown Brothers of Milawa, is a centre for wine tasting visitors to the region.

Other drawcards include Milawa Mustards, conveniently located in the centre of town; Milawa Cheese Co, which offers a restaurant and tastings of its award-winning Milawa Blue cheese; and King River Café in Oxley, renowned for offering one of the region's finest dining experiences.

King Valley wineries include: Avalon Winery, King River Estate, La Cantina King Valley, Chrismont Wines, and Dal Zotto Estate Wines. Wineries located in Milawa and Oxley include: John Gehrig Wines, Brown Brothers Milawa Vineyard, Ciavarella Wines, Miranda Wines King Valley, Reads Oxley Winery, and Wood Park Wines.

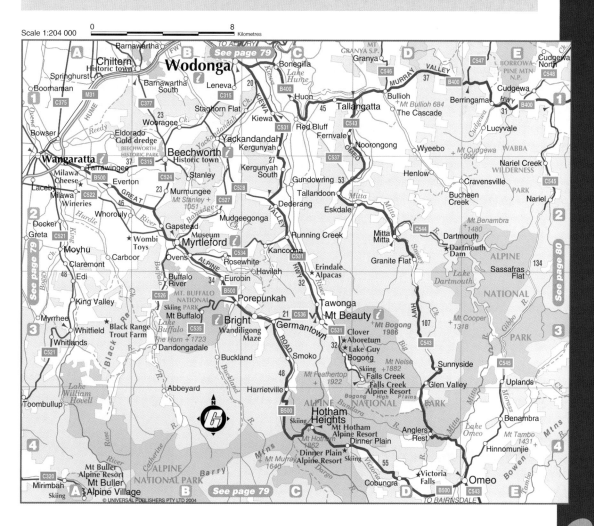

Scale 1:204 000

Wilsons Promontory

Sealers Cove

Once part of the ancient land bridge to Tasmania, Wilsons Promontory is the southern-most point of the mainland and is protected by one of Victoria's oldest and most spectacular national parks, reserved in 1898.

Its pristine beaches and coves formed by granite masses, rivers, creeks and rugged mountain ranges are preserved by their remoteness: despite this, the accommodation and camping grounds at Tidal River are busy during holiday times.

Highlights include the area's majestic coastline and botanical diversity: 'the Prom' features more than 700 native plant species. There are tall eucalypts, moist and luxuriant fern gullies, groves of brown and yellow stringy-barks, copses of banksias and ti-trees, salt marshes and stands of white mangroves. The 500 square kilometres national park has 130km of coastline and more than 100km of walking trails. Permits are required for overnight hiking and a ballot system is used for camping sites and holiday cabins during peak periods.

When to visit 'the Prom'

In spring, see abundant wildflowers or visit in the autumn when temperatures are cool and ideal for walking. Conditions can be cold and bleak in winter, while in summer the Prom is very crowded.

Tourist information

Wilsons Promontory
National Park

Park Office and Visitors Centre, Tidal River Vic. 3960
Freecall: 1800 350 552
www.parkweb.vic.gov.au
www.promcountrytourism.com.au

Main Attractions

◈ **Mt Oberon** Popular for its panoramic views of the surrounding bays and islands.

◈ **Norman Bay** This sweeping bay is worth visiting for its lovely views stretching to the horizon.

◈ **Sealers Cove** Pack a picnic lunch to enjoy the day walk (20km return) to this spectacular sheltered cove. The shallow waters allow for excellent, secluded swimming.

◈ **West Coast Beaches** A string of stunning beaches on the Promontory's west coast face the waters of Bass Strait.

◈ **Wilsons Promontory Lightstation (1859)** Providing breathtaking vistas of the promontory, the lighthouse is a 37km return walk, best done as an overnight hike. Cottage accommodation must be booked in advance.

◈ **Wilsons Promontory National Park** Many of the Prom's beaches are safe for swimming or surfing and bushwalking trails cater for all levels.

Mt Bishop

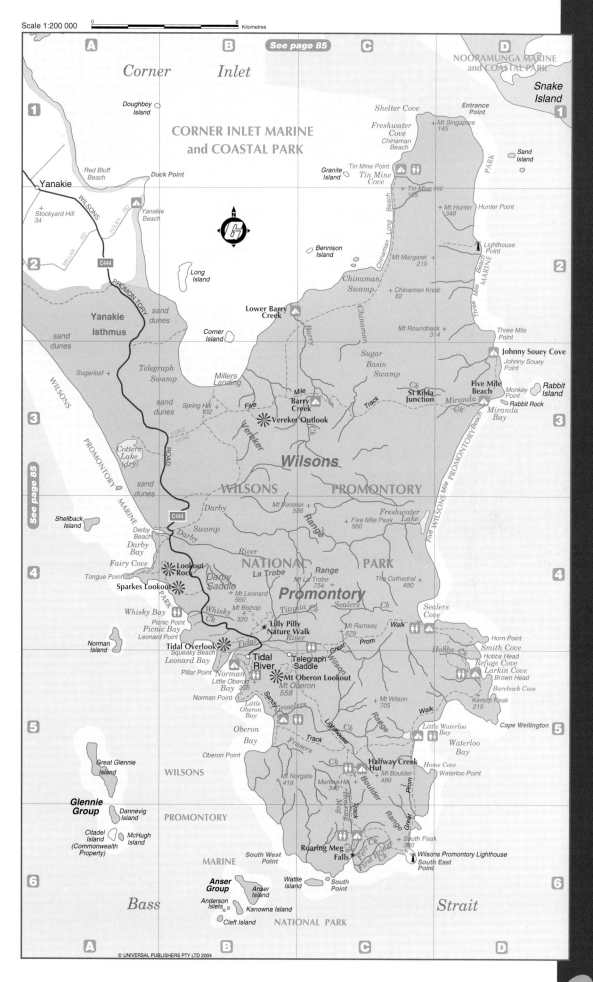

Queensland
The Sunshine State

The state of Queensland occupies the north-east area of the Australian continent and is the country's second largest state. There are seven distinct tourist regions: Gold Coast, Brisbane Region, Darling Downs, Central Coast, Northern Queensland, Great Barrier Reef and Outback Queensland. Queensland has 5207km of stunning coastline and beaches and islands are among its major attractions.

From north to south the state's greatest distance is 2092km, while the greatest distance from east to west is 1448km. This huge expanse of land features a diversity of terrains, ranging from the lush, tropical rainforests of Cape York, to the temperate sub-tropical climes around the capital Brisbane, and the rugged and dry landscape of the state's interior.

Although weather conditions vary from one region to another – the northernmost tip has just two seasons, wet and dry – Queensland's abundant sunshine and warmth make it an ideal destination for holidays and touring. Brisbane, for example, boasts an average temperature of 25°C and dry winters.

Despite the steady growth of Brisbane and its urban areas, Queensland still has Australia's most rural population – it is the only state with a higher proportion of people living outside its capital than in it.

Tourist information

i Queensland
Travel Centre

30 Makerston St,
Brisbane Qld 4000
Ph: 138 833
www.queenslandtravel.com.au

| Area = 1,727,530 sq km | Occupies 22.5% of Australia | Length of coast = 5207 km |

Queensland Key Map & Distance Chart

All distances shown in the chart below have been measured over highways and major roads, not necessarily by the shortest route.

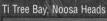
Ti Tree Bay, Noosa Heads

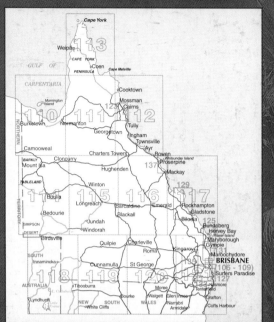

Approximate Distance	Bourke NSW	Bowen	Brisbane	Bundaberg	Cairns	Charleville	Charters Towers	Emerald	Gladstone	Longreach	Mackay	Maryborough	Moree NSW	Mt Isa	Rockhampton	Roma	Toowoomba	Townsville	Tweed Heads	Warwick
Bourke NSW		1690	1062	1228	2078	454	1596	1123	1309	968	1503	1164	877	1610	1304	722	937	1737	1135	952
Bowen	1690		1143	873	542	1236	330	567	646	980	187	900	1304	1086	520	968	1180	195	1243	1301
Brisbane	1062	1143		346	1659	753	1359	886	535	1185	956	243	471	1827	623	485	125	1338	100	158
Bundaberg	1228	873	346		1415	919	1094	621	265	1034	686	103	817	1676	353	651	402	1068	450	504
Cairns	2078	542	1659	1415		1624	482	955	1188	1368	729	1442	1840	1238	1062	1356	1716	347	1759	1800
Charleville	454	1236	753	919	1624		1142	669	855	514	1049	855	752	1156	850	268	628	1277	831	712
Charters Towers	1596	330	1359	1094	482	1142		473	867	886	517	1121	1358	756	741	874	1234	135	1437	1318
Emerald	1123	567	886	621	955	669	473		394	413	380	648	885	1055	268	401	761	608	964	845
Gladstone	1309	646	535	265	1188	855	867	394		807	459	292	789	1449	126	587	660	841	639	693
Longreach	968	980	1185	1034	1368	514	886	413	807		793	1061	1184	642	681	700	1060	1021	1263	1144
Mackay	1503	187	956	686	729	1049	517	380	459	793		713	1117	1273	333	781	993	382	1056	1077
Maryborough	1164	900	243	103	1442	855	1121	648	292	1061	713		722	1703	380	587	368	1095	343	401
Moree NSW	877	1304	471	817	1840	752	1358	885	789	1184	1117	722		1826	784	484	346	1493	557	321
Mt Isa	1610	1086	1827	1676	1238	1156	756	1055	1449	642	1273	1703	1826		1323	1342	1702	891	1905	1786
Rockhampton	1304	520	623	353	1062	850	741	268	126	681	333	380	784	1323		582	660	715	727	744
Roma	722	968	485	651	1356	268	874	401	587	700	781	587	484	1342	582		360	1009	563	444
Toowoomba	937	1180	125	402	1716	628	1234	761	660	1060	993	368	346	1702	660	360		1285	203	84
Townsville	1737	195	1338	1068	347	1277	135	608	841	1021	382	1095	1493	891	715	1009	1285		1442	1453
Tweed Heads	1135	1243	100	450	1759	831	1437	964	639	1263	1056	343	557	1905	727	563	203	1442		236
Warwick	952	1301	148	504	1800	712	1318	845	693	1144	1077	401	321	1786	744	444	84	1453	236	

Brisbane

Brisbane River and Brisbane city

Main Attractions

◈ **City Botanic Gardens** Formal gardens, bicycle tracks and duck ponds are some of the gardens' attractions.

◈ **Fortitude Valley, Chinatown** This cosmopolitan area boasts a range of cafes, restaurants and clubs and a shopping mall.

◈ **Mt Coot-tha Lookout** Brisbane's other official botanical gardens feature a scented garden and the Sir Thomas Brisbane Planetarium.

◈ **Queen St Mall** The mall brings life to the city's shopping centre with a blend of traditional and modern architecture.

◈ **Queensland Cultural Centre** Located on Brisbane River's south bank, this cultural centre consists of Queensland Museum, Queensland Art Gallery, State Library and the huge Performing Arts Complex.

◈ **South Bank Parklands** This is a recreation area providing entertainment for all with gardens, waterways, riverside walkways, cafes, restaurants, BBQ facilities and a man-made beach.

Australia's northernmost capital is an attractive and relaxed sub-tropical city. Located 14 km inland on the banks of the Brisbane River, it is a central base for touring the magnificent coastline of the Gold Coast to the south and Sunshine Coast to the north. While in the past Brisbane was a capital with the atmosphere of a large country town, visitors now discover a modern and sophisticated city that is full of vitality.

In 1825, a detachment of 45 convicts and their guards established a penal settlement at Redcliffe, north of Brisbane. A year later, the settlement was moved to Brisbane's present site on the river, where there was a more reliable fresh water supply. The riverside position has since played a pivotal role in the life of this vibrant, steamy city. Paddlesteamers, yachts, floating restaurants, ferries, cruise boats and bridges can be seen from many vantage points on Brisbane River's picturesque banks, which form a focal point for the outdoor lifestyle of the city's 1.7 million residents.

The compact city centre is situated on a single bend of the river and museums, galleries, heritage buildings and parks and gardens are all easily accessible on foot, or by high-speed catamaran along the river.

Places of Interest

Ⓐ Anzac Square **B3**
Ⓑ Brisbane City Hall and Tower **B3**
Ⓒ Brisbane Convention and Exhibition Centre **A4**
Ⓓ Brisbane Cricket Ground (Gabba) **D6**
Ⓔ City Botanic Gardens **C4**
Ⓕ Conrad Treasury Brisbane (Casino) **B4**
Ⓖ Customs House **C3**
Ⓗ Eagle St Pier and Riverside Markets **C4**

Ⓘ Kangaroo Point **D3**
Ⓙ Old Commissariat Store **B4**
Ⓚ Old Government House **C5**
Ⓛ Old Windmill Observatory **B3**
Ⓜ Parliament House **C4**
Ⓝ Queen St Mall **B4**
Ⓞ Queensland Art Gallery and Museum **A4**
Ⓟ Queensland Maritime Museum **B5**
Ⓠ Queensland Performing Arts Complex **B4**

Ⓡ Queensland Sciencentre **B4**
Ⓢ Riverside Centre **C3**
Ⓣ South Bank **B5**
Ⓤ State Library of Queensland **A4**
Ⓥ Story Bridge **D3**
Ⓦ Victoria Barracks **A3**
Ⓧ Victoria Park **B1**

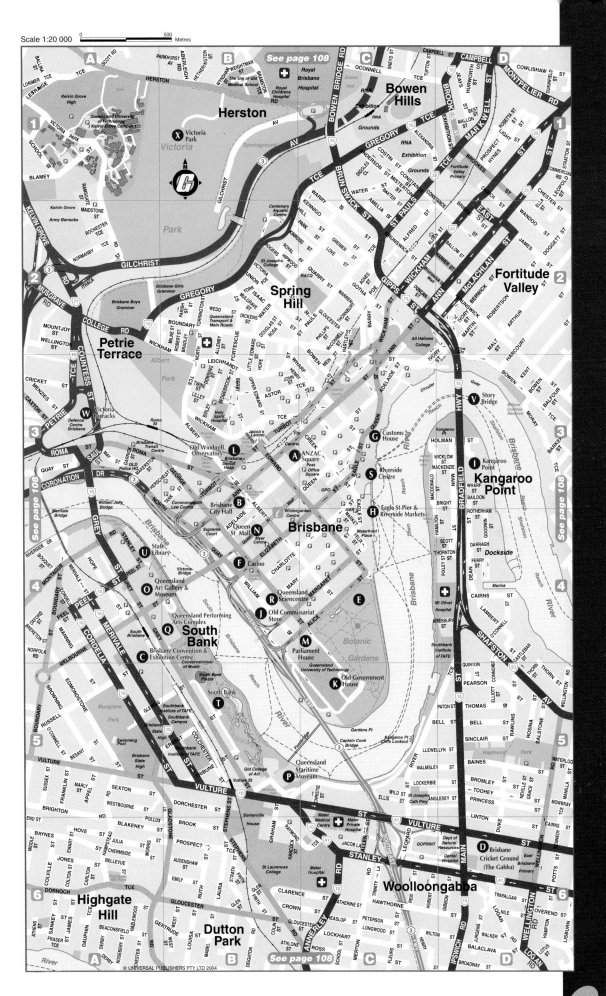

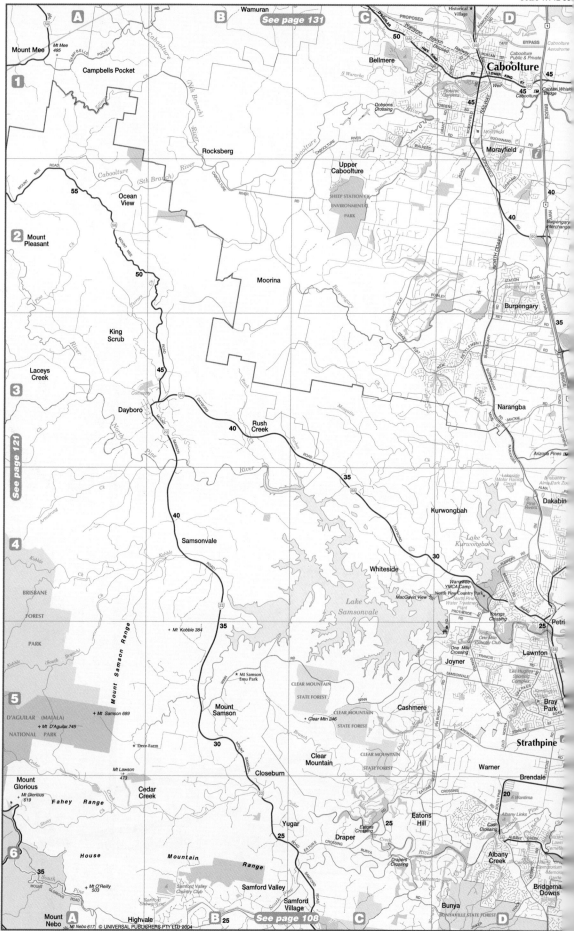

See page 131

Mount Mee

Campbells Pocket

Wamuran

Bellmere

Historical ★ Village

PROPOSED

BYPASS

Caboolture Aerodrome

Caboolture Public & Private

Caboolture

Morayfield

Rocksberg

Upper Caboolture

SHEEP STATION CK ENVIRONMENTAL PARK

Ocean View

55

Mount Pleasant

50

Moorina

Burpengary

Burpengary Interchange

King Scrub

Laceys Creek

45

Dayboro

Rush Creek

40

35

Narangba

Kurwongbah

Dakabin

Samsonvale

40

Lake Kurwongbah

Lake Samsonvale

Whiteside

30

Petri

BRISBANE FOREST PARK

+ Mt Kobble 384

35

MacGavin View

Warralee YMCA Camp North Pine Country Park

Youngs Crossing

25

Lawnton

Mount Samson Range

+ Mt Samson Emu Park

CLEAR MOUNTAIN STATE FOREST

One Mile Crossing

Joyner

Cashmere

Bray Park

D'AGUILAR (MAIALA) NATIONAL PARK

+ Mt Samson 689

+ Mt D'Aguilar 745

* Deer Farm

Mount Samson

30

+ Clear Mtn 246

CLEAR MOUNTAIN STATE FOREST

CLEAR MOUNTAIN STATE FOREST

Strathpine

Mount Glorious

+ Mt Glorious 619

Fahey Range

Mt Lawson 473

Cedar Creek

Closeburn

Clear Mountain

Warner

Brendale

20

Yugar

25

Eatons Crossing

Draper

25

Eatons Hill

Cash Crossing

Albany Creek

House

Mountain Range

35

+ Mt O'Reilly 503

Samford Valley Country Club

Samford Valley

Drapers Crossing

Bunya

Bridgema Downs

Mount Nebo

Mt Nebo 617

Highvale

25

See page 108

Samford Village

Bunya

© UNIVERSAL PUBLISHERS PTY LTD 2004

5 Kilometres

Tea Tree Swamp

Abbey Museum ★

Restricted Vehicle Access

State   Forest   ROAD

50

Ningi   BRIBIE   ISLAND   Ningi Island

Silver Shores

Bellara   65   Bribie Island   Woorim

BRIBIE ISLAND N.P.

Welsby   Bongaree   Bribie

Bribie Pines   Island

Sandstone Point   Sandstone Point   Bribie Bridge

Godwin Beach

FIRST   Skirmish Pt

Buckleys Hole   Woody Bay

South Pt   BUCKLEYS HOLE C.P.

Red Beach   Bald Pt

Caboolture

BEACHMERE ENVIRONMENTAL PARK

1

Beachmere

Burpengary   Creek

River   ROAD

Deception

2

Vehicular Ferry

OLD BAY

Bay

Moreton

Caboolture Lawn Cemetery

TETWATER N.P.

DECEPTION BAY

Endeavour   Four Star

35   Deception Bay

North Reef   Castlereagh (or Reef) Pt

Scarborough Boat Harbour   Scarborough Boat Harbour

Oyster Pt   HAYS   Scarborough Pt

3

Redcliffe Aerodrome   35   Scarborough Beach

Rothwell   **NEWPORT MARINA**   Scarborough   Drury Pt

30   NATHAN ROAD WETLANDS RESERVE   Queens Beach Nth

Rothwell Memorial   ANZAC   30   KLUNGNER   Osbourne Pt

30   Queens Beach

Kippa - Ring   30   ANZAC   Queens Beach South

HAYS INLET C.P. NO.2   ✚   Redcliffe Jetty

Kallangur   Mango Hill   **Redcliffe**   Settlement Cove Lagoon

Redcliffe Pt

Museum ★

Murrumba Downs   Clontarf   Margate   30   Marine Sutton Beach   **4**

HAYS INLET C.P. NO.3   DUFFIELD   KING   Scotts Pt

Griffin   Bramble Bay   Woody   Picnic Pt

25   Clontarf Beach   Bells Beach   Woody Point Beach   Woody Pt

25   Clontarf Pt

HAYS INLET C.P. NO.1

Bay

TINCHI TAMPA WETLANDS RESERVE

Brighton

20   **Bramble**   **5**

Babinburra Bushland Res   NORTH   Brighton

20   20   **Bay**

20   Sandgate Foreshores

DEAGON WETLANDS

WATERWAY   Passenger Ferry (Tangalooma Flyer)

Sandgate

Bald Hills   Bracken Ridge   Deagon   Shorncliffe   Cabbage Tree Head

North Boondall   Brisbane Ent Centre

Fitzgibbon   Boondall Wetlands Visitor Centre   Nudgee Beach   **6**

15   Taigum   Boondall   18   Nudgee Beach

Carseldine   Colonial Village   BOONDALL WETLANDS PARK

QUT Carseldine Campus   15   Juno Point

Zillmere   Boondall   Port of Brisbane

Aspley   Geebung   Banyo   Nudgee   **See page 109**   Luggage Point Whale Water Treatment Plant   BISHOP

© UNIVERSAL PUBLISHERS PTY LTD 2004

See page 106

See page 121

See page 133

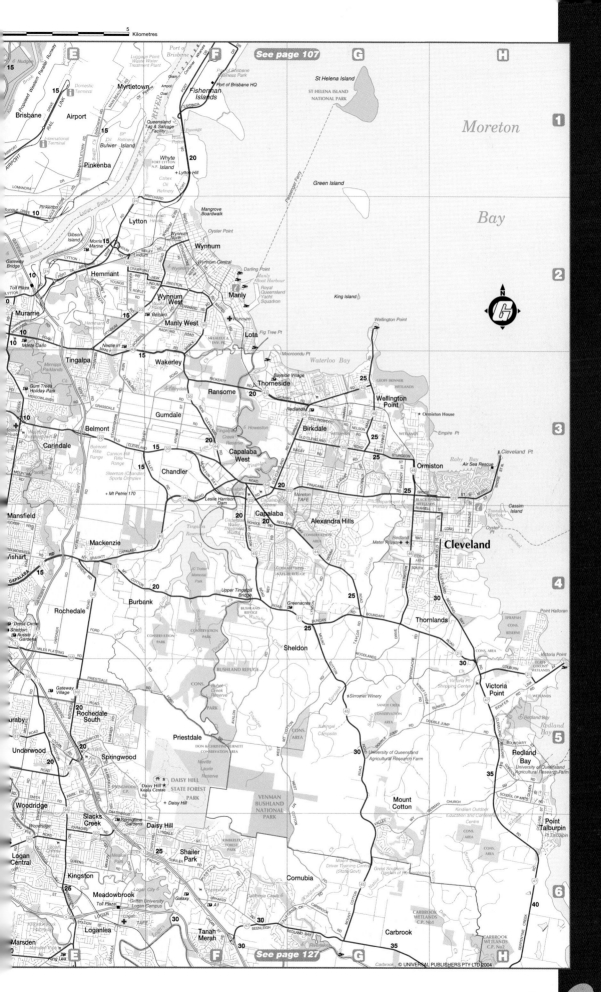

5 Kilometres

Moreton

Bay

© UNIVERSAL PUBLISHERS PTY LTD 2004

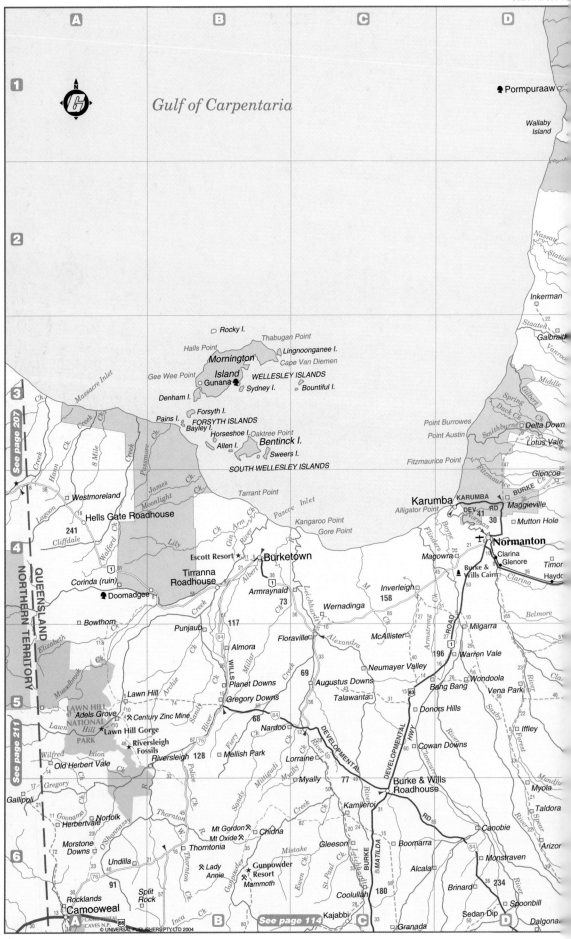

Scale 1:2 600 0C

See page 207
See page 211
See page 114

Gulf of Carpentaria

Pormpuraaw

Wallaby
Island

Nassau
Statio

Inkerman

Staaten

Galbrait

Vanroo

Rocky I.

Thabugan Point

Halls Point

Lingnoonganee I.

Mornington
Island   Cape Van Diemen

Gee Wee Point   WELLESLEY ISLANDS

Gunana   Sydney I.   Bountiful I.
Denham I.

Middle

Spring

Point Burrowes   Gilber

Point Austin   Duck Ck   Delta Down

Smithburne   Lotus Vale

Forsyth I.

Pains I.   FORSYTH ISLANDS
Bayley I.
Horseshoe I.Oaktree Point
Allen I.   Bentinck I.

Sweers I.

SOUTH WELLESLEY ISLANDS

Fitzmaurice Point   Glencoe

Fitzmaurice

Tarrant Point

Massacre Inlet

Hann Ck   Creek

8 Mile   Creek   Passmore Ck   James Ck   Moonlight Ck

Pascoe Inlet   Kangaroo Point   Karumba   KARUMBA   BURKE

Gore Point   Alligator Point   DEV 41   RD   Maggieville
30   Mutton Hole

Westmoreland   Lily Ck   Gin Arm   River   Forman   Normanton

Hells Gate Roadhouse   Magowra   Clarina   Timor

241   Escott Resort   11 5   Burketown   Burke &   Glenore   Hayde
Cliffdale   Tirranna   Albert   38   Wills Cairn   Clarina   39
Corinda (ruin)   81   Roadhouse   21   1   Inverleigh   45   53

Doomadgee   Armraynald   Leichhardt   158   Armstrong   196   Warren Vale
73   Wernadinga   McAllister   Milgarra
Bowthorn   117   Neumayer Valley   Wondoola
Punjaub   Floraville   Alexandra   Bang Bang   Vena Park
Almora   69   Augustus Downs   83   Donors Hills   Iffley
Lawn Hill   Planet Downs   Talawanta   60   Cowan Downs
Adels Grove   Gregory Downs   68   Nardoo   DEVELOPMENTAL   Burke & Wills   Myola
Century Zinc Mine   84   Lorraine   77   Roadhouse   Taldora
Lawn Hill Gorge   Mellish Park   Myally   Kamileroi   RD   Canobie   Arizor
Riversleigh   Old Herbert Vale   128   Mt Gordon   Chidna   Gleeson   Boomarra   Monstraven
Gallipoli   Norfolk   Mt Oxide   Thorntonia   MATILDA   Alcala   Brinard   234
Herbertvale   Lady   Gunpowder   Coolullah   180   Spoonbill
Morstone   Annie   Resort   Sedan Dip   Dalgona
Downs   Undilla   Mammoth   Kajabbi   Granada
91   Split
Rocklands   Rock
Camooweal   CAVES N.P.
66
© UNIVERSAL PUBLISHERS PTY LTD 2004

QUEENSLAND
NORTHERN TERRITORY

LAWN HILL
NATIONAL
PARK

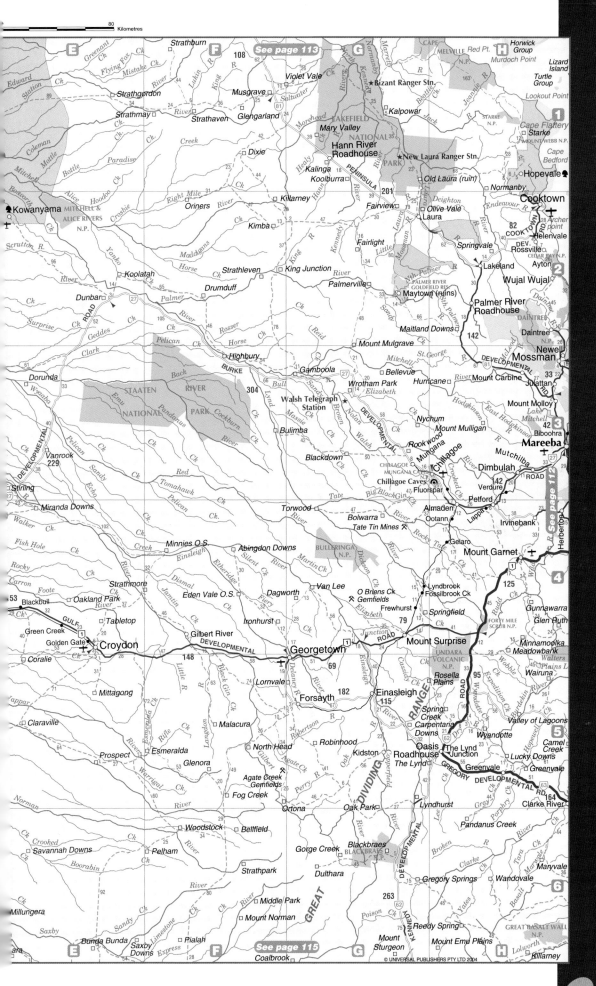

See page 113

See page 115

© UNIVERSAL PUBLISHERS PTY LTD 2004

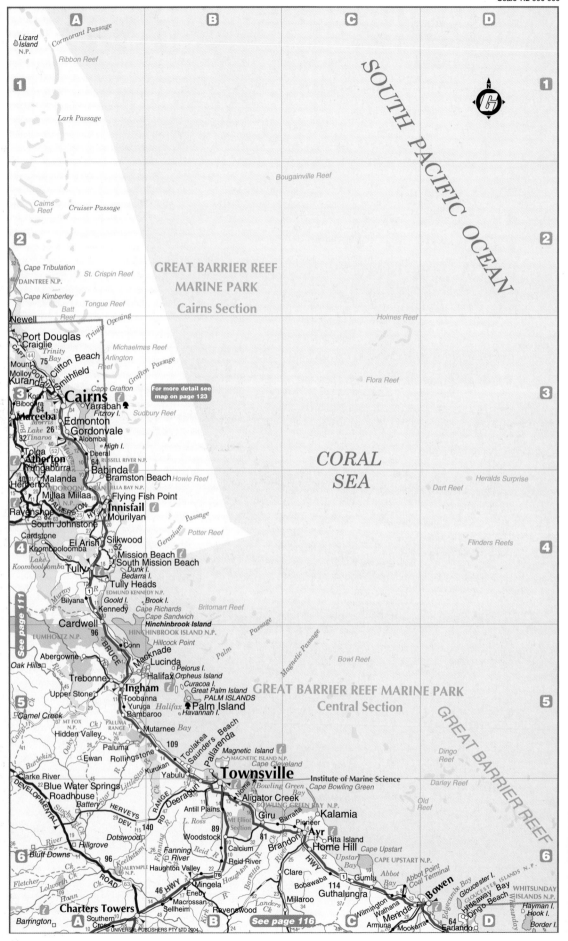

Scale 1:2 600 000

SOUTH PACIFIC OCEAN

CORAL SEA

GREAT BARRIER REEF MARINE PARK
Cairns Section

GREAT BARRIER REEF MARINE PARK
Central Section

GREAT BARRIER REEF

© UNIVERSAL PUBLISHERS PTY LTD 2004

For more detail see map on page 123

See page 111

See page 116

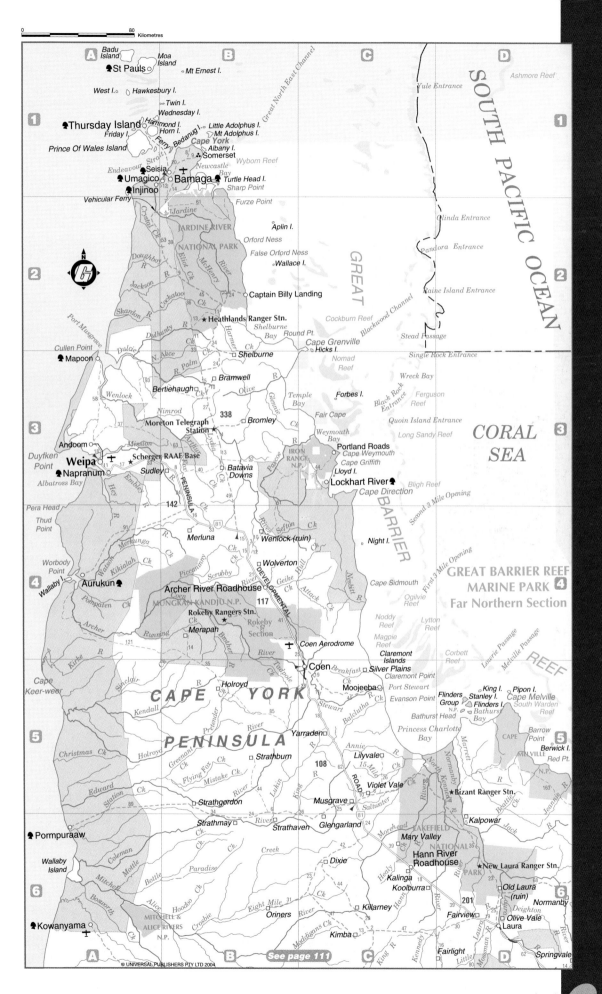

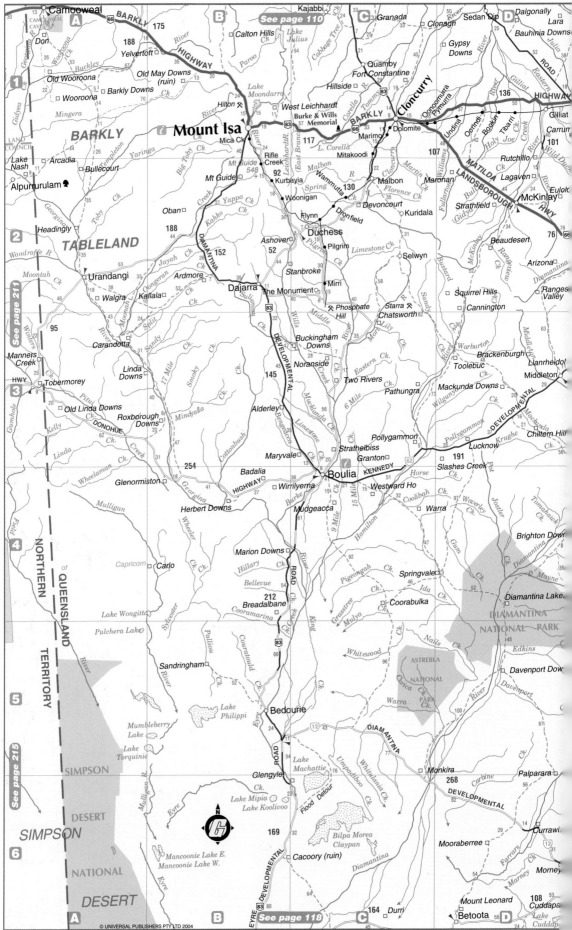

Scale 1:2 600 000

Camooweal

© UNIVERSAL PUBLISHERS PTY LTD 2004

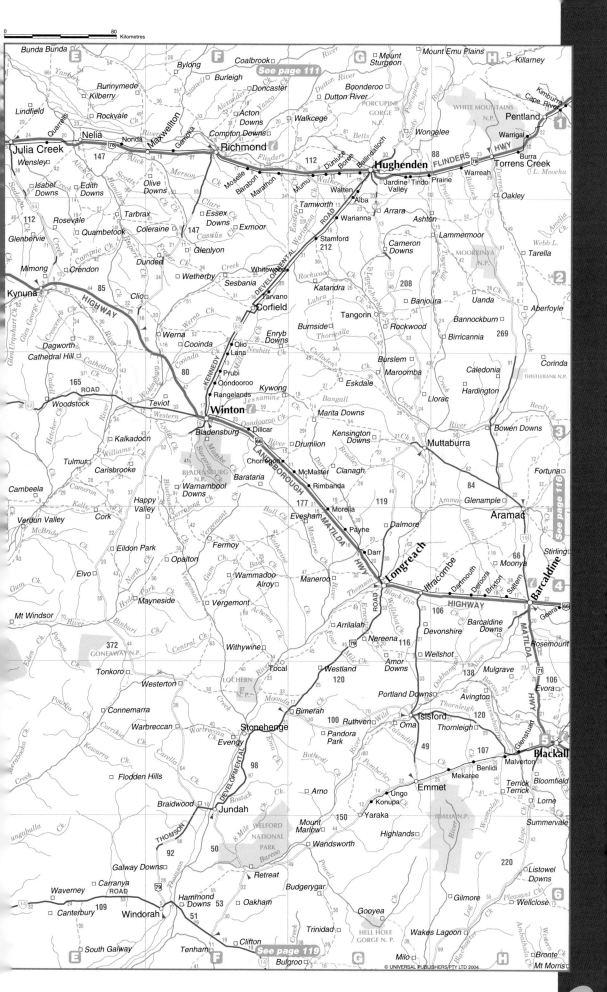

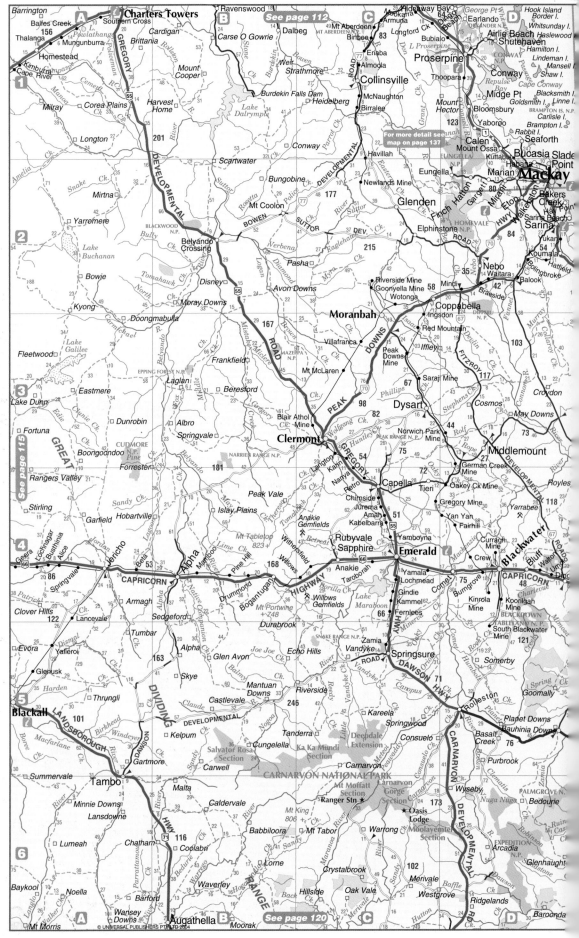

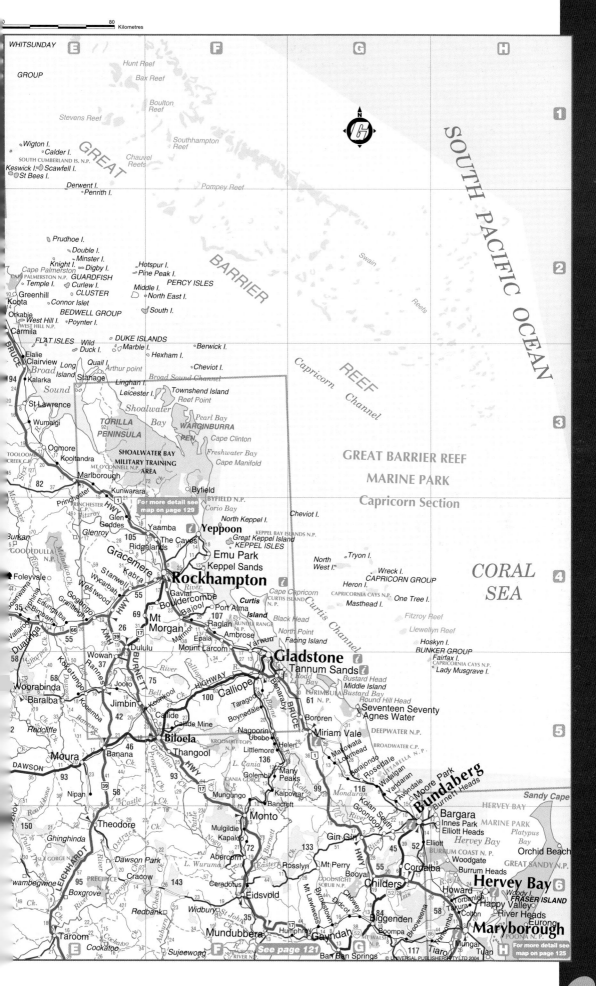

GROUP

Kilometres

E   F   G   H

1

Hunt Reef
Bax Reef

Boulton
Reef

Stevens Reef

GREAT

Southhampton
Reef

N

SOUTH PACIFIC OCEAN

2

Wigton I.
Calder I.
SOUTH CUMBERLAND IS. N.P.
Keswick I. Scawfell I.
St Bees I.

Chauvel
Reefs

BARRIER

Swain

Pompey Reef

Reefs

Derwent I.
Penrith I.

Prudhoe I.

Double I.
Minster I.
Knight I. Digby I.
Cape Palmerston GUARDFISH
CAPE PALMERSTON N.P. Curlew I.
Temple I. CLUSTER
Greenhill Connor Islet
Kobta
Orkabie BEDWELL GROUP
West Hill I. Poynter I.
Carmila

Hotspur I.
Pine Peak I.

PERCY ISLES

Middle I.
North East I.

South I.

REEF

3

FLAT ISLES Wild
Elalie Duck I.
Clairview Long Quail I.
Kalarka Island Stanage
St Lawrence Sound
Wumalgi

DUKE ISLANDS

Marble I.
Hexham I.

Berwick I.

Cheviot I.

Broad Sound Channel

Capricorn

Channel

BRUCE
194
24
20
16
19

Ogmore
Kooltandra

TOOLOOMBAH
CREEK C.P.

Marlborough

82 37

Burkan

GOODEDULLA
N.P.

Foleyvale

Linghan I.
Leicester I.

Townshend Island
Reef Point

Shoalwater

TORILLA
PENINSULA

Bay

Pearl Bay
WARGINBURRA
PEN.

Cape Clinton

SHOALWATER BAY
MILITARY TRAINING
AREA
MT. O'CONNELL N.P.

Freshwater Bay
Cape Manifold

GREAT BARRIER REEF

MARINE PARK

Capricorn Section

CORAL
SEA

4

Kunwarara

Byfield
BYFIELD N.P.

For more detail see
map on page 129

Corio Bay

Princhester
PRINCHESTER
N.P.
Glen Fitzroy
Geddes
Glenroy 105
Gracemere Ridglands
Stanwell Kabra
Westwood Wycarbah
Granliegh
Gogango Edungalba
Duaringa Bimbam

Yaamba
The Caves
Ridglands

North Keppel I.

Cheviot I.

KEPPEL BAY ISLANDS N.P.
Great Keppel Island
KEPPEL ISLES

Tryon I.

Yeppoon

Emu Park
Keppel Sands

North
West I.

Wreck I.
CAPRICORN GROUP
Heron I. CAPRICORNIA CAYS N.P. One Tree I.
Masthead I.

Rockhampton

River

Gavial
Bouldercombe
Bajool
Mt Raglan
Morgan Marmor
Epala
Mount Larcom

Port Alma
107
RUNDLE RANGE
N.P.

Curtis
Island

Cape Capricorn
CURTIS ISLAND
N.P.

Fitzroy Reef

Llewellyn Reef

5

35
44
66

Wowan
Rannes
Jooro

69 Mt
26 Morgan
17
39 Dululu

Black Head

North Point
Facing Island

Yarwun

Gladstone

Hoskyn I.
BUNKER GROUP
Fairfax I. CAPRICORNIA CAYS N.P.
Lady Musgrave I.

58 12

Woorabinda

Baralba

68

River

Jimbin

42

Bell

Kokotungo
Kooemba

BURNETT

Calliope

HIGHWAY

Calliope

Taragoola

100

Tannum Sands

Rodd
Bay

Bustard Head
Middle Island
Bustard Bay
EURIMBULA Round Hill Head
N.P.

Seventeen Seventy
Agnes Water

DEEPWATER N.P.

BROADWATER C.P.

Moura

Banana

93

Nipan

2
Redcliffe

150

Theodore

Ghinghinda

DAWSON

11

58

21

Calide
Callide Mine

Biloela
Thangool

BRUCE

61

Boynedale

Bororen

Miriam Vale

Matowata
Lowmead

Beraiondo
Rosedale

BUNDABERG

HERVEY BAY
MARINE PARK

Sandy Cape

Bargara
Innes Park
Elliott Heads

Platypus
Bay

Orchid Beach

KROOMBIT TOPS
N.P.

Helen

Littlemore

136

Golemba
CANIA GORGE
N.P.

L. Cania

Many
Peaks

Mungungo

Kalpowar

Bancroft

Monto

99

Kolan

L.
Monduran

116

Goondoon

Kolan South

Watalgan
Yardaran
Avondale

Moore Park
Burnett Heads

LITTABELLA
N.P.

52

Elliott
Woodgate
BURRUM COAST N.P. Burrum Heads

Hervey Bay

GREAT SANDY N.P.

Dawson Park

95 PRECIPICE

Boxgrove

wambegwine

Cracow

143

Mulgildie

Kapaldo

Abercorn

72

Ceradotus

Eidsvold

Gin Gin

Mt Perry

133

Rosslyn

Cordalba

55

Childers

52

Howard
Torbanlea
Takura

HERVEY BAY

Woody I. FRASER ISLAND
Happy Valley
River Heads
Colton
Eurong

Redbank

Widbury

Mundubbera

See page 121

Taroom

Cockatoo

Sujeewong

Gayndah

Ban Ban Springs

GOODNIGHT
SCRUB N.P.

Booyal

Biggenden

MT WALSH

Boompa

Didcot

Chowey

Biggenden

84

58

Tiaro

Mungar
Tuan

Maryborough

POONA N.P.

117

For more detail see
map on page 125

© UNIVERSAL PUBLISHERS PTY LTD 2004

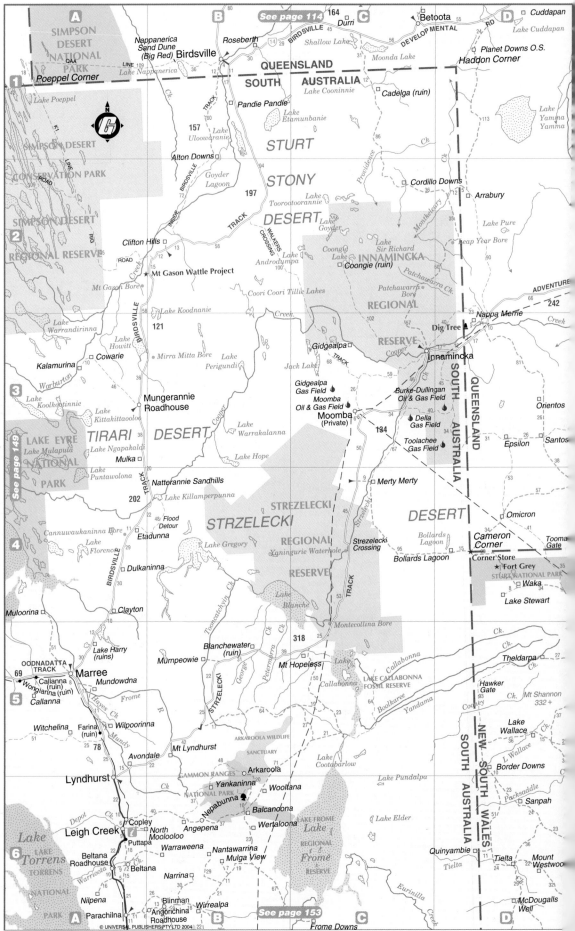

See page 114

© UNIVERSAL PUBLISHERS PTY LTD 2004

See page 153

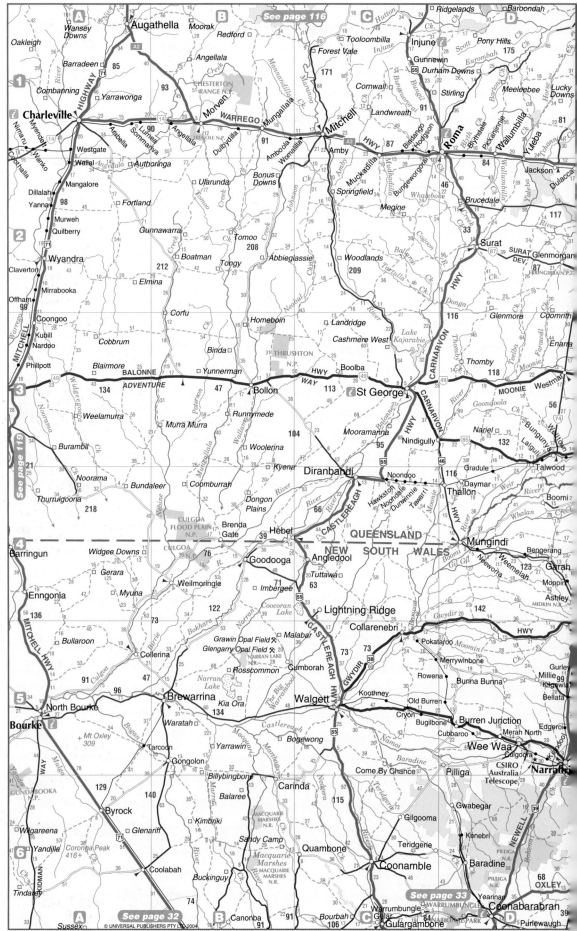

© UNIVERSAL PUBLISHERS PTY LTD 2004

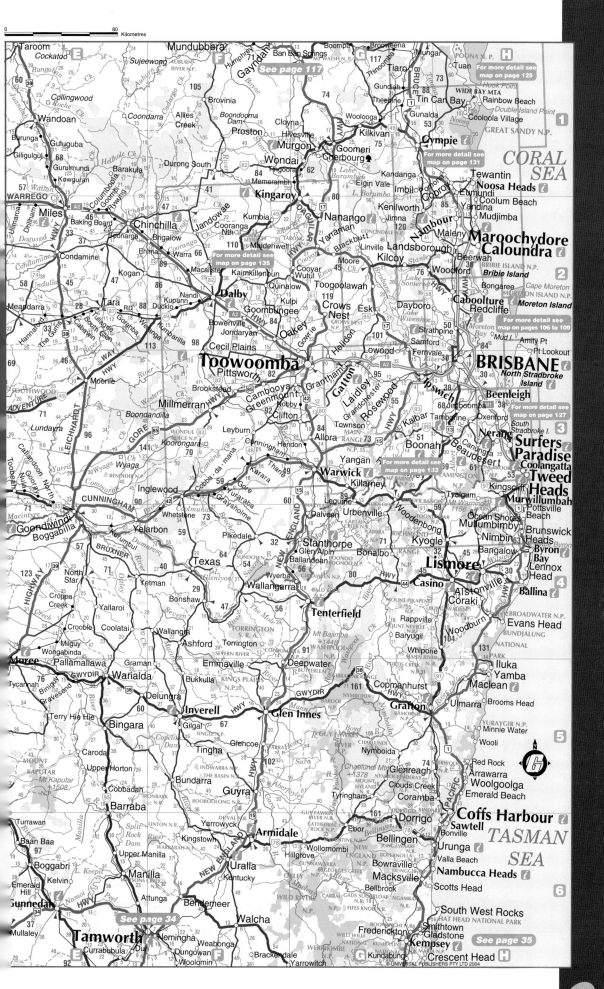

Cairns

Diving on the Great Barrier Reef

The Eden-like environment of Cairns and its surrounding districts is a lush tropical belt bordered by the Coral Sea's temperate waters and the brilliant green plains that sweep from the northernmost section of the Great Dividing Range. Inland from the balmy, humid coast, the Atherton Tableland is elevated 600 to 900m above sea level. Known as the 'cool tropics', it is usually warm and sunny during the day, while the night provides relief from the heat.

The region is blessed with an abundance of waterfalls, rolling hills, rainforests, idyllic tropical beaches, extinct volcanoes and crater lakes, and takes pride of place as an international holiday destination. It features an eclectic combination of colonial tropical architecture, modern resorts and wild forest vegetation.

The Great Barrier Reef is the world's largest and most complex coral reef system, stretching more than 2000km along Queensland's north-east coast. It has thousands of individual coral reefs and hundreds of continental islands, reef islands and cays.

While Cairns is the most popular gateway to the Great Barrier Reef, the reef can also be accessed from many points along the Queensland coast. A wide range of tours is available and visitors can choose to snorkel or scuba dive, or to view the reef from underwater observatories.

Crater Lakes

Lake Barrine (below) and Lake Eacham have formed in the craters of extinct volcanoes, each millions of years old. Lake Eacham was an early settler's camp; Aborigines believed it to be haunted and steered clear of the vicinity for fear of upsetting the lake's spirits, who in ancestral stories had brought on volcanic destruction.

Tourist information

i Gateway Discovery Centre
51 The Esplanade, Cairns Qld 4870
Ph: (07) 4051 3588
www.tropicalaustralia.com.au

Main Attractions

◈ **Daintree National Park** This national park features crocodile tours, bird watching, and walks through lush rainforest.

◈ **Kuranda** The resort town's attractions include markets, a butterfly sanctuary, a scenic railway, and rainforest tours by boat.

◈ **Mossman Gorge** The Kuku Yalangi Aboriginal community give guided tours of this river gorge, which is surrounded by rainforest.

◈ **Port Douglas & Palm Cove** These are upmarket tourist resorts north of Cairns.

◈ **Skyrail Rainforest Cableway** Cable cars make a 7.5km journey hovering above the tree tops.

◈ **Tjapukai Aboriginal Cultural Park** This park showcasing the Tjapukai Aboriginal Dance Theatre has a traditional campsite, history theatre, and restaurant.

◈ **Wooroonooran National Park** Within this park are Josephine Falls, Babinda Boulders, Walshs Pyramid, and Qld's highest mountain, Bartle Frere.

Daintree Lodge

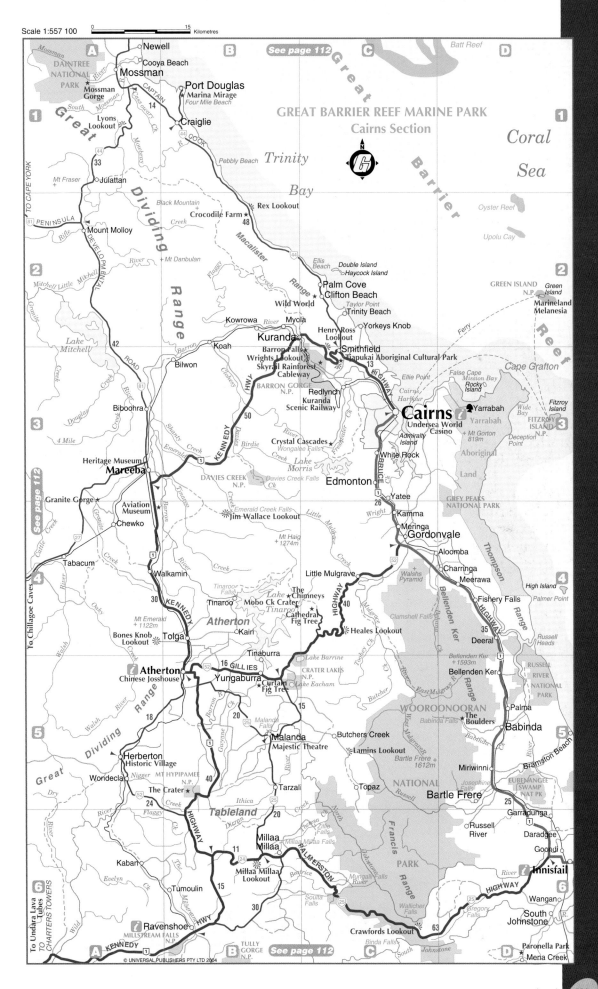

Fraser Coast

Sunset on Fraser Island

The magnificent natural playground of the Fraser Coast features diverse and unique landscapes, from intriguing coloured sands, silent rainforests, giant sand dunes and towering cliffs to tranquil lakes, spectacular scenery, pristine beaches and lush national parks.

Boasting the world's largest sand island and magnificent waterways, the Fraser Coast offers a wide range of watersports including swimming, fishing, scuba diving and boating. The seaside townships dotting the mainland coast, such as Tuan, Tinnanbar and Poona, provide both adventure tourism opportunities and more sedate and relaxed activities.

A major attraction for visitors is the sight of majestic humpback whales and their calves passing through Hervey Bay on their migration to Antarctica, after giving birth in the waters of northern Queensland.

Shipwreck Survivor

After the wreck of the *Stirling Castle* in 1836, Eliza Fraser was cast ashore on Fraser Island where she lived with the local Kabi Aboriginal people. After several months she was led back towards Brisbane by 'Wandi', the escaped convict, David Bracefell.

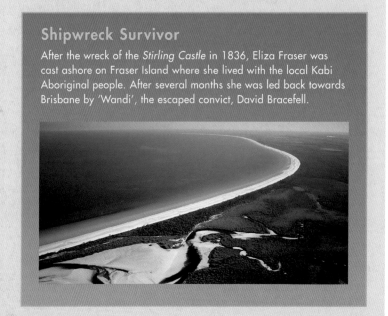

Tourist information

Fraser Coast South Burnett Regional Tourism Board

388 Kent St, Maryborough
Qld 4650
Ph: (07) 4122 3444
www.frasercoastholidays.info

Main Attractions

◈ **'The Cathedrals'** These strikingly coloured sand cliffs at Cathedral Beach on Fraser Island change colour depending on the light and time of day.

◈ **Eli Creek** The crystalline Eli Creek is the largest creek on the east coast of Fraser Island and is ideal for swimming.

◈ **Fraser Island** This island is famous for its coloured sands, vast sand dunes and rainforests.

◈ **Great Sandy National Park** Bushwalking tracks let visitors explore this 165,000ha wilderness, with 43 short walks ranging in levels of difficulty.

◈ **Maryborough** Picturesque Maryborough has many historic buildings.

◈ **Neptunes Reef World** A natural reef aquarium with live coral, tropical fish, seals, turtles and sharks.

◈ **Whale Watching** A good time to see migrating humpback whales and calves is between late July and early November.

Whale breaching in Harvey Bay

Gold Coast

Snapper Rocks, Coolangatta

Just one hour south of Brisbane and stretching along 70 km of coastline lies Australia's biggest, busiest and brassiest tourist resort: the Gold Coast. The narrow coastal strip is crammed with high-rise accommodation, eateries, tourist shops and nightclubs, while all roads lead to one of Australia's most famous stretches of beach, the aptly named Surfers Paradise.

With its idyllic climate – the Coast boasts an annual average temperature of 23°C and 300 sunny days per year – and a stunning hinterland of cooler, sub-tropical mountain ranges, the Gold Coast has become a magnet for both tourists and retirees. Behind the commercial strip, expensive canal developments cater for people who have been attracted to the Gold Coast's sunshine and breezy lifestyle, many of them escapees from cooler southern climes.

Boasting 40 beaches and five key waterways, the Gold Coast offers every imaginable watersport. Surfing, windsurfing, swimming, sailing, scuba diving, jet-skiing, fishing and canoeing make this a prime holiday destination for sun lovers and surfers.

A plethora of theme parks jostle for attention with the shops, restaurants and outdoor activities on offer to the 4.3 million-plus visitors flocking to the Gold Coast each year. This vibrant resort town does not sleep – a casino, nightclubs and bustling bars provide for a hectic nightlife.

Tourist information

Surfers Paradise Visitor Information Centre

Cavill Ave,
Surfers Paradise Qld 4217
Ph: (07) 5538 4419
www.goldcoasttourism.com.au

Main Attractions

◈ **Burleigh Heads National Park**
Several tracks wander through the rainforest, open forest and grassy hills of this park.

◈ **Currumbin Wildlife Sanctuary**
Visitors can feed lorikeets, see koalas, visit the snake pit and the animal nursery and see daily performances by Aboriginal dancers.

◈ **Coolangatta** Greenmount Beach at Coolangatta is delightfully calm and ideal for families.

◈ **Dreamworld** This fantasy adventure park offers rides, a wildlife park, theme 'worlds' and a huge cinema screen.

◈ **Sea World** Sea World features a dolphin show, rides and water-ski displays.

◈ **Surfers Paradise** With popular beaches and a waterfront promenade, this tourist hotspot is the heart of the Gold Coast.

◈ **Warner Bros. Movie World**
Billed as 'Hollywood on the Gold Coast', this is a film and TV-based theme park.

Dreamworld

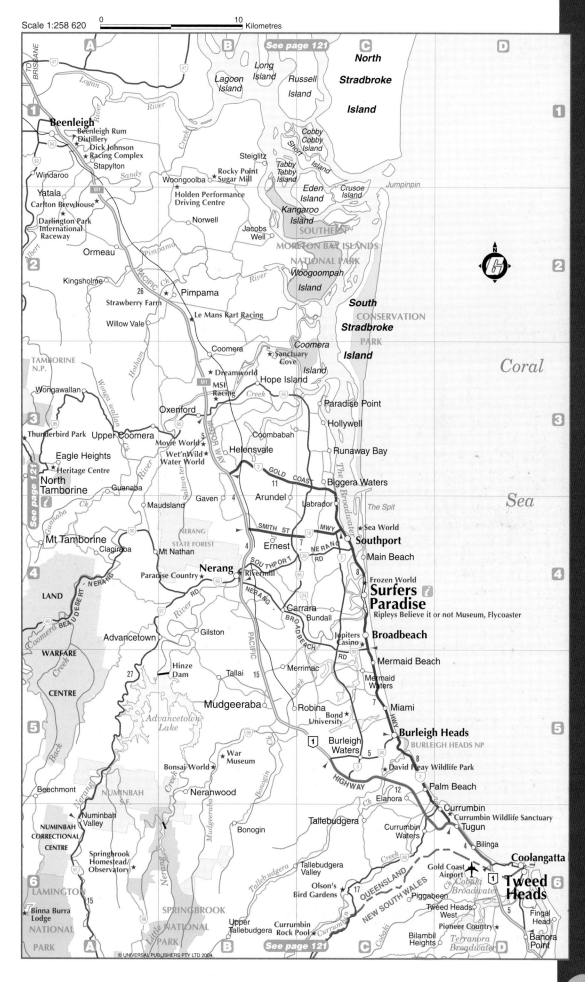

Scale 1:258 620

0 — 10 Kilometres

See page 121

A **B** **C** **D**

TO BRISBANE

Logan River

Beenleigh
Beenleigh Rum Distillery
Dick Johnson
Racing Complex
Windaroo
Stapylton
Yatala
Carlton Brewhouse
Darlington Park International Raceway
Ormeau

Woongoolba
Rocky Point Sugar Mill
Holden Performance Driving Centre
Norwell

1

Lagoon Island
Long Island
Russell Island

Steiglitz

North
Stradbroke
Island

Cobby Cobby Island
Tabby Tabby Island
Eden Island
Crusoe Island

Jumpinpin

Jacobs Well

Kangaroo Island

SOUTHERN
MORETON BAY ISLANDS
NATIONAL PARK

Woogoompah Island

2

Kingsholme
Pimpama
26
Pimpama
Strawberry Farm
Willow Vale
Le Mans Kart Racing

Coomera
Coomera Island
Sanctuary Cove

South
Stradbroke
Island

CONSERVATION
PARK

Coral

TAMBORINE N.P.
Wongawallan

Dreamworld
MSI Racing
Hope Island
Oxenford

Paradise Point
Hollywell

3

Thunderbird Park
Upper Coomera
Eagle Heights
Heritage Centre
Movie World
Wet'nWild Water World
Helensvale
Guanaba
North Tamborine

Coombabah

Runaway Bay

GOLD COAST
Biggera Waters

Sea

Maudsland
Gaven
Arundel
Labrador

The Broadwater

The Spit

4

Mt Tamborine
Clagiraba
Mt Nathan

NERANG
STATE FOREST

SMITH ST
Ernest
7

Sea World

Southport
Main Beach

Nerang
Paradise Country
Rivermill

NERANG RD

8
Frozen World
Surfers
Paradise
Ripleys Believe it or not Museum, Flycoaster

LAND
WARFARE
CENTRE

Advancetown
Gilston

Carrara
Bundall
Jupiters Casino
Broadbeach

Mermaid Beach

Hinze Dam
27
Tallai
15
Merrimac
Mermaid Waters

5

Advancetown Lake

Mudgeeraba
Robina
Bond University
7
Miami

Burleigh Heads
BURLEIGH HEADS NP

Burleigh Waters
5
8
David Fleay Wildlife Park
Palm Beach

Beechmont
NUMINBAH S.F.

War Museum
Bonsai World
Neranwood

HIGHWAY
12
Elanora
Currumbin
Currumbin Wildlife Sanctuary
Tugun

NUMINBAH CORRECTIONAL CENTRE
Numinbah Valley
Springbrook Homestead/Observatory

Bonogin
Tallebudgera
Currumbin Waters
Bilinga

4
Coolangatta

6

LAMINGTON
15

Binna Burra Lodge

SPRINGBROOK NATIONAL PARK

Upper Tallebudgera
Currumbin Rock Pool
Tallebudgera Valley
Olson's Bird Gardens
17
QUEENSLAND
NEW SOUTH WALES
Gold Coast Airport
Piggabeen
Tweed Heads West
Pioneer Country
Bilambil Heights
Cobaki Broadwater

Tweed
Heads
5
Fingal Head
Banora Point
Terranora Broadwater

NATIONAL PARK

See page 121

Rockhampton and Capricorn Coast

Customs House, Rockhampton

The Capricorn Coast straddles the Tropic of Capricorn and is an inviting combination of glorious beaches, raging rivers, intricate reef islands and rugged, sun-bathed outback towns. A contrast of dramatic volcanic outcrops, hazy beaches, vast grazier's estates, estuarine mudflats, scenic headlands and wooded hills, the region is dotted with historic townships where elegant buildings hint at the wealth of former times.

Rich in history, the area was once the site of a gold rush, and flourished due to its abundant natural resources: from gold and copper mines, to vast cattle country properties. Relics provide evidence of this prosperous past.

The region's Aboriginal history is another drawcard for visitors: there are bora rings, museums and artefacts of the Darumbal people, whose lands once stretched from inland Mt Morgan to the Keppel Bay coastline. Diverse landscapes offer the delights of rainforest, rugged gorges and tropical beaches; this is a place where visitors can enjoy some of the world's best fishing and scuba diving, bushwalking, caving, camping and sightseeing.

Dreamtime Cultural Centre

This centre is located on an important ancient site where Aboriginal people once gathered for tribal meetings. The museum aims to promote understanding of 40,000 years of Aboriginal history.

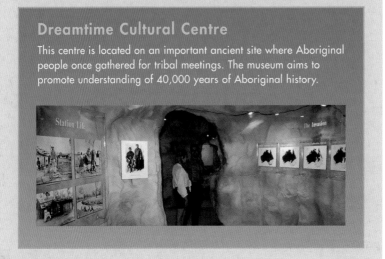

Tourist information

 Capricorn Visitor Information Centre

'The Spire', Gladstone Rd, Rockhampton Qld 4700
Ph: (07) 4927 2055
Freecall: 1800 676 701
www.capricorntourism.com.au

 Gladstone Visitor Information Centre

Gladstone Marina Ferry Terminal, Bryan Jordan Dr, Gladstone Qld 4680
Ph: (07) 4972 4000
www.gladstoneregion.org.au

Main Attractions

◈ **Byfield National Park** See beautiful rainforest, visit local artisans, or hire a canoe on Waterpark Creek.

◈ **Capricorn Caverns** A spectacular system of 16 limestone caves. The Cathedral is one of these, with fantastic natural acoustics and old church pews to sit on.

◈ **Curtis Island** This is a serene island of sweeping coastline, remote beaches and rugged headlands.

◈ **Great Keppel Island** This lively, sun-drenched island is accessible via ferry from Rosslyn Bay harbour in Yeppoon.

◈ **Heritage Village** A township museum where visitors can experience Rockhampton's colourful history.

◈ **Koorana Crocodile Farm** This farm is famed for breeding estuarine crocodiles.

◈ **Lake Maraboon** This large man-made dam near Emerald is a haven for waterbirds and water sports.

◈ **Mt Morgan** This former gold mine closed in 1981 and now houses a history and railway museum.

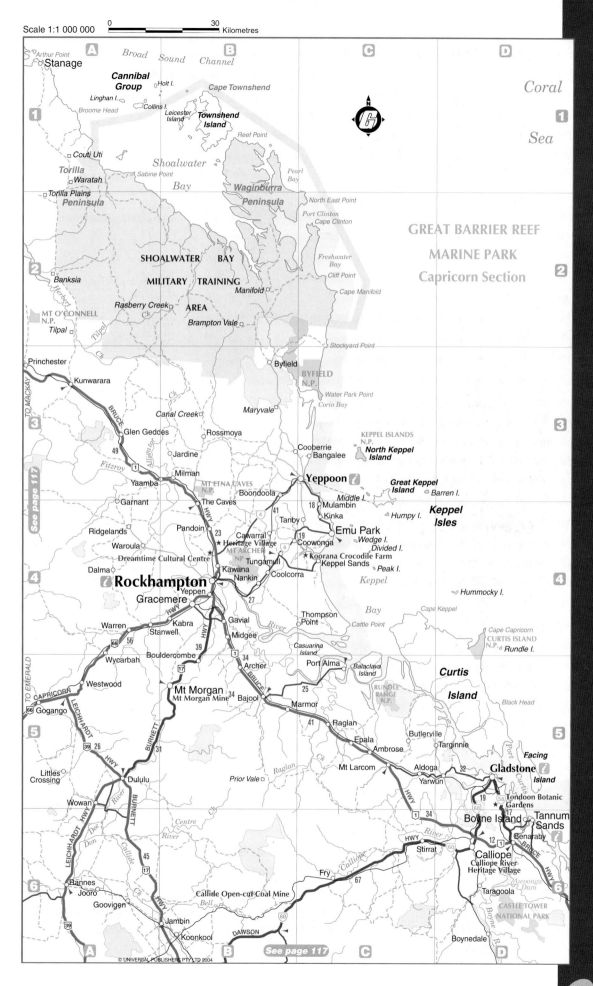

0   30
Kilometres

Broad   Sound   Channel

Arthur Point
Stanage

Cannibal Group
Holt I.
Cape Townshend
Linghan I.
Broome Head
Collins I.
Leicester Island
Townshend Island
Reef Point

Couti Uti
Torilla
Waratah
Shoalwater
Sabine Point
Bay
Pearl Bay
Waginburra
Torilla Plains
Peninsula
North East Point
Port Clinton
Cape Clinton

Coral

Sea

Banksia
SHOALWATER   BAY
Manifold
Freshwater Bay
Cliff Point
Cape Manifold

GREAT BARRIER REEF
MARINE PARK
Capricorn Section

MT O'CONNELL
N.P.
MILITARY   TRAINING
Tilpal
Rasberry Creek
Ck
AREA
Brampton Vale
Stockyard Point

Princhester
Kunwarara
Byfield
BYFIELD
N.P.
Water Park Point
Corio Bay

TO MACKAY
BRUCE
Canal Creek
Ck
Maryvale

Glen Geddes
49
Rossmoya
Cooberrie
Bangalee
KEPPEL ISLANDS
N.P.
North Keppel Island

Jardine
Fitzroy
Milman
1
Yeppoon i
Great Keppel Island
Barren I.
Keppel
Yaamba
Garnant
MT ETNA CAVES
N.P.
Boondoola
Middle I.
18 Mulambin
Kinka
Humpy I.
Isles

Ridgelands
Pandoin
23
Tanby
41
4
Emu Park
Wedge I.
Waroula
Cawarral
★ Heritage Village
19 Coowonga
★ Koorana Crocodile Farm
Divided I.

Dalma
Dreamtime Cultural Centre
MT ARCHER
NP
Tungamull
Keppel Sands
Peak I.

i **Rockhampton**
Kawana
Nankin
Coolcorra
Keppel

Gracemere
Yeppen
27
Cape Keppel
Hummocky I.

Warren
Kabra
Stanwell
Gavial
Midgee
River
Thompson Point
Cattle Point
Bay
Cape Capricorn
CURTIS ISLAND
N.P.
Rundle I.

66   56
Wycarbah
Bouldercombe
39
17
34
Archer
Casuarina Island
Port Alma
Balaclava Island
RUNDLE RANGE N.P.
Curtis

Westwood
Mt Morgan
Mt Morgan Mine
34
Bajool
25
Marmor
Island
Black Head

CAPRICORN
66 Gogango
LEICHHARDT
BURNETT
31
41
Raglan
Epala
Ambrose
Butlerville
Targinnie
Port

Littles Crossing
39 26
Dululu
BURNETT
Prior Vale
Mt Larcom
Aldoga
Yarwun
32
Gladstone i
Facing
Island

Wowan
River
Centre
River
1 34
19
Tondoon Botanic Gardens
Boyne Island
Tannum Sands

HWY
Stirrat
60
12 1
Benaraby
i

Rannes
45
17
Calliope
Calliope River Heritage Village

Jooro
Goovigen
Ck
Fry
67
Taragoola
Awoonga Dam

39
Jambin
Koonkool
DAWSON
Callide Open-cut Coal Mine
Bell
60
Boynedale
CASTLE TOWER
NATIONAL PARK

LEICHHARDT HWY
Dee River
Don
Callide
Ck
Raglan
Ck
Calliope
River
Boyne R.

See page 117

Sunshine Coast

Surf near Maroochydore

 Maroochy Tourism

Cnr Sixth Ave and Melrose Pde,
Maroochydore Qld 4558
Freecall: 1800 882 032
www.maroochytourism.com

Main Attractions

◈ **Australia Zoo** The home of Crocodile Hunter Steve Irwin features a wildlife and conservation park.

◈ **The Big Pineapple** This park is based on a working pineapple and macadamia plantation. The Big Pineapple itself has a lookout at the top.

◈ **Dolphin Viewing** Tin Can Bay is a great place for viewing humpback whales and dolphins.

◈ **Eumundi Market** The popular market sells all manner of produce and wares.

◈ **Maroochydore** This modern beachside town features the Sunshine Plaza entertainment and shopping centre.

◈ **Mooloolaba** The seal show at UnderWater World is one of the attractions of this thriving beach town.

◈ **Noosa Heads** Noosa offers great beaches, world-class shopping and chic restaurants, surrounded by the Noosa National Park.

Ｎorth of Brisbane, the 48km coastal stretch bounded by Caloundra to the south and Noosa Heads to the north is called the Sunshine Coast. It is an apt name for a region that offers sun-drenched surf beaches, picturesque lakes, unspoilt rainforests and cliffs of rainbow-coloured sand.

The Sunshine Coast presents a quieter, more relaxed alternative to the Gold Coast. With an average annual temperature that does not drop below 20°C and a wide choice of accommodation to suit every taste and budget, the Sunshine Coast lures visitors with its laid-back way of life. Some of these once-sleepy coastal villages and modest holiday destinations have become glamorous retreats for the glitterati; others retain the quiet charm of earlier times.

Legend of the Coloured Sands

According to the Kabi Kabi Aborigines, the coloured sands at Rainbow Beach were formed when the Rainbow Spirit was shattered by a boomerang in a fight over a woman. The pieces fell onto the sand cliffs, colouring them forever.

UnderWater World, Mooloolaba

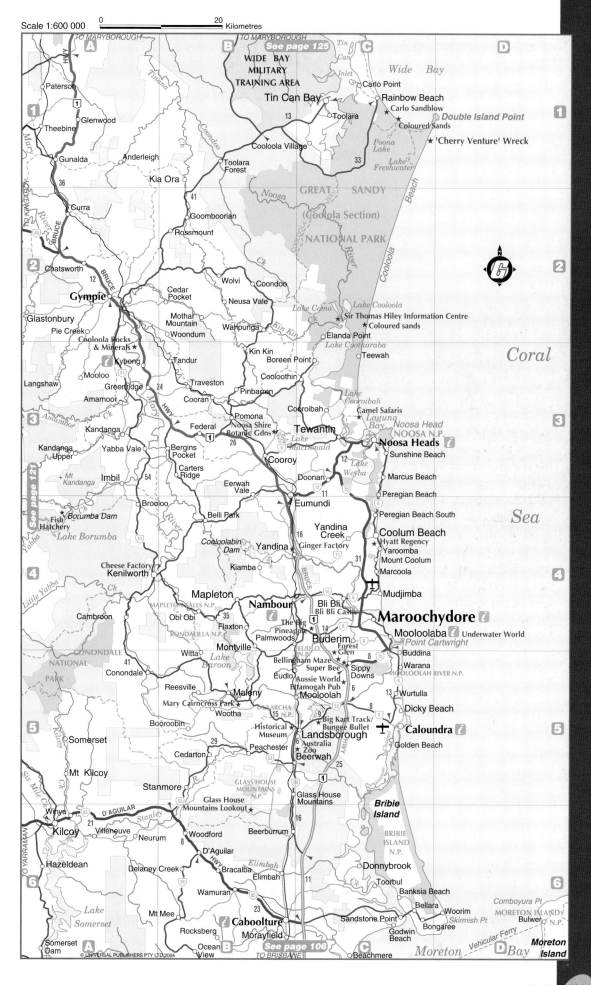

Scale 1:600 000

0   20

Kilometres

TO MARYBOROUGH

TO MARYBOROUGH
See page 125

WIDE BAY
MILITARY
TRAINING AREA

Tin Can Bay

Carlo Point
Rainbow Beach
Carlo Sandblow
Coloured Sands
Double Island Point
'Cherry Venture' Wreck

Toolara

13

33

Wide Bay

Paterson
Theebine
Glenwood
Gunalda
Anderleigh
Kia Ora
Cooloola Village
Toolara Forest

GREAT SANDY
(Coloola Section)
NATIONAL PARK

36
41

Curra
Goomboorian
Rossmount

Chatsworth

12

Gympie
Glastonbury
Pie Creek
Cooloola Rocks
& Minerals
Kybong
Mooloo
Langshaw
Greenridge
Amamoor
Kandanga
Kandanga
Upper
Mt
Kandanga
Imbil
Yabba Vale
Bergins
Pocket
Carters
Ridge
Brooloo

Cedar
Pocket
Mothar
Mountain
Woondum
Tandur
Traveston
Cooran
Federal
Pomona
Noosa Shire
Botanic Gdns
Cooroy

Wolvi
Neusa Vale
Wahpunga
Kin Kin
Boreen Point
Cooloothin
Pinbarren
Cooroibah

Sir Thomas Hiley Information Centre
Coloured sands
Elanda Point
Teewah

Lake Como
Lake Cooloola
Lake Cootharaba

Coral

Camel Safaris
Laguna
Bay
Noosa Head
NOOSA N.P.
Noosa Heads
Sunshine Beach

Tewantin

Coroibah

Eerwah
Vale
Eumundi

Doonan
12
Lake
Weyba
Marcus Beach
Peregian Beach

Lake
Cooroibah

26
54

Fish
Hatchery
Lake Borumba
Borumba Dam

Belli Park

Yandina
Creek
Ginger Factory
Yandina

Peregian Beach South
Coolum Beach
Hyatt Regency
Yaroomba
Mount Coolum
Marcoola
Mudjimba

16
31
11

Cooloolabin
Dam
Kiamba

Cheese Factory
Kenilworth

Mapleton

Nambour
The Big
Pineapple
Palmwoods
Bli Bli
Bli Bli Castle

Maroochydore

Obi Obi
Flaxton

Buderim
Forest
Glen

Mooloolaba
Point Cartwright
Underwater World
Buddina
Warana

35

Cambroon

Montville
Witta

Lake
Baroon

Bellingham Maze
Super Bee
Aussie World
Eudlo
Etamogah Pub
Mooloolah

Sippy
Downs

8

70
8

Wurtulla

41

Conondale

Reesville

Maleny
Mary Cairncross Park
Wootha
DULARCHA
N.P.

Historical
Museum
Landsborough
Peachester
Cedarton
Australia
Zoo
Beerwah

Big Kart Track/
Bungee Bullet

13
8

Dicky Beach

Caloundra
Golden Beach

NATIONAL
PARK

CONONDALE

Booroobin

29

15

6

25

Somerset
Mt Kilcoy
Stanmore

GLASS HOUSE
MOUNTAINS
N.P.

Glass House
Mountains Lookout

Glass House
Mountains

Bribie
Island

Winya
Kilcoy
Villeneuve
Neurum
Woodford
Beerburrum

16

BRIBIE
ISLAND
N.P.

21
8

D'AGUILAR

Hazeldean
Delaney Creek
D'Aguilar
Bracalba
Elimbah

Donnybrook
Toorbul

Banksia Beach

11

Wamuran

58

Mt Mee

Rocksberg
Ocean
View

23

Caboolture
Morayfield

Sandstone Point
Godwin
Beach

Bellara
Woorim
Bongaree

Combuyura Pt
MORETON ISLAND
Skirmish Pt
Bulwer
N.P.

Lake
Somerset

Somerset
Dam

Moreton
Vehicular Ferry

Bay

Moreton
Island

See page 106
TO BRISBANE

Beachmere

85

Sea

© UNIVERSAL PUBLISHERS PTY LTD 2004

The Scenic Rim

Luke's Bluff, Lamington National Park

Tourist information

 Ipswich Visitor Information
Centre

14 Queen Victoria Pde,
Ipswich 4305
Ph: (07) 3281 0555
www.ipswichtourism.com.au

Main Attractions

⬦ **Binna Burra** Binna Burra Lodge
is a privately-run ecotourism resort
in the north-east portion of
Lamington National Park.

⬦ **Helidon** Helidon is renowned
for its natural and sandstone spas.

⬦ **Ipswich** Qld's oldest provincial
city features heritage buildings and
the Workshops Rail Museum.

⬦ **Karoomba Vineyard** This
popular vineyard offers wine
tasting, a restaurant, and a
lavender farm.

⬦ **Lamington National Park** This
park protects Australia's largest
remaining sub-tropical rainforest.
Highlights include panoramic
views at Green Mountains and the
Treetop Walk at O'Reilly's
Rainforest Guesthouse.

⬦ **Springbrook National Park** This
showcases the Springbrook
Plateau, Mt Cougal and Natural
Bridge.

⬦ **Tamborine Mountain** Mt
Tamborine features sweeping
views, galleries, cafes and
gardens.

South of Brisbane, the Scenic Rim's mountain rainforests form a temperate region between the Darling Downs and the coastal flats of the Gold Coast. This lush expanse of sub-tropical rainforest reveals wild national parks, the breathtaking Lamington Plateau, majestic waterfalls, remote river valleys and fertile farmlands, all with the backdrop of stunning mountain ranges.

A bushwalker's paradise, the Scenic Rim offers much to explore for day-trippers, bushwalkers, campers, and those with time to explore. The region has both well-trodden paths and more isolated tracks, so visitors have the choice of either joining or escaping the crowds. The three mountain groups which dominate the landscape provide the source of rivers and streams that keep this verdant region fresh and well watered.

Slow Progress

The cliffs, waterfalls and dense rainforest in the Springbrook area made the going so difficult that in 1863 it took a surveyor six months to survey a distance of just 5km from Springbrook to the Numinbah Valley.

Abseiling at Binna Burra

Lockyer Valley

This secluded valley encapsulates the Scenic Rim's charms. It boasts a combination of stunning views, rural farmlands and homesteads, and natural attractions. Schultz's Lookout provides the best vantage point for viewing the valley from above, with panoramic vistas of Mt Beau Brummel and Mt Castle.

Attractions include Qld's oldest railway station, Grandchester, and Bigge's Camp, marking the original settlement of Grandchester. Bigge's Camp Park has picnic facilities, shelter sheds and monuments to local Aboriginal history among the spotted-gum forest.

In Laidley, the Pioneer Village contains a century old school, blacksmith's shop, police cells, pioneer cottage and stores. Das

Das Neumann Haus, Laidley

Neumann Haus is an unusual timber building constructed in 1893 which now houses a museum, arts and crafts shop, and a German cafe. Laidley market is held on the last Saturday of each month, and each Friday there is a market in the main street. Laidley Bakery is housed in a two-storey brick building that dates back to

1904. Narda Lagoon, set picturesquely opposite the Pioneer Village, provides a welcome habitat for the region's wildlife. Denbigh Farm and Teahouse, which offers bed and breakfast accommodation, is an ode to the valley's pioneering past. For a change of pace, the tiny township of Forest Hill features many historic pubs.

Scale 1:1 100 000

0   30 Kilometres

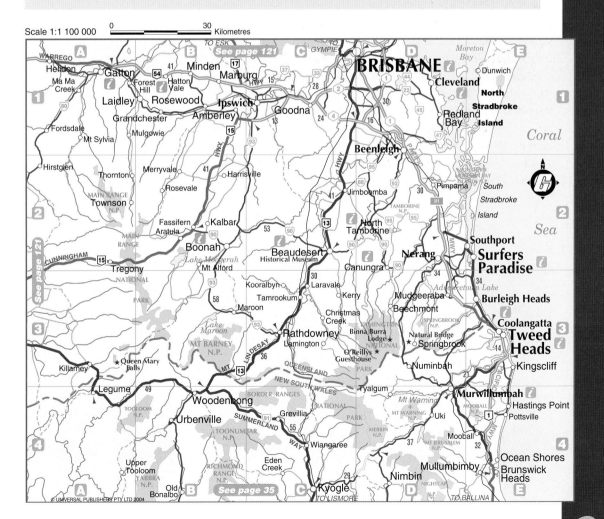

Toowoomba and Eastern Downs

Horse-riding on the National Trail

L ocated 100km inland from Brisbane, the verdant plains of the Darling Downs are dotted with farmhouses, pastures, crops and grazing lands. The rich black soil is a by-product of ancient volcanic activity, as are the mountain peaks of the Great Dividing Range that form the eastern boundary of this region.

Sprawling from Crows Nest in the north to Dalby in the west, the Eastern Downs offers visitors many diversions. Among the farmlands and cotton country there are also wineries, national parks, quaint villages, bustling townships, grand colonial architecture and physical reminders of the stories told by author Steele Rudd about the realities of rural life in the early 1900s. The Darling Downs is often associated with the grand old pastoralists of south-east Queensland. The region is ideal for combining outdoor activities – bushwalking, camping, cycling, horseriding and golf – with more sedate pursuits such as antique shopping, bed and breakfast stays, historical tours, Devonshire teas and exploring rural villages.

Toowoomba, the largest inland regional city in Australia, is known as Queensland's Garden City and celebrates its Carnival of Flowers in late September.

Tourist information

 Toowoomba Visitor Information Centre

86 James St (Warrego Hwy),
Toowoomba Qld 4350
Freecall: 1800 331 155
www.toowoombaholidays.info

Main Attractions

◈ **Cobb and Co Museum, Toowoomba** This museum houses many types of horse-drawn carriage.

◈ **Crows Nest** This picturesque town provides an intriguing insight into pioneer life.

◈ **Crows Nest National Park** Inside the park lies the renowned Valley of Diamonds, named for the shimmering effect of sunlight streaming onto the rock face of the gorge.

◈ **Empire Theatre, Toowoomba** This heritage-listed theatre is the largest regional theatre in Australia.

◈ **Jondaryan Woolshed** Approaching 150 years old, the historic woolshed is Queensland's oldest.

◈ **Rimfire Vineyards and Winery** This winery is located in Maclagan, 35km north of Jondaryan.

◈ **R. M. Williams Toowoomba** The hometown store of iconic boot maker R. M. Williams.

◈ **Rudd's Pub** This is a museum and pub at the birthplace of Arthur Hoey Davis, otherwise known as Steele Rudd – creator of the 'Dad 'n Dave' tales.

Road Rage

The famous transport company Cobb & Co had rules for passengers displayed on notices in its carriages. These included: no discussion of bushrangers, accidents, politics or religion; and no snoring or removal of shoes.

Rudd's Pub, Nobby

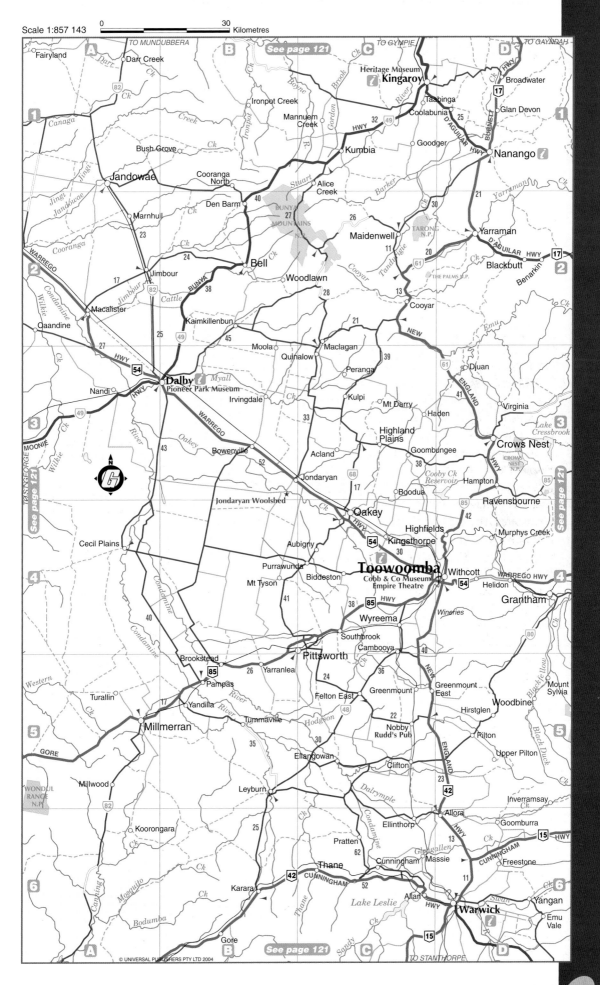

Scale 1:857 143

See page 121

See page 121

Whitsunday Islands

Wilderness Lodge, Long Island

When Captain James Cook entered what is now known as the Whitsunday Passage on Whit Sunday, 1770, he spent time surveying the beautiful islands he encountered. The 74 tropical islands, only eight of which are now inhabited, lie off the stretch of mainland coast between Mackay to the south and Bowen to the north.

With an estimated 8.25 hours of sunshine per day and an average yearly temperature of 23°C, the sun-bathed Whitsunday coast is an idyllic retreat.

The region has all you would expect from a tropical island oasis: coral-fringed islands, pristine beaches, luminescent waters, balmy weather and alluring seaside resorts. The Whitsunday coast is a dream destination for beach-lovers, offering consistently perfect conditions for swimming, snorkelling, scuba diving, fishing, sailing and cruising in the warm turquoise waters. The Great Barrier Reef surrounds the Whitsundays and its warm shallow waters are home to some of the most colourful fish and coral formations in the Great Barrier Reef Marine Park.

Charter and tour companies based on the mainland offer a wide variety of tour and recreation options. Explore the area by boat or seaplane; sightsee from a scenic flight; or try parasailing, bungy jumping and tandem skydiving with the region's spectacular scenery as a backdrop. Excellent fishing opportunities can be found at Funnel Bay, Dingo Beach and Hydeaway Bay. The Whitsundays offer a full range of accommodation to suit all tastes and budgets, from camping on a deserted island to a suite in a luxurious five-star resort.

Tourist information

 Whitsunday Information Centre

Bruce Highway, Proserpine Qld 4800
Freecall: 1800 801 252
www.whitsundaytourism.com

Main Attractions

◈ **Barefoot Bushman's Wildlife Park** This park features a collection of native animals and birds.

◈ **Brampton Island** This National Park has a 280-person resort.

◈ **Conway National Park** The park protects lush rainforest.

◈ **Daydream Island** This is a resort island.

◈ **Hamilton Island** The resort is the key landmark.

◈ **Hayman Island** A resort island close to the outer reef.

◈ **Lindeman Island** This island is home to Australia's first Club Med resort.

◈ **Long Island** There are three resorts on this Great Barrier Reef island.

◈ **South Molle Island** This unspoilt National Park fringed by scenic beaches is great for family groups.

◈ **Whitehaven Beach** This 9-km stretch of pristine beach is on Whitsunday Island.

Airlie Beach

With the exotic perimeters of the Great Barrier Reef and Conway National Park, Airlie Beach is a prime holiday destination. The town offers a range of accommodation and is a perfect base for exploring the region. A recent free attraction is Whitsunday Lagoon, a man-made 'stinger free' lagoon for year-round swimming.

Yacht off Hayman Island

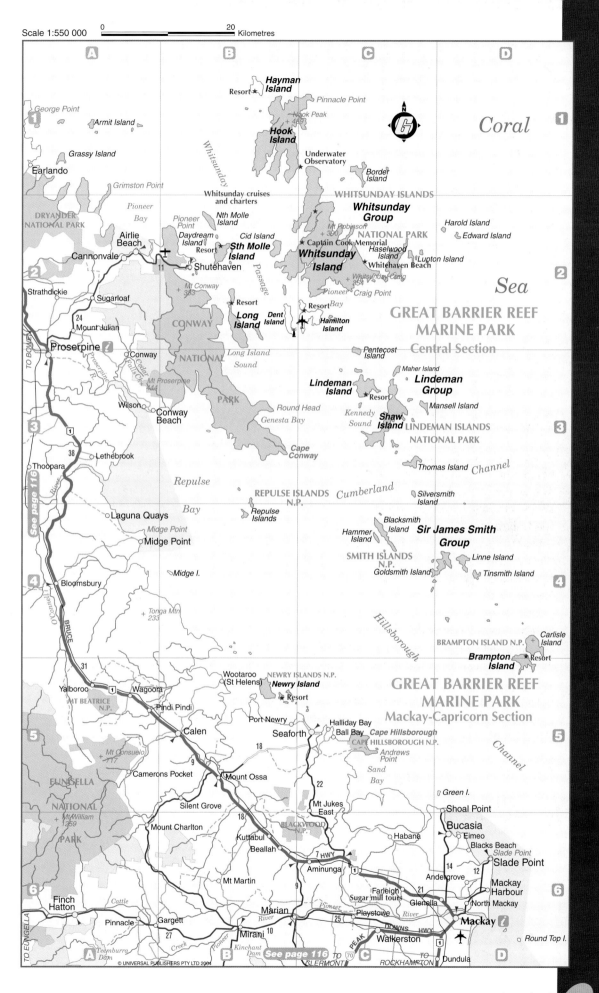

A   B   C   D

1 George Point
Armit Island
Grassy Island
Earlando

Coral

Hayman Island
Resort ★

Pinnacle Point
Hook Peak
+ 459

Hook Island

Underwater Observatory

Border Island

Harold Island
Edward Island

WHITSUNDAY ISLANDS

1

Whitsunday cruises and charters

Grimston Point
Pioneer Bay
DRYANDER NATIONAL PARK

Pioneer Point
Daydream Island Resort

Nth Molle Island
Cid Island
Sth Molle Island

Whitsunday Group

NATIONAL PARK

Mt Robinson
+ 390
Captain Cook Memorial

Haselwood Island

Lupton Island

Sea

2 Airlie Beach
Cannonvale
11
Shutehaven

+ Mt Conway
383

CONWAY

Long Island Passage

Whitsunday Island

Whitehaven Beach

Whitsunday Peak
359

Pioneer Bay
Craig Point

2

Strathdickie
Sugarloaf
24
Mount Julian

Resort

Resort
Dent Island
Long Island
Hamilton Island

GREAT BARRIER REEF MARINE PARK
Central Section

3 Proserpine
Conway

NATIONAL

Mt Proserpine
444

Cedar Falls Ck

Wilson
Conway Beach

PARK

Long Island Sound

Round Head
Genesta Bay

Pentecost Island

Maher Island

Lindeman Island

Lindeman Group
Resort

Mansell Island

3

38
Letchebrook
Thoopara

Kennedy Sound

Shaw Island

LINDEMAN ISLANDS
NATIONAL PARK

Cape Conway

Thomas Island *Channel*

Repulse

REPULSE ISLANDS N.P.

Cumberland

Silversmith Island

4 Laguna Quays

Bay

Midge Point
Midge Point

Repulse Islands

Blacksmith Island

Hammer Island

Sir James Smith Group

Linne Island

Carlisle Island

4

Bloomsbury

+ Tonga Mtn
233

Midge I.

SMITH ISLANDS N.P.
Goldsmith Island

Tinsmith Island

BRAMPTON ISLAND N.P.

Brampton Island ★ Resort

31

Hillsborough

5 Yalboroo
Wagoora
Pindi Pindi

MT BEATRICE N.P.

Wootaroo (St Helens)
NEWRY ISLANDS N.P.
Newry Island
Resort

Port Newry

GREAT BARRIER REEF MARINE PARK
Mackay-Capricorn Section

Channel

5

Calen
18

Seaforth
Halliday Bay
Ball Bay
Cape Hillsborough
CAPE HILLSBOROUGH N.P.
Andrews Point

EUNGELLA

Mt Consuelo
717

9
Camerons Pocket
Mount Ossa

22

Sand Bay

Green I.
Shoal Point

6 NATIONAL
Mt William
1359
PARK
Mount Charlton

Silent Grove

18

Kuttabul
Beallah

BLACKWOOD N.P.

Mt Jukes East

7 HWY

Aminunga
1

Habana

Bucasia
Eimeo
Blacks Beach
Slade Point
Slade Point

14   12
Andergrove

6

Finch Hatton
Pinnacle
Gargett
27

Mt Martin

9

Marian
Mirani
10

Pioneer River

Kinchant Dam
Teemburra Dam

© UNIVERSAL PUBLISHERS PTY LTD 2004

Farleigh
Sugar mill tours
Playstowe

21
Glenella

25

DOWNS HWY

Walkerston

River

Mackay Harbour
North Mackay

Mackay

1

Round Top I.

Dundula

A   B   C   D

See page 116
TO CLERMONT

TO 70
ROCKHAMPTON

South Australia
The Festival State

S outh Australia is in the unique position of bordering all the country's mainland states. The fourth largest state (including the Northern Territory) and the driest in Australia, SA has a predominantly flat, low-lying terrain consisting of large tracts of desert, broken by the Flinders and Musgrave Ranges, and gigantic saline lakes.

In contrast to the arid lands of the north and west are the gulf lands, which include the Eyre, Yorke and Fleurieu peninsulas, fringed by quiet beaches and fishing towns; the rolling hills of the Mount Lofty Ranges; and the dry south-east plains watered by the Murray River.

Many of the state's varied attractions are within a three-hour radius of its capital, Adelaide. There are many reasons to visit South Australia, including spectacular scenery, fishing, fauna and national parks; however, wine and food touring are often at the top of the list. South Australia's wineries are legendary: the Barossa Valley, McLaren Vale, Clare Valley and Coonawarra are sought out by many visitors.

While the outback is quite isolated, it still has much to offer including the opal fields of Coober Pedy and Andamooka, and Lake Eyre, Australia's largest lake.

Tourist information

 South Australian Visitor
& Travel Centre

18 King William St,
Adelaide SA 5000
Tollfree: 1300 655 276
www.southaustralia.com

| Area = 984,381 sq km | Occupies 12.5% of Australia | Length of coast = 3540 km |

South Australia Key Map & Distance Chart

All distances shown in the chart below have been measured over highways and major roads, not necessarily by the shortest route.

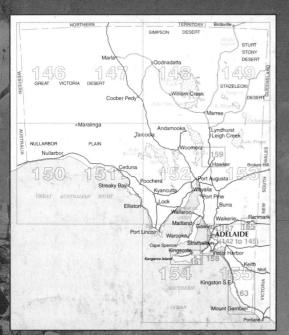

Adelaide city architecture

Approximate Distance	Adelaide	Bordertown	Broken Hill NSW	Ceduna	Coober Pedy	Eucla WA	Innaminka	Kulgera NT	Leigh Creek	Mount Gambier	Murray Bridge	Peterborough	Pinnaroo	Port Augusta	Port Lincoln	Port Pirie	Renmark	Streaky Bay	Whyalla	Woomera
Adelaide		267	514	773	841	1260	1033	1255	548	435	74	261	239	309	646	227	244	699	382	488
Bordertown	267		787	1040	1108	1527	1300	1522	815	183	193	528	132	576	913	494	279	966	649	755
Broken Hill NSW	514	787		878	946	1365	1064	1360	579	986	594	281	671	414	751	387	550	804	487	593
Ceduna	773	1040	878		996	487	1213	1410	728	1208	847	597	967	464	399	546	859	107	449	643
Coober Pedy	841	1108	946	996		1483	1281	414	796	1276	915	665	1035	532	869	614	901	922	605	369
Eucla WA	1260	1527	1365	487	1483		1700	1897	1215	1695	1334	1084	1454	951	886	1033	1346	594	936	1130
Innaminka	1033	1300	1064	1213	1281	1700		1695	485	1445	1107	882	1227	749	1086	831	1106	1139	822	928
Kulgera NT	1255	1522	1360	1410	414	1897	1695		1210	1690	1329	1079	1473	946	1283	1028	1352	1336	1019	783
Leigh Creek	548	815	579	728	796	1215	485	1210		983	622	298	742	264	601	346	621	654	337	435
Mount Gambier	435	183	986	1208	1276	1695	1445	1690	983		361	696	315	744	1081	662	462	1134	817	923
Murray Bridge	74	193	594	847	915	1334	1107	1329	622	361		335	165	383	720	301	218	773	456	562
Peterborough	261	528	281	597	665	1084	882	1079	298	696	335		418	133	470	106	297	523	206	312
Pinnaroo	239	132	671	967	1035	1454	1227	1473	742	315	165	418		527	864	434	147	918	600	706
Port Augusta	309	576	414	464	532	951	749	946	264	744	383	133	527		337	82	395	390	73	179
Port Lincoln	646	913	751	399	869	886	1086	1283	601	1081	720	470	864	337		419	732	292	264	516
Port Pirie	227	494	387	546	614	1033	831	1028	346	662	301	106	434	82	419		313	472	155	261
Renmark	244	266	550	833	901	1346	1106	1352	621	462	218	297	147	395	732	313		785	468	574
Streaky Bay	699	966	804	107	922	594	1139	1336	654	1134	773	523	918	390	292	472	785		375	569
Whyalla	382	649	487	449	605	936	822	1019	337	817	456	206	600	73	264	155	468	375		252
Woomera	488	755	593	643	369	1130	920	783	435	923	562	312	706	179	516	261	574	569	252	

Adelaide

Adelaide at night

As Australia's first planned city for free settlers, Adelaide has no convict history. Settlement began due to overcrowding in NSW, and South Australia was officially declared a state in 1836.

The state capital was named after Queen Adelaide, the wife of England's King William IV, and its boom times are evident in its glorious architecture. Adelaide's historic churches and gracious 19th century buildings are interspersed with those built with gold rush wealth in the Italian Renaissance style. King William St and the tree-lined North Terrace are the site of many of the city's finest buildings.

Although it has more than one million residents, this planned city is easy to navigate due to its grid design. Its position on the banks of the picturesque Torrens River, among superb gardens with the blue haze of the Adelaide Hills as a backdrop, gives the city a relaxed atmosphere. Adelaide experiences four distinctly different seasons, adding to its charm.

Its long history of immigration has influenced the city's development: cafe culture has long been part of Adelaide life and its ethnic diversity is reflected in the city's markets and restaurant scene. Adelaide is renowned for its restaurants, wines, fine produce, and colourful festivals.

Tourist information

ℹ️ South Australian Visitor & Travel Centre

18 King William St,
Adelaide SA 5000
Tollfree: 1300 655 276
www.adelaide.southaustralia.com

Main Attractions

◈ **Adelaide Botanic Gardens** These beautifully landscaped gardens house the oldest glasshouse in an Australian botanic garden.

◈ **Adelaide Festival Centre** This imposing building hosts world-class productions, and free concerts during summer.

◈ **Central Market** The markets are a culinary adventure and reflect Adelaide's diverse ethnic population. Adelaide's Chinatown is in the market area.

◈ **Glenelg** Connected to the city by the Bay Tram, Glenelg Beach is the most popular of Adelaide's long, sandy beaches.

◈ **Gouger St** One of Adelaide's premier 'eat streets' features food from around the world.

◈ **Rundle Mall** The retail hub of Adelaide.

◈ **South Australian Museum** This museum features a fascinating collection of Aboriginal artefacts.

Palm House, Adelaide Botanic Gardens

Places of Interest

- Ⓐ Adelaide Botanic Gardens **C3**
- Ⓑ Adelaide Festival Centre **B3**
- Ⓒ Adelaide Town Hall **C4**
- Ⓓ Adelaide Zoo **C3**
- Ⓔ Art Gallery of South Australia **C3**
- Ⓕ Ayers House **C3**
- Ⓖ Central Market **B4**
- Ⓗ Edmund Wright House **B4**

- Ⓘ Elder Park **B3**
- Ⓙ Government House **C3**
- Ⓚ Light's Vision **B3**
- Ⓛ Lion Arts Centre **B4**
- Ⓜ Migration Museum **C3**
- Ⓝ Mortlock Library of South Australiana **C3**
- Ⓞ National Wine Centre **D3**

- Ⓟ Old Adelaide Gaol **A3**
- Ⓠ Parliament House & Old Parliament House **B3**
- Ⓡ Performing Arts Collection **B3**
- Ⓢ Skycity Adelaide **B3**
- Ⓣ South Australian Museum **C3**
- Ⓤ Tandanya **C4**

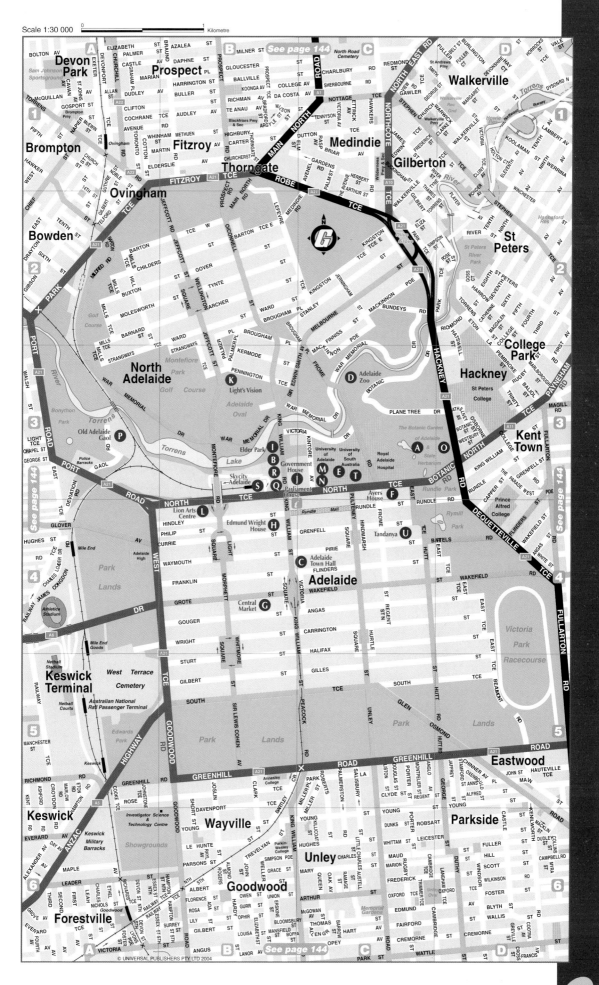

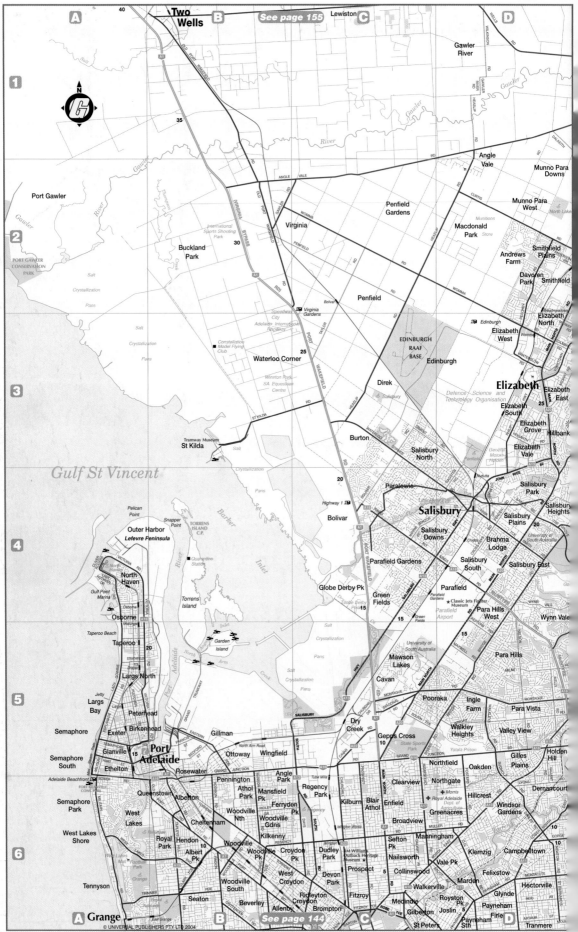

Scale 1:142 850

Two Wells

See page 155   Lewiston

Gawler River

Angle Vale

Munno Para Downs

Port Gawler

Munno Para West

PORT GAWLER CONSERVATION PARK

Buckland Park

Virginia

Penfield Gardens

Macdonald Park

Andrews Farm

Smithfield Plains

Davoren Park

Smithfield

International Sports Shooting Park

Salt Crystallization Pans

Penfield

Elizabeth North

Elizabeth West

Speedway City Adelaide International Raceway

Virginia Gardens

Bolivar

Elizabeth

EDINBURGH RAAF BASE

Edinburgh

Elizabeth South

Salt Crystallization Pans

Constellation Model Flying Club

Waterloo Corner

Direk

Defence Science and Technology Organisation

Elizabeth East

Elizabeth Grove

Hillbank

Winston Park SA Equestrian Centre

Burton

Elizabeth Vale

Tramway Museum

St Kilda

Salt Crystallization

Salisbury North

Gulf St Vincent

Paralowie

Salisbury Park

Salisbury Heights

Highway 1

Salisbury

Salisbury Plains

Bolivar

Salisbury Downs

Brahma Lodge

University of South Australia

Pelican Point

Snapper Point

TORRENS ISLAND C.P.

Parafield Gardens

Salisbury South

Salisbury East

Outer Harbor

Lefevre Peninsula

Quarantine Station

Globe Derby Pk

Green Fields

Parafield

Classic Jets Fighter Museum

Para Hills West

Wynn Vale

North Haven

Torrens Island

Parafield Airport

Para Hills

Gulf Point Marina

Osborne

University of South Australia

Mawson Lakes

Taperoo Beach

Taperoo

Garden Island

Cavan

Pooraka

Ingle Farm

Para Vista

Largs North

Salt Crystallization Pans

Largs Bay

Dry Creek

Walkley Heights

Valley View

Semaphore

Peterhead

Birkenhead

Gillman

Wingfield

Gepps Cross

Northfield

Oakden

Gilles Plains

Holden Hill

Exeter

Glanville

Port Adelaide

Ottoway

Rosewater

Angle Park

Regency Park

Clearview

Northgate

Semaphore South

Ethelton

Pennington

Mansfield Pk

Kilburn

Blair Athol

Enfield

Hillcrest

Dernancourt

Adelaide Beachfront

Queenstown

Alberton

Athol Park

Ferryden Pk

Regency Pk

Broadview

Greenacres

Windsor Gardens

Semaphore Park

West Lakes

Cheltenham

Woodville Nth

Woodville Gdns

Sefton Pk

Manningham

Klemzig

Campbelltown

West Lakes Shore

Hendon

Royal Park

Albert Pk

Kilkenny

Woodville

Croydon Pk

Dudley Park

Nailsworth

Vale Pk

Felixstow

Tennyson

Seaton

Woodville South

Woodville Pk

West Croydon

Croydon

Devon Park

Prospect

Collinswood

Walkerville

Marden

Hectorville

Beverley

Ridleyton

Brompton

Fitzroy

Medindie

Royston Joslin

Glynde

Payneham

Grange

See page 144

Allenby

St Peters

Gilberton

Payneham Sth

Tranmere

© UNIVERSAL PUBLISHERS PTY LTD 2004

See page 157
See page 155
See page 145

© UNIVERSAL PUBLISHERS PTY LTD 2004

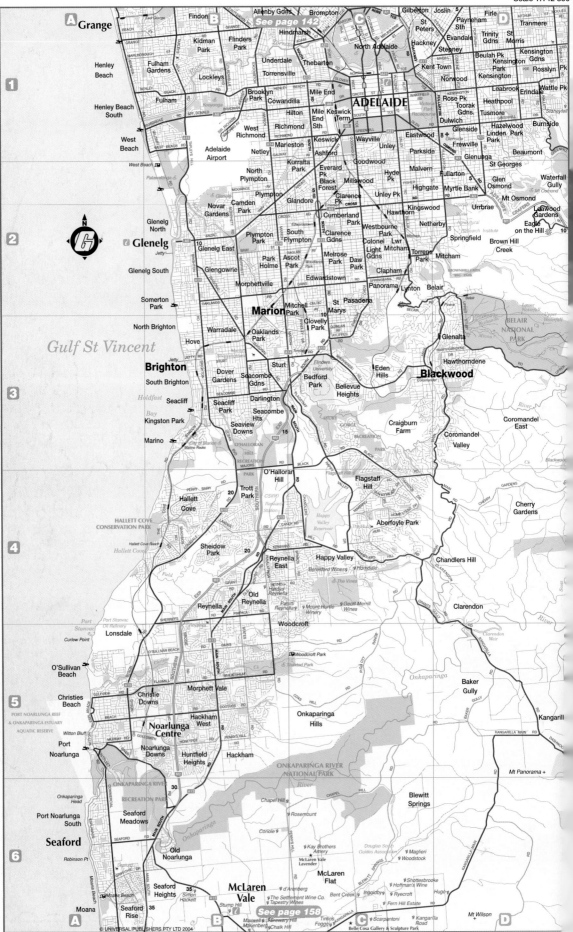

Scale 1:142 850

See page 142

See page 158

© UNIVERSAL PUBLISHERS PTY LTD 2004

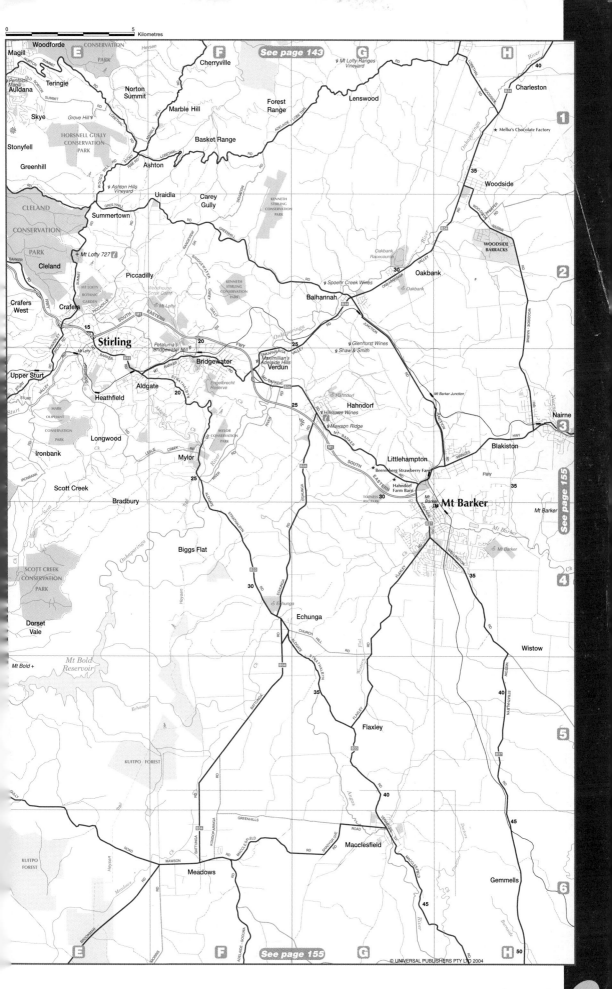

See page 143
See page 155
See page 155

South Australia 145

PETERMAN

See page 212

NORTHERN TERRITORY

Mann

Ranges

Mulga Park

Jones

Surveyor Generals Corner

+ Mt Whinham
1231

SOUTH AUSTRALIA

ROAD 83

64

Ck.

Irrunytju
(Wingellina)   Pipalyatjara

GILES · MULGA PARK   124

Amata

Mt Woodroffe
1440

Musgrave   Ranges

126

+ Mt Kintore
1070

Churie Ck.

149

188

+ Mt Linsay
819

PITJANTJATJARA

See page 184

SOUTH WESTERN AUSTRALIA

Waigen
Lakes

GREAT   208   VICTORIA

UNNAMED CONSERVATION PARK

ANNE   BEADELL   172

HWY 105

Vokes Hill
Corner

Serpentine
Lakes

Nurrari
Lakes

Wyola Lake

Halinor Lake

Lake
Dey Dey

Forrest
Lakes

Lake
Maurice

258

MARALINGA - TJARUTJA

GREAT
VICTORIA
DESERT
NATURE
RESERVE

See page 150

Maralinga

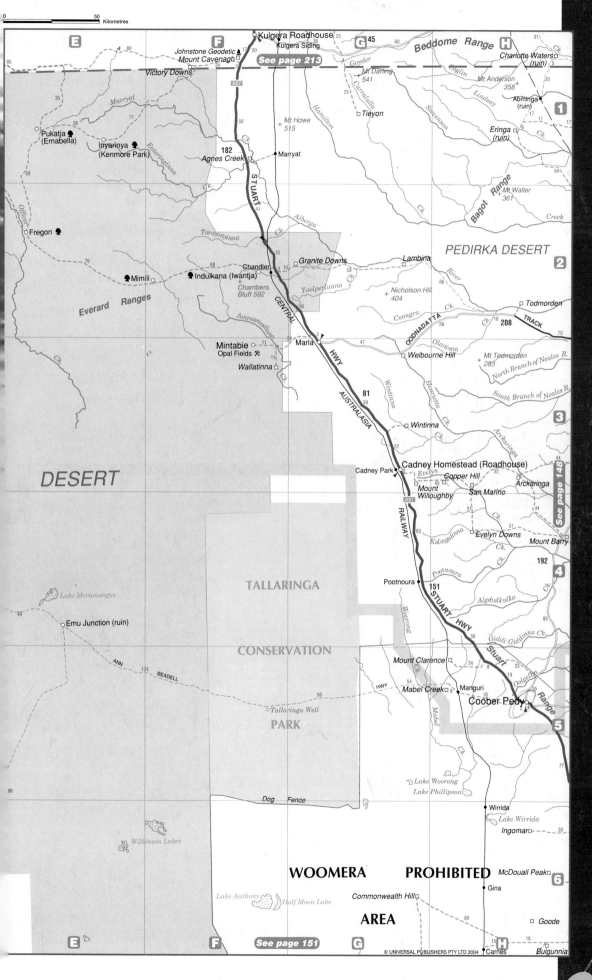

See page 213

0   50   Kilometres

Kulgera Roadhouse 25
Kulgera Siding
Johnstone Geodetic
Mount Cavenagh
Victory Downs

Beddome Range
Charlotte Waters (ruin)
Mt Darling 541
Mt Anderson 358
Abminga (ruin)
Tieyon
Eringa (ruin)

Marryat

182
Agnes Creek   Marryat

Pukatja (Ernabella)
Inyarinya (Kenmore Park)

Mt Howe 515

Mt Walter 361
Bagot Range

Creek

Fregon

Alberga
Tarcoonyinna

Lambina
PEDIRKA DESERT

Nicholson Hill 404

Chandler
Mimili   Indulkana (Iwantja)
Chambers Bluff 592

Granite Downs
Yoolperlunna

River

Todmorden

Everard Ranges
Ammaroodinna

Coongra

208   TRACK

Welbourne Hill
Mt Todmorden 283
North Branch of Neales R.

Mintabie   Marla
Opal Fields
Wallatinna

South Branch of Neales R.

Wintinna

81

Wintinna

DESERT

Cadney Homestead (Roadhouse)
Cadney Park   Evelyn
Copper Hill
Arckaringa
Mount Willoughby
San Marino

Evelyn Downs
Mount Barry

192

TALLARINGA

Kuduigalinna

Pootnoura
Pootnoura   151

Algebuckulha

Giddi Giddinna Ck

Emu Junction (ruin)

CONSERVATION

Mount Clarence

Mabel Creek
Manguri   Oolgelina Range

Tallaringa Well

PARK

Mabel   Coober Pedy

Lake Woorong
Lake Phillipson

Dog   Fence

Wirrida
Lake Wirrida
Ingomar

Wilkinson Lakes

Lake Anthony   Half Moon Lake

WOOMERA   PROHIBITED   McDouall Peak

Commonwealth Hill   Gina

AREA

Goode

See page 151

© UNIVERSAL PUBLISHERS PTY LTD 2004

Carnes   Bulgunnia

South Australia 147

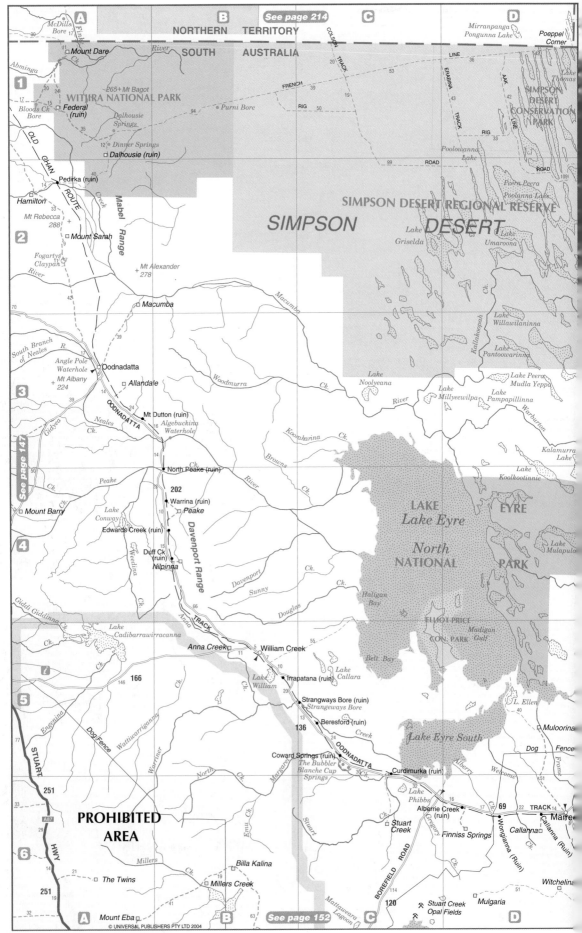

Scale 1:1 900 000

McDills Bore
Mount Dare
Finke River
NORTHERN TERRITORY
SOUTH AUSTRALIA
COLSON TRACK
Mirranpanga
Pongunna Lake
Poeppel Corner
Abminga
265+ Mt Bagot
WITJIRA NATIONAL PARK
Purni Bore
FRENCH
RIG
LINE
ERABINA
TRACK
AAK
LINE
SIMPSON DESERT CONSERVATION PARK
Lake Thomas
Bloods Ck Bore
Federal (ruin)
Dalhousie Springs
Dinner Springs
Dalhousie (ruin)
RIG
ROAD
Poolowanna Lake
ROAD
Peera Peera Poolanna Lake
Hamilton
OLD GHAN ROUTE
Pedirka (ruin)
Mabel Range
Creek
SIMPSON DESERT REGIONAL RESERVE
SIMPSON DESERT
Mt Rebecca 288
Mount Sarah
Fogartys Claypan
Mt Alexander 278
Lake Griselda
Lake Umaroona
River
Macumba
Macumba
Kallakoopah
Lake Willawilaninna
South Branch of Neales R.
Angle Pole Waterhole
Mt Albany 224
Oodnadatta
Allandale
OODNADATTA
Mt Dutton (ruin)
Algebuckina Waterhole
Woodmurra
Ck
Lake Noolyeana
Lake Millyeewilpa
Lake Peera Mudla Yeppa
Lake Pampapillinna
Lake Pantoowarinna
Warburton
Gidyea Ck.
Neales Ck.
Koonakarina
Ck.
Kalamurra Lake
Peake Ck.
North Peake (ruin)
Ck.
Browns
River
Lake Koolkootinnie
Mount Barry
202
Warrina (ruin)
Peake
Lake Conway
Edwards Creek (ruin)
Weedina
Duff Ck (ruin)
Nilpinna
Davenport Range
Ck.
LAKE EYRE
Lake Eyre
North
NATIONAL
PARK
Lake Mulapula
Davenport
Sunny
Douglas
Ck.
Haligan Bay
Gidgi Giddinna Ck.
Lake Cadibarrawirracanna
Anna
TRACK
Anna Creek
William Creek
Lake William
Irrapatana (ruin)
Lake Callara
Belt Bay
ELLIOT PRICE CON. PARK
Madigan Gulf
EYRE
L. Ellen
Engenina
Dog Fence
Wattiwarrigannia
Worriner
North
Ck.
Strangways Bore (ruin)
Strangeways Bore
Beresford (ruin)
Creek
136
OODNADATTA
Coward Springs (ruin)
The Bubbler
Blanche Cup Springs
Lake Eyre South
Curdimurka (ruin)
Alberry
Welcome
Muloorina
Dog Fence
Frome
STUART HWY
251
PROHIBITED AREA
Millers Ck.
Emu Ck.
Stuart Ck.
Margaret Ck.
Lake Phibbs
Alberrie Creek (ruin)
Stuart Creek
Finniss Springs
Gregory
TRACK
Marree
Callanna
Wongianna (Ruin)
Callanna (Ruin)
The Twins
251
Billa Kalina
Millers Creek
Mount Eba
BOREFIELD ROAD
Stuart Creek Opal Fields
Mulgaria
Witcheline
Mattawara Lagoon

© UNIVERSAL PUBLISHERS PTY LTD 2004

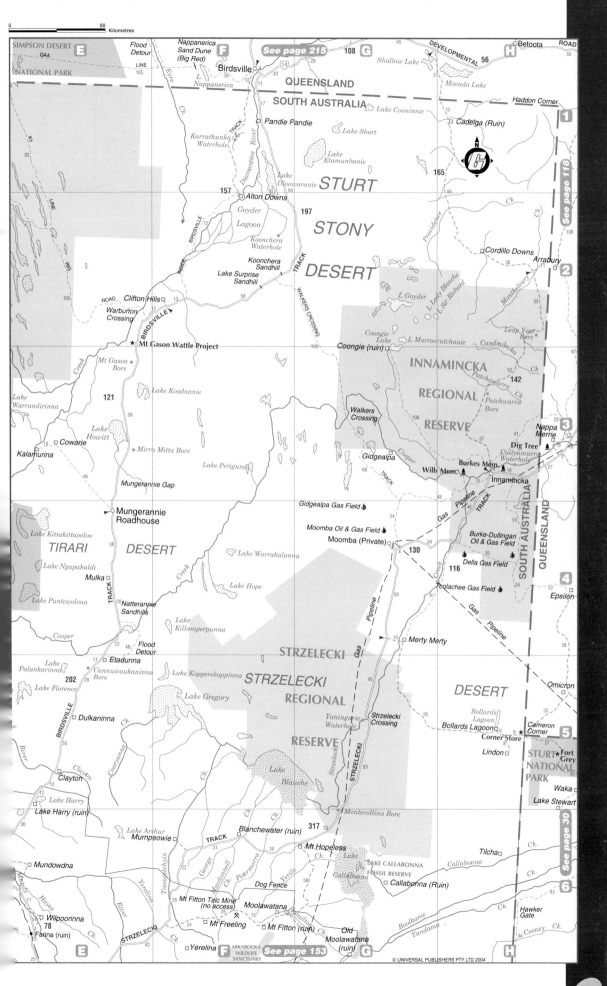

Scale 1:1 900 000

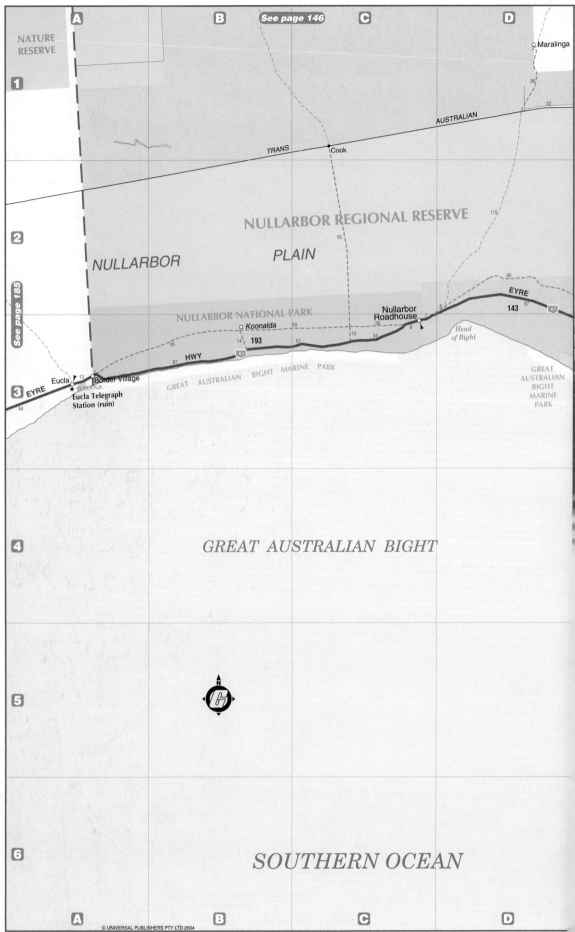

NATURE
RESERVE

A   B   See page 146   C   D

Maralinga

36

32

AUSTRALIAN

TRANS   Cook

NULLARBOR REGIONAL RESERVE

NULLARBOR   PLAIN

95

115

95

EYRE

143   A1

87

Nullarbor
Roadhouse   8

NULLARBOR NATIONAL PARK   Head
of Bight

Koonalda   59   193   110   34   8

85   57   GREAT
AUSTRALIAN
BIGHT
MARINE
PARK

87   HWY   14   A1

Eucla   12   Border Village
EUCLA N.P.   GREAT   AUSTRALIAN   BIGHT   MARINE   PARK

EYRE   Eucla Telegraph
Station (ruin)

64

GREAT AUSTRALIAN BIGHT

SOUTHERN OCEAN

A   B   C   D

© UNIVERSAL PUBLISHERS PTY LTD 2004

See page 185

150 *Gregory's Road Atlas of Australia*

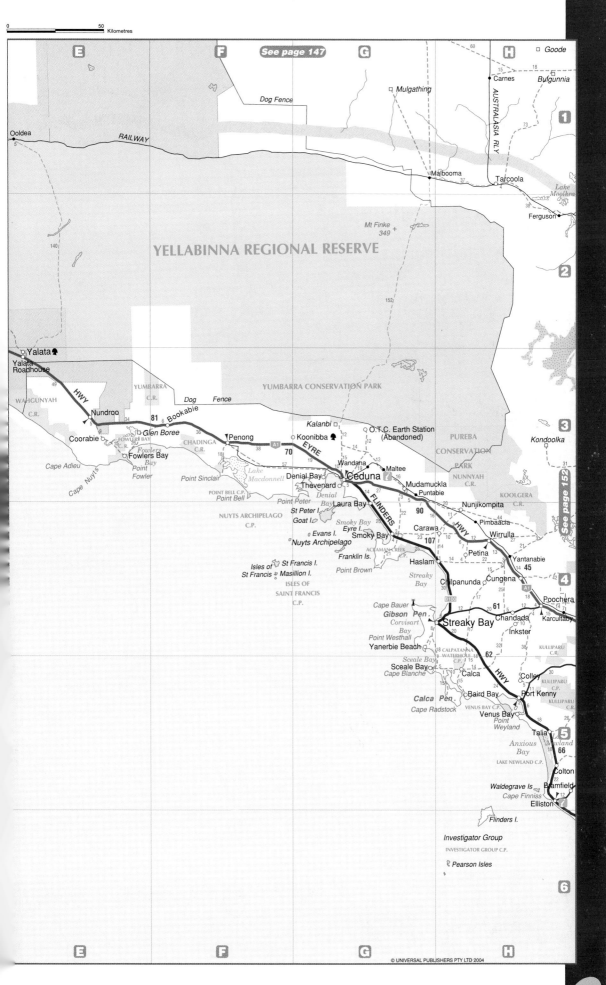

See page 147

0   50
Kilometres

□ Goode

Carnes ●   □ Bulgunnia

Dog Fence

Mulgathing □

AUSTRALASIA RLY

RAILWAY

Ooldea ●

Malbooma ●

Tarcoola ●

Lake Moolkra

Ferguson ●

Mt Finke
349 +

YELLABINNA REGIONAL RESERVE

Yalata ●
Yalata
Roadhouse ●

YUMBARRA
C.R.

Dog Fence

YUMBARRA CONSERVATION PARK

PUREBA

Kondoolka

HWY

Nundroo ●
81
Bookabie

Coorabie ●
Glen Boree □
34

FOWLERS BAY
C.R.
Fowlers Bay ●

CHADINGA
C.R.

Kalanbi □
Koonibba ●
70
A1

O.T.C. Earth Station
(Abandoned)

CONSERVATION

Cape Adieu

Point
Fowler

*Fowlers
Bay*

Penong ●
38
EYRE

Wandana ●

PARK

NUNNYAH
C.R.

Cape Nuyts

Point Sinclair
57
19

Denial Bay ●

Ceduna ●
Maltee ●

Mudamuckla ●
Puntabie ●

KOOLGERA
C.R.

POINT BELL C.P.
Point Bell

Point Peter

Thevenard ●

*Denial
Bay*
Laura Bay

Nunjikompita ●

NUYTS ARCHIPELAGO
C.P.

St Peter I.
Goat I.

FLINDERS
90

Pimbaacla ●
HWY
Wirrulla ●

Evans I.
Nuyts Archipelago

Smoky Bay
Eyre I.
Smoky Bay ●
107

Carawa ●

Petina ●

Yantanabie ●
45

ISLES OF
SAINT FRANCIS
C.P.

Franklin Is.

ACRAMAN CREEK

Haslam ●

Cungena ●
A1

Isles of
St Francis
St Francis I.
Masillion I.
Point Brown

*Streaky
Bay*

Chilpanunda ●

Poochera ●

Karcultaby ●
B100
61

Cape Bauer

Gibson Pen.
*Corvisart
Bay*

Streaky Bay ●

Chandada ●
Inkster ●

Point Westhall
Yanerbie Beach ●

CALPATANNA
WATERHOLE
C.P.

KULLIPARU
C.R.

Sceale Bay
Sceale Bay ●
Cape Blanche

62
HWY

Calca ●

Colley ●

KULLIPARU
C.P.

Calca Pen.
Cape Radstock

Baird Bay ●

Port Kenny ●

KULLIPARU
C.R.

VENUS BAY C.P.
Venus Bay ●
Point
Weyland

Talia ●
66

Newland

*Anxious
Bay*

LAKE NEWLAND C.P.

Colton ●

Waldegrave Is
Cape Finniss

Bramfield ●
Elliston ●

Flinders I.

Investigator Group

INVESTIGATOR GROUP C.P.

Pearson Isles

© UNIVERSAL PUBLISHERS PTY LTD 2004

South Australia

151

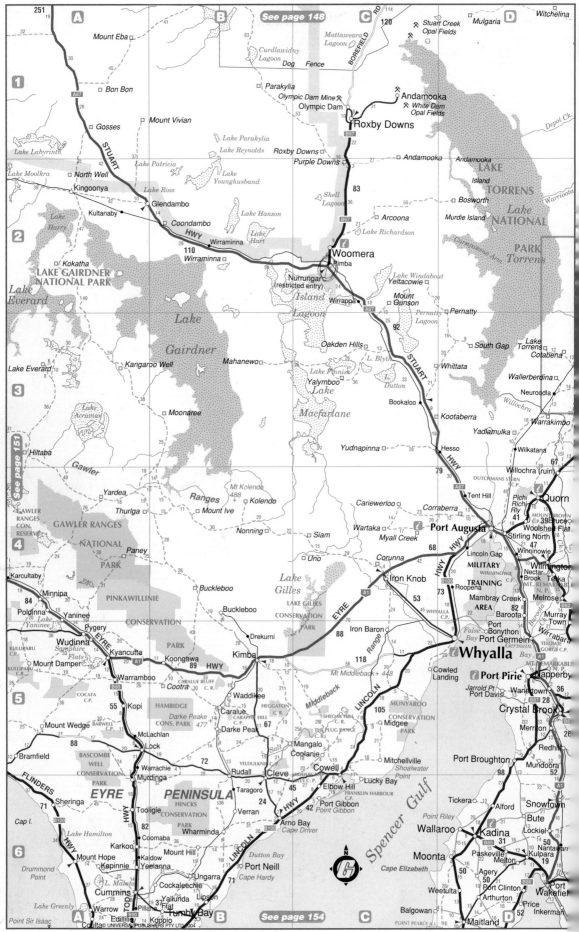

Scale 1:1 900 000

See page 148

See page 151

See page 154

© UNIVERSAL PUBLISHERS PTY LTD 2004

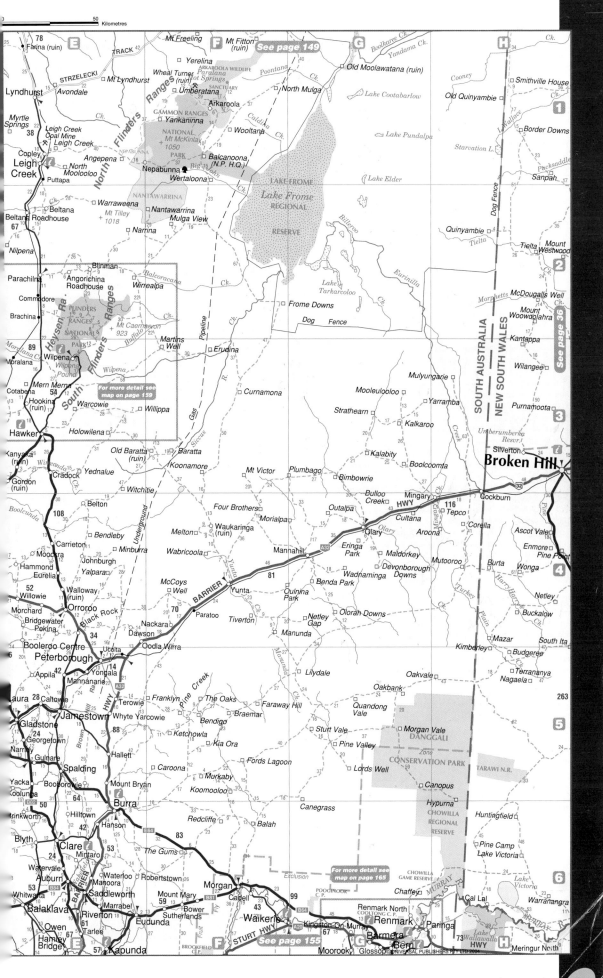

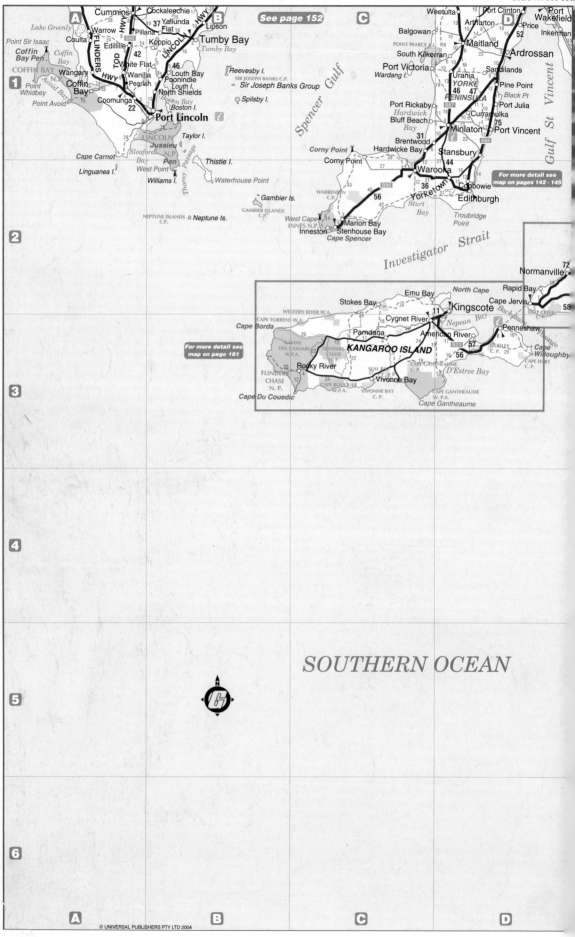

Scale 1:1 900 000

See page 152

For more detail see
map on pages 142 - 145

For more detail see
map on page 161

SOUTHERN OCEAN

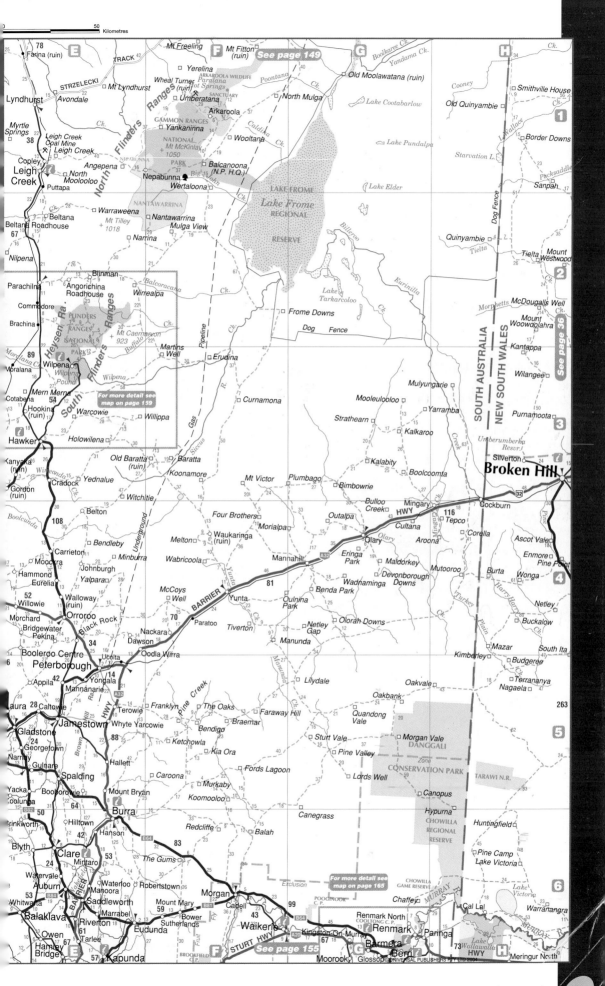

See page 149
See page 36
See page 155

Scale
50 Kilometres

SOUTH AUSTRALIA
NEW SOUTH WALES

For more detail see
map on page 159

For more detail see
map on page 165

Glossop © UNIVERSAL PUBLISHERS P/L LTD 200?

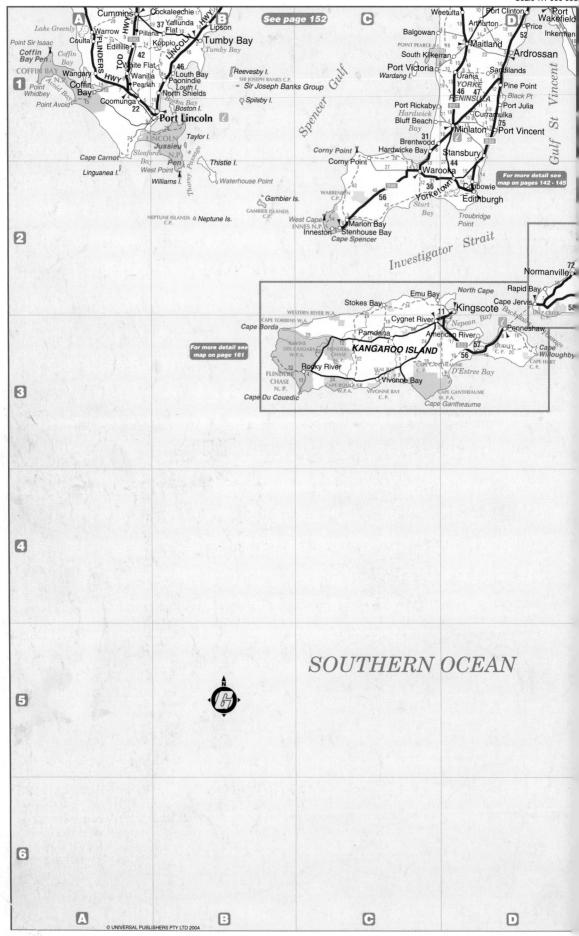

Scale 1:1 900 000

See page 152

SOUTHERN OCEAN

© UNIVERSAL PUBLISHERS PTY LTD 2004

Barossa Valley

Wine tasting in the barrel room

Although relatively small in area, the Barossa Valley is Australia's best-known wine region. Thousands of visitors tour the region each year, tasting the wines and making purchases at the cellar door. German immigrants initially settled the area and the valley's first vines were planted at Orlando vineyards in 1847. The Barossa's Mediterranean-like climate and differing soil types make it an ideal place for growing diverse varieties of grapes, from shiraz and chardonnay to excellent riesling and cabernet sauvignon.

While the Barossa Valley boasts over 60 wineries, from household names such as Penfolds to boutique wineries like Charles Melton and Grant Burge Wines, this historic region offers lots of other attractions. The valley is dotted with small Lutheran churches, another legacy of the German settlers escaping religious persecution. There are also quaint townships with antique stores, old-fashioned pubs, restaurants, cafes and bakeries. The Barossa Farmers' Market, featuring fresh local produce, is held every Saturday morning, and the renowned Maggie Beer's Farm Shop offers gourmet food and wine.

The Barossa's proximity to Adelaide makes it an ideal day trip destination. The region is easy to get around and, with a range of great accommodation options, is also an excellent place to stay for a few days.

Tourist information

i Barossa Wine and Visitor Information Centre

66–68 Murray St, Tanunda SA 5352
Ph: (08) 8563 0600
Tollfree: 1300 852 982
www.barossa-region.org

Main Attractions

◈ **Angaston** This picturesque town is home to some of the Barossa's oldest wineries.

◈ **Bethany Wines** This hillside winery offers great views, wine and white port.

◈ **Chateau Tanunda** An historic bluestone mansion and panoramic views are the highlights of this winery.

◈ **Lyndoch** This historic town settled in 1839 offers wineries and the Lyndoch Lavender Farm.

◈ **Penfolds Wines** Established in 1844, Penfolds showcases some of Australia's best-known wines.

◈ **Seppeltsfield** One of the Barossa's most spectacular wineries, founded in 1851.

◈ **Wolf Blass** This winery consistently produces prize-winning wines.

◈ **Yaldara Estate** Housed in a restored 19th century flourmill, this winery offers 35 wines for tasting.

◈ **Yalumba** Founded in 1849, this is Australia's oldest family-owned winery.

Barossa Festivals

German influence remains with some of the Barossa festivals. The biennial Vintage Festival, held from Easter Monday during odd-numbered years, attracts more than 100,000 people. Other events include Melodienacht (in May), the Barossa Under the Stars concert (February) and the Barossa Jazz Weekend (August).

Vineyards, Eden Valley

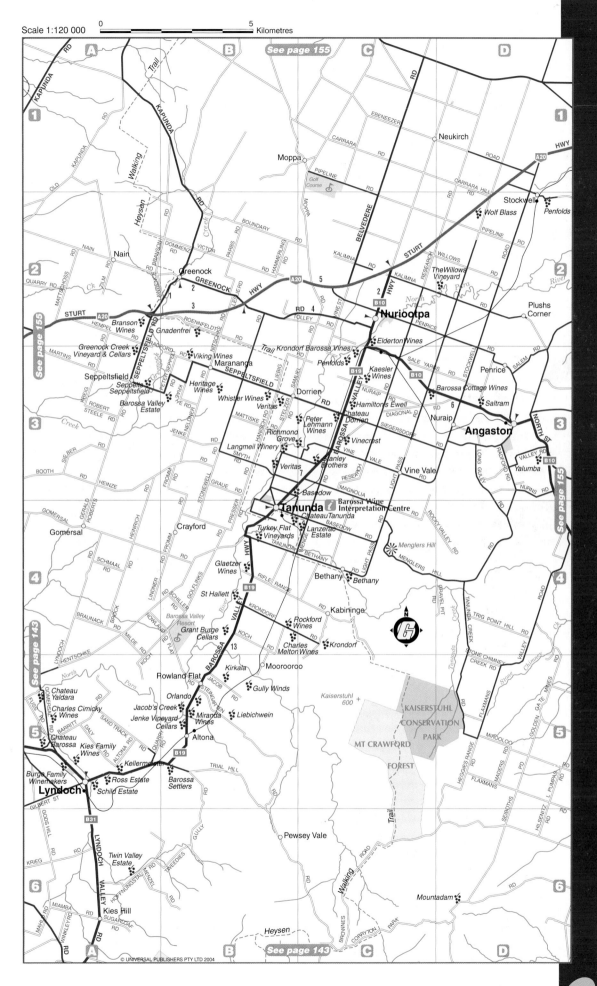

Neukirch

Moppa

Stockwell

Wolf Blass

Penfolds

Nain

Greenock

The Willows Vineyard

Plushs Corner

Nuriootpa

STURT HWY

Branson Wines

Gnadenfrei

Greenock Creek Vineyard & Cellars

Elderton Wines

Krondorf Barossa Vines

Viking Wines

Marananga

Penfolds

Kaesler Wines

Penrice

Seppeltsfield

Seppelts Seppeltsfield

Heritage Wines

Barossa Cottage Wines

Barossa Valley Estate

Whistler Wines

Veritas

Dorrien

Hamilton's Ewell

Saltram

Peter Lehmann Wines

Chateau Dorrien

Nuraip

Angaston

Richmond Grove

Vinecrest

Langmeil Winery

Veritas

Stanley Brothers

Vine Vale

Yalumba

Basedow

Barossa Wine Interpretation Centre

Tanunda

Chateau Tanunda

Menglers Hill

Turkey Flat Vineyards

Lanzerac Estate

Glaetzer Wines

Bethany

Bethany

St Hallett

Kabininge

Barossa Valley Resort

Rockford Wines

Grant Burge Cellars

Charles Melton Wines

Krondorf

Kirkala

Moorooroo

Rowland Flat

Gully Winds

Chateau Yaldara

Orlando

Charles Cimicky Wines

Jacob's Creek

Liebichwein

Jenke Vineyard Cellars

Miranda Wines

Chateau Barossa

Altona

Kies Family Wines

Kaiserstuhl 600

KAISERSTUHL CONSERVATION PARK

Kellermeister

MT CRAWFORD FOREST

Burge Family Winemakers

Ross Estate

Lyndoch

Schild Estate

Barossa Settlers

Pewsey Vale

Twin Valley Estate

Kies Hill

Mountadam

Heysen

Fleurieu Peninsula

Horseriding above Yankalilla Bay

Its close proximity to Adelaide and outstanding combination of seaside resorts surrounded by idyllic rural townships, each set among rolling hills and vineyards, make the Fleurieu Peninsula an ideal holiday destination.

The region starts near the southern coast of Adelaide and continues to Cape Jervis at the tip of the Peninsula, where a vehicular ferry runs to Kangaroo Island.

Both sides of the Peninsula's coast offer great surfing and swimming beaches, islands that are home to penguins, and waters frequently visited by southern right whales.

In contrast, the lush green interior hosts more than 20 conservation parks, 1500km of nature trails, sleepy villages and world-class wineries. The region's noted natural beauty has made it a haven for artists and craftspeople, whose works can be seen in galleries and at weekend craft markets.

Tourist information

i McLaren Vale and Fleurieu Visitor Centre

Main Rd, McLaren Vale SA 5171
Ph: (08) 8323 9944
Freecall: 1800 628 410
www.visitorcentre.com.au

Must Visit

◈ Cape Jervis
◈ Granite Island, Victor Harbor
◈ Deep Creek Conservation Park
◈ McLaren Vale wineries

Scale 1:450 000

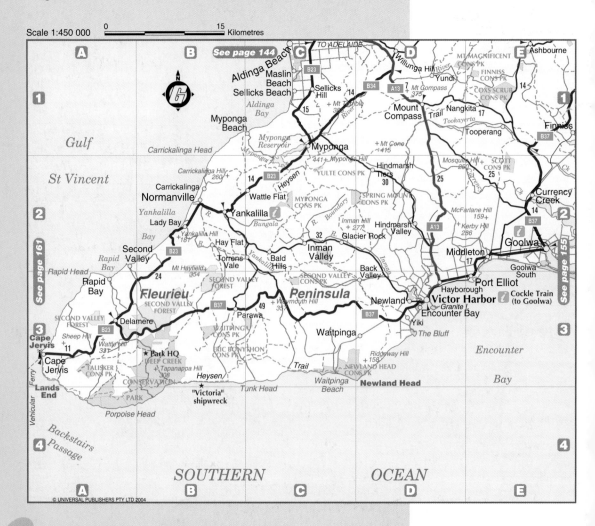

Flinders Ranges

Emus at Parachilna

This isolated area of rugged mountains, deep gorges and tranquil valleys tells tales of adventure, hardship, success and failure. North of Adelaide, the ancient landscape of the Flinders Ranges has been reshaped through the ages: granite in the area has been dated at 600 million years old. Remnants of fossilised palm trees, seashell remains in the inland deserts, and fossils in the walls of the gorge at Mount Billy Creek point to the area once having been an ancient seabed.

Aborigines lived in this area for more than 40,000 years and ceremonial grounds, cave paintings and carvings maintain these people's links with the land.

There are many natural attractions to explore here including vast salt lakes, historic mining areas, rock formations, gorges, waterholes, and rare wildlife and plants. The area is ideal for 4WD tours, driving or even camel trekking, but it is important to be adequately prepared and to check weather conditions before setting out, as these are infamously changeable.

Tourist information

i Wadlata Outback Centre
41 Flinders Tce,
Port Augusta SA 5700
Ph: (08) 8642 4511
www.flindersoutback.com

Must Visit

- ◈ Arkaroola Wilderness Sanctuary
- ◈ Historic Beltana outback settlement
- ◈ Flinders Ranges National Park
- ◈ Gammon Ranges National Park
- ◈ Wilpena Pound

Scale 1:750 000   0   20 Kilometres

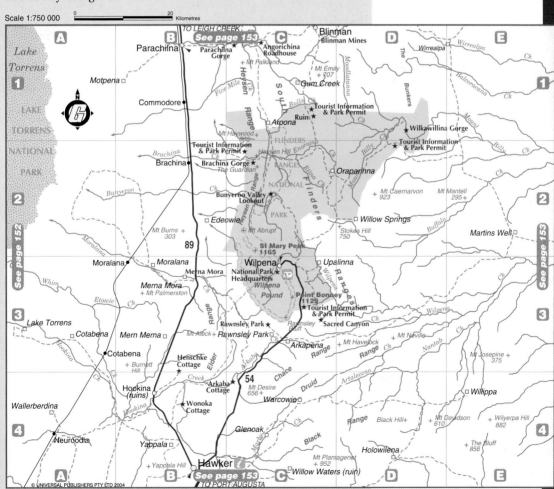

Kangaroo Island

Sea lions, Seal Bay

The third largest island off the Australian coastline, Kangaroo Island surprises many visitors with its size: 155km long and 55km at its widest point. It has a well-deserved reputation as a haven for native wildlife and flora, with 50% of the island never cleared and 30% of its total area covered by national parks.

Even in peak season, the island's size protects it from feeling crowded, although its small townships swell considerably. It offers a relaxed lifestyle and endless opportunities for water-based activities such as fishing, swimming, sailing, surfing, scuba diving and boating.

Kangaroo Island has become well known as a place to see wildlife – some of which is rare or extinct on the Australian mainland – in its natural habitat. Visitors have the opportunity to see little penguins, Australian sea lions, New Zealand fur seals, koalas and the kangaroos that give the island its name.

The spectacular coastline also offers magnificent views, historic lighthouses and remnants of shipwrecks.

History

Kangaroo Island was discovered in 1802 by Matthew Flinders, who named it after the dark-furred kangaroos he saw there. For some years the island was a hideout for escaped convicts, ship deserters and renegade whalers, who lived a violent and harsh life.

Tourist information

i Gateway Information Centre
Howard Dr, Penneshaw SA 5222
Ph: (08) 8553 1185
Freecall: 1800 811 080
www.tourkangarooisland.com.au

Main Attractions

◈ **Cape Willoughby Lighthouse** The first lighthouse in South Australia, this was completed in 1852.

◈ **Emu Bay** With shallow, clear water, this is one of the island's popular swimming spots.

◈ **Flinders Chase National Park** Highlights of the park include the Remarkable Rocks and Cape Borda Lighthouse.

◈ **Kingscote** SA's first settlement site. Nearby Reeves Point is also rich in history.

◈ **Penneshaw Penguin Tour** See little penguins at dusk as they come ashore to nest in the sand hills.

◈ **Seal Bay Conservation Park** This sandy beach provides a resting place and breeding habitat for Australian sea lions.

◈ **Stokes Bay** Rock pools offer protected swimming, while small caves provide shelter from the sun.

Crayfishing, Vivonne Bay

Island Produce

Due to its relative seclusion and limited industry, Kangaroo Island has been able to preserve a clean and green environment. Enterprising Islanders have seized this opportunity to develop Kangaroo Island into one of Australia's premier alternative primary production areas, offering an increasing and diverse range of regional produce with a growing export market. The fox-free island produces high quality, corn fed, free-range chickens, while its location makes it ideal for fresh seafood: King George whiting is a regional specialty, featured on many local restaurant menus. To taste the island's treats visit:

Picnic, Kangaroo Island

◈ **Clifford's Honey Farm** – Believed to be the only place in the world with a pure strain of Ligurian bee, the farm offers free tastings and sells home-made honey icecream.

◈ **Dudley Partners, Kangaroo Island** – Offering locally grown and produced red and white wines, Hog Bay River Vineyards is developing a reputation for its fine Cabernet Merlot.

◈ **Emu Ridge Eucalyptus** – Distilled from the indigenous Kangaroo Island Narrow Leaf Mallee known for its strong aroma, Emu Ridge eucalyptus products include sweets, eucalyptus soap and gift packs.

◈ **Island Pure Sheep Dairy** – Producing world-class sheep cheeses and yoghurts based on Greek, Cypriot, Italian and Spanish recipes, the dairy offers opportunities to observe milking, plus tastings and sales.

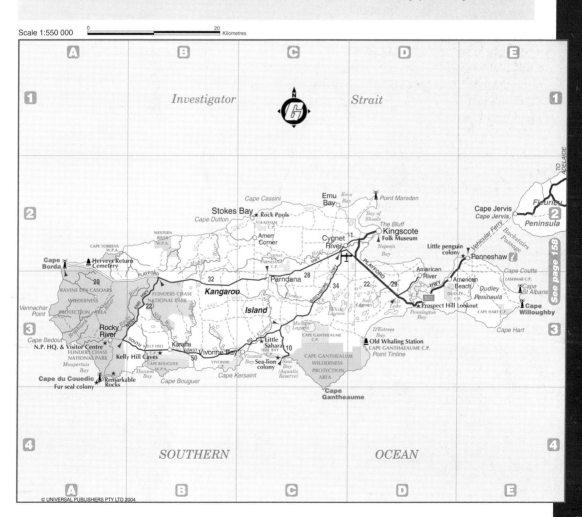

Mt Gambier District

Cave at Naracoorte Caves National Park

Known as the 'Limestone Coast', SA's south-east corner is rich in natural attractions, with an arc of pristine beaches and lobster-fishing ports stretching along the coastline to the Victorian border. The region, which centres on Mount Gambier, is named for its incomparable concentration of limestone craters, caves and cliffs, and offers visitors a range of activities and attractions in a spectacular natural setting. The limestone base gives the famous Coonawarra and Padthaway wine regions their distinctive terra rossa soil.

Volcanic activity sculpted the landscape, forming the Crater Lakes that are among the region's most stunning natural attractions. Inland, the World Heritage-listed Naracoote Caves are a major fossil cave system; re-creations of prehistoric animals that once inhabited the caves are displayed at Wonambi Fossil Centre.

Along the coast are significant wetlands and coastal conservation areas in the Coorong National Park and Canunda National Park, and historic fishing ports at Robe, Beachport and Kingston S.E.

Tourist information

i 'The Lady Nelson' Visitor and Discovery Centre

Jubilee Hwy East,
Mt Gambier SA 5290
Ph: (08) 8724 9750
Freecall: 1800 087 187
www.thelimestonecoast.com

Main Attractions

◈ **Blue Lake** This is the district's most famous tourist destination and was originally a volcanic crater.

◈ **Camp Coorong** Learn about traditional Aboriginal life by visiting the Ngarrindjeri people in the area where they have lived for thousands of years.

◈ **Coonawarra** One of Australia's best-known wine districts.

◈ **Coorong National Park** These wetlands are home to a breeding colony of Australian pelicans, and host migratory birds from as far away as Siberia.

◈ **Naracoorte Caves** The region's largest limestone cave system is in this World Heritage-listed park.

◈ **Penola** Visit Mary MacKillop's first schoolhouse built in 1867, with displays of her life's work.

◈ **Robe** This historic fishing village has been a holiday destination for more than 150 years.

Visit Beachport

This historic whaling port offers excellent fishing from the jetty at Rivoli Bay. Visit the Butcher's Gallery in SA's first butcher shop, the National Trust Museum and Beachport Conservation Park. The nearby Pool of Siloam is a small lake claimed to have healing qualities.

Vineyard in the Coonawarra

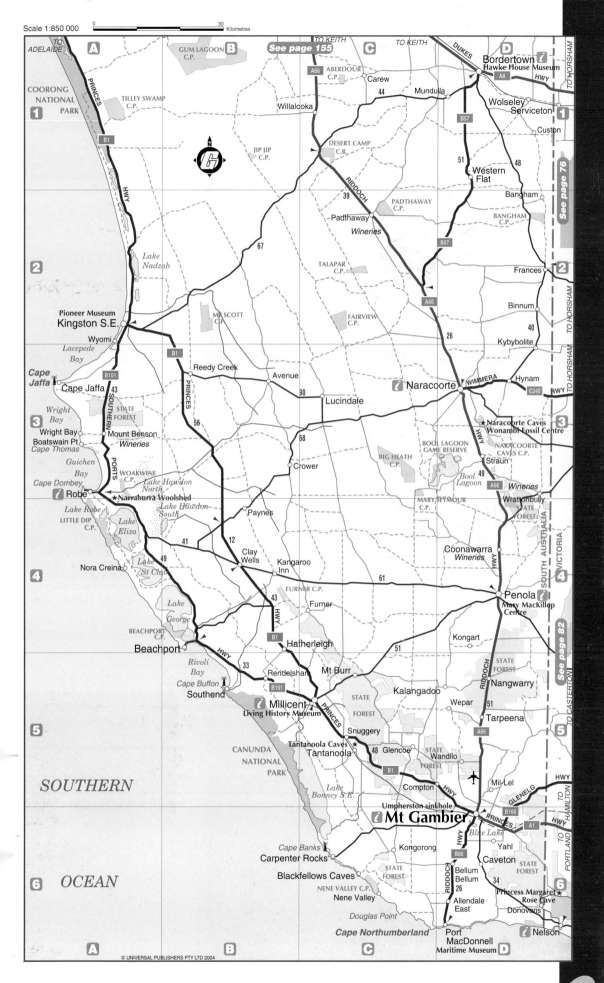

Riverland

Portee Station, Blanchetown

This region features around 300km of the Murray River, one of the world's great waterways, meandering its way through a changing landscape. Not only does the river dominate the region's landscape, it also influences its economy, providing the lifeblood for its orchards, vineyards and dairy pastures.

Riverland produces almost half of SA's wine grapes and is becoming increasingly known as a wine-producing region in its own right. It is the 'fruit bowl' of SA, where more than 90% of the state's citrus, stone fruit, and nuts are grown. Local produce can be sampled from stalls along the roadside.

There is no better way to explore the mighty Murray River than by travelling along it. Fully-equipped houseboats, with home comforts, are one holiday option. The river is ideal for anglers, and catches of the day include Murray cod, redfin and fresh yabbies. Dotted with tiny towns and rich in pioneering history, Riverland offers much to explore.

Tourist information

i Renmark /
Paringa Visitor Centre

84 Murray Ave, Renmark SA 5341
Ph: (08) 8586 6704
www.riverland.info

Main Attractions

◈ **Banrock Station Winery** Visit this unique combination of a winery and wetlands conservation project.

◈ **Barmera** SA's country music capital has hosted the state's annual country music festival for more than 25 years.

◈ **Berri** Renowned for its citrus and stone fruits, Berri is an ideal base for exploring the region.

◈ **Loxton Historical Village** An award-winning attraction of 30 furnished buildings on the waterfront.

◈ **Renmark** This Murray River town offers an insight into early river history. Worth visiting is Ruston's Rose Garden, containing 50,000 rose bushes.

◈ **The Big Orange** Located on the Sturt Hwy in Berri, The Big Orange is a tribute to the region's citrus industry, featuring sales of local produce and a lookout.

The Overland Corner Hotel

Constructed in 1858, this hotel was the first stone building in the Riverland. Weary bullock teamsters used it as a stop on the original stock route to Adelaide. The hotel remains at Overland Corner and now includes a museum of its history.

Water-skiing on the Murray

Cruising the Mighty Murray

Since the first paddlesteamer, the *Mary Ann*, was launched in 1853 near Mannum, river transport has been a popular way to travel along the Murray River. Today, the river can be cruised by houseboats, paddleships and historic paddlesteamers past quaint townships, vineyards, orchards, ancient terrain and scenic wilderness. Options also include eco-cruises focusing on native flora and fauna.

For a Murray adventure contact the operators below, or the Renmark / Paringa, Berri, or Murray Bridge Visitor Information Centres for more details.

◈ **Big River Holidays:** Offers a fully equipped and easy-to-operate houseboat for 2–12 people from Berri.

◈ **Green and Gold Houseboats:** Available for hire for overnight cruises, these luxury houseboats for 2–12 are based in Waikerie.

◈ **Proud Australia Holidays:** Board the elegant *Proud Mary* from Renmark for eco-cruises.

◈ **PS Industry:** This historic paddlesteamer operates 90-minute cruises from Renmark.

◈ **PS Murray Princess:** Offering luxury cruising on SA's largest inland water

paddlewheeler. Trips depart from Mannum and include visits to an Aboriginal site and water-skiing.

◈ **River Murray Houseboats:** These self-drive, fully equipped houseboats sleeping 2–10 people are based in Renmark.

◈ *PS Princess Andrea; MV Barrangul:* Both offer an hour-long afternoon tea cruises from Murray Bridge.

The paddlesteamer *PS Industry*

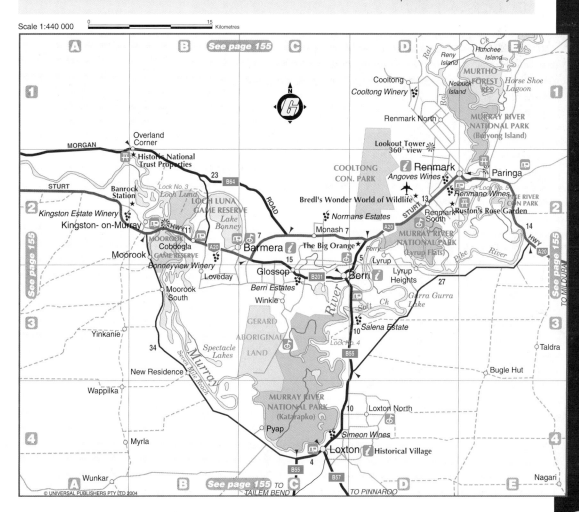

Western Australia
Wildflower State

F lanked by desert to the east and 12,500 km of coastline to the west, Western Australia covers approximately one third of the Australian continent and encompasses a number of climatic zones.

Outside the major cities, this vast land mass is sparsely populated and WA's population makes up just 10 per cent of the national total. Almost three quarters of the state's residents – around 1.3 million people – live in and around the capital, Perth, which is closer to Jakarta and Singapore than to Sydney or Melbourne.

Rich in natural resources including iron ore, gold, gas, petroleum products, wheat, wool and minerals, WA is essentially a primary industry state, although the fastest growing industry is tourism. The state has many national parks with spectacular natural attractions, ranging from magnificent desert landscapes and wildflower-carpeted forests, to pristine coastline, drawing visitors in increasing numbers.

The state has a combination of tropical, temperate and arid climes. The southern region experiences cool winters and hot, dry summers. The monsoonal north has consistently high, humid temperatures in its wet and dry seasons. In contrast, the interior crackles with a dry heat rising to over 40°C in the middle of its summer days.

Tourist information

Western Australian Visitor Centre

Forrest Pl, cnr Wellington St,
Perth WA 6000
Tollfree: 1300 361 351
www.westernaustralia.com

| Area = 2,527,633 sq km | Occupies 32.9% of Australia | Length of coast = 7000 km |

Western Australia Key Map & Distance Chart

All distances shown in the chart below have been measured over highways and major roads, not necessarily by the shortest route.

Cottesloe Beach

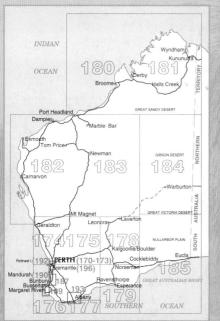

Approximate Distance	Albany	Broome	Bunbury	Busselton	Carnarvon	Derby	Esperance	Eucla	Geraldton	Halls Creek	Kalgoorlie/Boulder	Kununurra	Mandurah	Meekatharra	Merredin	Narrogin	Norseman	Northam	Perth	Port Hedland
Albany		2582	361	372	1292	2736	474	1386	819	3196	799	3554	468	1116	463	269	676	439	406	1988
Broome	2582		2538	2592	1461	222	912	3082	1934	682	2185	1040	2441	1466	2304	2313	2372	2143	2372	614
Bunbury	361	2538		54	1069	2554	687	1599	596	3004	764	3362	1027	924	422	170	889	261	182	1796
Busselton	372	2592	54		1123	2608	698	1610	650	3058	818	3416	161	978	482	224	900	315	236	1850
Carnarvon	1292	1461	1069	1123		1615	1600	2300	473	2075	1161	2433	972	620	1125	1078	1590	964	903	867
Derby	2736	222	2554	2608	1615		2728	3236	2088	544	2267	902	2447	1620	2458	2467	2526	2297	2378	768
Esperance	474	912	687	698	1600	2728		912	1319	3188	389	3486	710	1108	562	535	202	828	714	1980
Eucla	1386	3082	1599	1610	2300	3236	912		1827	3696	897	4054	1502	1616	1175	1433	710	1336	1433	2488
Geraldton	819	1934	596	650	473	2088	1319	1827		2548	988	2906	499	540	652	605	1117	491	430	1340
Halls Creek	3196	682	3004	3058	2075	544	3188	3696	2548		2799	358	2907	2080	2918	2927	2986	2757	2838	1228
Kalgoorlie/Boulder	799	2185	764	818	1161	2267	389	897	988	2799		3157	663	719	336	594	187	497	594	1591
Kununurra	3554	1040	3362	3416	2433	902	3486	4054	2906	358	3157		3265	2438	3276	3285	3344	3115	3196	1586
Mandurah	468	2441	1027	161	972	2447	710	1502	499	2907	663	3265		827	327	175	792	166	75	1698
Meekatharra	1116	1466	924	978	620	1620	1108	1616	540	2080	719	2438	827		838	847	906	677	758	872
Merredin	463	2304	422	482	1125	2458	562	1175	652	2918	336	3276	327	838		258	465	161	258	1710
Narrogin	269	2313	170	224	1078	2467	535	1433	605	2927	594	3285	175	847	258		723	170	192	1719
Norseman	676	2372	889	900	1590	2526	202	710	1117	2986	187	3344	792	906	465	723		626	723	1778
Northam	439	2143	261	315	964	2297	828	1336	491	2757	497	3115	166	677	161	170	626		97	1549
Perth	406	2372	182	236	903	2378	714	1433	430	2838	594	3196	75	758	258	192	723	97		1630
Port Hedland	1988	614	1796	1850	867	768	1980	2488	1340	1228	1591	1586	1698	872	1710	1719	1778	1549	1630	

Perth

Matilda Bay marina

Founded in 1829 and built on the banks of the Swan River, Perth is a scenic and sophisticated city, renowned for its abundant sunshine, relaxed lifestyle and easy-going manner.

Perth's modern skyline blends with magnificent colonial architecture, housing excellent retail outlets, particularly around Hay and Murray Streets and the malls running between them. King St, the historic and lovingly-restored commercial precinct, is now renowned for its fashion houses, cafes, art galleries and specialist book stores.

Within minutes of the CBD are Australia's oldest operating mint, a number of art galleries and museums, historic buildings and numerous parklands.

Perth's prime location, straddling both the broad reaches of the Swan River and the open waters of the Indian Ocean, makes it an ideal place for enjoying alfresco dining. The riverside, beach front, and the entertainment precinct of Northbridge all boast an array of cafes and restaurants, while nearby stretch more than 80km of white sandy beaches. Many of WA's key attractions are located within close proximity to Perth, which makes the capital an ideal base for exploring the surrounding regions.

Tourist information

i Western Australian Visitor Centre

Forrest Pl, cnr Wellington St, Perth WA 6000
Ph: (08) 9483 1111
Tollfree: 1300 361 351
www.westernaustralia.com

Main Attractions

◈ **Art Gallery of Western Australia** See one of the finest collections of Aboriginal Art in Australia.

◈ **Kings Park** Experience stunning views from Mt Eliza, natural bushland, WA's famed wildflowers, and a walk among the treetops on the new Federation Walkway.

◈ **London Court** This Tudor-style shopping arcade is a popular attraction.

◈ **Perth Mint** Visit the past in the Mint's Old Melting House; see gold bar pouring demonstrations and watch the workings from the viewing gallery.

◈ **The Swan Bells** The historic Swan Bells together make one of the world's largest musical instruments.

Kings Park

Places of Interest

Ⓐ Art Gallery of Western Australia **B3**
Ⓑ Barracks Archway **A3**
Ⓒ Fire Safety Education Centre and Museum **B3**
Ⓓ Francis Burt Law Education Centre and Museum **B4**
Ⓔ His Majesty's Theatre **A3**
Ⓕ London Court **B3**

Ⓖ Parliament House **A3**
Ⓗ Perth Cultural Centre **D4**
Ⓘ Perth Institute of Contemporary Arts **B3**
Ⓙ Perth Mint **C3**
Ⓚ Perth Town Hall **B3**
Ⓛ Perth Zoo **A6**
Ⓜ Queens Gardens **D4**

Ⓝ Scitech Discovery Centre **A2**
Ⓞ Stirling Gardens **B3**
Ⓟ Supreme Court Gardens **B4**
Ⓠ The Old Mill **A4**
Ⓡ The Swan Bells **B4**
Ⓢ WACA Oval **D4**
Ⓣ Western Australian Museum **B3**

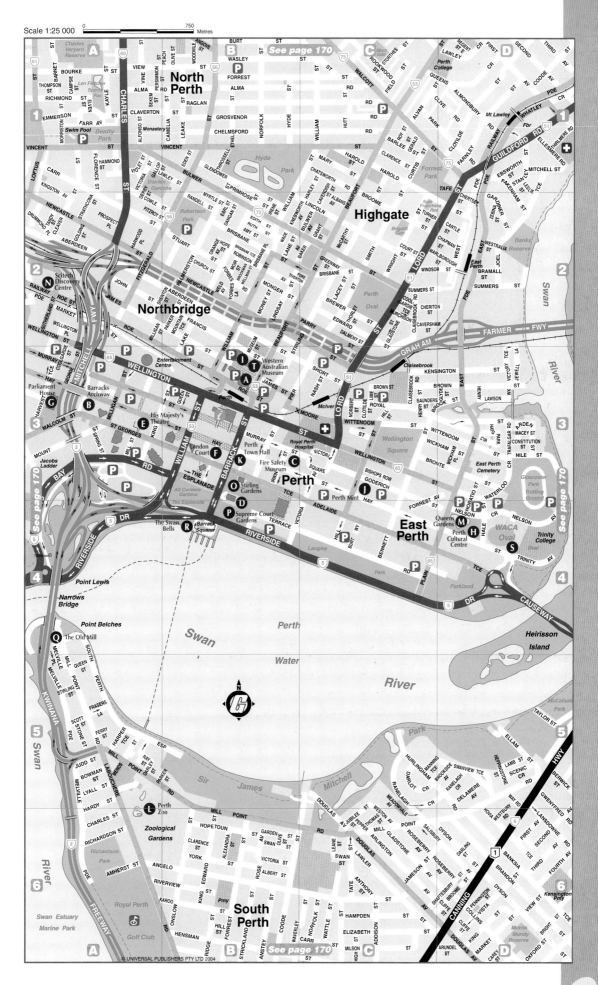

Scale 1:25 000

0   750
Metres

See page 170

North Perth

Highgate

Northbridge

Perth

East Perth

South Perth

Swan

Water

River

Heirisson Island

See page 170

See page 170

See page 170

© UNIVERSAL PUBLISHERS PTY LTD 2004

INDIAN

OCEAN

See page 176

See page 172

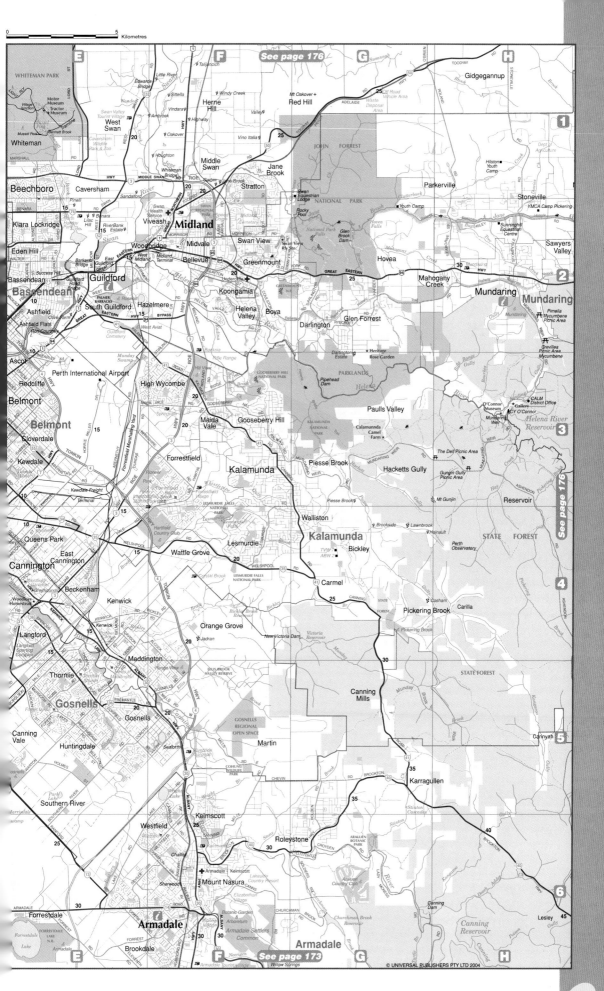

See page 176

See page 176

See page 173

© UNIVERSAL PUBLISHERS PTY LTD 2004

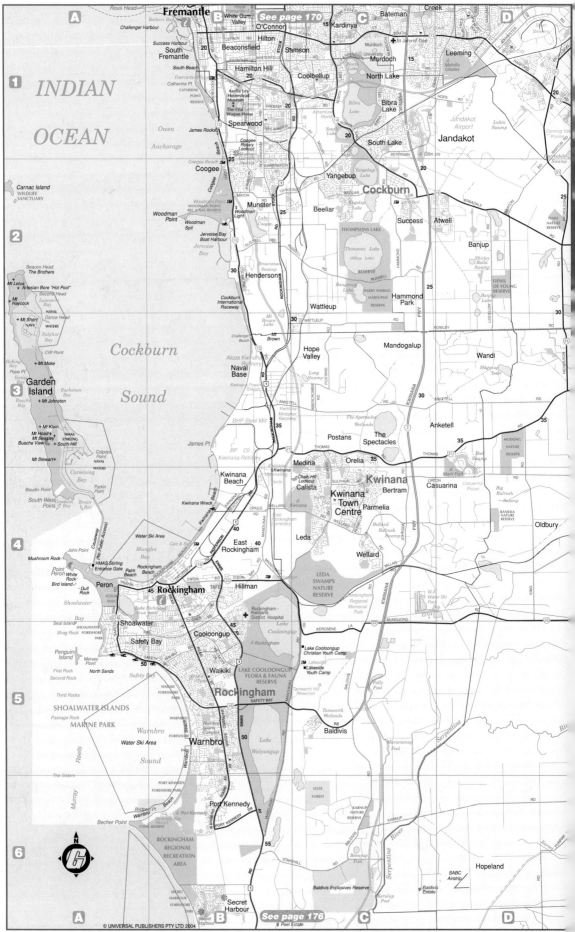

INDIAN

OCEAN

Cockburn

Sound

© UNIVERSAL PUBLISHERS PTY LTD 2004

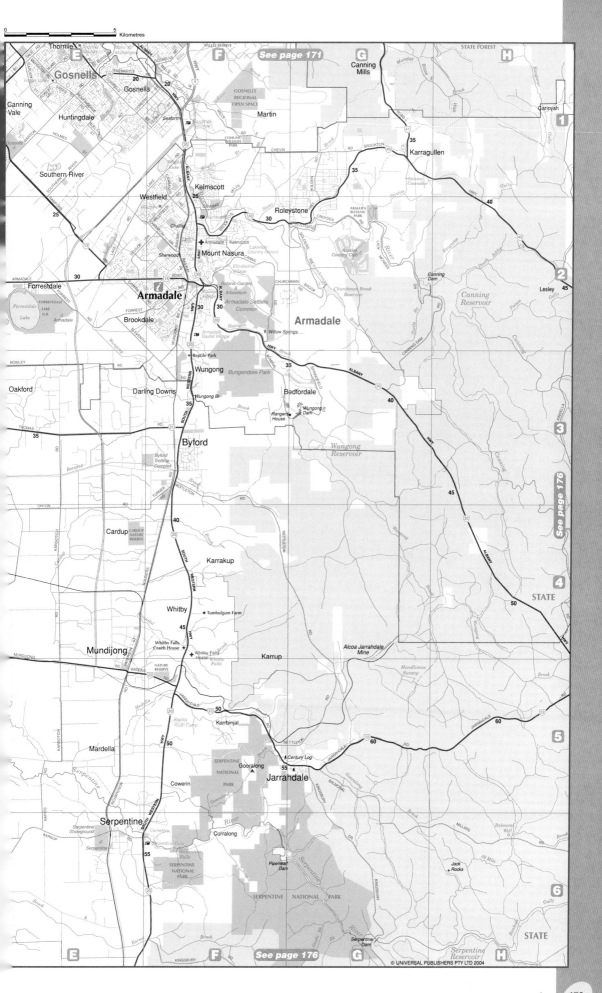

0   5   Kilometres

Thornlie

Gosnells

Gosnells

Canning
Vale

Huntingdale

Canning
Mills

Carinyah

Southern River

Martin

STATE FOREST

Westfield

Kelmscott

Roleystone

Karragullen

Lesley

Araluen
Country Club

Canning
Reservoir

Forrestdale

Armadale

Mount Nasura

Armadale

Canning
Dam

Brookdale

Armadale Settlers
Common

Oakford

Wungong

Bungendore Park

Willow Springs

Darling Downs

Wungong Br

Bedfordale

Wungong
Dam

Byford

Rangers
House

Wungong
Reservoir

Byford
Trotting
Complex

Cardup

CARDUP
NATURE
RESERVE

Karrakup

Whitby

Tumbulgum Farm

Mundijong

Whitby Falls
Coach House

Whitby Falls
Hostel   Whitby
Falls

Karrup

Alcoa Jarrahdale
Mine

NATURE
RESERVE

Mandlimup
Swamp

Mardella

Korbinjal

Baptist
Youth Camp

Century Log

SERPENTINE
NATIONAL
PARK

Gooralong

Jarrahdale

STATE

Cowerin

Balmoral
Well

Serpentine
Showground

Serpentine

Curralong

Millars

39 Mile

Jack
Rocks

Serpentine
Falls

SERPENTINE
NATIONAL
PARK

Pipehead
Dam

SERPENTINE   NATIONAL   PARK

Serpentine
Dam

Serpentine
Reservoir

STATE

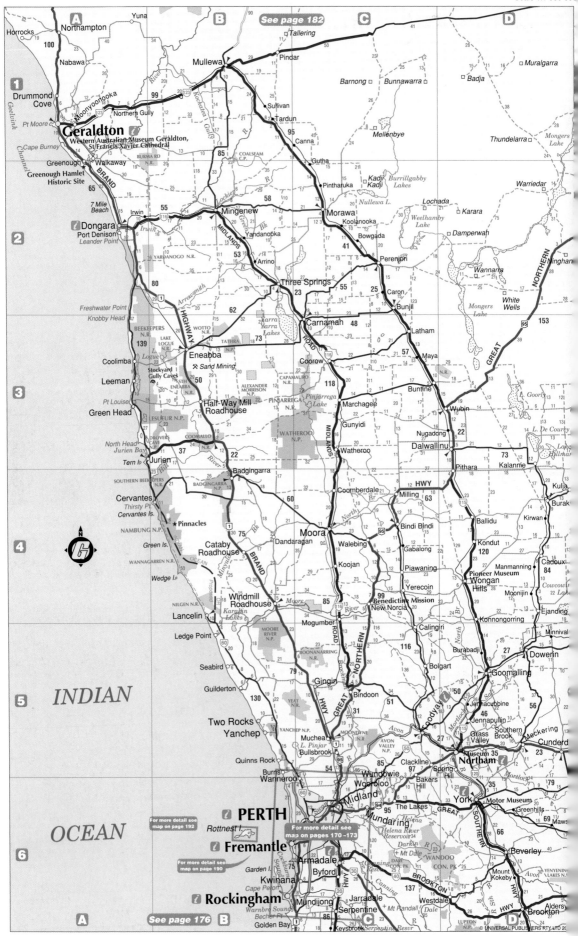

INDIAN

OCEAN

PERTH

Fremantle

Rockingham

See page 182

See page 176

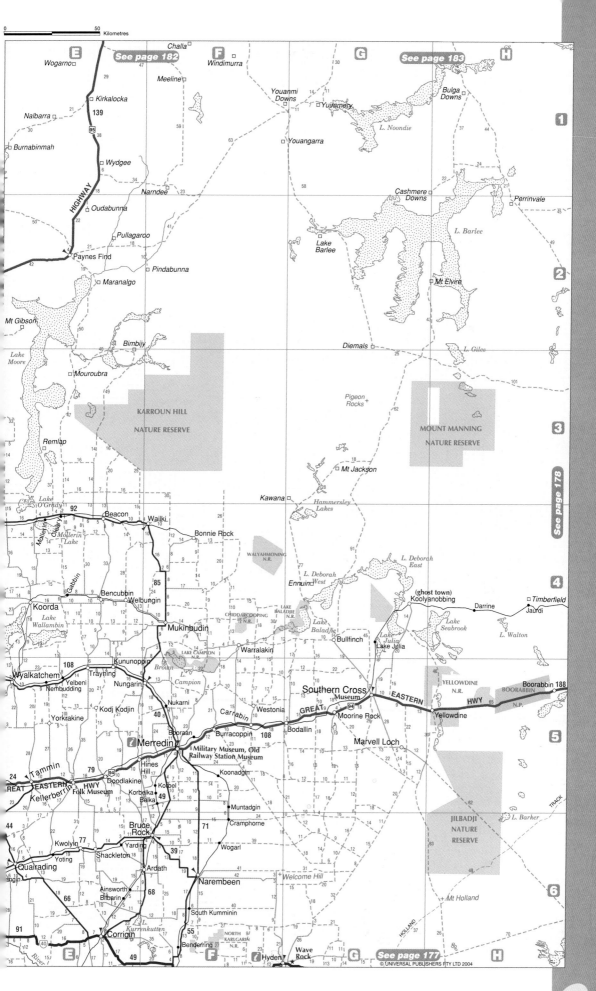

0   50   Kilometres

E   F   G   H

Wogarno
Challa
Windimurra
Meeline

1

Nalbarra
Kirkalocka
139
Youanmi Downs
Yuinmery
Bulga Downs
L. Noondie

Burnabinmah
95
38
Wydgee
Youangarra
Cashmere Downs
Perrinvale

HIGHWAY
Narndee
L. Barlee

2
Oudabunna
Lake Barlee
Mt Elvire

Pullagaroo
Paynes Find
Pindabunna

Maranalgo

Mt Gibson
Bimbijy
Diemals
L. Giles

Lake Moore
Mouroubra
Pigeon Rocks

KARROUN HILL
NATURE RESERVE
MOUNT MANNING
NATURE RESERVE

3

Remlap

See page 178

Lake O'Grady
Mt Jackson
Kawana
Hammersley Lakes

92
Beacon
Wailki
L. Deborah East

Mollerin
Mollerin Lake
Bonnie Rock
WALYAHMONING N.R.
L. Deborah West
Koolyanobbing (ghost town)
Darrine
Timberfield

Gabbin
85
Welbungin
Ennuin
CHIDDARCOOPING N.R.
LAKE BALADJIE N.R.
Lake Baladjie
Koolyanobbing
Lake Seabrook
Jaurdi

Koorda
Bencubbin
L. Walton

Lake Wallambin
Mukinbudin
LAKE CAMPION N.R.
Bullfinch
Lake Julia

108
Kununoppin
Warralakin
Lake Julia

Wyalkatchem
Brown
L. Campion

Trayning
Yelbeni
Nungarin
Nukarni
Southern Cross
Museum
EASTERN
YELLOWDINE N.R.
Boorabbin **188**

Nembudding
40
Carrabin
Westonia
GREAT
94
Moorine Rock
Yellowdine
BOORABBIN N.P.

Kodj Kodjin
Booraan
Burracoppin
108
Bodallin

Yorkrakine
Merredin
Marvell Loch

Tammin
79
Hines Hill
Military Museum, Old
Railway Station Museum
Koonadgin

24
94
Doodlakine
JILBADJI
NATURE
RESERVE

EASTERN HWY
Kellerberrin
Folk Museum
Korbel
Korbelka
Balka
49
Muntadgin

44
Kwolyin
77
Bruce Rock
71
Cramphorne
L. Barker

Yoting
Yarding
Shackleton
39
Wogarl
Welcome Hill
Mt Holland

Quairading
Ardath
Narembeen

66
Ainsworth
Bilbarin
68

91
South Kumminin

L. Kurrenkutten
Corrigin
55
NORTH KARLGARIN N.R.

40
49
Benderring
E   F
Hyden
Wave Rock
G   H

Western Australia **175**

Scale 1:1 900 000

See page 174

INDIAN

OCEAN

PERTH

Fremantle

Rockingham

Mandurah

Bunbury

Dunsborough

Margaret River

Augusta

D'ENTRECASTEAUX
NATIONAL PARK

WALPOLE - NORNALUP N.P.

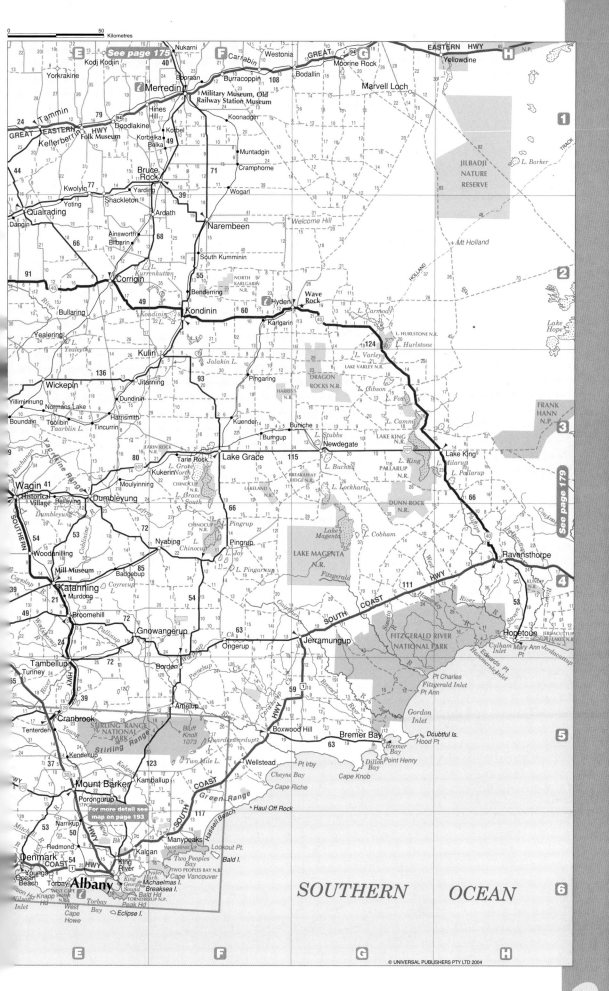

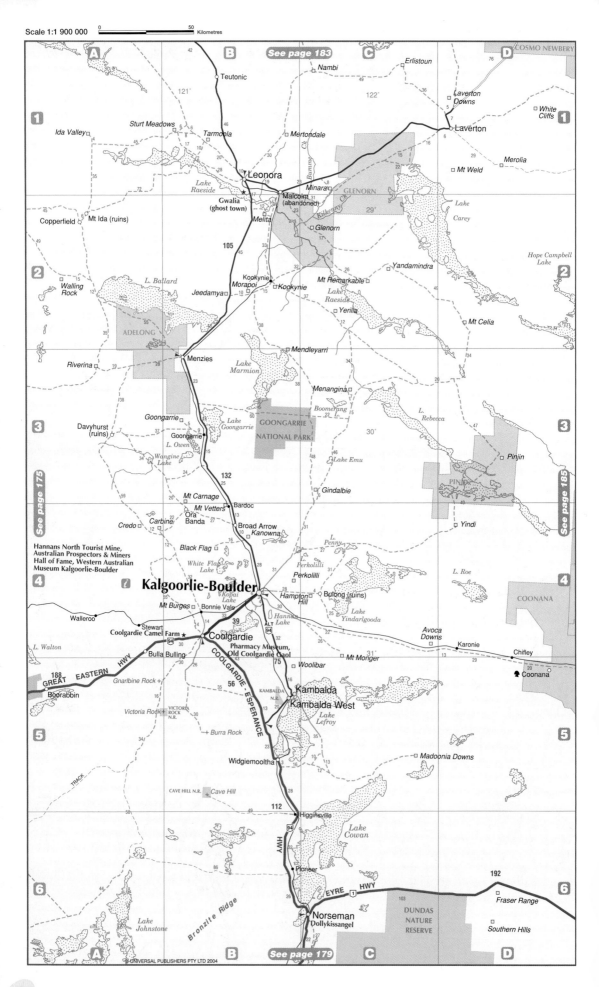

See page 183

COSMO NEWBERY

Teutonic

Nambi

Erlistoun

Laverton Downs

White Cliffs

Ida Valley

Sturt Meadows

Tarmoola

Mertondale

Laverton

Merolia

Mt Weld

Leonora

Minara

GLENORN

Lake Carey

Hope Campbell Lake

Copperfield
Mt Ida (ruins)

Gwalia (ghost town)

Malcolm (abandoned)

Melita

Glenorn

105

Kookynie
Morapoi

Kookynie

Yandamindra

Walling Rock

L. Ballard

Jeedamya

Mt Remarkable

Lake Raeside

Yerilla

Mt Celia

ADELONG

Menzies

Mendleyarri

Riverina

Lake Marmion

Menangina

Goongarrie

Lake Goongarrie

Boomerang L.

L. Rebecca

Davyhurst (ruins)

Goongarrie

GOONGARRIE NATIONAL PARK

Pinjin

L. Owen

Lake Emu

PINJIN

Wangine Lake

132

Mt Carnage

Mt Vetters
Bardoc

Gindalbie

Yindi

Credo
Carbine

Ora Banda

Broad Arrow
Kanowna

L. Penny

Black Flag

White Flag Lake

L. Perkolilli

Perkolilli

L. Roe

See page 175

Hannans North Tourist Mine, Australian Prospectors & Miners Hall of Fame, Western Australian Museum Kalgoorlie-Boulder

Kalgoorlie-Boulder

Kopai Lake

Hampton Hill

Butong (ruins)

COONANA

Mt Burges
Bonnie Vale

Hannan Lake

Lake Yindarlgooda

Walleroo

Stewart

Coolgardie Camel Farm

Coolgardie

Avoca Downs

Karonie

Chifley

L. Walton

Bulla Bulling

Pharmacy Museum, Old Coolgardie Gaol

Woolibar

Mt Monger

Coonana

GREAT EASTERN HWY

188

Gnarlbine Rock

75

COOLGARDIE - ESPERANCE

56

KAMBALDA N.R.

Kambalda

Boorabbin

Victoria Rock

VICTORIA ROCK N.R.

Kambalda West

Lake Lefroy

Madoonia Downs

Burra Rock

Widgiemooltha

CAVE HILL N.R.
Cave Hill

112

Higginsville

Lake Cowan

See page 185

HWY

94

Pioneer

192

EYRE HWY

Fraser Range

Bronzite Ridge

Lake Johnstone

Norseman
Dollykissangel

DUNDAS NATURE RESERVE

Southern Hills

See page 179

© UNIVERSAL PUBLISHERS PTY LTD 2004

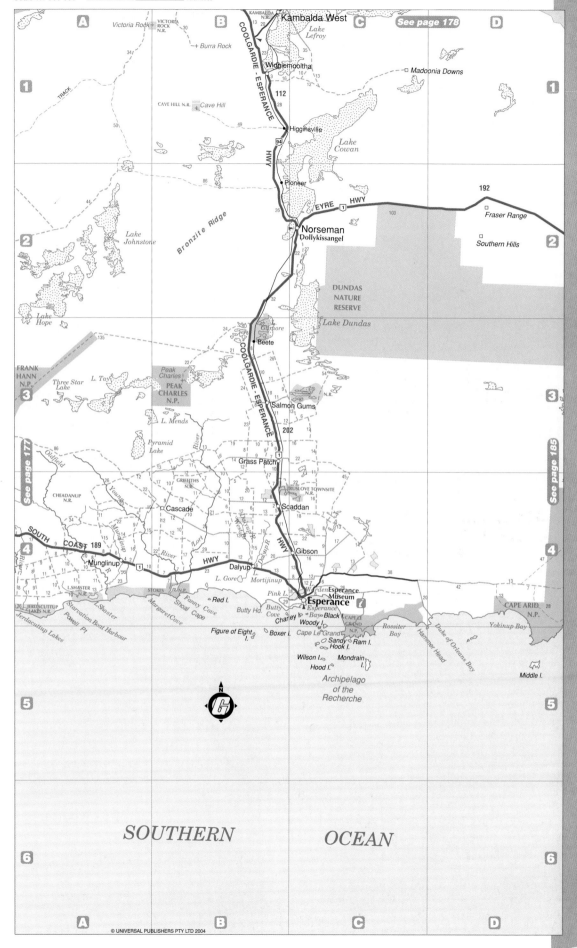

SOUTHERN

OCEAN

INDIAN OCEAN

Seringapatam Reef

Scott Reef

SCOTT REEF
NATURE RES.

Browse I.

Adele I.

Buccaneer
Archipelago

Koolan I.
Cockatoo I.
Cockatoo Island Resort
Koolan

Hidden I.

Cape Leveque
One Arm
Kooljaman Resort
Point (Bardi)
Lombardina
(Djarindjin)
PENDER BAY
Pender
Pender Bay
King
Sound

Beagle Bay
BEAGLE BAY

Derby

Country
Downs
Fraser R.
Mowanjum
Yeeda
Willare Bridge Roadhouse
146
Kilto
Logue
Bedunburru
Tjarramba
Yakka
Munga
Roebuck Roadhouse
Roebuck Plains

COULOMB POINT
N.R.

Rowley Shoals
ROWLEY SHOALS
MARINE PARK
Clerke Reef
Mermaid Reef

Imperieuse Reef

Malcolm Douglas
Crocodile Park
Waterbank
Cable Beach
Chinatown, Japanese Cemetery
Broome
Broome Bird Observatory
Thangoo
Roebuck Bay
34

Eco Beach Wilderness Retreat
Cape Latouche Treville
Port Smith Caravan & Bird Park
Lagrange Bay
Cape Bossut
Admiral Bay
Frazier Downs
Shamrock
Bidyadanga
(Lagrange)
FRAZIER
DOWNS
287
Nita Downs

Dampier
Downs

Mowla Bluff
Mowla Bluff +
203

HWY
112

Anna Plains

Eighty Mile Beach
Mandora
Sandfire Roadhouse

GREAT
SANDY
DESERT
DRAGON TREE N.R
KIDSON

Cape Keraudren
Wallal Downs
141
NORTHERN
(WAPET RD)
TRACK
375

North Turtle I.
Poissonnier Pt
Mining Museum,
Pioneer & Pearlers Cemetery
De Grey
Pardoo
Pardoo Roadhouse
GREAT
Nimingarra
Port
Hedland
Cape Thouin
Boodarie
South
Hedland
Strelley
142
De Grey
Muccan
Callawa
Mundabullangana
32
Carlindie
Coongan
Wallareenya
Tabba
Tabba
Lalla Rookh
Eginbah
Bamboo
Creek
Mine
Warrawagine
143

See page 182
See page 183
© UNIVERSAL PUBLISHERS PTY LTD 200

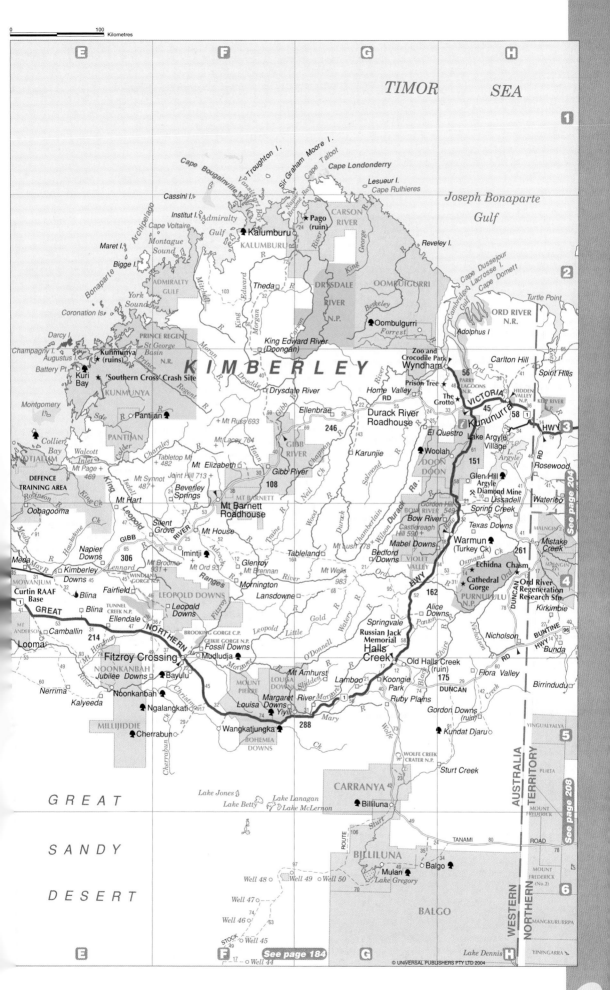

TIMOR SEA

Joseph Bonaparte
Gulf

Cape Bougainville
Vansittart Bay
Sir Graham Moore I.
Cape Talbot
Cape Londonderry
Lesueur I.
Cape Rulhieres

Cassini I.

Institut I.
Admiralty
Gulf
★ Pago
(ruin)
CARSON
RIVER
Reveley I.

Maret I.
Montague
Sound
● Kalumburu
KALUMBURU

Bigge I.
Bonaparte
Archipelago
Cape Voltaire
ADMIRALTY
GULF
York
Sound
Theda
DRYSDALE
RIVER
N.P.
OOMBUIGURRI
Cape Dussejour
Cape Lacrosse I.
Cape Dornett
Turtle Point

Coronation Is
Berkeley
● Oombulgurri
Forrest
ORD RIVER
N.R.

Darcy I.
Champagny I.
Augustus I.
St George
Basin
PRINCE REGENT
N.R.
● Kunmunya
(ruins)
King Edward River
(Doongan)
Adolphus I.

Battery Pt.
● Kuri
Bay
★ 'Southern Cross' Crash Site
K I M B E R L E Y
Zoo and
Crocodile Park ●
Wyndham
Carlton Hill
Spirit Hills

Montgomery
Is.
KUNMUNYA
● Drysdale River
Home Valley
RD
Prison Tree ★
56
PARRY
LAGOONS
N.R.
HIDDEN
VALLEY
N.P.
KEEP RIVER
N.P.

Collier
Bay
PANTIJAN
● Pantijan
Ellenbrae
Durack River
Roadhouse
The
Grotto ★
VICTORIA
45
58
HWY

DEFENCE
TRAINING AREA
246
● Kunununurra
Lake Argyle
Village
Rosewood

Oobagooma
Charnley
Tabletop Mt
Mt Elizabeth
GIBB
RIVER
El Questro
● Karunjie
● Woolah
DOON
DOON
151
Glen Hill
Argyle
Diamond Mine
Lissadell
Waterloo

Meda
Napier
Downs
GIBB
306
Gibb River
108
Mt Barnett
Roadhouse
MALNGIN

Kimberley
Downs
Silent
Grove
Mt House
Mt Broome
931+
Imintji
Glenroy
Mt Ord 937
Mt Brennan
Tableland
Bedford
Downs
Mabel Downs
Castlereagh
River
Warmun
(Turkey Ck)
Texas Downs
Spring Creek
Mistake
Creek

Curtin RAAF
Base
● Blina
● Blina
TUNNEL
CREEK N.P.
LEOPOLD DOWNS
Leopold
Downs
Fairfield
Mornington
Lansdowne
Mt Wells
983
VIOLET
VALLEY
162
Echidna Chasm
Cathedral
Gorge
PURNULULU
N.P.
Ord River
Regeneration
Research Stn.
Kirkimbie

GREAT
Camballin
214
Looma
NORTHERN
BROOKING GORGE C.P.
GEIKIE GORGE N.P.
Fossil Downs
Alice
Downs
Springvale
Russian Jack
Memorial
Halls
Creek ●
Old Halls Creek
(ruin)
175
Flora Valley
Bunda
Birrindudu
HWY
BUNTINE

Ellendale
Fitzroy Crossing
Mudludja
Mt Amhurst
Lamboo
Koongie
Park
Ruby Plains
DUNCAN
Gordon Downs
(ruin)

NOONKANBAH
Jubilee Downs
Bayulu
MOUNT
PIERRE
LOUISA
DOWNS
Margaret River
Louisa
Downs
Yiyili
288
Mary
Kundat Djaru

Nerrima
Noonkanbah
Ngalangkati
Wangkatjungka
BOHEMIA
DOWNS
Gordon Downs
(ruin)

Kalyeeda
MILLIJIDDIE
Cherrabun

G R E A T
Lake Jones
Lake Lanagan
Lake Betty
Lake McLernon
CARRANYA
● Billiluna
Sturt Creek
YINGUALYALYA

S A N D Y
ROUTE
106
Sturt
TANAMI
ROAD

D E S E R T
Well 48
Well 49
Well 50
BILLILUNA
● Mulan
Balgo
MOUNT
FREDERICK
(No.2)

Well 47
Well 46
Lake Gregory
BALGO
MANGKURURRPA

Well 45
STOCK
Well 44
Lake Dennis
YININGARRA

See page 184
See page 204
See page 208

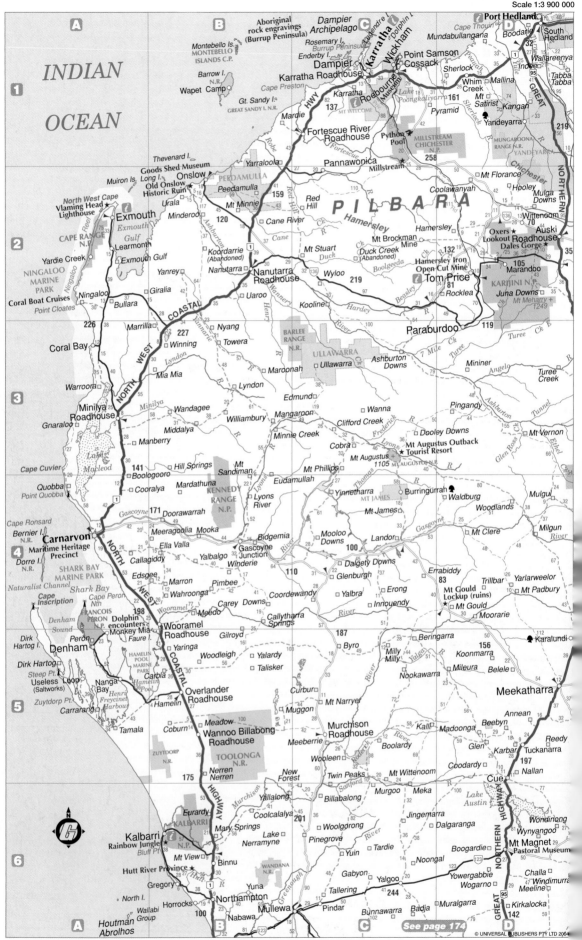

INDIAN

OCEAN

Aboriginal rock engravings (Burrup Peninsula)

Dampier Archipelago

Montebello Is.
MONTEBELLO ISLANDS C.P.

Barrow I.
Wapet Camp

Gt. Sandy Is.
GREAT SANDY I. N.R.

Cape Preston

Port Hedland

Mundabullangana

South Hedland

Wallareenya

Indee

Tabba Tabba

Karratha
Wickham
Point Samson
Cossack

Dampier
Karratha Roadhouse
Roebourne

Sherlock
Whim Creek
Mallina

Karratha
Mardie
Lake Poongkaliyarra
Pyramid

Mt Satirist
Kangan
Yandeyarra

GREAT NORTHERN

Fortescue River Roadhouse

Python Pool

MILLSTREAM CHICHESTER N.P.
258

Mungaboona Range N.R.
YANDEYARRA

Pannawonica
Millstream

Mt Florance
Hooley
Mulga Downs

Thevenard I.
Goods Shed Museum
Muiron Is. Long I.
Old Onslow Historic Ruin
Onslow
PERDAMULLA

Peedamulla
159

Urala

Mt Minnie

Red Hill
Red Hill

Coolawanyah
Wittenoom

North West Cape
Vlaming Head Lighthouse
Exmouth

CAPE RANGE N.P.
Exmouth Gulf
Learmonth
Exmouth Gulf

Minderoo

Cane River

P I L B A R A

Hamersley
Hamersley

Oxers Lookout
Auski Roadhouse
Dales Gorge

Koordarrie (Abandoned)
Nanutarra

Mt Stuart
Duck

Mt Brockman Mine
Duck Creek (Abandoned)

132

KARIJINI N.P.
105
Marandoo

NINGALOO MARINE PARK

Yanrey

Nanutarra Roadhouse

Wyloo
219

Hamersley Iron Open Cut Mine
Tom Price
81
Rocklea

Juna Downs
Mt Meharry 1249

Coral Boat Cruises
Point Cloates

Yardie Creek

Ningaloo
Bullara

Giralia

Uaroo

Kooline
Hardey

Paraburdoo
119

Turee

Turee Creek

226

Marrilla
227

Nyang
Towera

BARLEE RANGE N.R.

Ashburton Downs

Mininer

Angelo

Coral Bay

Winning

Maroonah

ULLAWARRA
Ullawarra

7 Mile

Pingandy

Mt Vernon

Warroora

Mia Mia
Lyndon

Edmund

Wanna

Ashburton

NORTH WEST COASTAL

Minilya Roadhouse
Gnaraloo

Wandagee
Middalya
Manberry

Williambury
Mangaroon
Minnie Creek

Clifford Creek
Cobra

Dooley Downs

Mt Vernon

Glen Ross

Cape Cuvier
Quobba
Point Quobba

Lake Macleod

141
Boologooro

Hill Springs

Mardathuna

KENNEDY RANGE N.P.

Mt Sandiman

Lyons River

Eudamullah

Mt Phillips

Mt Augustus
1105 MT AUGUSTUS N.P.

Mt Augustus Outback Tourist Resort

Mulgul

Milgun

Cape Ronsard
Bernier I. N.R.

171
Doorawarrah

Cooralya

Yinnetharra
Mt James

Burringurrah
Waldburg
Woodlands

Carnarvon
Maritime Heritage Precinct

Dorre I. N.R.

SHARK BAY MARINE PARK

Meeragoolia
Mooka
Ella Valla
Callagiddy
Edsgee
Marron

Yalbalgo
Winderie

Bidgemia
Gascoyne Junction

Mooloo Downs
Landor

100

Mt Clere
Mt James

Errabiddy
83

Trillbar
Mt Gould

Yarlarweelor
Mt Padbury

Naturalist Channel
Cape Inscription
Cape Peron Nth
FRANCOIS PERON N.P.

Shark Bay
Monkey Mia
Denham
Peron
Faure I.

Pimbee
Wahroonga
Meedo

110

Glenburgh
Daigety Downs

Erong

Mt Gould Lockup (ruins)

Moorarie

Dirk Hartog I.

Dirk Hartog

HAMELIN POOL MARINE PARK

Wooramel Roadhouse

198

Yaringa
Woodleigh

Carey Downs
Coordewandy
Callytharra Springs

Yalbra
Innouendy

Karalundi

Steep Pt.
Useless Loop (Saltworks)
Zuytdorp Pt.

Nanga Bay

Gilroyd

187

Byro

Milly Milly

Beringarra
Koonmarra

156

Carrarang
Henri Freycinet Harbour

Hamelin
Carbla

Talisker
Yalardy

Nookawarra
Mileura
Belele

Tamala

Overlander Roadhouse

Curbur

Muggon

Mt Narryer

Annean
Beebyn

Meekatharra

Reedy

Coburn
Meadow
100

Wannoo Billabong Roadhouse

Meeberrie

Murchison Roadhouse

Kalli
Madoonga

Glen
Karbar

Tuckanarra
197

Nallan

ZUYTDORP N.R.

TOOLONGA N.R.

Nerren Nerren

Wooleen

Boolardy

Coodardy

Cue

175

New Forest

Twin Peaks

Mt Wittenoom

Lake Austin

NORTHERN

Eurardy

KALBARRI

Yallalong

Billabong

Murgoo
Meka

123

Wondinong
Wynyangoo

Kalbarri
Rainbow Jungle
Bluff Pt

KALBARRI N.P.

Mary Springs
Coolcalalya
201

Lake Nerramyne

Woolgorong

Jingemarra

Dalgaranga

Boogardie

Mt Magnet
Pastoral Museum

Mt View
Binnu

Pinegrove

Yuin

Tardie

Noongal

Yowergabbie
Wogarno

Challa
Windimurra
Meeline

Hutt River Province

Gregory
North I.

Yuna

Gabyon

Yalgoo

Tallering

244

NORTHERN

Kirkalocka

Horrocks

Northampton
Nabawa

Pindar

Bunnawarra

Badja

Muralgarra

142

Wallabi Group

Houtman Abrolhos

100

Mullewa

See page 174

GREAT

© UNIVERSAL PUBLISHERS PTY LTD 2004

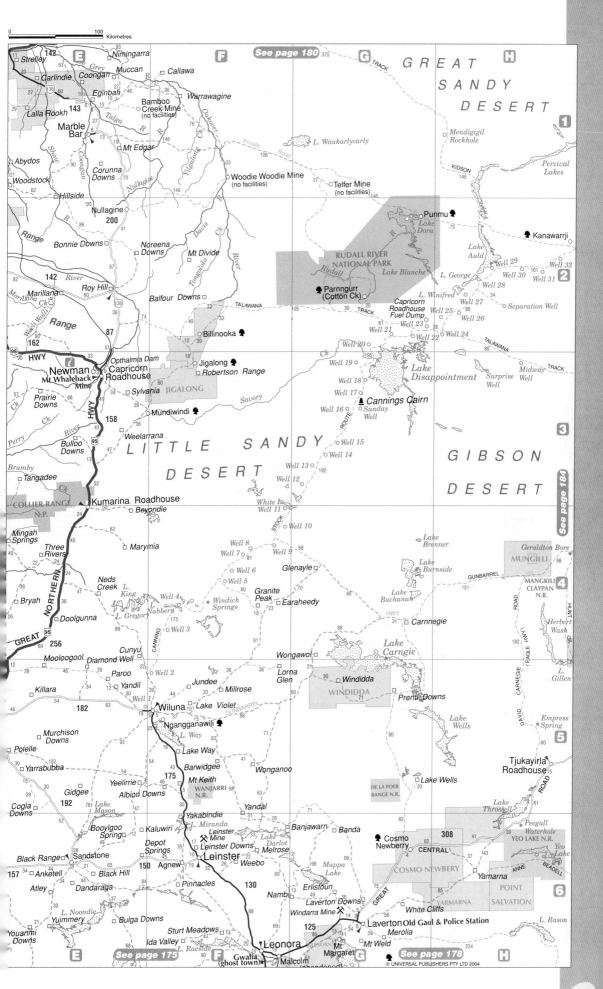

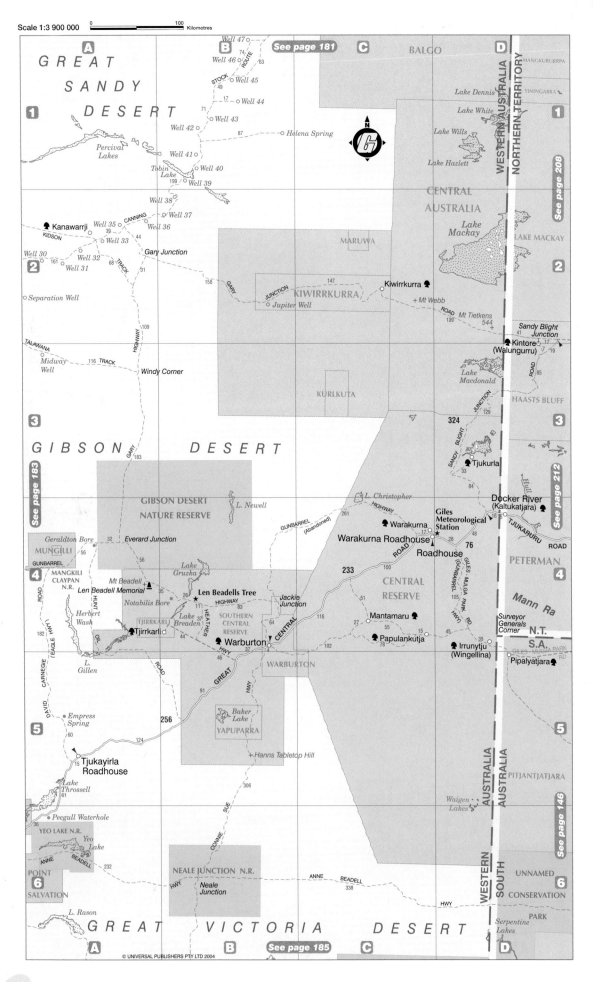

Scale 1:3 900 000

GREAT SANDY DESERT

See page 181

BALGO

Mangkururrpa

Yiningarra

Lake Dennis
Lake White
Lake Wills
Lake Hazlett

WESTERN AUSTRALIA
NORTHERN TERRITORY

See page 208

Well 47
Well 46
Well 45
Well 44
Well 43
Well 42
Well 41
Well 40
Well 39
Well 38
Well 37
Well 36
Well 35
Well 33
Well 32
Well 31
Well 30

STOCK ROUTE
KIDSON
CANNING

Kanawarrji
Gary Junction

Separation Well

CENTRAL AUSTRALIA

Lake Mackay

LAKE MACKAY

Helena Spring

MARUWA

KIWIRRKURRA
Jupiter Well
JUNCTION

Kiwirrkurra
+ Mt Webb
ROAD   Mt Tietkens
544 +

Sandy Blight Junction
Kintore (Walungurru)

GARY
HIGHWAY
TALAWANA
Midway Well
Windy Corner

KURLKUTA

Lake Macdonald

HAASTS BLUFF

GIBSON DESERT

L. Newell

L. Christopher

324

Tjukurla

See page 212

GIBSON DESERT NATURE RESERVE

GUNBARREL (Abandoned)

Highway
Warakurna
Giles Meteorological Station
Warakurna Roadhouse
Roadhouse

Docker River (Kaltukatjara)

TJUKARURU ROAD

PETERMAN

Geraldton Bore
MUNGILLI
GUNBARREL
MANGKILI CLAYPAN N.R.

Everard Junction

Lake Gruzka

Mt Beadell
Len Beadell Memorial
Notabilis Bore

Herbert Wash

TJIRRKARLI

Len Beadells Tree

HIGHWAY
SOUTHERN CENTRAL RESERVE

Lake Breaden
Tjirrkarli
L. Gillen

HUNT
HEATHER

Jackie Junction

CENTRAL RESERVE

Mantamaru
Papulankutja

Irrunytju (Wingellina)
Pipalyatjara

Mann Ra
Surveyor Generals Corner
N.T.
S.A.

GILES-MULGA PARK RD

Warburton

WARBURTON

GREAT
CARNEGIE (EAGLE HWY)
DAVID

Empress Spring

Baker Lake
YAPUPARRA

Hanns Tabletop Hill

PITJANTJATJARA

WESTERN AUSTRALIA
SOUTH AUSTRALIA

Tjukayirla Roadhouse

Lake Throssell

Peegull Waterhole

YEO LAKE N.R.
Yeo Lake

CONNIE SUE

Waigen Lakes

POINT SALVATION
ANNE BEADELL

NEALE JUNCTION N.R.
Neale Junction

ANNE   BEADELL
HWY

UNNAMED CONSERVATION PARK

Serpentine Lakes

L. Rason

GREAT   VICTORIA   DESERT

See page 185

See page 146

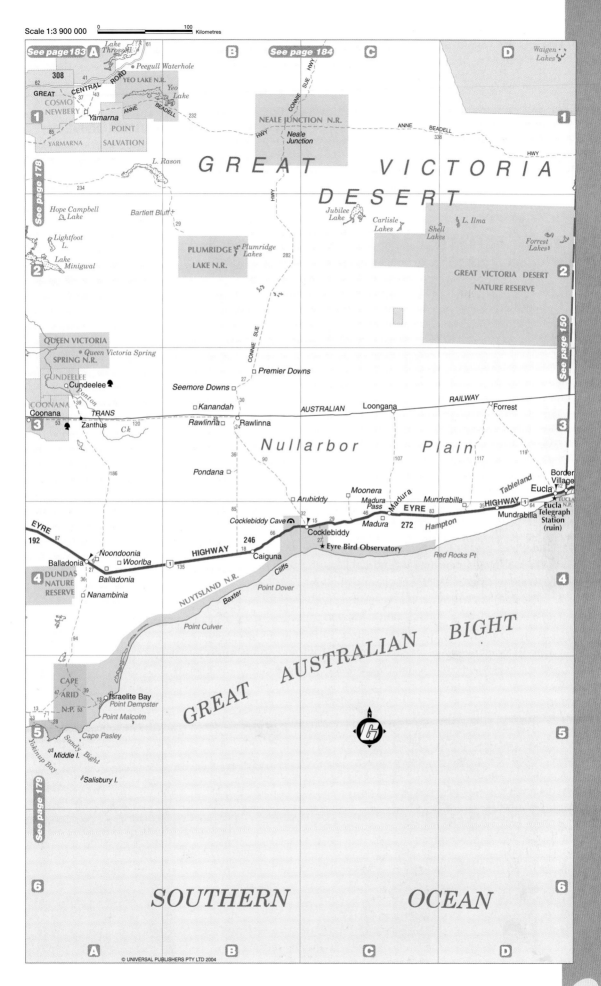

Scale 1:3 900 000

0   100   Kilometres

See page 183

A

B

See page 184

C

D

Waigen Lakes

Lake Throssell

• Peegull Waterhole

308

GREAT CENTRAL ROAD

YEO LAKE N.R.

Yeo Lake

See page 178

COSMO NEWBERY

GREAT

Yamarna

POINT SALVATION

YARMARNA

ANNE

BEADELL

232

ANNE

BEADELL

338

HWY

1

NEALE JUNCTION N.R.

Neale Junction

HWY

CONNIE SUE HWY

G R E A T   V I C T O R I A

D E S E R T

L. Rason

Hope Campbell Lake

Bartlett Bluff

234

29

Jubilee Lake

Carlisle Lakes

Shell Lakes

L. Ilma

Forrest Lakes

Lightfoot L.

Lake Minigwal

PLUMRIDGE LAKE N.R.

Plumridge Lakes

282

GREAT VICTORIA DESERT NATURE RESERVE

2

See page 150

QUEEN VICTORIA SPRING N.R.

• Queen Victoria Spring

Premier Downs

CONNIE SUE

27

GUNDEELEE

Cundeelee ♣

Seemore Downs □

30

□ Kanandah

AUSTRALIAN

Loongana

RAILWAY

Forrest

COONANA

Ponton

TRANS

Zanthus

Ck

120

□ Rawlinna

Rawlinna

24

N u l l a r b o r   P l a i n

107

117

119

Coonana

53

39

3

186

36

Pondana □

90

Moonera

Madura Pass

Madura

Mundrabilla

Tableland

Eucla

Border Village

EUCLA N.P.

□ Arubiddy

85

32

15

29

46

EYRE

83

35

HIGHWAY

Eucla

Cocklebiddy Cave ☉

246

66

Madura

272

Hampton

Mundrabilla

Eucla Telegraph Station (ruin)

EYRE

192

87

Noondoonia

□ Woorlba

HIGHWAY

18

Caiguna

★ Eyre Bird Observatory

Red Rocks Pt

135

27

Balladonia

6

27

Balladonia

Cliffs

Point Dover

DUNDAS NATURE RESERVE

36

□ Nanambinia

NUYTSLAND N.R.

Baxter

Point Culver

4

94

G R E A T   A U S T R A L I A N   B I G H T

CAPE ARID

N.P.

47

39

53

13

Israelite Bay

Point Dempster

13

13

7

28

Point Malcolm

Cape Pasley

See page 179

Torkinup Bay

Middle I.   Sandy Bight

Salisbury I.

S O U T H E R N

O C E A N

5

6

A

B

C

D

Western Australia   **185**

Bunbury

Rose Hotel

Main Attractions

◈ **Australind** This historic town is popular for boating, sailing, fishing, prawning, crabbing and windsurfing.

◈ **Bunbury** Bunbury offers a cosmopolitan seaside atmosphere of beaches, cafes, shopping, and nature-based attractions.

◈ **Dolphin Discovery Centre** Experience the sight and sounds of these amazing creatures through an audiovisual show.

◈ **Koombana Bay dolphins** The bay is famed for the dolphins which frolic in its protected waters.

◈ **Mangrove Boardwalk** Bunbury's white mangroves are estimated to be 20,000 years old.

◈ **Old Goldfields Orchard and Cider Factory** See the workings of Donnybrook's historic gold-rush era and sample brews at the boutique cider factory.

Bunbury is the capital of the region known as the South West, and marks the point where the warm Indian Ocean waters collide with those of the cooler Southern Ocean. This area is renowned for its abundant wildlife as well as its bountiful rivers.

The city was named more than 150 years ago after Lt Henry William St Pierre Bunbury, who was sent to further explore the region in 1836. It is now an excellent base for visitors to begin their own regional explorations, although the city itself offers many attractions: a stretch of golden beaches, caves and inlets, beach and sea-fishing opportunities, tranquil lagoons, superior yachting facilities, picturesque picnic spots, and dolphin cruises.

The surrounding hinterland features superb karri forest, pretty orchards, verdant grassland, farm-stay opportunities, and towns known for their fresh produce. Visitors can sample Capel Vale wines; Donnybrook's apples, pears, stone fruit and cider; while Harvey boasts some of WA's best oranges and prime beef.

Manjimup

This region is best known for its karri forests and is home to the 'Four Aces' – four giant karri trees more than 400 years old – and the 'King Jarrah', estimated to be 600 years old. Other karri trees are nearly as ancient and up to 75m tall.

Swimming with dolphins

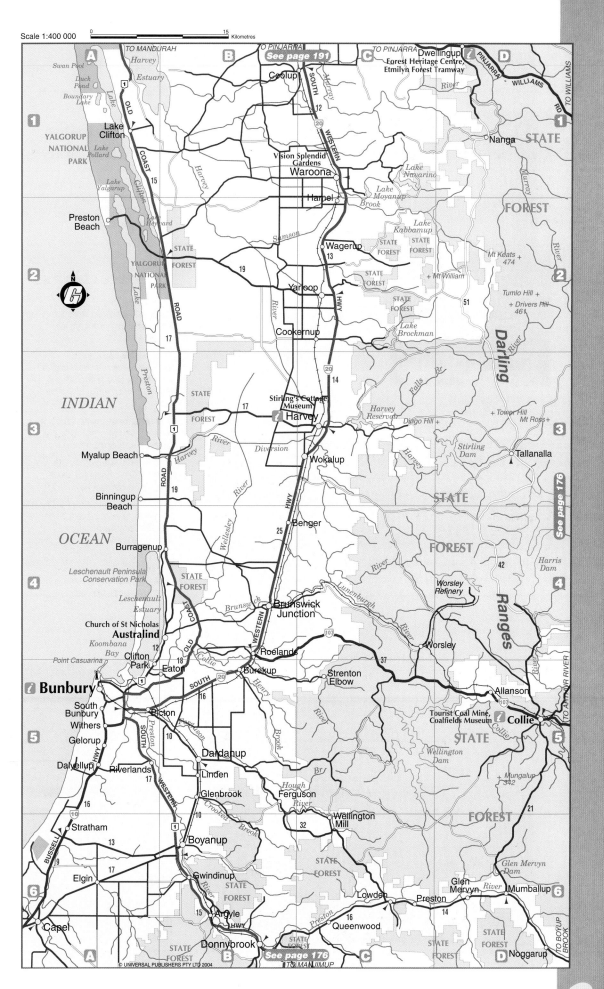

Scale 1:400 000

0   15
Kilometres

A

TO MANDURAH

Swan Pool
Duck Pond
Boundary Lake

Harvey Estuary

TO PINJARRA
See page 191

TO PINJARRA
Dwellingup
Forest Heritage Centre,
Etmilyn Forest Tramway

D

TO WILLIAMS

B

Coolup

Harvey River

1

YALGORUP
NATIONAL
PARK

Lake Clifton

Lake Pollard

Lake Yalgorup

Nanga

STATE

1

Vision Splendid
Gardens

Waroona

Lake Navarino

Murray River

FOREST

Harpel

Lake Moyanup Brook

Preston Beach

Lake Heyward

STATE FOREST

Samson River

Wagerup

13

Lake Kabbamup

STATE FOREST

STATE FOREST

Mt Keats 474

2

YALGORUP NATIONAL PARK

19

Yarloop

STATE FOREST

+ Mt William

Tumlo Hill +
+ Drivers Hill 461

51

2

Lake Brockman

STATE FOREST

17

Cookernup

Darling

INDIAN

ROAD

14

20

Falls Br.

Tower Hill +
Mt Ross +

3

State Forest

17

Stirling's Cottage Museum

Harvey

Harvey Reservoir

Dingo Hill +

Stirling Dam

Tallanalla

Myalup Beach

Harvey River

Diversion

Wokalup

Harvey

STATE

3

Binningup Beach

19

Wellesley River

25

Benger

River

FOREST

42

Harris Dam

4

OCEAN

Leschenault Peninsula
Conservation Park

Burragenup

STATE FOREST

Brunswick River

Brunswick Junction

Lunenburgh River

Worsley Refinery

Ranges

4

Leschenault Estuary

Church of St Nicholas

Australind

12

COAST

OLD

Collie River

Roelands

107

Worsley

River

Koombana Bay

Point Casuarina

Clifton Park

Eaton

18

Burekup

Strenton Elbow

37

Allanson

107

5

Bunbury

SOUTH

20

Henry River

Tourist Coal Mine,
Coalfields Museum

Collie

5

South Bunbury

Picton

16

Brook

STATE

TO ARTHUR RIVER

Collie River

Withers

Gelorup

10

Dardanup

Wellington Dam

Dalyellup

Riverlands

Linden

Hough Br.

Ferguson River

Mungalup 342

17

Glenbrook

32

Wellington Mill

FOREST

21

6

16

Stratham

WESTERN

10

Crooked Brook

1

STATE FOREST

Glen Mervyn Dam

13

Boyanup

Glen Mervyn

Mumballup

6

9

Elgin

17

Gwindinup

River

STATE FOREST

Lowden

Preston

14

15

Argyle

HWY

Preston River

Queenwood

16

STATE FOREST

Capel

STATE FOREST

Donnybrook

See page 176

TO MANJIMUP

TO BOYUP BROOK

Noggarup

BUSSELL

A

© UNIVERSAL PUBLISHERS PTY LTD 2004

B

C

D

The Caves District boasts spectacular and varied attractions: one of the world's most extensive limestone cave systems, one of Australia's most dynamic wine-producing regions, and coastline that is a beacon for surfers from around the world.

The region is known as the 'Cape to Cape' area due to its swathe of promontories, from Cape Naturaliste in the north to Cape Leeuwin in the south.

It is an ideal holiday destination, with a winning combination of caves and

Cape Leeuwin Lighthouse

rolling pastures in the hinterland, bordered by a beautiful coastline of reefs and bays, with wineries, sophisticated restaurants and gourmet produce stores dotted in between.

Margaret River wines have quickly gained an international reputation for character and quality, and the region's many wineries produce varieties including chardonnay, sauvignon blanc, cabernet and merlot.

The infamous Roaring Forties winds create challenging surf conditions, and waves of up to six metres can greet competitors in the Salomon Margaret River Masters, held in late March. In contrast, the tranquil waters of Geographe Bay attract anglers, water-skiers, snorkellers and beach-lovers, while the network of some 300 caves draws abseilers, cavers, and bushwalkers from around the globe.

Tourist information

 Margaret River Visitor Centre

Bussell Hwy,
Margaret River WA 6285
Ph: (08) 9757 2911
www.margaretriver.com

Main Attractions

◈ **Augusta**
This beautiful fishing town is surrounded by pristine countryside.

◈ **Busselton**
With 30km of white sandy beaches, this seaside resort town also features the 2km-long Busselton Jetty.

◈ **Dunsborough** Home of the *HMAS Swan* dive wreck, peaceful coves, and gateway to the Leeuwin-Naturaliste National Park.

◈ **Jewel Cave** Regarded as the region's best cave, it features complex formations such as helictites.

◈ **Lake Cave** Guarded by an ancient karri tree, the cave features a unique table suspended over a subterranean lake.

◈ **Margaret River** The success of the vineyards here, only established in the early 1970s, is legendary world-wide.

The Magical Cave System

Weathering over the eons has resulted in the formation of caves in the long limestone range between Cape Leeuwin and Cape Naturaliste. Of the 120–200 known caves, seven of the most spectacular are open to the public.

South-west vineyard

0   15   Kilometres

| A | B | C | D |

See page 176

Cape Naturaliste
★ Lighthouse & Museum
Rocky Point
Eagle Bay
★ HMAS Swan dive site
Geographe
Peppermint Grove Beach
Penola
Sugarloaf Rock
Point Picquet
Meelup
TUART FOREST N.P.
HWY

1

LEEUWIN - NATURALISTE NATIONAL PARK
★ Whaling Station Site
Point Darling
Bay
Wonnerup Estuary

Ngilgi Cave
Dunsborough
Quindalup
CAVES
Busselton Jetty, Underwater Observatory, Old Butter Factory Museum
Wonnerup
Vasse Estuary
Ludlow

Yallingup
Quindalup Fauna Park
15
RD
Busselton
Abba
14

Smiths Point
Gunyulgup
Happs
Marybrook
Vasse
8
11
VASSE
6
Sabrina

Canal Rocks
Deep Woods
Yallingup Shearing Shed
Marybrook
8
Ambergate
Yoongarillup
HWY

Cape Clairault
Wildwood
Amberley
Rivendell
18
Carbunup River
River
104

2

LEEUWIN - NATURALISTE NATIONAL PARK
Abbeys
Clairault
STATE FOREST
North Jindong
Jindong
Boallia
Walsall
Acton Park
Range

Driftwood
Yelverton
Island Brook
Becketts Flat
RD

Injidup Point
Mary
Brook
Chapmans Creek
Metricup
Woody Nook
The Grove
Vasse
River
North STATE

Moss Brothers
Walburra
Fermoy
CAVES
Harmans
Hay Shed Hill
Ashbrook
Arlewood
Treeton
Palandri
Whicher
FOREST

Lenton Brae
Moss Wood
Sandalford
Willespie
20
Margaret
SUES

Evans & Tate
Pierro
8
Gralyn
Bettenay
Howard Park
River

Woodlands
Ribbon Vale
Cullen
Stellar Ridge
Cowaramup
Cape Grace

3

Vasse Felix
Juniper
Ellensbrook Homestead
Adinfern
Edwards
Wirring
Osmington
52
FOREST

North Point
Cowaramup Point
Gracetown
LEEUWIN - NATURALISTE NATIONAL PARK
13
ROAD
BUSSELL
10
STATE FOREST
Margaret

INDIAN
Cape Mentelle
Old Settlement Museum
Margaret River
Rosa Brook
STATE

Cape Mentelle
5
Xanadu
Berry Farm
By

Prevelly
Eagle's Heritage
8
Minot
Voyager
9
East Witchcliffe
Marron Farm
Swallows Welcome
Rosa Glen
Rockfield
FOREST

4

Redgate
7
Leeuwin
Witchcliffe
Shell Museum
10
Chapman
Upper Chapman
S.F.

OCEAN
"Georgette" Wreck ★
Mammoth Cave
Forrest Grove
Serventy
Br
Blackwood
FOREST

Lake Cave
Green Valley
250
McLeod
BUSSELL
STATE FOREST
STATE

Cape Freycinet
20
Warner Glen
FOREST

LEEUWIN - NATURALISTE
27
Alexandra Bridge
BROCKMAN
10
HWY
10

5

North Point
NATIONAL
Bonanup Maze
Hamelin Bay
Alexandra Bridge
30

PARK
Karridale
Creek
10
SCOTT NATIONAL PARK

Hamelin Bay
Foul Bay
5
Glenarty
Ck

Knobby Head
Cosy Corner
Cape Hamelin
Kudardup
250
16
ROAD
10
Hardy Inlet
Scott
River
Milyeannup
GINGILUP SWAMPS NATURE RESERVE

Jewel Cave
Hillview Lookout
Historical Museum, Lumen Christi Church
Augusta
Gingilup Swamps

6

LEEUWIN - NATURALISTE NATIONAL PARK
Duke Head
Finders Bay
White Point

Cape Leeuwin
Cape Leeuwin Lighthouse
250
Point Matthew
SOUTHERN OCEAN

Fremantle

'Freo', as it is affectionately known to locals, is Perth's port and maritime playground. It has a lively street life, a thriving cafe culture, and an alternative arts scene amid the workings of a fully functioning port.

Since hosting the 1987 America's Cup, this once sleepy harbour village has become a cosmopolitan tourism and recreation centre. Its renowned markets – such as the National Trust-classified Fremantle Markets and the E Shed Markets – sidewalk cafes and seaside ambience attract weekenders and holiday-makers.

Tourist information

i Fremantle Tourist Bureau

Town Hall, Kings Square, High St
Fremantle WA 6160
Ph: (08) 9431 7878
www.fremantlewesternaustralia.
com

Must Visit

- ◈ Fremantle Fishing Boat Harbour
- ◈ Fremantle History Museum
- ◈ Old Fremantle Prison
- ◈ The Round House
- ◈ WA Maritime Museum

Places of Interest

- Ⓐ Army Museum of WA **E1**
- Ⓑ E Shed Markets **C2**
- Ⓒ Esplanade Hotel **D2**
- Ⓓ Fremantle Fishing Boat Harbour **D3**
- Ⓔ Fremantle History Museum and Arts Centre **E1**
- Ⓕ Fremantle Markets **D2**
- Ⓖ Fremantle Town Hall **C2**
- Ⓗ Shipwreck Museum **C2**
- Ⓘ Old Fremantle Prison **D2**
- Ⓙ Old Fire Station **C2**
- Ⓚ Samson's House Museum **E2**
- Ⓛ Success Harbour **D4**
- Ⓜ The Round House **C2**
- Ⓝ WA Maritime Museum **C2**
- Ⓞ World of Energy **D1**

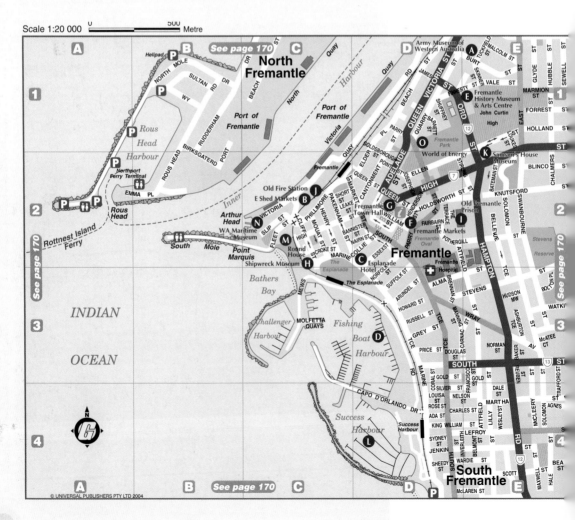

Mandurah-Pinjarra

Peel Inlet

Mandurah-Pinjarra is one hour's drive south of Perth, and encompasses 5700 square kilometres of diverse landscape, from rolling farm pastures and striking jarrah forests in the east, and the calm waters of Peel Inlet and Harvey Estuary in the west, to the white sandy beaches that fringe the Indian Ocean.

The protected inlet waters provide excellent boating, swimming and fishing opportunities, while the foreshores offer scenic picnic spots with BBQ facilities. The long stretches of ocean beaches are perfect for crabbing, prawning, windsurfing, scuba diving and yachting. The area is famous for its blue swimmer crabs and locals look forward to the beginning of the 'crab run', when boat owners armed with drop nets arrive to lure away the bountiful crabs. The region boasts three world-renowned golf courses as well as wineries, white-water rafting on the Murray River, and Yalgorup National Park.

Tourist information

i Mandurah Visitor Centre

75 Mandurah Tce,
Mandurah WA 6210
Ph: (08) 9550 3999
www.peeltour.net.au

Must Visit

◈ Hotham Valley Tourist Railway
◈ Pinjarra Heritage Trail
◈ Harvey Estuary
◈ Peel Inlet
◈ Peel wineries

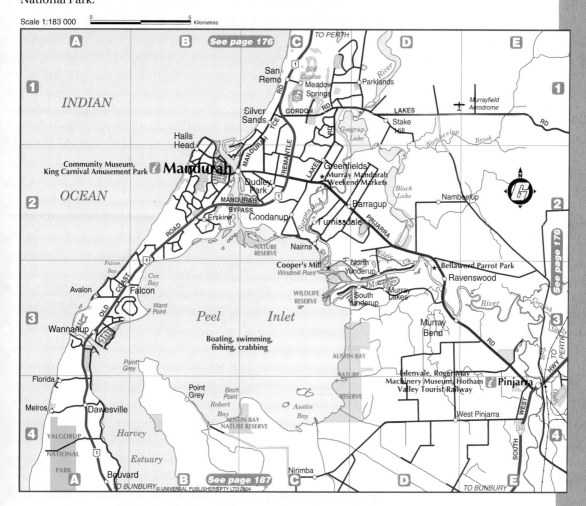

Scale 1:183 000

Rottnest Island

Bathurst Lighthouse

This limestone island is home to a population of quokkas, small indigenous marsupials that were mistakenly identified as rats in 1696 by a Dutch explorer, who subsequently named the island 'Rats' Nest'. Today, holiday-makers join the quokkas on Rottnest Island in their thousands each year. Bicycles are the main mode of transport and are widely available for hire, so there is almost no motorised traffic on the island.

'Rotto', 18km west of Fremantle, is only 11km long and less than half that wide. Its beaches are a major drawcard, as they have crystal-clear water and some of the world's southern-most coral reefs. Over 360 species of fish and 20 species of coral are found within Rottnest's waters, and the sheltered bays provide idyllic conditions for snorkelling, surfing, scuba diving, swimming or just soaking up the sun. Colonial streetscapes and architecture are also a feature of this historic island. With regular connections from Perth and Fremantle by ferry or aeroplane, Rottnest is an ideal day trip destination, and has much to offer visitors who choose to stay longer.

Tourist information

Rottnest Island Visitor and Information Centre

Thomson Bay,
Rottnest Island WA 6161
Ph: (08) 9372 9752
www.rottnest.wa.gov.au

Must Visit

- Rottnest's colonial architecture
- Rottnest Museum
- Historic Oliver Hill light railway
- Thomson Bay

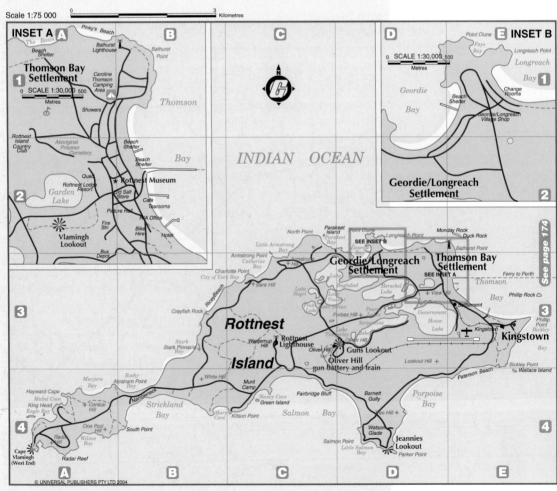

Stirling Range National Park to Albany

Hikers atop Toolbrunup Peak, Stirling Range National Park

Blessed with immense natural beauty, the Great Southern region is ideal for holidaymakers. Its diverse landscape features sweeping rural vistas, rugged coastline, sheltered coves and bays, rivers and dramatic mountain ranges. Unspoilt national parks of majestic karri and tingle forest are dotted with ancient rock formations, while the tranquil bays invite calving southern right and humpback whales to give birth to their young each year. Some of WA's most beautiful wildflowers carpet the granite ranges, which date back 1000 million years and today offer excellent hiking and bushwalking opportunities.

This region was settled before Perth; its de facto capital, Albany was WA's first European settlement, and the site of its original farm still remains. The Great Southern is increasingly feted for its rural charm and regional produce, and is fast becoming one of Australia's largest wine-growing regions, with over 30 wineries to visit.

Tourist information

i Albany Visitor Centre
Old Railway Station,
Proudlove Pde, Albany WA 6330
Ph: (08) 9841 1088
Freecall: 1800 644 088
www.albanygateway.com.au

Must Visit

- Albany Whale World
- Albany Wind Farm
- Middleton Beach
- Mt Barker wine-producing region
- Valley of the Giants Treetop Walk

Scale 1:800 000

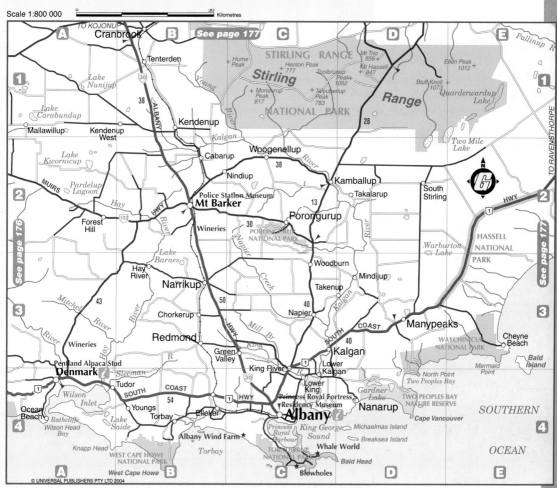

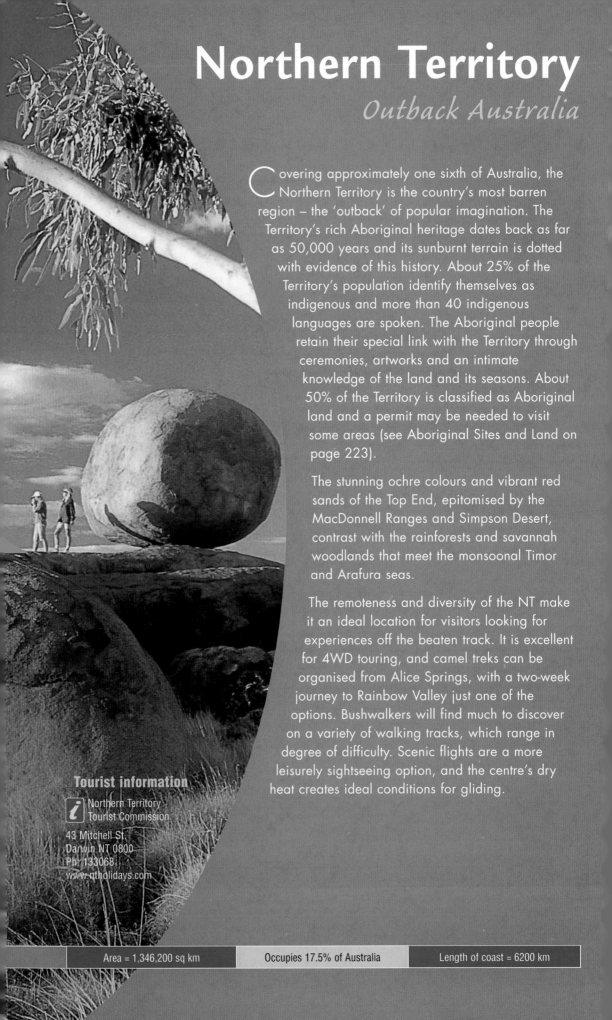

Northern Territory
Outback Australia

Covering approximately one sixth of Australia, the Northern Territory is the country's most barren region – the 'outback' of popular imagination. The Territory's rich Aboriginal heritage dates back as far as 50,000 years and its sunburnt terrain is dotted with evidence of this history. About 25% of the Territory's population identify themselves as indigenous and more than 40 indigenous languages are spoken. The Aboriginal people retain their special link with the Territory through ceremonies, artworks and an intimate knowledge of the land and its seasons. About 50% of the Territory is classified as Aboriginal land and a permit may be needed to visit some areas (see Aboriginal Sites and Land on page 223).

The stunning ochre colours and vibrant red sands of the Top End, epitomised by the MacDonnell Ranges and Simpson Desert, contrast with the rainforests and savannah woodlands that meet the monsoonal Timor and Arafura seas.

The remoteness and diversity of the NT make it an ideal location for visitors looking for experiences off the beaten track. It is excellent for 4WD touring, and camel treks can be organised from Alice Springs, with a two-week journey to Rainbow Valley just one of the options. Bushwalkers will find much to discover on a variety of walking tracks, which range in degree of difficulty. Scenic flights are a more leisurely sightseeing option, and the centre's dry heat creates ideal conditions for gliding.

Tourist information

i Northern Territory
Tourist Commission
43 Mitchell St,
Darwin NT 0800
Ph: 133068
www.ntholidays.com

| Area = 1,346,200 sq km | Occupies 17.5% of Australia | Length of coast = 6200 km |

Northern Territory Key Map & Distance Chart

All distances shown in the chart below have been measured over highways and major roads, not necessarily by the shortest route.

Twin Falls, Kakadu National Park

Approximate Distance	Adelaide River	Alice Springs	Ayers Rock/Yulara	Borroloola	Camooweal QLD	Darwin	Erldunda	HiWay Inn	Jabiru	Katherine	Kulgera	Kununurra WA	Mataranka	Nicholson WA	Pine Creek	Tennant Creek	Ti-Tree	Top Springs	Tobermorey	Wauchope
Adelaide River		1385	1827	860	1293	107	1584	477	288	202	1660	714	313	902	111	407	1180	492	1799	985
Alice Springs	1385		442	1214	988	1492	199	908	1468	1183	275	1695	1070	1464	1274	504	195	1054	570	400
Ayers Rock/Yulara	1827	442		1656	1430	1934	243	1350	1910	1625	319	2137	1512	1906	1716	956	647	1496	1012	842
Borroloola	860	1214	1656		746	967	1413	383	943	658	1489	1151	545	1011	749	700	1009	601	1628	814
Camooweal QLD	1293	988	1430	746		1400	1187	816	1376	1091	1263	1603	978	1372	1182	474	783	962	1402	588
Darwin	107	1492	1934	967	1400		1691	584	243	309	1767	821	422	1009	218	978	1287	599	1906	1092
Erldunda	1584	199	243	1413	1187	1691		1107	1667	1382	76	1803	1269	1663	1473	713	404	1253	760	600
HiWay Inn	477	908	1350	383	816	584	1107		560	275	1183	768	162	628	366	394	703	218	1322	508
Jabiru	288	1468	1910	943	1376	243	1667	560		285	1743	797	398	985	194	954	1263	575	1882	1068
Katherine	202	1183	1625	658	1091	309	1382	275	285		1458	512	113	700	91	669	978	290	1597	783
Kulgera	1660	275	319	1489	1263	1767	76	1183	1743	1458		1879	1345	1739	1549	789	480	1329	845	675
Kununurra WA	714	1695	2137	1151	1603	821	1803	768	797	512	1879		625	319	603	1090	1399	550	2018	1204
Mataranka	313	1070	1512	545	978	422	1269	162	398	113	1345	625		797	197	556	865	380	1484	670
Nicholson WA	902	1464	1906	1011	1372	1009	1663	628	985	700	1739	319	797		791	950	1259	410	1878	1064
Pine Creek	111	1274	1716	749	1182	218	1473	366	194	91	1549	603	197	791		760	1069	381	1688	874
Tennant Creek	407	504	956	700	474	978	713	394	954	669	789	1090	556	950	760		309	540	928	114
Ti-Tree	1180	195	647	1009	783	1287	404	703	1263	978	480	1399	865	1259	1069	309		849	619	195
Top Springs	492	1054	1496	601	962	599	1253	218	575	290	1329	550	380	410	381	540	849		1468	654
Tobermorey	1799	570	1012	1628	1402	1906	769	1322	1882	1597	845	2018	1484	1878	1688	928	619	1468		814
Wauchope	985	400	842	814	588	1092	599	508	1068	783	675	1204	670	1064	874	114	195	654	814	

Darwin

The Territory's capital, perched on a picturesque harbour, is closer to Jakarta and Singapore than it is to Sydney and Melbourne. Home to the Larrak Aboriginal people for thousands of years, it was first settled by Europeans in 1869 when South Australian Surveyor-General Goyder arrived to establish a city in the Top End. Darwin was the terminus for the Overland Telegraph link to England, which began operating in 1872 and provided Darwin's first economic and migrant boom. Darwin now serves primarily as an administrative centre for government and the Australian Defence Force, while tourism is becoming an increasingly important part of the local economy.

Darwin is one of Australia's most modern cities, with few historic buildings remaining after the Japanese air raids during World War II and the devastation caused by Cyclone Tracy on Christmas Day in 1974.

Its isolation and steamy tropical climate give Darwin a relaxed, easygoing atmosphere and way of life. The Mindil Beach Sunset Markets are extremely popular. Held on one of Darwin's favourite beaches, the markets feature food and craft stalls that reflect the city's eclectic multicultural mix. The historic Wharf Precinct was once the domain of anglers and skateboarders; now the old wharves are becoming a tourist attraction, with restaurants, museums and tours.

Sunset on a Darwin beach

Tourist information

Tourism Top End

Cnr Mitchell St & Knuckey St,
Darwin NT 0800
Ph: (08) 8936 2499
www.ntholidays.com

Main Attractions

◈ **Aquascene** Witness the spectacular sight of hundreds of fish – milkfish, mullet, catfish and others – being hand-fed each day at high tide.

◈ **Australian Pearling Exhibition** This exhibit provides an insight into the romance of the local pearling industry.

◈ **Crocodylus Park** This wildlife park offers croc-feeding sessions and the chance to hatch a crocodile egg.

◈ **Darwin Botanic Gardens** Explore 42ha of mangroves, orchids, rainforest, open woodlands and other tropical habitats.

◈ **East Point Reserve** A dusk visit will reveal Fannie Bay's spectacular sunset and mobs of wallabies. The 200ha reserve features natural mangroves, forest, and safe saltwater swimming.

◈ **Indo-Pacific Marine** Boasting living coral reef ecosystems, the night program offers a torchlight tour and seafood buffet dinner.

Juggler at Mindil Beach Sunset Market

Places of Interest

Ⓐ Aquascene **B5**

Ⓑ Australian Pearling Exhibition **D6**

Ⓒ Cenotaph **C5**

Ⓓ Chinese Temple **C5**

Ⓔ Darwin Botanic Gardens **C3**

Ⓕ Darwin Entertainment Centre **B5**

Ⓖ Darwin Wharf Precinct **D6**

Ⓗ Fannie Bay Gaol Museum **B1**

Ⓘ Government House **C6**

Ⓙ Indo Pacific Marine **D6**

Ⓚ MGM Grand Darwin (Casino) **B3**

Ⓛ Mindil Beach Lookout **A3**

Ⓜ Mindil Beach Market **B3**

Ⓝ Museum and Art Gallery of the NT **B2**

Ⓞ Old Court House **C5**

Ⓟ Parliament House **C6**

Ⓠ Smith Street Mall **C5**

Ⓡ Vesteys Beach **B2**

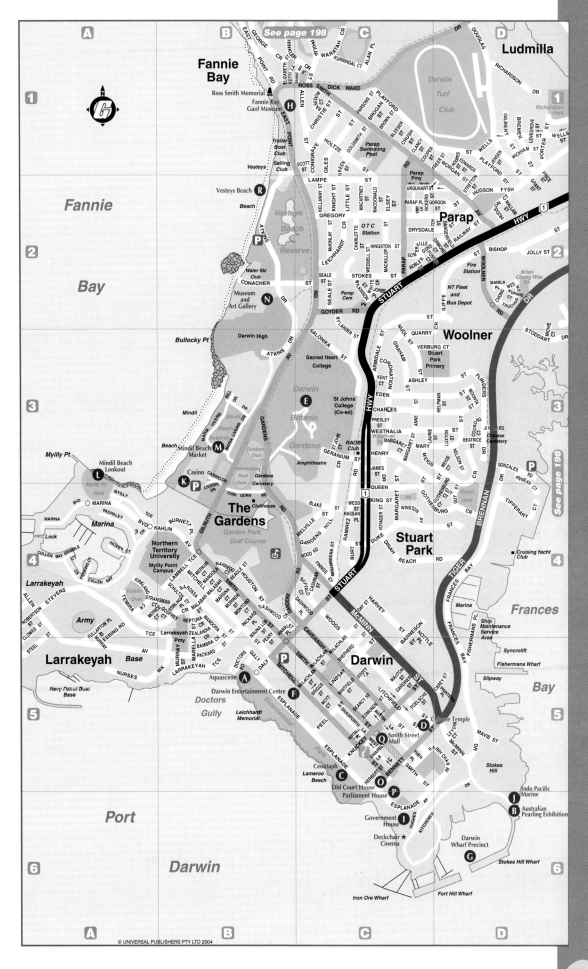

Ludmilla

Darwin Turf Club

Fannie Bay

Ross Smith Memorial
Fannie Bay Gaol Museum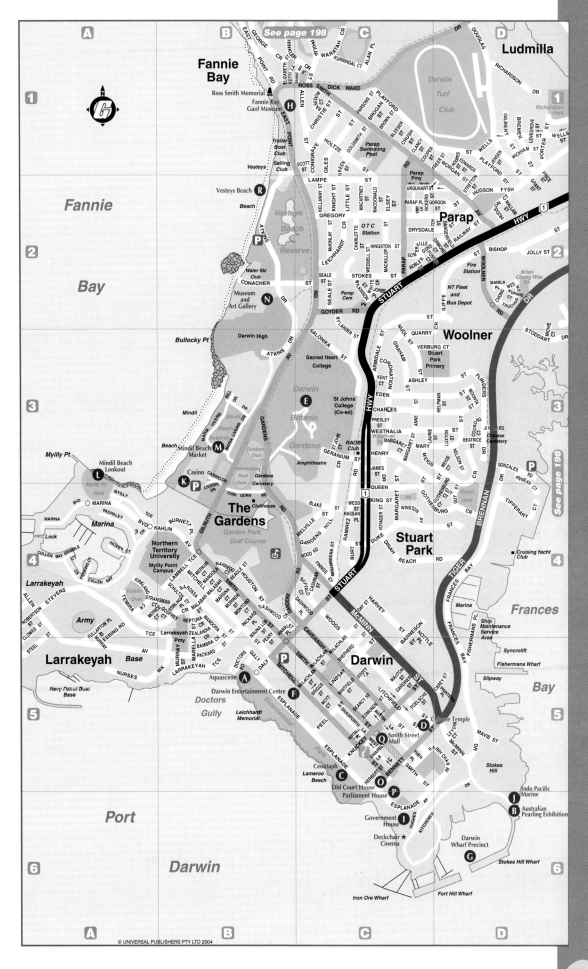

Richardson Park

Trailer Boat Club
Sailing Club

Fannie

Vesteys

Vesteys Beach

Beach

Parap

Parap Swimming Pool

Vesteys Beach Reserve

Bay

Water Ski Club CONACHER

OTC Station

Parap Cem Pk

Museum and Art Gallery

Fire Station

NT Fleet and Bus Depot

Brian Chong Wee Pk

Bullocky Pt

Darwin High

Woolner

Sacred Heart College

VERBURG CT
Stuart Park Primary

Chinese Cemetery

Darwin Botanic Gardens

Mindil Beach

St Johns College (Co-ed)

Mindil Beach Market

RAOB Club

Myilly Pt

Mindil Beach Lookout

Myilly Pt Park

Gardens Oval

Amphitheatre

Casino

Palmerston Park Oval

Gardens Cemetery

Marina

The Gardens

Clubhouse

Stuart Park

Garden Park Golf Course

Northern Territory University
Myilly Point Campus

Kahlin Oval

Cruising Yacht Club

Larrakeyah

Army Base

Marina

Ship Maintenance Service Area

Syncrolift

Frances

Navy Patrol Boat Base

Larrakeyah

Fishermans Wharf

Slipway

Bay

Aquascene

Darwin Entertainment Centre

Doctors Gully

Leichhardt Memorial

Darwin

Chinese Temple

Smith Street Mall

Stokes Hill

Bicentennial Park

Cenotaph

Lameroo Beach

Old Court House
Parliament House

Indo Pacific Marine
Australian Pearling Exhibition

Port

Government House

Deckchair Cinema

Darwin Wharf Precinct

Darwin

Stokes Hill Wharf

Iron Ore Wharf

Fort Hill Wharf

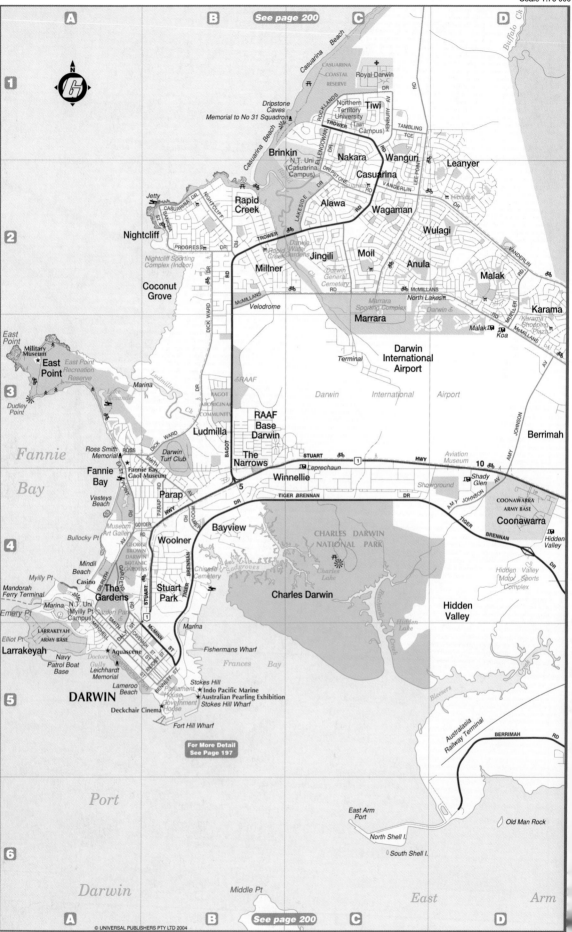

Royal Darwin

CASUARINA
COASTAL
RESERVE

Casuarina Beach

Buffalo Ck

Dripstone
Caves
Memorial to No 31 Squadron

Northern
Territory
University
(Tiwi
Campus)

Tiwi

TAMBLING
TCE

Brinkin

N.T. Uni
(Casuarina
Campus)

Nakara

Wanguri

Leanyer

Casuarina

Jetty

**Rapid
Creek**

Alawa

Wagaman

Wulagi

Nightcliff

Nightcliff Sporting
Complex (Indoor)

Millner

Jingili

Moil

Anula

Malak

**Coconut
Grove**

Darwin
Water
Gardens

Rapid
Creek

Darwin
General
Cemetery

Marrara

Marrara
Sporting
Complex

North Lakes

Darwin

Karama

Velodrome

Malak

Koa

Karama
Shopping
Plaza

East
Point

Military
Museum

**East
Point**

East Point
Recreation
Reserve

Terminal

**Darwin
International
Airport**

Marina

Dudley
Point

BAGOT
ABORIGINAL
COMMUNITY

Darwin

International

Airport

Ludmilla

**RAAF
Base
Darwin**

Berrimah

Fannie

Ross Smith
Memorial

**Fannie
Bay**

Darwin
Turf Club

**The
Narrows**

Leprechaun

HWY

Aviation
Museum

10

Bay

Fannie Bay
Gaol Museum

Vesteys
Beach

Parap

Museum
Art Gallery

Woolner

GEORGE
BROWN
DARWIN
BOTANIC
GARDENS

Winnellie

5

Shady
Glen

Showground

COONAWARRA
ARMY BASE

Coonawarra

TIGER BRENNAN

Bayview

CHARLES DARWIN
NATIONAL PARK

Charles
Lake

Hidden
Valley
Motor
Sports
Complex

Hidden
Valley

Myilly Pt

Mindil
Beach

Casino

**The
Gardens**

Garden Park

N.T. Uni
(Myilly Pt)
Campus)

Bullocky Pt

**Stuart
Park**

Chinese
Cemetery

Charles Darwin

Hidden
Lake

**Hidden
Valley**

Mandorah
Ferry Terminal

Marina

Emery Pt

Elliot Pt

LARRAKEYAH
ARMY BASE

Larrakeyah

Navy
Patrol Boat
Base

Aquascene

Doctors
Gully

Leichhardt
Memorial

Marina

Fishermans Wharf

Frances   Bay

Blue

BERRIMAH
RD

Lameroo
Beach

DARWIN

Parliament
House
Government
House

Stokes Hill
Indo Pacific Marine
Australian Pearling Exhibition
Stokes Hill Wharf

Deckchair Cinema

Fort Hill Wharf

East Arm
Port

Australasia
Railway Terminal

Old Man Rock

For More Detail
See Page 197

North Shell I.

South Shell I.

Port

Darwin

Middle Pt

East   **Arm**

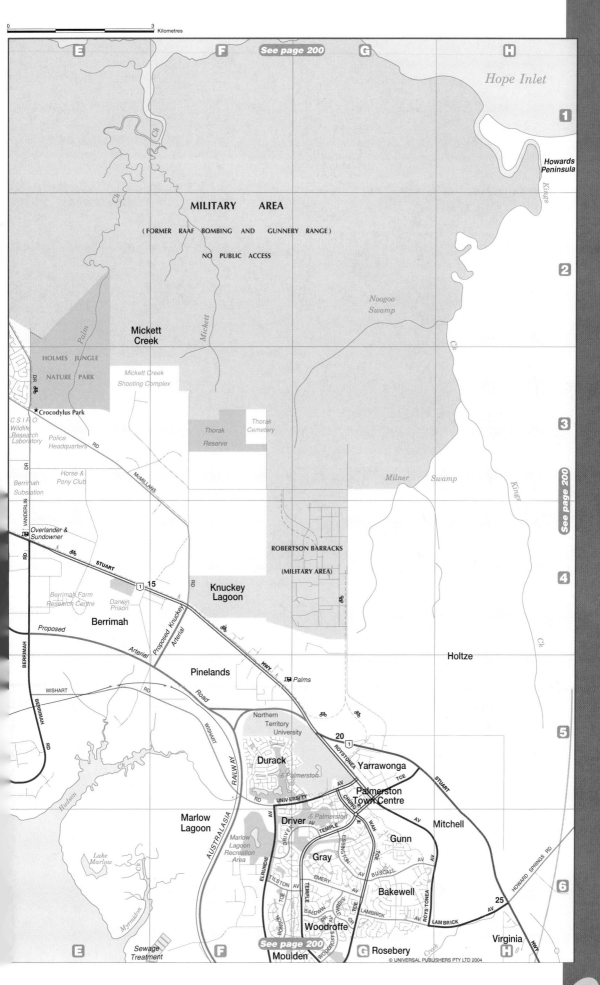

E   F   *See page 200*   G   H

Hope Inlet

1

*Howards
Peninsula*

MILITARY   AREA

(FORMER   RAAF   BOMBING   AND   GUNNERY   RANGE)

NO   PUBLIC   ACCESS

2

*Noogoo
Swamp*

**Mickett
Creek**

HOLMES   JUNGLE

NATURE   PARK

*Mickett Creek
Shooting Complex*

★ Crocodylus Park

C S I R O
*Wildlife
Research
Laboratory*

*Thorak
Reserve*

*Thorak
Cemetery*

3

*Police
Headquarters*

Milner   *Swamp*

*Berrimah
Substation*

*Horse &
Pony Club*

*Overlander &
Sundowner*

ROBERTSON BARRACKS

(MILITARY AREA)

4

STUART

1   **15**

*Berrimah Farm
Research Centre*

*Darwin
Prison*

**Knuckey
Lagoon**

Berrimah

Proposed

Arterial

Holtze

*Proposed Knuckey
Arterial*

WISHART

Pinelands

HWY

Palms

Road

WISHART   RD

Northern
Territory
University

5

20

1

Hudson

Durack

Yarrawonga

TCE

*Lake
Marlow*

**Marlow
Lagoon**

AUSTRALASIA   RAILWAY

RD

UNIVERSITY

S Palmerston

**Palmerston
Town Centre**

STUART

S Palmerston

Driver

AV

Mitchell

HOWARD SPRINGS RD

*Marlow
Lagoon
Recreation
Area*

Myrmidon

Gray

Gunn

TEMPLE

BUSCALL

Bakewell

6

ELRUNDIE

TILSTON   TCE

EMERY

LAMBRICK

25

*Sewage
Treatment*

Woodroffe

See page 200

Roseberry

Virginia

HWY

E   F   **Moulden**   G   H

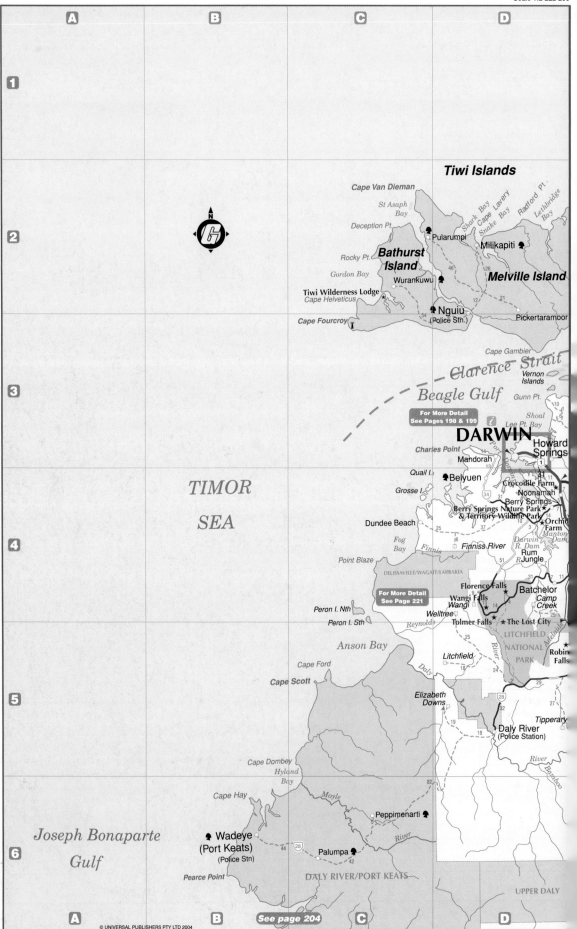

Scale 1:2 222 200

Tiwi Islands

Cape Van Dieman

St Asaph Bay

Deception Pt.

Shark Bay
Cape Lavery
Snake Bay
Radford Pt.
Lethbridge Bay

♠ Pularumpi

Milikapiti ♠

Rocky Pt. **Bathurst Island**

Gordon Bay

46

126 **Melville Island**

Wurankuwu

Tiwi Wilderness Lodge
Cape Helveticus

12

21

♠ Nguiu
(Police Stn.)

54

Cape Fourcroy

Pickertaramoor

Cape Gambier

Clarence Strait

Vernon Islands

Beagle Gulf

Gunn Pt.

10

Shoal
Lee Pt. Bay

For More Detail
See Pages 198 & 199 *i*

DARWIN

Howard Springs

Charles Point

1

Mandorah

13

11

Quail I.

♠ Belyuen

Crocodile Farm

Grosse I.

31

Noonamah
Berry Springs
Berry Springs Nature Park ★
& Territory Wildlife Park

34

14

Orchid Farm

Dundee Beach

25

37

Manton Dam

3

1

Fog Bay

Finniss

16

□ Finniss River

Darwin R. Dam

Rum Jungle

TIMOR

SEA

51

Point Blaze

DELISSAVILLE/WAGAIT/LARRAKIA

11

Florence Falls

Batchelor

For More Detail
See Page 221

Wangi Falls
Wangi
13 14

Camp Creek

Peron I. Nth

Welltree

★ The Lost City

Peron I. Sth

Reynolds

Tolmer Falls

25

LITCHFIELD

★

Anson Bay

25

Daly

NATIONAL

Robin Falls

Cape Ford

Litchfield

□
18

River

PARK

24

Cape Scott

Elizabeth Downs

29

28

27

19

32

Tipperary

18

Daly River
(Police Station)

Cape Dombey
Hyland Bay

River

Bamboo

82

Cape Hay

Moyle

Joseph Bonaparte

Peppimenarti ♠

River

Gulf

♠ Wadeye
(Port Keats)
(Police Stn)

44

28

Palumpa ♠

42

Pearce Point

DALY RIVER/PORT KEATS

UPPER DALY

See page 204

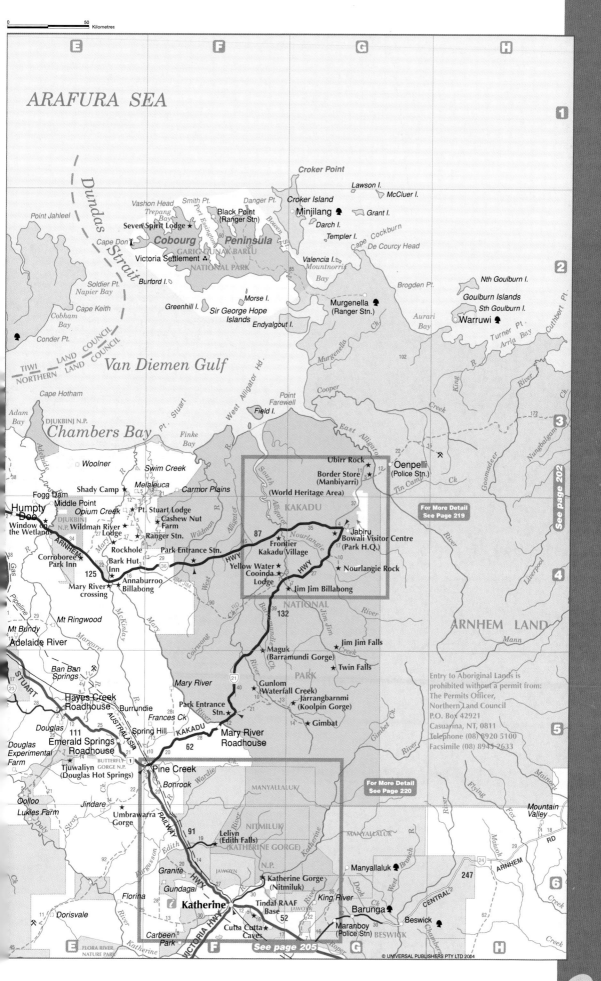

ARAFURA SEA

Dundas Strait

Point Jahleel

Croker Point

Lawson I.   McCluer I.

Vashon Head
Trepang Bay   Smith Pt.   Danger Pt.   Croker Island
Seven Spirit Lodge ★   Black Point   Minjilang ♣
                                   (Ranger Stn.)   Darch I.   Grant I.
Cape Don   Cobourg   Peninsula   Templer I.   Cape Cockburn   De Courcy Head
Victoria Settlement ♣   GARIG GUNAK BARLU
                                   NATIONAL PARK   Valencia I.
Soldier Pt.   Burford I.   Mountnorris   Nth Goulburn I.
Napier Bay   Bay   Goulburn Islands
Cape Keith   Greenhill I.   Morse I.   Aurari   Sth Goulburn I.
Cobham   Sir George Hope   Murgenella ♣   Bay   Warruwi ♣
Bay   Islands   Endyalgout I.   (Ranger Stn.)   Turner Pt.
♣   Conder Pt.   Arra Bay   Cuthbert Pt.

TIWI   NORTHERN   LAND COUNCIL   LAND COUNCIL

Van Diemen Gulf

Cape Hotham   Point   Cooper   King   River   102   172
                    Farewell
Adam   DJUKBINJ N.P.   West Alligator Rd.   Field I.
Bay   Chambers Bay   Pt. Stuart   Finke   East   Alligator
          Bay
                    Woolner   Swim Creek   Ubirr Rock ★   Oenpelli
          Shady Camp   Melaleuca   Carmor Plains   Border Store   (Police Stn.)
          Middle Point   Opium Creek   (World Heritage Area)   (Manbiyarri) ★   Tin Camp   Ck
Fogg Dam   Pt. Stuart Lodge   KAKADU   37
Humpty   Window on   Cashew Nut   South   Nourlangie   Jabiru
Doo   the Wetlands   Farm   87   Frontier   Bowali Visitor Centre
          DJUKBINJ   Wildman River   Alligator   Kakadu Village   (Park H.Q.)
ARNHEM   N.P.   Lodge   Yellow Water   Nourlangie Rock ★
          Corroboree   Rockhole   Park Entrance Stn.   HWY   Cooinda
          Park Inn   Bark Hut   West   Lodge
          125   Inn   HWY   Jim Jim Billabong ★
Gas   Mary River   Annaburroo   ARNHEM LAND
Pipeline   crossing   Billabong   132   Mann
Mt Ringwood   NATIONAL
Mt Bundy   Jim Jim Falls ★
Adelaide River   Maguk   Liverpool
          Ban Ban   (Barramundi Gorge) ★   PARK   Twin Falls ★
          Springs   Mary River
Hayes Creek   Gunlom   Jarrangbarnmi
Roadhouse   (Waterfall Creek) ★   (Koolpin Gorge)
          Burrundie   Park Entrance   Gimbat ★
STUART   Frances Ck   Stn.
Douglas   Spring Hill   Mary River   Entry to Aboriginal Lands is
Emerald Springs   KAKADU   Roadhouse   prohibited without a permit from:
Roadhouse   111   62   The Permits Officer,
Douglas   BUTTERFLY   Northern Land Council.
Experimental   GORGE N.P.   P.O. Box 42921
Farm   Tjuwaliyn   Pine Creek   Casuarina, NT, 0811
          (Douglas Hot Springs)   Bonrook   MANYALLALUK   For More Detail   Telephone (08) 8920 5100
Oolloo   Jindare   See Page 220   Facsimile (08) 8945 2633
Lukles Farm   RAILWAY   NITMILUK   Mountain
          Umbrawarra   91   Leliyn   Valley
          Gorge   (Edith Falls)   MANYALLALUK   R   ARNHEM   RD
          Granite   (KATHERINE GORGE)   247
          Gundagai   N.P.   Manyallaluk ♣
Florina   JAWOYN   Katherine Gorge ★   West   CENTRAL
Dorisvale   HWY   Katherine   (Nitmiluk)   King River   Barunga ♣
          Carbeen   VICTORIA HWY   Tindal RAAF   52   Beswick ♣
          Park   See page 205   Base   Maranboy   BESWICK
FLORA RIVER   Cutta Cutta   (Police Stn.)   Creek
NATURE PARK   Caves

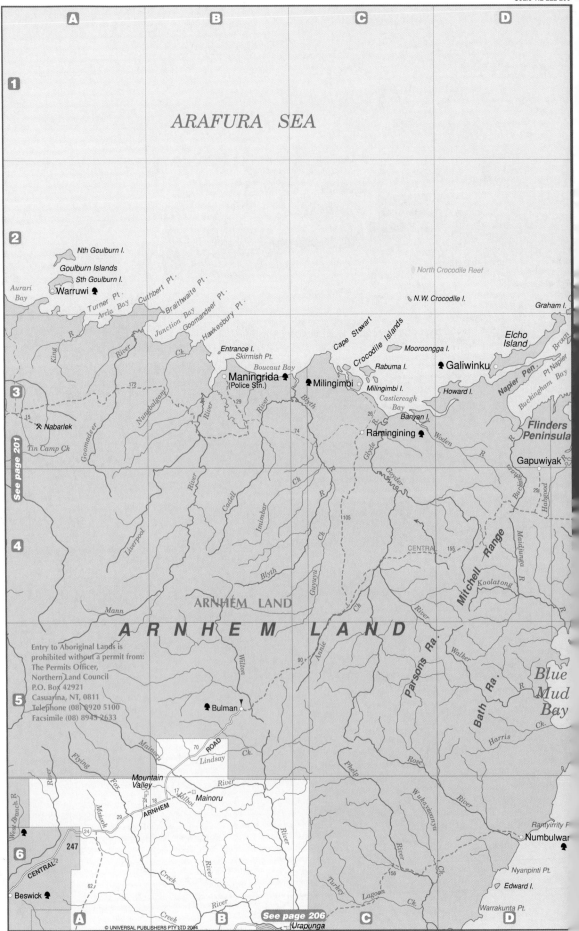

ARAFURA SEA

A B C D

1

2

Nth Goulburn I.

Goulburn Islands
Sth Goulburn I.

Aurari Bay

Warruwi ♣

Turner Pt. *Culbert Pt.* *Braithwaite Pt.* *Hawkesbury Pt.* *Goomandeer Pt.*

Arrla Bay *Junction Bay*

North Crocodile Reef

⚓ *N.W. Crocodile I.*

Graham I.

Cape Stewart

Crocodile Islands *Mooroongga I.*

Elcho Island

Rabuma I.

♣ **Galiwinku**

King R.

172

Goomadeer River

Nungbolgam

Entrance I.
Skirmish Pt.

Boucaut Bay

Maningrida ♣
(Police Stn.)

29

♣ **Milingimbi**

Milingimbi I.

Howard I.

Napier Pen. *Pt Napier*

Braun R.

Buckingham Bay

3

⤢ 15 ⚔ **Nabarlek**

Tin Camp Ck

Goomadeer

Liverpool River

Cadell River

River *Blyth*

74

Ck

Clyde

Castlereagh Bay

26

Banyan I.

Ramingining ♣

Woden R.

Flinders Peninsula

Gapuwiyak ○

See page 201

4

Imimbar

Guyuyu R.

1105

Goyder River

CENTRAL 155

Mitchell Range

Maidjunga R.

Koolatong

25

Habgood R.

Blyth

ARNHEM LAND

Mann R.

A R N H E M   L A N D

Walher R.

Parsons Ra.

Bath Ra.

Blue Mud Bay

5

Entry to Aboriginal Lands is
prohibited without a permit from:
The Permits Officer,
Northern Land Council
P.O. Box 42921
Casuarina, NT, 0811
Telephone (08) 8920 5100
Facsimile (08) 8945 2633

Wilton River

♣ **Bulman** ⚑

90

Annie Ck

Ck

Phelp River

Rose River

Wukabuanya R.

Harris Ck.

Flying Fox River

70

ROAD

Lindsay

Ck.

Mountain Valley

17

74 18 *Wilboi*

Mainoru

Maaork

29

ARNHEM

River

River

Rantyirrity P.

Numbulwar ♣

Nyanpinti Pt.

6

♣

247

West Branch R.

CENTRAL 12

♣ **Beswick**

24

62

Turkey Ck

Lagoon

156

Ck.

○ *Edward I.*

Warrakunta Pt.

Creek *River* *Creek*

See page 206

Urapunga

A B C D

E F G H

1

Cape Wessel
Rimbija I.

Marchinbar
Island

Wessel Islands

Stevens I.
Guluwuru I.

Drysdale I.

Raragala I.
Companys Is.
Truant I.
Jirrgari I.
Bumaga I.
Wigram I.
Wamawi I.
English
Alger I.
Cotton I.
Astell I.
Cape Wilberforce

The
Inglis I.

Probable I.
Melville
Bay
Bremer I.

Mallison I.
Nhulunbuy
Yirrkala
Gove
Peninsula

Arnhem
Bay
Cape Arnhem

Gulf of

Port Bradshaw

ROAD

ARNHEM
Warryanmera Pt.

Carpentaria

Pt. Alexander

Durnbudhoi
Caledon Bay
182

Cape Grey

Trial Bay

Myaoola
Bay

Cape Shield

Nicol I.

Isle Woodah

Bruney I.

Cape Barrow
Hawksnest I.
North East Is.
Bartalumba
Bay

Bickerton
Island
Winchelsea I.
Port Langdon
Scott Pt.
Milyakburra
Alyangula
(Police Stn)
Umbakumba

Wanuch Ck.
Angurugu
Groote
Eylandt
Dalumbu Bay
Ungwariba Pt.

Laurie Ck.

South Pt.
ARNHEM LAND

Cape Beatrice

ANINDILYAKWA LAND COUNCIL

E F G H

2

3

4

5

6

See page 207

Joseph Bonaparte Gulf

See page 200

Peppimenarti

Wadeye
(Port Keats)
(Police Stn)

Palumpa

DALY RIVER/PORT KEATS

UPPER DALY

Pearce Point

Wombungi

Cape Dusséjour

Lacrosse I.

Cape Domett

Rocky I.

Pelican I.

Turtle Point

Quoin I.

Cambridge Gulf

Keyling Inlet

Queens Channel

Fitzmaurice

River

River

River

ORD RIVER N.R.

Legune

Bradshaw

Angalarri

Carlton Hill

Spirit Hills

Bullo River

Coolibah

Ord

Baines R.

Victoria

River

Fitzroy

PARRY LAGOONS N.R.

Ivanhoe

VICTORIA

Kununurra

KEEP RIVER N.P.

Auvergne

VICTORIA

Timber Creek
(Police Stn)

158

Lake Kununurra

R.

Newry

HWY

170

East

Baines

NGALIWURRU/
NUNCAH

WANIMIYN

Dunham

Pilot Dam

Lake Argyle Village

HWY

Limestone Gorge

Bullita

GREGORY

Kidman Springs

Woolah

Lake Argyle

ROAD

Rosewood

NAGURUNGURU

NATIONAL

Humbert River
(Ranger Station)

Victoria River Downs

Yarralin

DOON DOON

Amanbidgi

Glen Hill

Waterloo

Baines

Leichhardt

PARK

Broadarrow

Ck

NORTHERN

Lissadell

River

DUNCAN

Wed

Ck

Negeri

Wickham

BOW RIVER

GREAT

Spring Creek

261

MALNGIN 2

Mt Sanford

Texas Downs

Darlu Darlu

Mistake Creek

Depot

Gordon

Warmun
(Turkey Ck)

Negri

Stirling

Limbunya

Gill

Stevens

Echidna Chasm

PURNULULU N.P.

Nelson Springs

MALNGIN

Ord River Regeneration
Research Stn.

River

Wattie

DAGURAGU

Ck

Daguragu

Kalkarindji
(Police Stn)

BUNTINE

Bungle Bungle Ra
Cathedral Gorge

Ord

Mt Napier

Ck

Swan

Creek

Gum Ck

HWY

240

Comfie

Kirkimbie

NORTHERN

WESTERN

Victoria

112

Eldrie R.

Nicholson

BUNTINE

Inverway

Riveren

DUNCAN

Nicholson

ROAD

Bunda

Maud Ck

Sturt

Ck

Hooker

AUSTRALIA

TERRITORY

Nongra Lake

HOOKER CREEK

Flora Valley

Bullion

Creek

Birrindudu

(Police Stn)

Lajamanu

DUNCAN

See page 208

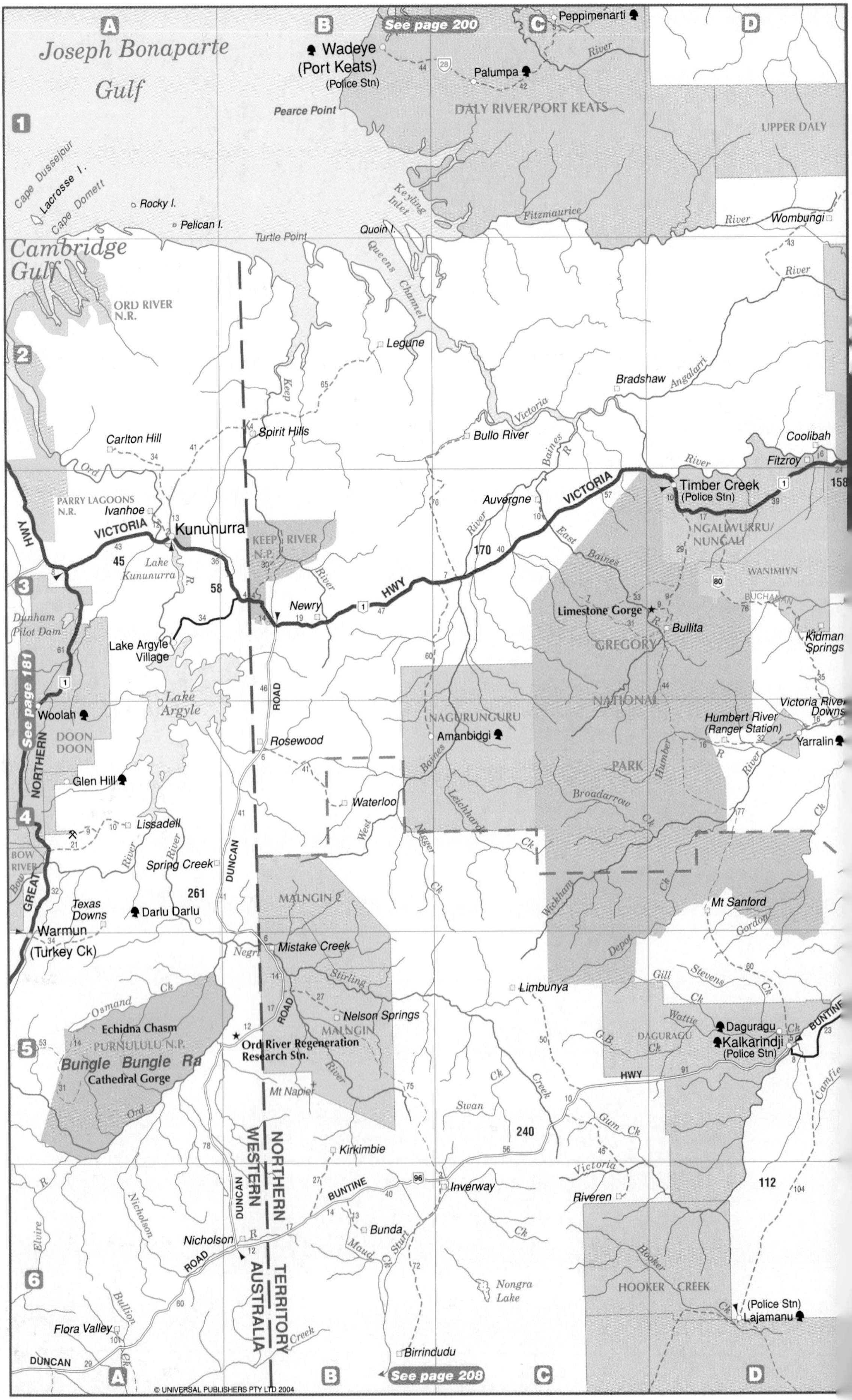

© UNIVERSAL PUBLISHERS PTY LTD 2004

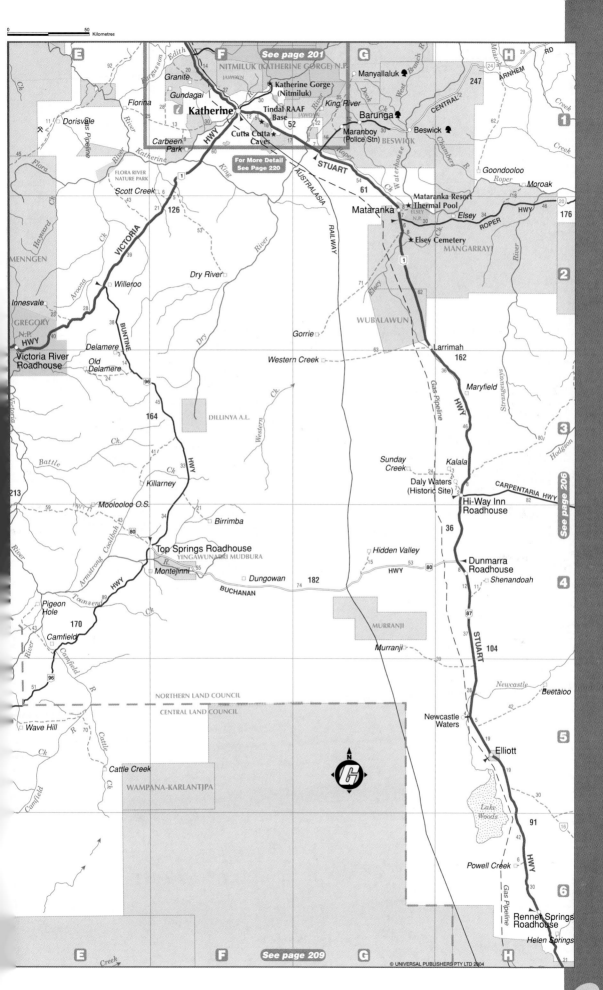

0   50   Kilometres

E   **F**   **G**   **H**

See page 201

NITMILUK (KATHERINE GORGE) N.P.
JAWOYN

Granite
Gundagai
Florina

★ Katherine Gorge (Nitmiluk)
Manyallaluk ♣

Katherine

King River

Tindal RAAF Base

Cutta Cutta Caves

Barunga ♣

Beswick ♣

BESWICK

Dorisvale

Carbeen Park

FLORA RIVER NATURE PARK

Maranboy (Police Stn)

For More Detail See Page 220

STUART

AUSTRALASIA

Goondooloo
Moroak

Mataranka Resort ★ Thermal Pool

Scott Creek

VICTORIA

126

MENNGEN

Willeroo

Dry River

Mataranka

Elsey

ROPER

176

★ Elsey Cemetery
MANGARRAYI

Innesvale

GREGORY N.P.

HWY

Delamere

Old Delamere

BUNTINE

WUBALAWUN

Gorrie

Elsey

Victoria River Roadhouse

96

Western Creek

Larrimah

162

DILLINYA A.L.

Maryfield

164

HWY

Gas Pipeline

213

Killarney

Sunday Creek

Kalala

Moolooloo O.S.

Birrimba

80

Daly Waters (Historic Site)

CARPENTARIA HWY

See page 206

Top Springs Roadhouse

YINGAWUNARRI MUDBURA

Hi-Way Inn Roadhouse

36

Montejinni

Hidden Valley

Dunmarra Roadhouse

Shenandoah

Pigeon Hole

BUCHANAN

Dungowan

182

HWY

MURRANJI

87

STUART

104

170

Camfield

Murranji

Newcastle

Beetaloo

96

NORTHERN LAND COUNCIL

CENTRAL LAND COUNCIL

Newcastle Waters

Wave Hill

Elliott

Cattle Creek

WAMPANA-KARLANTJPA

Lake Woods

91

Powell Creek

Gas Pipeline

Rennet Springs Roadhouse

Helen Springs

E   **F**   **G**   **H**

See page 209

© UNIVERSAL PUBLISHERS PTY LTD 2004

Northern Territory   **205**

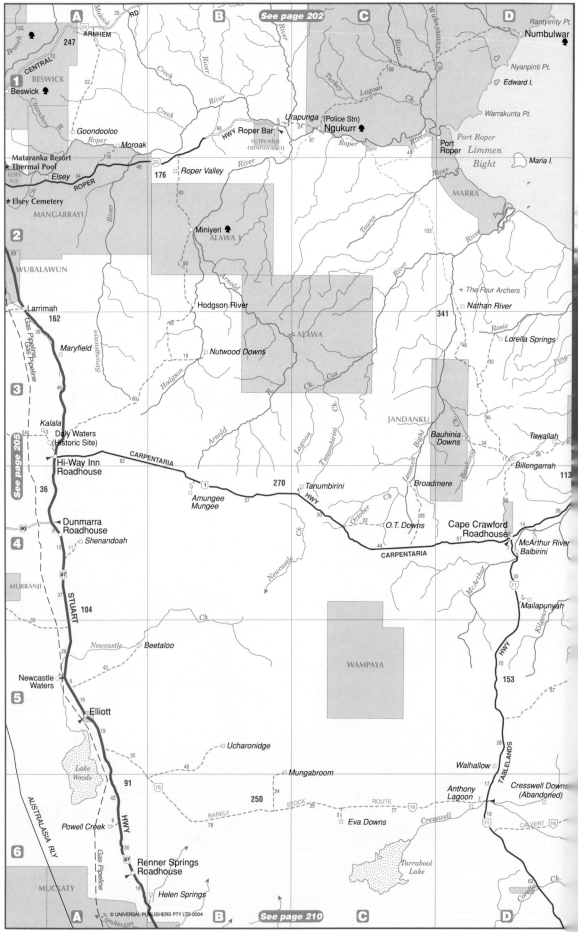

A — ARNHEM — RD
247
CENTRAL
BESWICK
Beswick ♣
Goondooloo
Moroak
Roper
Mataranka Resort
Thermal Pool
Elsey
ELSEY
N.P.
★ Elsey Cemetery
MANGARRAYI
WUBALAWUN
Larrimah
162
Maryfield
Gas Pipeline
Kalala
Daly Waters
(Historic Site)
Hi-Way Inn
Roadhouse
36
Dunmarra
Roadhouse
Shenandoah
MURRANJI
STUART
104
Newcastle
Beetaloo
Newcastle
Waters
Elliott
Lake
Woods
91
STUART HWY
Powell Creek
AUSTRALASIA RLY
Gas Pipeline
87
Renner Springs
Roadhouse
MUCKATY
Helen Springs

B — See page 202
Roper River
Roper Bar
HWY Roper Bar
YUTPUNDJI
-DJINDIWIRRITJ
Roper Valley
176
Miniyeri ♣
ALAWA
Hodgson River
Arnold
ALAWA
Nutwood Downs
Hodgson
Arnold
CARPENTARIA
Amungee
Mungee
1
270
Tanumbirini
CARPENTARIA HWY
Ucharonidge
Mungabroom
250
BARKLY
STOCK
Eva Downs
Tarrabool
Lake

C — Urapunga (Police Stn)
Ngukurr ♣
Port Roper
Turkey Lagoon
Port Roper
Limmen
Bight
Maria I.
MARRA
The Four Archers
Nathan River
341
Rosie
Lorella Springs
Pine
JANDANKU
Bauhinia
Downs
Tawallah
Billengarrah
113
Broadmere
O.T. Downs
Cape Crawford
Roadhouse
McArthur River
Balbirini
Mailapunyah
WAMPAYA
Walhallow
Anthony
Lagoon
ROUTE
16
Cresswell Downs
(Abandoned)
CALVERT
16

D — Rantyirrity Pt.
Numbulwar ♣
Nyanpinti Pt.
Edward I.
Warrakunta Pt.

See page 205

See page 210

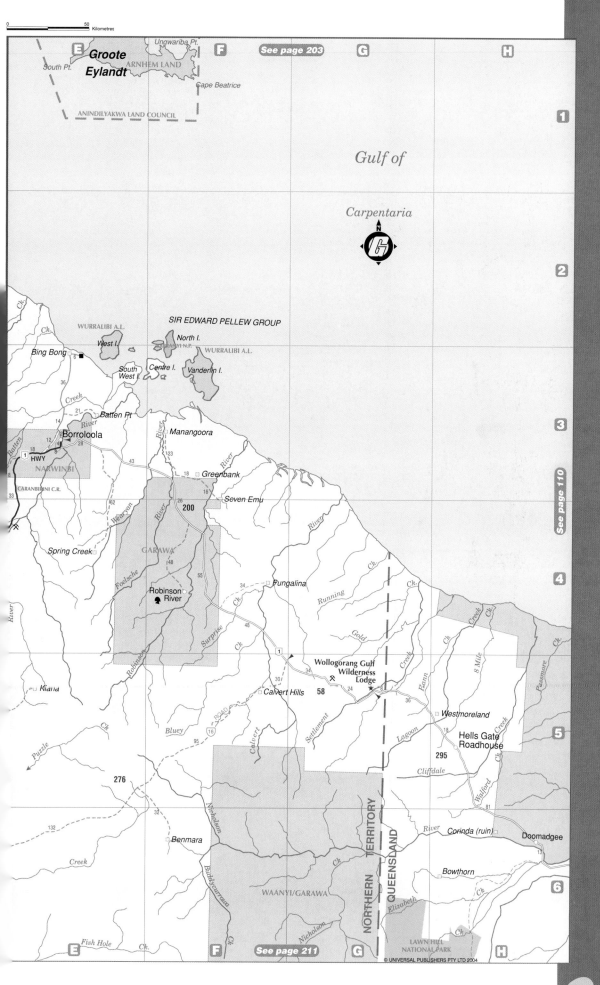

See page 203

See page 110

0   50
            Kilometres

E   Groote
    Eylandt

South Pt.   Ungwariba Pt.

ARNHEM LAND

ANINDILYAKWA LAND COUNCIL

Cape Beatrice

Gulf of

Carpentaria

SIR EDWARD PELLEW GROUP

WURRALIBI A.L.

West I.   North I.

Ck.

Bing Bong   WAANYI N.P.   WURRALIBI A.L.

Centre I.

South
West I.   Vanderlin I.

36

Creek

21

Batten Pt   River

14

Borroloola   Manangoora

28   123

NARWINBI   43

HWY   18

CARANBIRINI C.R.   Greenbank

33   62   200   Seven Emu

16

GARAWA   River

148

Spring Creek

River   River

55

Robinson
River   34   Pungalina

Surprise   Running

48

Kiana   Ck.   1   Gold   Wollogorang Gulf
                                                                    Wilderness
                                                                    Lodge

30   34

Calvert Hills   58   24

Bluey   16   36   Westmoreland

95   18   Hells Gate
                                      Roadhouse

276   Cliffdale   295

132   32   Corinda (ruin)   Doomadgee

Benmara   River

Bowthorn

WAANYI/GARAWA   Elizabeth   Ck.

NORTHERN TERRITORY

QUEENSLAND

LAWN HILL
NATIONAL PARK

Fish Hole   Ck.

E   F   See page 211   G   H

© UNIVERSAL PUBLISHERS PTY LTD 2004

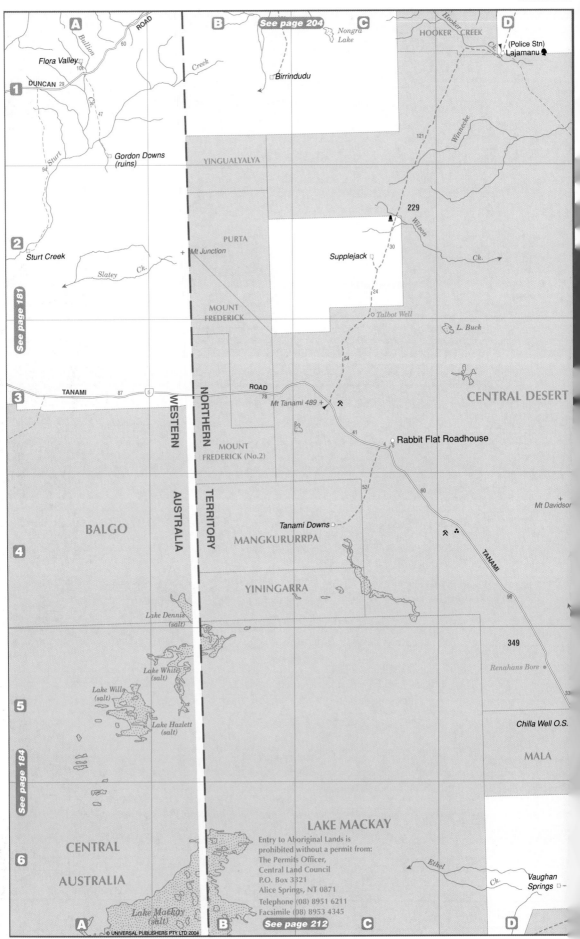

A
ROAD
Bullion
Flora Valley
60
10
DUNCAN 29

B
Creek
See page 204
Nongra Lake
Birrindudu

C
HOOKER CREEK
Hooker
Ck.

D
(Police Stn)
Lajamanu

1

Gordon Downs (ruins)
Sturt
94
Ck.
47

YINGUALYALYA

121
Winnecke

Ck.

2
Sturt Creek
Slatey
Ck.

Mt Junction
PURTA

229
Wilson
30
Supplejack
24

Ck.

See page 181

MOUNT FREDERICK
Talbot Well
L. Buck

54

3
TANAMI
87
1
ROAD
78
Mt Tanami 489

CENTRAL DESERT

WESTERN
NORTHERN
41

Rabbit Flat Roadhouse
4
5

MOUNT FREDERICK (No.2)

AUSTRALIA
TERRITORY

52
60
Mt Davidson

4
BALGO
MANGKURURRPA
Tanami Downs
YININGARRA

TANAMI
96

Lake Dennis (salt)

349
Renahans Bore

5
Lake White (salt)
Lake Wills (salt)
Lake Hazlett (salt)

33
Chilla Well O.S.

MALA

See page 184

6
CENTRAL

AUSTRALIA

LAKE MACKAY

Entry to Aboriginal Lands is prohibited without a permit from:
The Permits Officer,
Central Land Council
P.O. Box 3321
Alice Springs, NT 0871
Telephone (08) 8951 6211
Facsimile (08) 8953 4345

Ethel
Ck.
Vaughan Springs

Lake Mackay (salt)

A
© UNIVERSAL PUBLISHERS PTY LTD 2004

B
See page 212

C
D

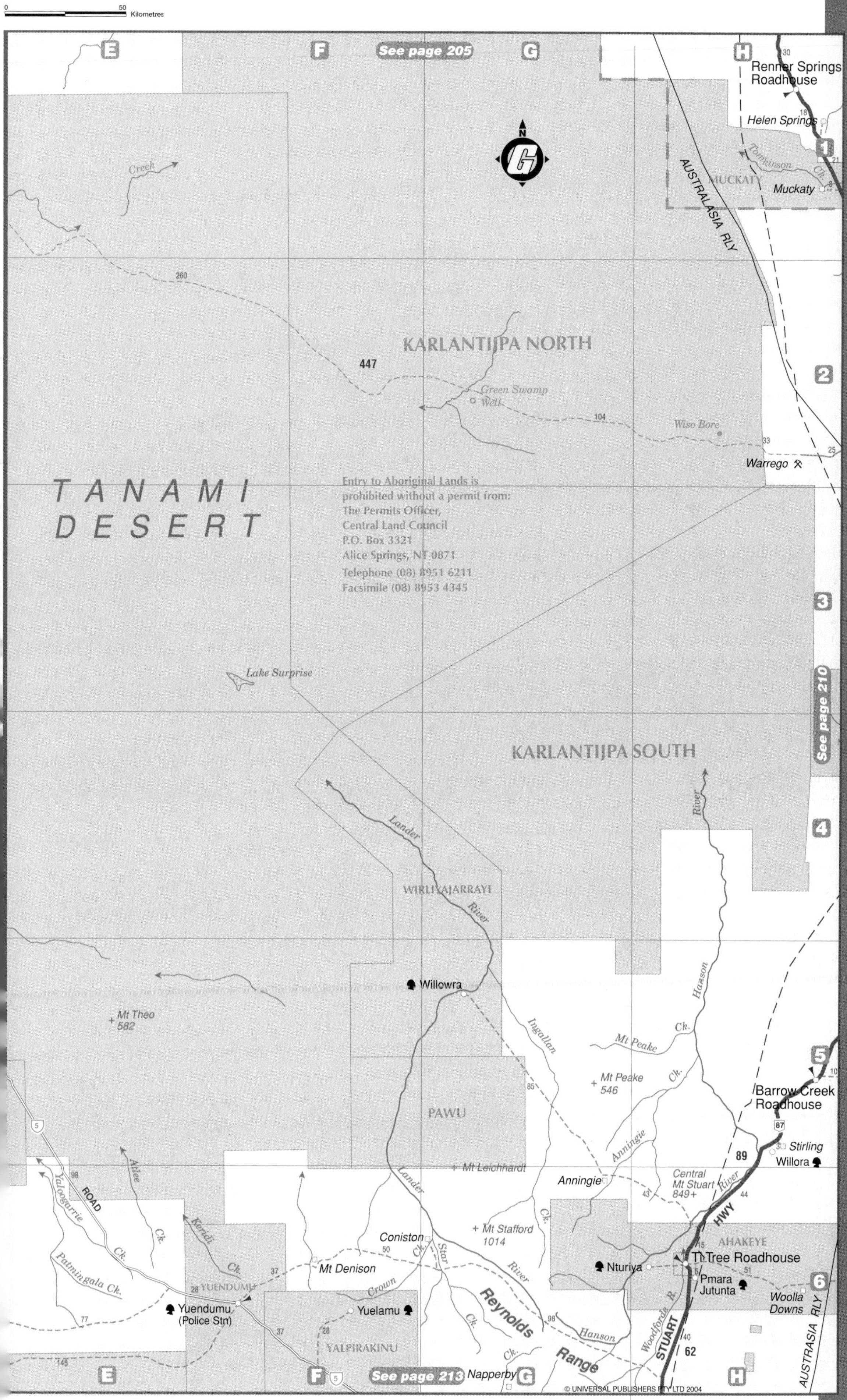

See page 205

Renner Springs
Roadhouse

Helen Springs

AUSTRALASIA RLY

MUCKATY

Muckaty

30

18

21

8

260

KARLANTIJPA NORTH

447

Green Swamp
Well

104

Wiso Bore

33

25

Warrego

T A N A M I
D E S E R T

Entry to Aboriginal Lands is
prohibited without a permit from:
The Permits Officer,
Central Land Council
P.O. Box 3321
Alice Springs, NT 0871
Telephone (08) 8951 6211
Facsimile (08) 8953 4345

See page 210

Lake Surprise

KARLANTIJPA SOUTH

River

Lander

River

WIRLIYAJARRAYI

Willowra

Ingallan

Hanson

Ck.

Mt Theo
582

Mt Peake

Ck.

Mt Peake
546

85

PAWU

Barrow Creek
Roadhouse

87

89

Stirling
Willora

10

31

Anningie

Anningie
Ck.

River

Central
Mt Stuart
849+

43

44

Lander

+ Mt Leichhardt

98

Alice

Ck.

Kerndi

ROAD

Yalogarrie

Ck.

Palmingala Ck.

Coniston

Mt Denison

Crown

Star

Ck.

+ Mt Stafford
1014

50

River

AHAKEYE

Nturiya

Ti Tree Roadhouse

Pmara
Jutunta

Woolla
Downs

51

62

40

Woodforde R.

STUART HWY

AUSTRALASIA RLY

Reynolds

Range

Hanson

Ck.

98

YUENDUMI

Yuendumu
(Police Stn)

77

YALPIRAKINU

Yuelamu

37

28

37

28

145

See page 213

Napperby

0   50
Kilometres

Northern Territory **209**

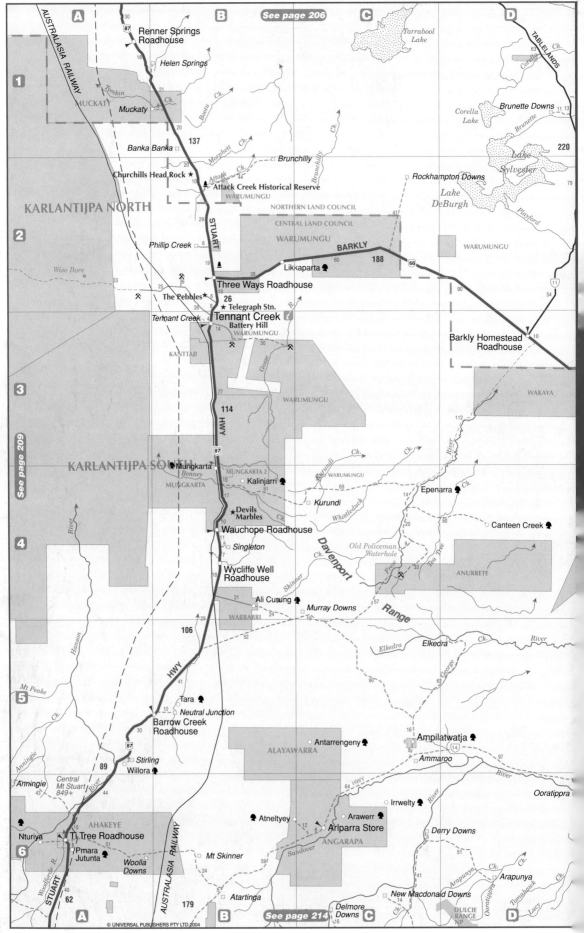

See page 206

Scale 1:2 222 200

Renner Springs
Roadhouse

Helen Springs

MUCKATY

Muckaty

Banka Banka

137

Brunchilly

Churchills Head Rock ★

Attack Creek Historical Reserve

WARUMUNGU

KARLANTIJPA NORTH

Phillip Creek

STUART

NORTHERN LAND COUNCIL

CENTRAL LAND COUNCIL

WARUMUNGU

BARKLY

188

Likkaparta

Three Ways Roadhouse

The Pebbles ★

26

★ Telegraph Stn.

Tennant Creek □
Battery Hill

Tennant Creek

WARUMUNGU

KANTTAJI

WARUMUNGU

HWY

114

WAKAYA

Barkly Homestead
Roadhouse

KARLANTIJPA SOUTH

Mungkarta

MUNGKARTA 2

Bonney

MUNGKARTA

Kalinjarri

WARUMUNGU

Kurundi

Epenarra

★ Devils
Marbles

Wauchope Roadhouse

Singleton

Old Policeman
Waterhole

Canteen Creek

ANURRETE

Wycliffe Well
Roadhouse

Skinner

Davenport

Ali Curung

WARRABRI

Murray Downs

Range

Elkedra

Elkedra

106

HWY

Tara

Neutral Junction

Barrow Creek
Roadhouse

ALAYAWARRA

Antarrengeny

Ampilatwatja

Ammaroo

Stirling

Willora

Central
Mt Stuart
849+

Anningie

AHAKEYE

Nturiya

Ti Tree Roadhouse

Pmara
Jutunta

Woolla
Downs

Mt Skinner

Irrwelty

Ooratippra

Atneltyey

Arawerr

Arlparra Store

ANGARAPA

Derry Downs

Arapunya

New Macdonald Downs

DULCIE
RANGE
NP

Atartinga

Delmore
Downs

179

See page 214

© UNIVERSAL PUBLISHERS PTY LTD 2004

STUART

AUSTRALASIA RAILWAY

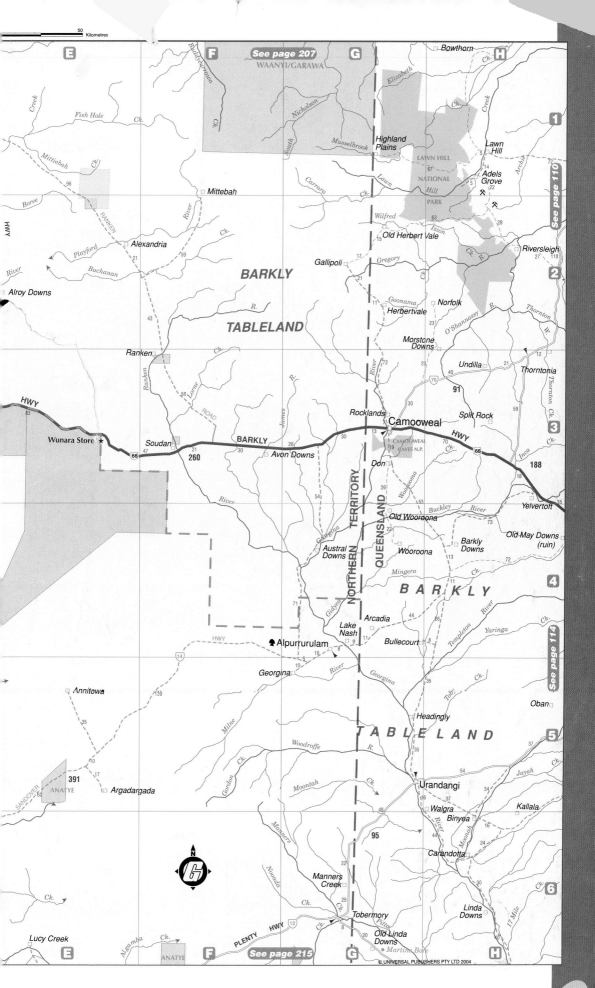

See page 207
WAANYI/GARAWA

Bowthorn

Highland
Plains

LAWN HILL
NATIONAL
Hill
PARK

Lawn
Hill

Adels
Grove

Mittebah

Fish Hole

Old Herbert Vale

Riversleigh

Alexandria

BARKLY

Gallipoli

Gregory

Goonama

Norfolk

Herbertvale

Alroy Downs

TABLELAND

Morstone
Downs

Ranken

Undilla

Thorntonia

91

HWY

Rocklands

Camooweal

Split Rock

Wunara Store

Soudan

BARKLY

HWY

66

260

Avon Downs

CAMOOWEAL
CAVES N.P.

188

Yelvertoft

Don

Old Wooroona

Old May Downs
(ruin)

Austral
Downs

Wooroona

Barkly
Downs

Mingera

B A R K L Y

Arcadia

Lake
Nash

Bullecourt

Templeton

Yaringa

Alpurrurulam

Annitowa

Georgina

Georgina

Oban

Headingly

T A B L E L A N D

391

ANATYE

Argadargada

Urandangi

Kallala

Walgra

Binyea

95

Carandotta

Lucy Creek

ANATYE

Manners
Creek

Tobermory

Linda
Downs

PLENTY HWY
12

Old Linda
Downs

See page 215

© UNIVERSAL PUBLISHERS PTY LTD 2004

NORTHERN TERRITORY

QUEENSLAND

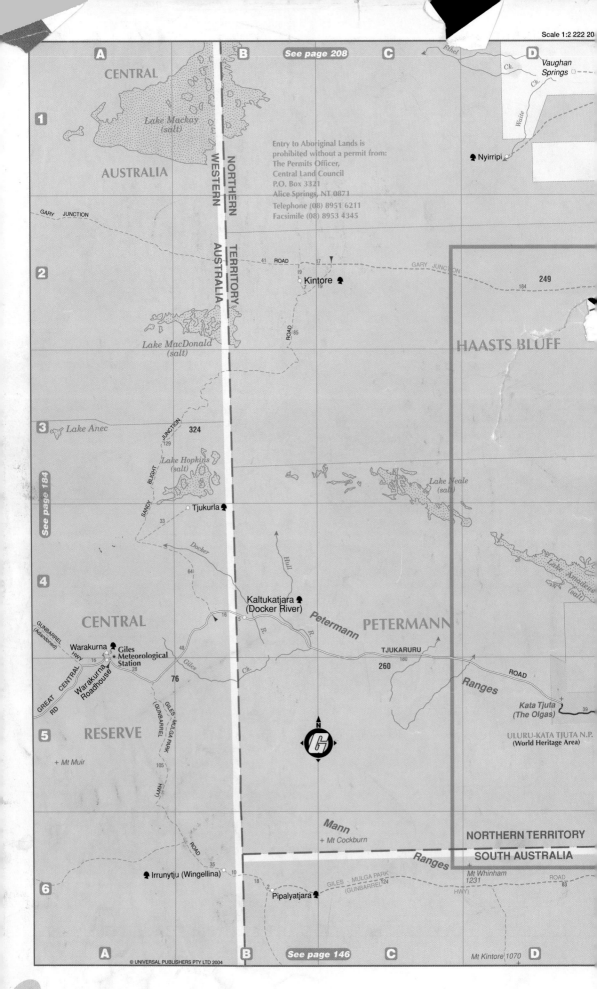

A   **B**   *See page 208*   **C**   **D**

CENTRAL

1

Lake Mackay
(salt)

AUSTRALIA

Vaughan
Springs

Ethel Ck.

Waite Ck.

Entry to Aboriginal Lands is
prohibited without a permit from:
The Permits Officer,
Central Land Council
P.O. Box 3321
Alice Springs, NT 0871
Telephone (08) 8951 6211
Facsimile (08) 8953 4345

Nyirripi

GARY JUNCTION

NORTHERN WESTERN AUSTRALIA TERRITORY

2

41 ROAD   17
19
19 Kintore
7   19

GARY JUNCTION

184   249

ROAD 85

HAASTS BLUFF

3

Lake Anec

JUNCTION
129

324

Lake Hopkins
(salt)

SANDY BLIGHT

Tjukurla

Lake Neale
(salt)

See page 184

33

Docker

64

Hull

4

Kaltukatjara
(Docker River)

Petermann

PETERMANN

Lake Amadeus
(salt)

R.

TJUKARURU

GUNBARREL
(Abandoned)

CENTRAL

16
48

R.

Ck.

260   180

ROAD

Ranges

Warakurna   Giles
★ Meteorological
   Station
28

Giles

Kata Tjuta
(The Olgas)   39

Warakurna
Roadhouse

GREAT CENTRAL RD

76

GILES MULGA PARK (GUNBARREL) HWY

ULURU-KATA TJUTA N.P.
(World Heritage Area)

5

RESERVE

+ Mt Muir

105

N
G

6

ROAD

35

Irrunytju (Wingellina)   10

18

Pipalyatjara

Mann

+ Mt Cockburn

Ranges

NORTHERN TERRITORY

SOUTH AUSTRALIA

Mt Whinham
1231

GILES MULGA PARK
(GUNBARREL) 124
HWY)

ROAD
83

A   **B**   *See page 146*   **C**   Mt Kintore 1070   **D**

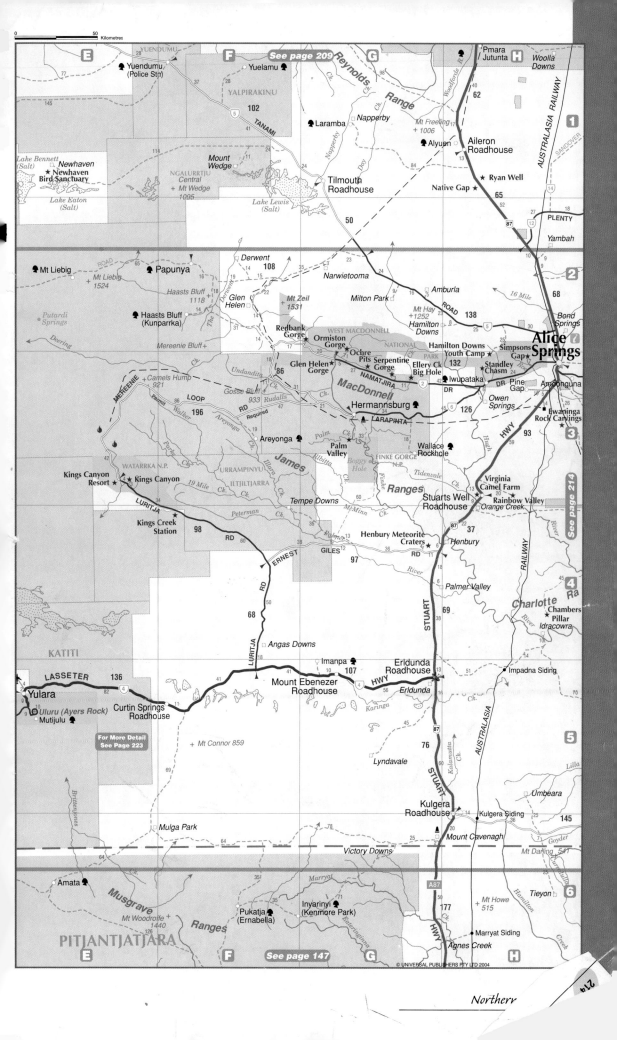

0 ___ 50 Kilometres

YUENDUMU

Yuendumu ♣ (Police Stn)

Yuelamu ♣

YALPIRAKINU

102   TANAMI

Laramba ♣   Napperby

Mt Freeling +1006

Alyuen ♣

Aileron Roadhouse

★ Ryan Well

Native Gap ★

65

52

PLENTY

Yambah

AUSTRALASIA RAILWAY

SANDOVER

1

Newhaven ★ Bird Sanctuary

Lake Bennett (Salt)

Lake Eaton (Salt)

Lake Lewis (Salt)

Mount Wedge

NGALURRTJU Central + Mt Wedge 1095

Tilmouth Roadhouse

50

Derwent 108

Narwietooma

Milton Park

Amburla

Mt Hay +1252

ROAD 138

5

Bond Springs

68

2

Mt Liebig ♣   + Mt Liebig 1524

Papunya ♣

Haasts Bluff 1118

Glen Helen □

Mt Zeil +1531

Redbank Gorge ★

WEST MACDONNELL

Hamilton Downs

16 Mile

Putardi Springs

Haasts Bluff (Kunparrka) ♣

The Deering

Mereenie Bluff +

Ormiston Gorge ★

NATIONAL PARK

Ochre Pits

Hamilton Downs Youth Camp

Simpsons Gap ★

Alice Springs ⊕

Glen Helen Gorge ★

Serpentine Gorge

Ellery Ck Big Hole

132

Standley Chasm

Iwupataka

Pine Gap

Amoonguna

7

MEREENIE + Camels Hump 921

86

LOOP 196

Gosse Bluff 933 Rudalls

Permit Walker required

NAMATJIRA

MacDonnell

DR 126

Owen Springs

Ewaninga Rock Carvings

3

Hermannsburg ▲

LARAPINTA

HWY 93

WATARRKA N.P.

Kings Canyon Resort ★

Kings Canyon

Areyonga ♣

James

Palm Valley ★

Boggy Hole

FINKE GORGE N-P

Ranges

Wallace Rockhole ♣

Virginia Camel Farm

See page 214

URRAMPINYU ILTJILTJARRA

19 Mile Ck   Ilbitta

Tempe Downs

Stuarts Well Roadhouse ★

Rainbow Valley ★

Orange Creek

Kings Creek Station ★

98 RD 60

Peterman Ck

Mt Minn

Henbury Meteorite Craters

Henbury

ERNEST 97

GILES 12

RD

RAILWAY

Palmer Valley

Charlotte

Ra

4

Chambers Pillar ★ Idracowra

STUART 69

68

LURITJA RD 50

Angas Downs

Imanpa ♣ 107

Mount Ebenezer Roadhouse

Erldunda Roadhouse

Erldunda

Impadna Siding

KATITI

LASSETER 136

Yulara ⊕

Uluru (Ayers Rock) ⊙

Mutijulu ♣

Curtin Springs Roadhouse

For More Detail See Page 223

+ Mt Connor 859

HWY

AUSTRALASIA

STUART

76

Lyndavale

Umbeara

145

5

Mulga Park

Kulgera Roadhouse

Kulgera Siding

Mount Cavenagh

Goyder Mt Darling 541

Lilla

Brittenjonas

Victory Downs

A87

Mt Howe +515

Tieyon

6

Amata ♣

Musgrave

Mt Woodroffe + 1440

Ranges

Pukatja (Ernabella)

Inyarinyi (Kenmore Park) ♣

HWY 177

Marryat Siding

PITJANTJATJARA

Agnes Creek

© UNIVERSAL PUBLISHERS PTY LTD 2004

Northern

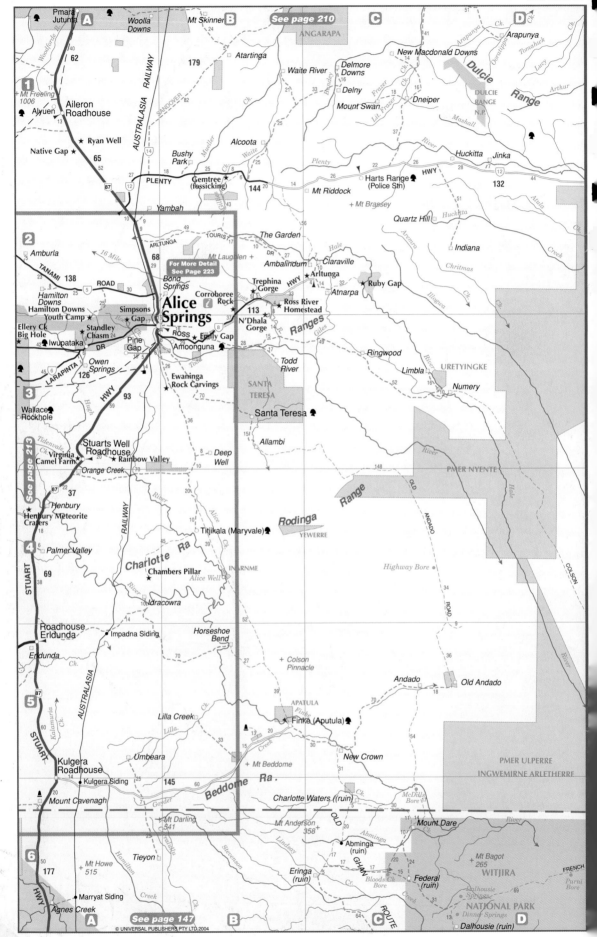

Scale 1:2 222 200

See page 210

For More Detail See Page 223

See page 213

See page 147

Pmara Jutunta

Woolla Downs

Mt Skinner

ANGARAPA

New Macdonald Downs

Arapunya

DULCIE RANGE N.P.

Dulcie Range

Mt Freeling 1006

Alyuen

Aileron Roadhouse

Atartinga

Waite River

Delmore Downs

Delny

Dneiper

Mount Swan

Huckitta

Jinka

Ryan Well

Native Gap

Bushy Park

Alcoota

Harts Range (Police Stn)

Mt Riddock

Mt Brassey

Quartz Hill

Indiana

PLENTY

Gemtree (fossicking)

Yambah

The Garden

Claraville

Amburla

Mt Laughlen

Ambalindum

Trephina Gorge

Arltunga

Ruby Gap

TANAMI

Bond Springs

Corroboree Rock

Atnarpa

ROAD

Hamilton Downs

Hamilton Downs Youth Camp

Simpsons Gap

Alice Springs

N'Dhala Gorge

Ross River Homestead

Ringwood

URETYINGKE

Ellery Ck Big Hole

Standley Chasm

Iwupataka

Pine Gap

ROSS

Emily Gap

Limbla

Numery

LARAPINTA

Owen Springs

Amoonguna

Todd River

SANTA TERESA

Ewaninga Rock Carvings

Wallace Rockhole

Santa Teresa

PMER NYENTE

Allambi

Stuarts Well Roadhouse

Deep Well

Virginia Camel Farm

Rainbow Valley

Orange Creek

Rodinga

YEWERRE

Titjikala (Maryvale)

Highway Bore

Henbury

Henbury Meteorite Craters

Palmer Valley

Chambers Pillar

Alice Well

INARNME

STUART

Idracowra

Roadhouse Erldunda

Impadna Siding

Horseshoe Bend

Colson Pinnacle

Andado

Old Andado

Erldunda

APATULA

Lilla Creek

Finke (Aputula)

New Crown

PMER ULPERRE

INGWEMIRNE ARLETHERRE

Kulgera Roadhouse

Umbeara

Mt Beddome

Kulgera Siding

Beddome Ra.

Charlotte Waters ((ruin))

McDills Bore

Mount Cavenagh

Mt Darling 541

Mt Anderson 358

Mount Dare

Mt Bagot 265

WITJIRA

FRENCH

Tieyon

Abminga (ruin)

Eringa (ruin)

Bloods Ck Bore

Federal (ruin)

Purni Bore

Mt Howe 515

Marryat Siding

Agnes Creek

NATIONAL PARK

Dinner Springs

Dalhousie (ruin)

© UNIVERSAL PUBLISHERS PTY LTD 2004

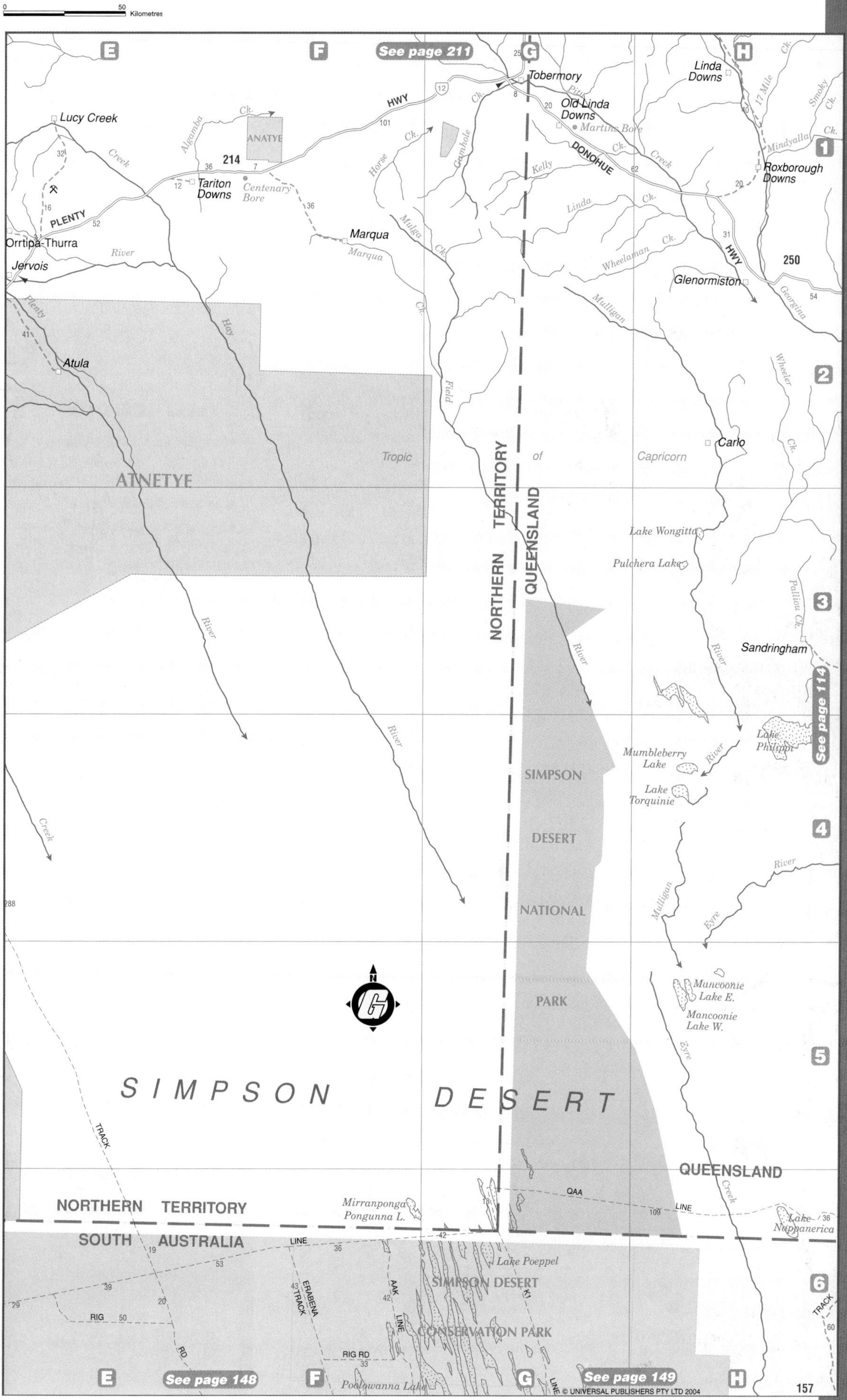

0   50   Kilometres

E   **F**   **G**   **H**

Linda Downs

Lucy Creek

Algambra Ck.

ANATYE

214

7

Tobermory

Old Linda Downs

Martins Bore

HWY

12

101

Horse Ck.

Gaynhole Ck.

DONOHUE

Kelly Ck.

25

8

20

17 Mile

Mindyalla Ck.

Smoky Ck.

Roxborough Downs

1

36

12

Tariton Downs

Centenary Bore

Creek

32

16

PLENTY

52

Orrtipa-Thurra

Jervois

River

Marqua

Marqua Ck.

Mulga Ck.

Field Ck.

36

Linda Ck.

Wheelaman Ck.

Mulligan

Glenormiston

HWY

31

250

Georgina

54

2

Atula

Plenty

41

Hoy River

Tropic

ATNETYE

NORTHERN TERRITORY

QUEENSLAND

of

Capricorn

Carlo

Wheeler Ck.

River

River

Lake Wongitta

Pulchera Lake

Polliou Ck.

Sandringham

See page 114

3

288

Creek

River

River

SIMPSON

DESERT

NATIONAL

PARK

Mumbleberry Lake

Lake Torquinie

River

Lake Philippi

Lake E.

4

Mulligan

Eyre

River

N

G

Mancoonie Lake E.

Mancoonie Lake W.

Eyre

5

TRACK

S I M P S O N   **D E S E R T**

QUEENSLAND

Creek

QAA LINE

109

Lake Nappanerica

36

NORTHERN TERRITORY

Mirranponga Ponggunna L.

SOUTH AUSTRALIA

LINE

42

36

19

53

20

ERABENA TRACK

AAK LINE

KY LINE

Lake Poeppel

SIMPSON DESERT

TRACK

60

6

29

39

RIG

50

20

43

33

CONSERVATION PARK

RIG RD

RD

Poolowanna Lake

157

LINE

E   **F**   **G**   **H**

See page 148
See page 149

Alice Springs

Devils Marbles

The largest settlement in the Australian interior, 'the Alice' is surrounded by the immense natural beauty of the MacDonnell Ranges, making it an excellent base for exploring the surrounding waterholes, gorges, creeks, national parks, flora and fauna.

Initially founded in 1870 as a staging post for the Overland Telegraph line, most of Alice Springs' growth has occurred in the past 30 years, particularly after a tourism boom in the 1980s. The Alice Springs Telegraph Station Historical Reserve is a memorial to the town's heritage. The site of the town's first settlement, the 2000-hectare reserve contains the telegraph station buildings and Alice's original waterhole.

Alice Springs has remained relatively isolated throughout most of its development: the southern road to Adelaide was only properly sealed in 1987. The Royal Flying Doctor Service and the Alice Springs School of the Air both operate from the town to service the remote communities and stations of central Australia. The Alice Springs Cultural Precinct is home to eight cultural and historical attractions including the Memorial Cemetery, the Central Australian Aviation Museum, and Frank McEllister Park.

Events in Alice Springs

Most famous is the Henley-on-Todd Regatta in September, when bottomless boats are raced along the dry bed of the Todd River. The annual Camel Cup races held in July are another unique outback event.

Tourist information

i Central Australian Tourism Industry Association

60 Gregory Tce,
Alice Springs NT 0870
Freecall: 1800 645 199
Ph: (08) 8952 5800
www.centralaustraliantourism.com

Main Attractions

◈ **Aboriginal Art & Culture Centre** Visitors can learn how to play the didgeridoo and try spear throwing.

◈ **Alice Springs Desert Park**

◈ **Anzac Hill** The most visited landmark in Alice Springs offers panoramic views of the MacDonnell Ranges.

◈ **Aruluen Centre for Arts and Entertainment** This centre showcases the work of famous Aboriginal artist Albert Namatjira.

◈ **Ghan Preservation Society** This museum celebrating the first Adelaide- to- Alice Springs train features the restored locomotive, the old loco shed and a tearoom.

◈ **Museum of Central Australia** This fascinating museum highlights the region's cultural and natural history.

◈ **Old Stuart Town Gaol** Alice Springs' oldest surviving building was constructed in 1907–1908.

◈ **The Alice Springs School of the Air** Visitors can observe radio lessons for children throughout central Australia.

Alice Springs Telegraph Station Historical Reserve

Scale 1:25 000

A   B   C   D

1

See page 214

DIXON
VALLEY CT
DRIVER CT
TURNER CT
SIMOUL VS
DIXON
SHADY CT
HEAD ST
CAMPBELL TCE
SARGENT ST
BIRD ST
MADIGAN ST
ANDREWS

Alice Springs

School of the Air ★
Campbell Pk
Rhonda Diano Park
Maynard Park
AMARA
MULARA
ANGGUNA
ERUMBA
ULUBA
DURIDA
McRAE
ALDIDJA
ABRAHAMS
BEBE
TIMBIRA
TUNGA CT
ERUA ST

Rotaract Park

Telegraph Station

Historical Reserve

River

Charles (Usually dry river bed)

Tucker Pk
LACKMAN
LUDGATE ST
TUCKER ST
CHEONG ST
LACKMAN
WOODS ST
ELLIOTT ST
CUMMINGS
KNUCKEY AV
PRIEST ST
Wintersun Gardens
McKINLAY ST
HARVEY ST
BARBOUR

STUART HWY

McCoy Pk
TIETKENS AV
KEKWICK ST
JARVIS ST
Kunoth Park
KUNOTH ST
STONE TCE
GREY ST
Grey Park
WOODS

2

Australasia
SMITH ST
Railway
SMITH
DR
DONALD CT
PRIEST ST
CRISPE ST
NDROW
PRIEST ST

River

KENNETT CT
SHIRLEY CT
DOWDY CT
ELDER ST
HELE CR
STOKES ST
WHITTAKER ST
McDONALD ST
COLSON ST

SCHWARZ
ANZAC HILL RD

Trevor Reid Park
RSL War Museum ★
Anzac Hill
★ War Memorial
Anzac Park
Snow Kenna

GOSSE ST
WINNECKE
GILES ST
LINDSAY
STURT
WARBURTON
CHEWINGS
MILLS ST
McMINN AV
HARVEY
RENNER ST

3

See page 214

IRVINE CR
SPICER ST
LOVEGROVE
CLARKE ST
GILMOUR ST
ALDRIDGE ST
NORMAN JONES ST
WILKINSON
PRICE ST
KIDMAN RD
COLTHARD ST
FOGARTY ST

Museum of Central Australia ★
Frank McEllister Community Park
Araluen Centre for Arts & Entmnt ★
Strehlow Research Ctr ★
Aviation Museum ★
Cemetery (Graves of Namatjira and Lasseter) ★

LARAPINTA
DE HAVILLAND DR
PIPER CT
AUSTER CT
HAVILLAND DR
COWLE ST
KENNA ST
BOJCAUT ST
MILNER ST
ASHWIN
LEWIS ST
NICKEL ST
HAWKINS CT
KIRK ST
HONG ST
GEORGET ST
GEORGE ST

Stuart Town Cemetery (Historic)
STUART HWY

WILLS ST
Pioneer Women's Hall of Fame ★
PARSONS ST
GREGORY TCE
Stuart Town Gaol ★
RAILWAY TCE
Aboriginal Art Centre
STOTT TCE
BATH ST
HARTLEY ST
TODD ST
TODD MALL
LEICHHARDT TCE
Civic Centre ★
ℹ

Alice Springs

Botanical Gardens

STURT TCE
GOYDER ST
LINDSAY
MUELLER CT
KHALICK CT
SADADEEN CR

UNDOOLYA RD
Main Causeway

4

PLOWMAN
VAN ST
BRUCE ST
SENDEN
SPENCER ST
BACON ST
ADAMSON
FLYNN ST
UNDERDOWN
SLOMAN
JOHANNSEN ST
A V
ROUNSEVELL ST
DAY ST
PLEW ST
BEECH CT
CRAFT CT
HABLETT ST
ROBERTS ST
MEMORIAL AV
MILNER ST
PEDLEY ST
LEWIS ST
EWART PL
GRUNDY ST
GEE ST
CAV AV
GASON ST
BLOOMFIELD ST
Ashwin Park
SIMPSON ST
SKINNER ST
WILLSHIRE ST
STUART
YARABAH
TCE
Royal Flying Doctor Service ★
BAGOT ST
TUNCKS

Olive Pink Flora Reserve

OLIVE PINK RD
STANDREWS CT
RANGE CR
THE FAIRWAY

5

BROMLEY ST
CHALMERS
OPA CR
Flynn Park
FRANCIS
PURVIS
CARRUTHERS
POEPPEL CR
PALMER CT
OGRADY
NEWLAND
SPEED ST
GAP RD
TRAEGER AV
BENSTEAD ST
Newland Park
Larapinta Park
🏛
ALLCHURCH ST
BALLINGALL ST
BREADEN ST
HAYES ST
Traeger Park
STREHLOW SOUTH

CROMWELL
REDSANDS CR
CATERPILLAR RD
Clubhouse ■

Alice Springs Golf Course

CROMWELL
COPPOCK CR
LINES CT
HIGGINS CT
DELAHANTY CT
MOORE CT
CONCORD CT

BRADSHAW
STANDLEY
FINLAYSON ST
WHITE ST
STANDLEY CR
CRANN ST
BARCLAY CR
GLEN LLOYD
BLOOMFIELD
FLINT ST
ACHILLA ST
KRAEGEN
GNOILA
KEMPE ST
PARKE CR
WALTER ST
MAHOMED ST

River
Todd (Usually dry river bed)

Lasseters Casino

♿

STEPHENS

6

Australasia
TELEGRAPH
GAP
WALMULLA
ALACIA ST
BROOKES ST
SUNSET TCE
BARRETT DR
SHANAHAN CL
HEAVITREE CT
MACONOCHIE RD
CLOO PL
MACDONNELL CT
SOUTH
Stuart Rotary Park
Todd

Heavitree Gap Historical Police Station ★

A   B   C   D

© UNIVERSAL PUBLISHERS PTY LTD 2004

Northern Territory

Kakadu National Park

Jim Jim Falls

A beacon for visitors to the NT, this World Heritage-listed national park contains a range of pristine ecosystems. Jointly managed by the traditional Aboriginal owners and Parks Australia, the park protects a cultural and ecological treasure trove of international importance.

Kakadu's 20,000 square kilometres are home to an estimated 10,000 species of insects, 65 mammal species, 1700 plant species, 280 bird species, 122 reptile species and 25 species of frog.

The diverse landscape is characterised by the wet and dry seasons. Although flocks of birds gather around the few remaining waterholes at the end of the dry season in September and October, the entire park springs to life during the rains from November to March. The creeks and floodplains fill with water and become a sea of bird life, and waterfalls reach their peak.

Aboriginal people have lived continuously in the area for at least 50,000 years, and the park is scattered with relics including grindstones, shelters, stone tools and ceremonial painting ochre. Dreamtime legends are presented at various significant sites throughout the park, with rock art 'galleries' showcasing images of hunters carrying barbed spears, and creation beings such as Ngalyod the Rainbow Serpent and Namarrgon the Lightning Man.

The Seasons of Kakadu

The weather is extreme and varied in Kakadu. Its Aboriginal people describe six distinct seasons in this region as opposed to just 'wet' and 'dry': Gunumeleng, Gudjewg, Banggereng, Yegge, Wurrgeng and Gurrung.

Tourist information

Bowali Visitor Centre
Kakadu Hwy, Kakadu National Park
NT 0886
Ph: (08) 8938 1120
www.deh.gov.au/parks/kakadu

Main Attractions

◈ **Gunlom** A striking combination of a waterfall and tranquil swimming-hole make this an idyllic picnic spot.

◈ **Jabiru** The town is set against the spectacular backdrop of the Arnhem Land Escarpment.

◈ **Koolpin Gorge** Access to this magical gorge is restricted, but well worth the effort of organising an entry permit in advance, and a key from the Southern Entry Station.

◈ **Nourlangie Rock** This 1.5km circular walk includes a visit to an ancient Aboriginal shelter and impressive art sites.

◈ **Ubirr** A 1km circular track past several fascinating rock art sites.

◈ **Yellow Water Billabong** Sunset is the ideal time to visit this pristine waterway, which supports a diverse ecosystem of animals, birds and plants.

Rock art – Nourlangie Rock

Kakadu's Crocs

The South Alligator River's entire drainage basin is within Kakadu National Park, providing an ideal wildlife habitat. The river was given its misleading name by an early British explorer who mistook its large community of crocodiles for alligators. The park's croc population was hunted almost to the point of extinction at the beginning of last century before the crocodile became a protected species in the Northern Territory in 1971.

Saltwater crocodile

The park provides a haven for two types of crocodile: saltwater and freshwater. 'Freshies' live in freshwater rivers and billabongs; they grow up to three metres long, eat small mammals, seafood and birds, and can be found in some of the park's swimming holes. Their neighbours the 'salties' inhabit both salt and fresh water, grow up to six metres in length, and have been known to take large mammals such as buffaloes and human beings.

Fully grown 'salties' are the largest reptiles on earth. An absence of warning signs does not necessarily mean that waterholes are safe for swimming, as the signs are popular souvenirs. A crocodile can remain underwater for up to an hour, as its heart rate can fall to as low as two or three beats per minute to conserve energy.

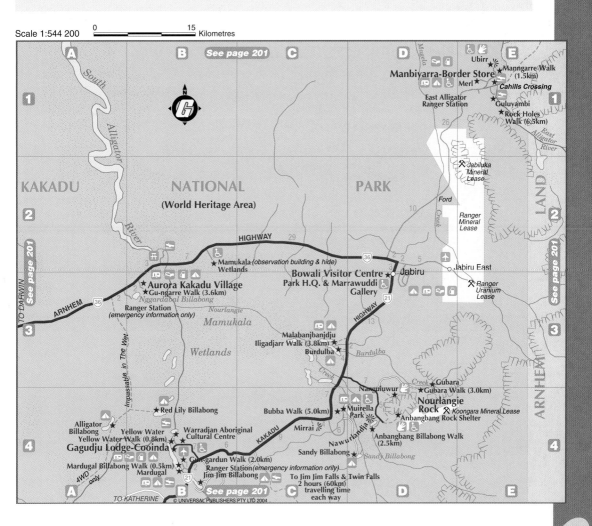

Katherine Gorge

Canoeing on Katherine Gorge

Nitmiluk is the traditional Jawoyn owners' word for 'Cicada Dreaming', an Aboriginal creation story. The national park contains beautiful gorges carved out over time by the Katherine River and separated by rapids. Rock art adorns the gorge walls and the park is home to prolific wildlife, including freshwater crocodiles, and offers more than 120km of walks. The park is the gateway to the Territory's 'Top End' and shares that region's monsoonal climate with a humid, hot, wet season between October and April, and a dry season from May to September.

The Katherine River functions both as a water source and a recreational attraction, with opportunities for swimming, canoeing and fishing along its picturesque shores. Other drawcards include croc-spotting tours, helicopter joy flights, horse trail rides and four-wheel driving.

Tourist information

Nitmiluk Visitor Centre

Gorge Rd, Nitmiluk National Park
Katherine NT 0851
Ph: (08) 8972 1886
www.krta.com.au

Must Visit

- ◈ Edith Falls
- ◈ Jatbula Trail
- ◈ Katherine Gorge
- ◈ Katherine River

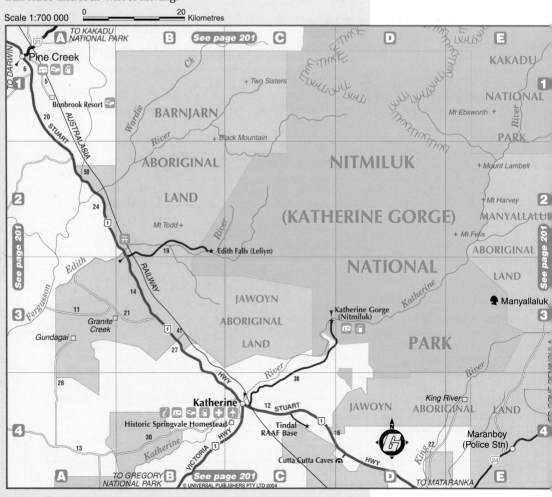

Litchfield National Park

Sandy Creek Falls (Tjaynera Falls)

Relatively unknown until it was declared a national park in 1986, Litchfield National Park is one of the Territory's underrated attractions. Its 1500 square kilometres encompass magnetic termite mounds, historic ruins, monsoonal rainforest, sandstone escarpments and spring-fed streams. The park's major attractions are accessible via sealed roads, with 4WD vehicles able to reach more remote locations. During the wet season, some areas may be inaccessible and waterholes may be closed due to water turbulence.

The park's permanent waterfalls are fed by the Tabletop Range's spring-fringed plateau, and its waterholes are generally crocodile-free and excellent for swimming. Permits are required for camping spots, with hotel accommodation available in the nearby towns of Adelaide River and Batchelor. Bushwalking is popular, and the lush wetlands provide fishing opportunities for anglers.

Tourist information

Litchfield National Park
cnr Pinaroo & Nurdina Sts,
Batchelor
NT 0845
Ph: (08) 8976 0282
www.nt.gov.au/ipe/pwcnt

Must Visit

◈ Adelaide River
◈ Batchelor Butterfly Farm
◈ Buley Rockhole
◈ Florence Falls
◈ Tjaynera Falls

Scale 1:509 300

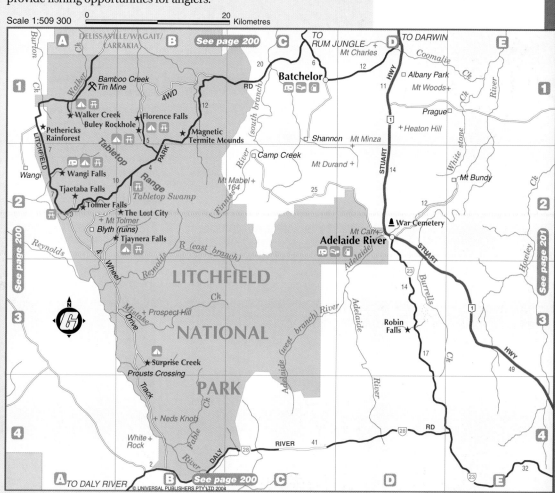

Uluru-Kata Tjuta National Park to Alice Springs

Uluru/Ayers Rock

The vast terrain west of Alice Springs to Uluru-Kata Tjuta National Park is the heart of the red centre, spanning the western section of the MacDonnell Ranges. This stunning but rugged area encompasses an ancient and unique terrain dotted with gorges, waterholes, unusual geological formations and strange landforms, carved out over hundreds of millions of years.

The arid and seemingly inhospitable landscape is home to an array of endemic flora and fauna: springtime sees the blossoming of colourful wildflowers, while rock wallabies are often seen around the steep ridges and rocky gaps of West MacDonnell National Park.

The Uluru-Kata Tjuta National Park covers 1325 square kilometres and contains two of the world's greatest natural wonders: Uluru (Ayers Rock) and Kata Tjuta (the Olgas) – both major tourist drawcards.

The park also offers much more, including Anangu Aboriginal heritage, guided walks, spectacular views, 416 plant species, 25 endemic mammals and 74 species of reptile.

The park first received international recognition in 1977, when it was declared an International Biosphere Reserve by UNESCO. In 1994 it became only the second World Heritage property listed for both its natural and cultural values.

Tourist information

Uluru-Kata Tjuta
Cultural Centre

Uluru-Kata Tjuta National Park
Yulara NT 0872
Ph: (08) 8956 3138
www.deh.gov.au/parks/uluru

Main Attractions

◈ **Yulara (Ayers Rock Resort)** This tourist resort and village is close to the district's major attractions.

◈ **Finke Gorge National Park** The main attraction here is Palm Valley, where prehistoric cycads and red cabbage palms have survived the barren terrain for more than 10,000 years.

◈ **Kata Tjuta** These extraordinary rock formations with 36 domes rise from the ground, and, like Uluru, their colours change with the light throughout the day. None of the domes can be climbed.

◈ **Standley Chasm** Sunlight bathes the 80m-high walls of this narrow chasm around noon. The chasm was formed by erosion of the softer rock from the red quartzite walls.

◈ **Uluru** At 348m high, Uluru is the world's largest monolith. The Mala and Kuniya guided walks provide an excellent grounding in Uluru's cultural significance to the Anangu people.

Kata Tjuta (The Olgas)

This group of 36 enormous and weathered domes, rising 546m, were described by explorer Ernest Giles as "monstrous pink haystacks". He named them after Queen Olga of Wurttemberg before they reverted to their original Aboriginal name meaning "many heads".

Uluru/Ayers Rock

Aboriginal Sites and land

As the Northern Territory encompasses terrain that is Aboriginal land, it is important that visitors who plan to travel through Aboriginal land away from designated highways obtain a permit. Permits can be obtained from the relevant Land Councils, although visitors travelling on organised tours will have their permits prepared for them. The Northern Territory also contains a number of sites that hold special significance to local Aboriginal people: some of these sites are protected by law. Although visitors are permitted to climb Uluru, the Aboriginal owners prefer they do not, because the climb is the traditional route ancestral Mala men took upon arriving at the rock.

The Land Councils for the NT are:

Central Land Council
31-33 Stuart Hwy,
Alice Springs NT 0871
Ph: (08) 8951 6211

Northern Land Council
9 Rowlings St,
Casuarina NT 0811
Ph: (08) 8920 5100

Tiwi Land Council
U5/3 Bishop St, Stuart Park,
Winnellie NT 0821
Ph: (08) 8981 4898

Aboriginal culture – Gove

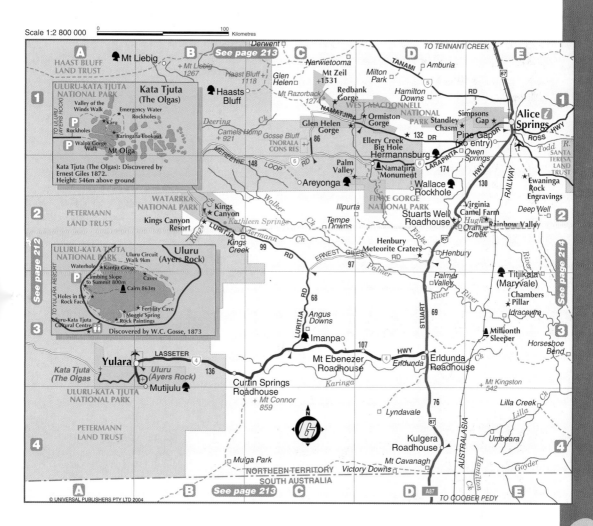

Tasmania
The Holiday Isle

The island state of Tasmania is Australia's smallest and southern-most state. It lies 240 km from the mainland and is surrounded by the turbulent waters of Bass Strait, the Southern Ocean and the Tasman Sea.

Tasmania's compactness makes it an ideal touring destination, as only relatively short distances separate its many attractions. Beaches circle its coastline, while national parks and reserves protect its spectacular terrain, which features approximately 1000km of world-class walking tracks.

Tasmania is also Australia's most mountainous state and has the highest percentage of national parks, comprising about one third of the island. It boasts stunning and remote World Heritage Areas that are home to rare flora and fauna, such as the Cradle Mountain-Lake St Clair National Park and the Franklin-Gordon Wild Rivers National Park.

The island's physical diversity ranges from dense rainforest to alpine moors covered in snow during winter, lush green pastures, long white beaches, rustic ports, and convict ruins, all crammed into a comparatively small area.

Much of Tasmania's colonial heritage has survived from the period when it was known as Van Diemen's Land, in well-preserved towns such as Richmond, New Norfolk and Ross. The small Aboriginal population is actively involved in maintaining its cultural identity through language and land management projects.

Tasmania is also renowned for its fresh produce and seafood including apples, cheeses, salmon, oysters, and superb ales and wines.

Tourist information

i Tasmanian Travel Centre
20 Davey St, Hobart Tas. 7000
Ph: (03) 6230 8233
Freecall: 1800 806 846
www.discovertasmania.com.au

| Area = 68,500 sq km | 240 km from mainland | Length of coast = 3200 km |

Tasmania Key Map & Distance Chart

All distances shown in the chart below have been measured over highways and major roads, not necessarily by the shortest route.

Tasmanian Devil

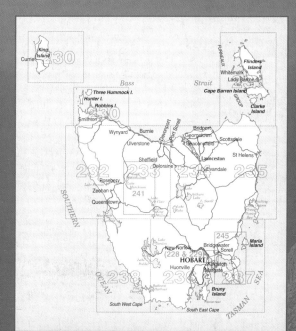

Approximate Distance	Burnie	Campbell Town	Deloraine	Devonport	Geeveston	George Town	Hobart	Launceston	New Norfolk	Oatlands	Port Arthur	Queenstown	Rosebery	St Helens	St Marys	Scottsdale	Smithton	Sorell	Swansea	Triabunna
Burnie		194	98	50	353	151	296	146	288	242	391	141	105	290	255	206	83	321	261	310
Campbell Town	194		98	148	184	113	127	68	126	48	205	317	301	120	85	128	273	118	67	116
Deloraine	98	98		50	255	89	198	50	190	146	303	218	205	205	159	110	177	223	165	214
Devonport	50	148	50		307	105	250	100	242	196	345	187	153	255	211	160	125	275	215	264
Geeveston	353	184	255	307		297	57	252	92	136	152	322	373	310	280	312	432	82	194	145
George Town	151	113	89	105	297		240	45	239	161	318	292	258	168	174	73	230	248	180	208
Hobart	296	127	198	250	57	240		106	35	79	95	265	314	247	212	255	402	25	137	88
Launceston	146	68	50	100	252	45	195		194	116	273	268	253	155	129	60	225	203	135	184
New Norfolk	288	126	190	242	92	239	35	194		78	130	230	267	246	211	254	367	60	151	123
Oatlands	242	48	140	196	136	161	79	116	78		157	269	306	168	133	176	321	87	115	164
Port Arthur	391	205	303	345	152	318	95	273	130	157		361	398	303	268	333	470	70	182	133
Queenstown	141	317	218	187	322	292	265	268	230	269	361		37	437	402	328	218	290	374	353
Rosebery	105	301	205	153	373	258	314	253	267	306	398	37		395	360	311	182	341	453	404
St Helens	290	120	205	255	310	168	247	155	246	168	303	437	395		35	95	380	228	116	165
St Marys	255	85	159	211	280	174	212	129	211	133	268	402	360	35		130	334	198	86	135
Scottsdale	206	128	110	160	312	73	255	60	254	176	333	328	311	95	130		285	263	211	260
Smithton	83	273	177	125	432	230	402	225	367	321	470	218	182	380	334	285		408	340	389
Sorell	321	118	223	275	82	248	25	203	60	87	70	290	341	228	198	263	408		112	63
Swansea	261	67	165	215	194	180	137	135	151	115	182	374	453	116	86	211	340	112		49
Triabunna	310	116	214	264	145	208	88	184	123	164	133	353	404	165	135	260	389	63	49	

Hobart

Constitution Dock, Hobart

Founded in 1804 and declared a city in 1842, Hobart is rich in reminders of its colonial past. It is Australia's second oldest city (after Sydney), and more than 90 of its buildings are classified by the National Trust. Most of these – including Australia's oldest theatre, the Theatre Royal – are located in historic Macquarie and Davey Sts.

Hobart is nestled on the western shore of the Derwent River and at the foot of Mt Wellington, which is often snow-capped in the winter months. There are panoramic vistas of the city from the mountain's superb lookouts.

Like most Australian capitals, Hobart's lifestyle is defined by water: it is a riverside city with picturesque warehouses hugging its bustling harbour. The harbour remains an integral part of the city's economy: only metres from the business district are the docks where overseas ships moor, supplies are loaded for Australia's Antarctic bases, and fishing vessels return with their catch.

The waterfront area is the site of many of the city's tourist attractions and events and is a focal point for visitors.

Hobart maintains a relaxed pace along with the benefits of a big city, including a thriving arts and crafts scene. Saturday's colourful Salamanca Market create a lively streetscape of buskers, string quartets and market stalls.

Tourist information

i Tasmanian Travel and Information Centre

20 Davey St, Hobart TAS 7000
Ph: (03) 6230 8233
Freecall: 1800 806 846
www.discovertasmania.com.au

Main Attractions

◈ **Battery Point** Hobart's oldest district, once home to sailors, fishermen and prostitutes, is now a fashionable inner-city neighbourhood.

◈ **Cadbury Chocolate Factory** Hobart is home to this well known chocolate manufacturer – a tour of the factory is a must for chocoholics.

◈ **Cascade Brewery** Australia's oldest brewery produces some of the finest beer in the country. Daily tours are available.

◈ **Royal Tasmanian Botanical Gardens** Established in 1818, these gardens house an extensive collection of native and exotic plants. Features include a cactus house, herb garden and Japanese Gardens.

◈ **Runnymede** This National Trust homestead built circa 1836 is set in exquisite gardens and is open to the public. Many original items remain in the house and rooms have been lovingly restored.

Places of Interest

Ⓐ Allport Library and Museum of Fine Arts **C3**
Ⓑ Anglesea Barracks **C4**
Ⓒ Antarctic Adventure **C4**
Ⓓ Battery Point **D4**
Ⓔ Cascade Brewery **A5**
Ⓕ Elizabeth Mall **C3**

Ⓖ Government House **C2**
Ⓗ Maritime Museum of Tasmania **C4**
Ⓘ Narryna Folk Museum **C4**
Ⓙ Parliament House **C4**
Ⓚ Princes Park **D4**
Ⓛ Royal Tasmanian Botanical Gardens **C2**

Ⓜ St Davids Park **C4**
Ⓝ Salamanca Place and Market **C4**
Ⓞ State Library of Tasmania **C3**
Ⓟ Sullivans Cove **D4**
Ⓠ Tasmanian Museum and Art Gallery **C3**
Ⓡ Wrest Point Hotel and Casino **D6**

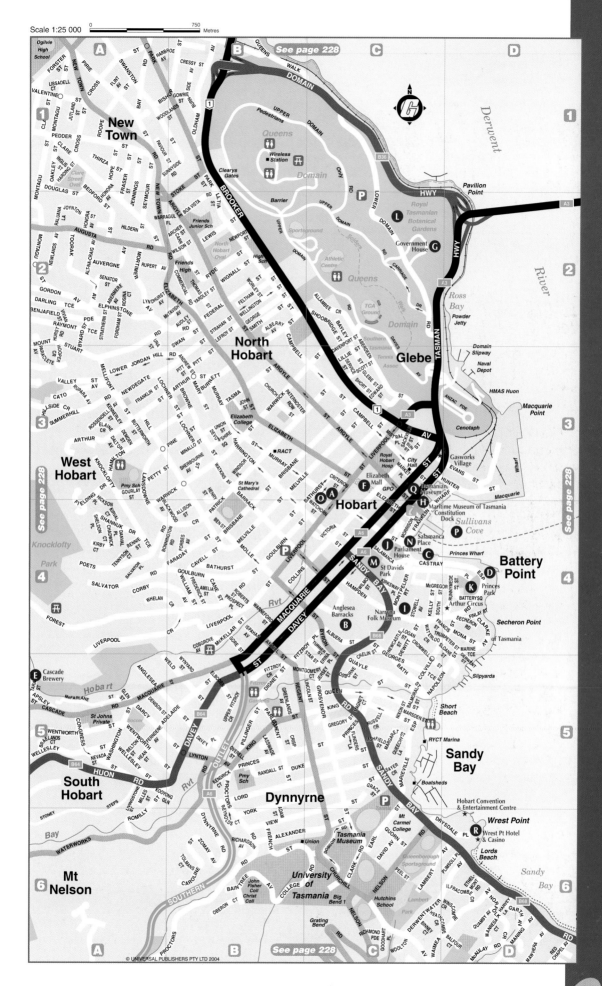

New Town

New
Town

Domain

Queens

Wireless
Station

Clearys
Gates

Barrier

Sportsground

North
Hobart Oval

North
Hobart

West
Hobart

Knocklofty
Park

Hobart

Glebe

Athletic
Centre

Queens

Domain

Royal
Tasmanian
Botanical
Gardens

Government
House

Ross
Bay

Powder
Jetty

Domain
Slipway

Naval
Depot

HMAS Huon

Macquarie
Point

Cenotaph

Gasworks
Village

Wharf

Macquarie

Maritime Museum of Tasmania

Constitution
Dock

Sullivans
Cove

Salamanca
Place

Parliament
House

CASTRAY

Princes Wharf

Battery
Point

Princes
Park

Arthur Circus

Secheron Point

of Tasmania

Slipyards

Short
Beach

RYCT Marina

Sandy
Bay

Hobart Convention
& Entertainment Centre

Wrest Point

Wrest Pt Hotel
& Casino

Lords
Beach

Sandy
Bay

Cascade
Brewery

Hobart

South
Hobart

Dynnyrne

Tasmania
Museum

University
of
Tasmania

Hutchins
School

Mt
Nelson

Derwent

River

Pavilion
Point

St Mary's
Cathedral

Elizabeth
Mall

City Hall

GPO

Tasmanian
Museum

St Davids
Park

Anglesea
Barracks

Narryna
Folk Museum

Mt Carmel
College

See page 228
See page 228
See page 228
See page 228

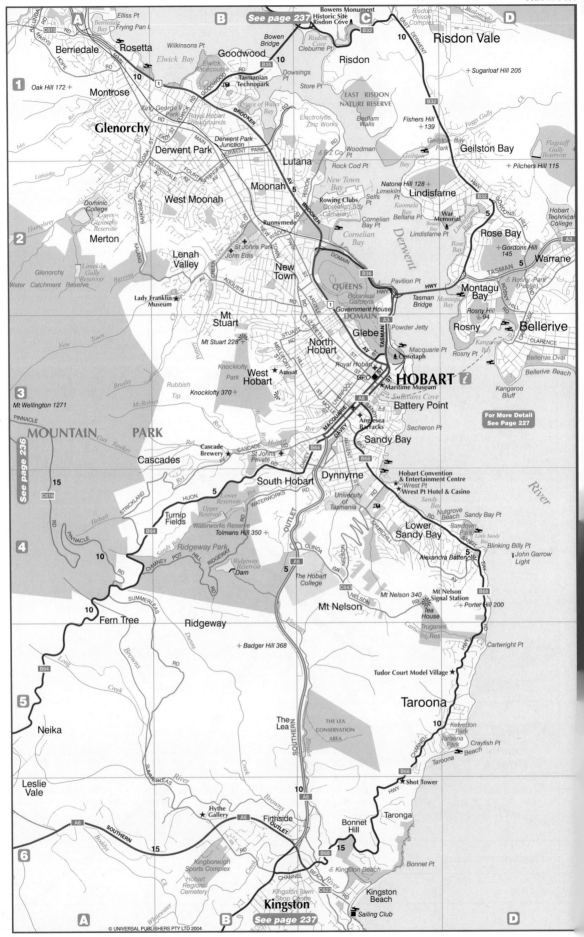

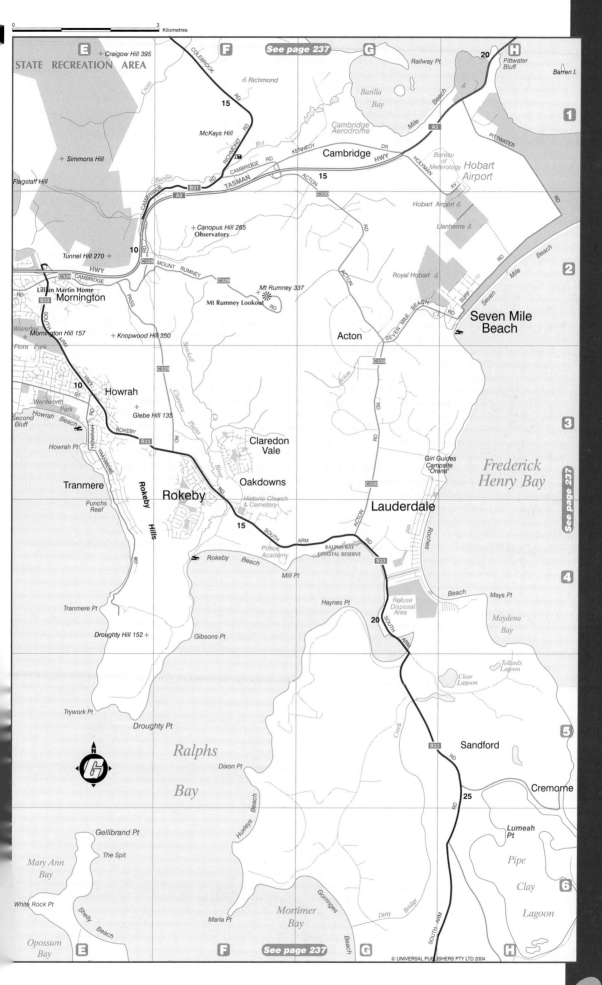

See page 237

STATE RECREATION AREA

+ Craigow Hill 395

COLEBROOK

& Richmond

Railway Pt

20

Pittwater Bluff

Barren I.

Barilla Bay

Cambridge Aerodrome

PITTWATER

McKays Hill

15

Hobart Airport

RICHMOND RD

KENNEDY RD

Cambridge

HOLYMAN

HWY

Bureau of Meteorology

+ Simmons Hill

CAMBRIDGE RD

TASMAN

B31

Barilla

A3

Rvt

DR

A3

15

ACTON RD

Hobart Airport &

AV

HOLYMAN

Flagstaff Hill

+ Canopus Hill 265
Observatory

C330

Llanherne &

Tunnel Hill 270 +

10

C329

MOUNT RUMNEY

ACTON RD

Royal Hobart &

SURF RD

Seven Mile Beach

HWY

C329

CAMBRIDGE

C328

Seven Mile Beach

RD

Lillian Martin Home

Mornington

B33

PASS

SOUTH ARM

Mt Rumney 337

Mt Rumney Lookout

RD

SEVEN MILE BEACH

Ck

Waverley

+ Mornington Hill 157

+ Knopwood Hill 350

Acton

Flora Park

Stackell

ACTON RD

Second Bluff

Wentworth Park

10

ST

Howrah

C328

Clarence Plains

Howrah Beach

+ Glebe Hill 135

Frederick Henry Bay

See page 237

HOWRAH

TRANMERE

River

Claredon Vale

Howrah Pt

ROKEBY

B33

RD

Girl Guides Campsite "Orana"

Tranmere

Rokeby Hills

Rokeby

Oakdowns

Historic Church & Cemetery

Lauderdale

Roches

Punchs Reef

15

SOUTH

Police Academy

RALPHS BAY COASTAL RESERVE

B33

Tranmere Pt

RD

Rokeby Beach

ARM

RD

Beach

Mays Pt

Mill Pt

Haynes Pt

Refuse Disposal Area

Maydena Bay

Droughty Hill 152 +

Gibsons Pt

20

SOUTH

Clear Lagoon

Tollards Lagoon

Trywork Pt

ARM

Droughty Pt

Ralphs

N
G

Dixon Pt

Sandford

B33

RD

5

Cremorne

Bay

25

RD

Gellibrand Pt

Huxleys Beach

Lumeah Pt

Mary Ann Bay

The Spit

Pipe

White Rock Pt

Shelly Beach

Maria Pt

Mortimer Bay

Gorringes

Dirty

Bridge

SOUTH-ARM RD

Clay

Lagoon

Beach

Opossum Bay

E

F

See page 237

G

H

© UNIVERSAL PUBLISHERS PTY LTD 2004

Tasmania

229

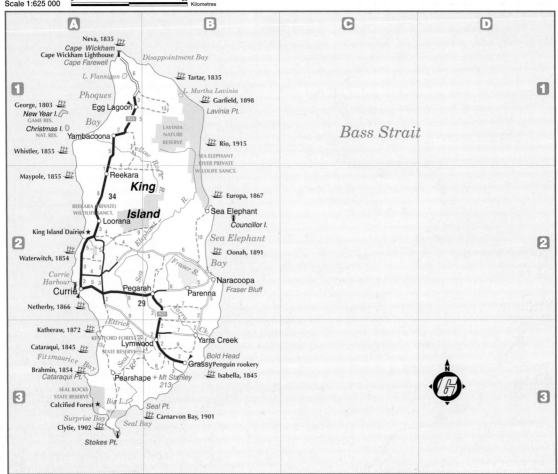

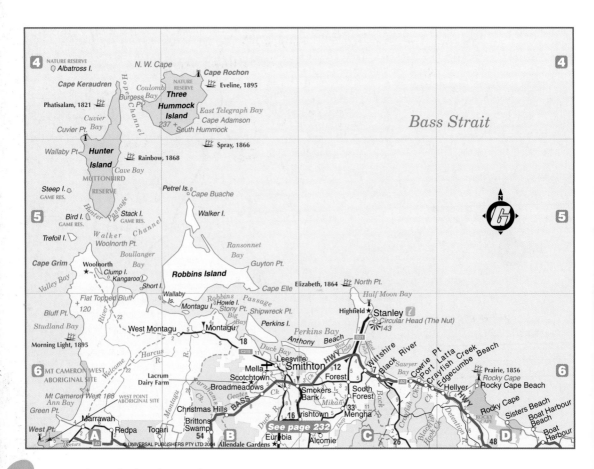

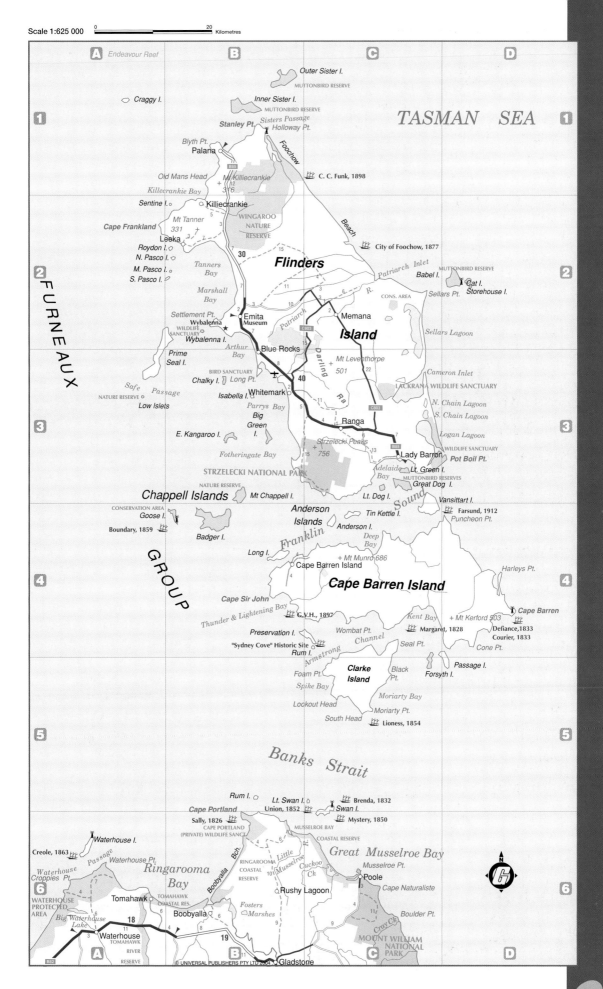

0   20   Kilometres

A   *Endeavour Reef*   **B**   **C**   **D**

Outer Sister I.
MUTTONBIRD RESERVE

Craggy I.
Inner Sister I.
MUTTONBIRD RESERVE

1

Stanley Pt.   Sisters Passage
Holloway Pt.

TASMAN SEA

Blyth Pt.
Palana

Foochow

Old Mans Head   Mt Killiecrankie
Killecrankie Bay   +   376

C. C. Funk, 1898

Sentine I.
Killiecrankie

Cape Frankland   Mt Tanner
331   +   WINGAROO
NATURE
RESERVE

Leeka
Roydon I.
N. Pasco I.
M. Pasco I.
S. Pasco I.

Beach

City of Foochow, 1877

2

Tanners
Bay

30

15

Flinders

Patriarch Inlet   MUTTONBIRD RESERVE
Babel I.   Cat I.
Storehouse I.

Marshall
Bay

11

3
10

R.   CONS. AREA

Sellars Pt.
Sellars Lagoon

Settlement Pt.
Wybalenna   Emita
WILDLIFE   Museum
SANCTUARY
Wybalenna

2
3
C803

2   Memana

Island

Arthur
Bay   Blue Rocks

Patriarch

Darling
Ra.

Mt Leventhorpe
+ 501   22

Cameron Inlet

Prime
Seal I.

BIRD SANCTUARY
Chalky I.   Long Pt.

8

40

LACKRANA WILDLIFE SANCTUARY

Safe
NATURE RESERVE   Passage
Low Islets

Whitemark
Isabella I.

C803

N. Chain Lagoon
S. Chain Lagoon

Parrys Bay
Big
Green
I.

11

5

Logan Lagoon

3

E. Kangaroo I.

Fotheringate Bay

Strzelecki Peaks
+ 756

Ranga

4
7

WILDLIFE SANCTUARY
Lady Barron   Pot Boil Pt.

15

V13

Lt. Green I.

Chappell Islands

STRZELECKI NATIONAL PARK

NATURE RESERVE
Mt Chappell I.

Adelaide
Bay

MUTTONBIRD RESERVES
Great Dog I.

Lt. Dog I.   Sound

Vansittart I.

CONSERVATION AREA
Goose I.

Anderson
Islands

Tin Kettle I.

Farsund, 1912
Puncheon Pt.

Boundary, 1859

Badger I.

Anderson I.

Franklin

Deep
Bay

4

GROUP

Long I.

+ Mt Munro 686
Cape Barren Island

Harleys Pt.

Cape Barren Island

Cape Sir John

Thunder & Lightening Bay   G.V.H., 1897

Kent Bay   + Mt Kerford 503
Margaret, 1828

Cape Barren

Defiance,1833
Courier, 1833

Preservation I.
"Sydney Cove" Historic Site
Rum I.

Wombat Pt.
Channel

Armstrong

Seal Pt.

Cone Pt.

Foam Pt.

Clarke
Island

Black
Pt.

Passage I.
Forsyth I.

Spike Bay

Moriarty Bay

Lookout Head
South Head   Lioness, 1854

Moriarty Pt.

5

Banks   Strait

Rum I.

Lt. Swan I.
Union, 1852   Swan I.

Brenda, 1832

Cape Portland
Sally, 1826
CAPE PORTLAND
(PRIVATE) WILDLIFE SANC.

Mystery, 1850

Waterhouse I.

MUSSELROE BAY
COASTAL RESERVE

Great Musselroe Bay

Creole, 1863

Waterhouse
Croppies Pt.

Passage
Waterhouse Pt.

Ringarooma
Bay

Bch.

Boobyalla

RINGAROOMA
COASTAL
RESERVE

Little
Musselroe

Cuckoo
Ck.

Musselroe Pt.
Poole
Cape Naturaliste

6

WATERHOUSE
PROTECTED
AREA

4
7

Tomahawk
TOMAHAWK
COASTAL RES.

Big Waterhouse
Lake

11

18

Waterhouse
TOMAHAWK
RIVER
RESERVE

B82

3

Boobyalla

Fosters
Marshes

Rushy Lagoon

4

Cray Ck.

Boulder Pt.

11

MOUNT WILLIAM
NATIONAL
PARK

19

© UNIVERSAL PUBLISHERS PTY LTD 2004

Gladstone

N

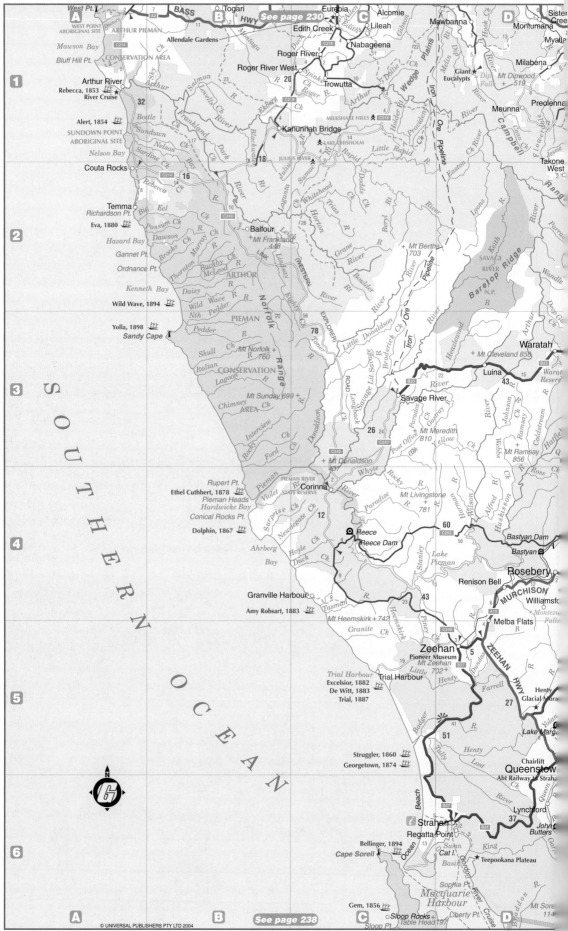

BASS HWY

West Pt.
A
WEST POINT
ABORIGINAL SITE
Mawson Bay
Bluff Hill Pt.
ARTHUR PIEMAN
CONSERVATION AREA

Togari
Allendale Gardens

B
See page 230
Edith Creek
Roger River
Roger River West
Trowutta

Eurebia
Alcomie
Lileah
Nabageena

C
Mawbanna
Sister
Cree
Montumana
Myalla

D
Milabena
Mt Dipwood +519

1

Arthur River
Rebecca, 1853
River Cruise

Alert, 1854
SUNDOWN POINT
ABORIGINAL SITE
Nelson Bay

Couta Rocks

32
Bottle
Sundown
Nelson

16

Kanunnah Bridge
MILKSHAKE HILLS
LAKE CHISHOLM

18
Julius River

20

Giant
Eucalypts
Meunna
Preolenna

Takone
West

2

Temma
Richardson Pt.
Eva, 1880
Hazard Bay
Gannet Pt.
Ordnance Pt.
Kenneth Bay
Wild Wave, 1894
Yolla, 1898
Sandy Cape

10
C249
Balfour
+ Mt Frankland 448
LINK

ARTHUR
PIEMAN
CONSERVATION
AREA
Mt Norfolk + /760
Skull
Italian
Lagoon
Chimney
Mt Sunday 699 +

78

+ Mt Bertha 703

SAVAGE
RIVER
N.P.

Waratah
+ Mt Cleveland 856

3

Rupert Pt.
Ethel Cuthbert, 1878
Pieman Heads
Hardwicke Bay
Conical Rocks Pt.
Dolphin, 1867

Corinna
PIEMAN RIVER
STATE RESERVE
+ Mt Donaldson 837

Mt Meredith 810 +

26 24

Savage River
60

Luina
43

4

Ahrberg
Bay

12

Granville Harbour
Amy Robsart, 1883
Mt Heemskirk + 742
Granite

Reece
Reece Dam

9

43

Mt Livingstone + 781
Lake
Pieman
Stanley

Bastyan Dam
Bastyan
Rosebery
Renison Bell
MURCHISON
Williamsfo
Melba Flats

5

Trial Harbour
Excelsior, 1882
De Witt, 1883
Trial, 1887

Struggler, 1860
Georgetown, 1874

Zeehan
Pioneer Museum
Mt Zeehan 702+
Trial Harbour

5

ZEEHAN
HWY
27
Henty
Glacial Mora
Lake Marg

6

Cape Sorell
Bellinger, 1894

Strahan
Regatta Point
Cape Sorell
Gem, 1856
Sloop Rocks
Table Head

51
41

Chairlift
Queenstow
Abt Railway to Stra
Lynchford
37
John
Butters
Teepookana Plateau
Macquarie
Harbour

SOUTHERN OCEAN

© UNIVERSAL PUBLISHERS PTY LTD 2004
See page 238

0   20   Kilometres

Bass Strait

★ Table Cape Lighthouse
Table Cape
★ Tulip Farm
Wynyard
Moorleah
Somerset
Seabrook
Camdale
Cooee
Burnie
Lapoinya
Wivenhoe
Chasm Creek
West Hd.
Lower
Mt Hicks
Calder
Oldina
Heybridge
Howth
Badger Hd.
Kellatier
Elliott
Mooreville
Sulphur Creek
Penguin
Pt Sorell
The Carbuncle
Yolla
Stowport
Cuprona
Ulverstone
Turners Beach
Hawley
Beach
Shearwater
Ridgley
Upper
West Pine
Penguin
Viewing
Leith
Devonport
Wright J.
Port Sorell
Squeaking Pt
Henrietta
West
Ridgley
Natone
Ferndene
Gawler
Leith
Forth
Ambleside
Wesley
Vale
Northdown
Thirlstane
Takone
Highclere
North
Motton
Riana
Abbotsham
Spreyton
Melrose
Moriarty
Harford
Tewkesbury
Camena
Spalford
Kindred
Paloona
Latrobe
East
Sassafras
Oonah
Upper
Natone
South
Riana
Preston
Sprent
Paloona
Sassafras
West Frankford
Hampshire
Gunns Plains
Loyetea
Heka
Gunns Plains
Warringa
Lower Barrington
Railton
Hellyer
Gorge
HELLYER GORGE
STATE PARK
Parrawe
South Preston
Upper
Castra
Lower
Wilmot
Barrington
Nook
Merseylea
Sunnyside
Parkham
Nietta
Wilmot
Devils
Gate
Sheffield
West Kentish
Kimberley
Cheese
Factory
Reedy
Marsh
Weetah
Guildford
Leven Canyon
Loongana
Narrawa
South
Nietta
Roland
Promised
Land
Paradise
Beulah
Moltema
Elizabeth
Town
Mt Pease
Erriba
Staverton
Claude
Road
Lower
Beulah
Weegena
Dunorlan
Chudleigh
Deloraine
Red Hills
Black Bluff
1339
Moina
Cethana
Murals
Gowrie
Park
Alum Cliffs
State Reserve
Folk
Museum
Mt Beecroft
1140
Wilmot
Lake
Cethana
Lorrinna
Liena
King
Solomon
Mayberry
Marakoopa
Mole Creek
Needles
Montana
Cradle Mountain
Lodge
★ Visitor Centre
Daisy Dell
Caveside
Western
Creek
Meander
Waldheim Chalet
★ Cradle Valley
Lemonthyme
Devils
Gullet
Jackeys Marsh
Mt Remas
1110
Dove Lake
Fisher
Fisher Bluff
1408
Ironstone Mtn
1443
Meander Falls
Mackintosh
Dam
Mackintosh
Cradle Mtn
1545
Rowallan
Lake
Rowallan
Central Plateau
Conservation Area
Breona
Tullah
★ Tullah
Wee Georgie
Wood Railway
Granite Tor
Conservation
Area
Lake Will
Lake
Louisa
Pillans L.
Lake Augusta
Rats Castle
1392
Reynolds I.
Reynolds Neck
Murchison
Dam
Mt Murchison
1273
Cradle Mountain
Lake St Clair
Mt Ossa
1617
Walls of Jerusalem
Lake Adelaide
Lake Ada
Liawenee
Tribute
Lake
Plimsoll
National Park
World
National Park
Double
Lagoon
Miena
Lake
Rolleston
Eldon
Eldon Pk
1439
Heritage
Travellers
Rest
L. Nugeleta
Lit. Pine Lagoon
Lake Margaret
Mt Sedgwick
1147
Lake St Clair
Travellers
Rest
Marlborough
Mt Lyell
Copper Mines
Gormanston
Area
Mt Olympus
1447
Visitor Centre
Bronte Park
Waddamana
Lyell Hwy
Raglan Ra.
Crotty Dam
Derwent
Bridge
Laughing
Jack Lag.
Bronte
Lake
Echo
Mt Mary
1012
Lake
King
William
Dee
Lake Echo
Darwin Dam
Mt King William I
1359
Butlers Gorge
Tungatinah
Frenchmans Cap
1445

For more detail see
map on page 241

See page 234

See page 236

© UNIVERSAL PUBLISHERS PTY LTD 2004

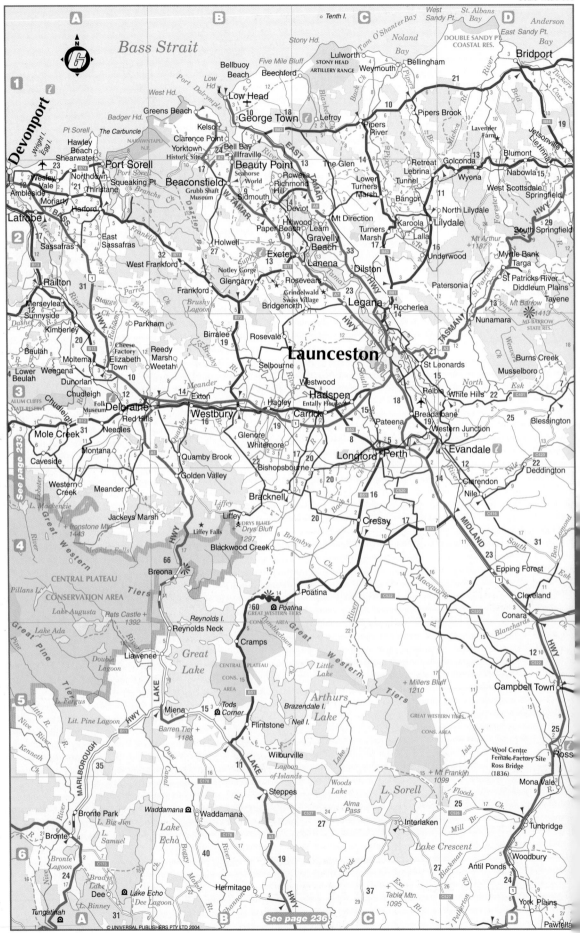

Bass Strait

West Sandy Pt.
St. Albans Bay
Anderson Bay
DOUBLE SANDY PT. COASTAL RES.
East Sandy Pt.

Bridport

Tenth I.
Stony Hd.
Tam O'Shanter Bay
Noland Bay

Bellbuoy Beach
Beechford
Lulworth
STONY HEAD ARTILLERY RANGE
Weymouth
Bellingham
21
Tuckers Rd.
19

Low Hd.
Five Mile Bluff
Blankeet Ck.
Back Ck.

West Hd.
Low Head
10
Pipers Brook
Jetsonville
Lietinna

Badger Hd.
Greens Beach
George Town
Lefroy
10
Pipers Brook
Lavender Farm
Blumont

Pt. Sorell
Wright I.
Egg I.
The Carbuncle
NARAWNTAPU N.P.
Kelso
Clarence Point
Yorktown
Historic Site
Bell Bay
Illfraville
Pipers River
Retreat
Lebrina
Golconda
Wyena
13
Nabowla
West Scottsdale
Springfield

Hawley Beach
Shearwater
Port Sorell
Squeaking Pt.
Beauty Point
Beaconsfield
Grubb Shaft Museum
Sidmouth
Seahorse World
Richmond Hill
Rowella
The Glen
Lower Turners Marsh
Tunnel
Bangor
North Lilydale
11
Myrtle Bank
Targa

Devonport
Wesley Vale
Northdown
Ambleside
Moriarty
Thirlstane
Harford
Deviot
Hillwood
Paper Beach
Leam
Gravelly Beach
Lanena
Mt Direction
Turners Marsh
Karoola
Lalla
Lilydale
Underwood
St Patricks River
Diddleum Plains
Tayene

Latrobe
Sassafras
East Sassafras
West Frankford
Holwell
Exeter
Notley Gorge
Glengarry
Rosevears
Grindelwald
Swiss Village
Bridgenorth
Legana
Dilston
Rocherlea
Patersonia
Nunamara
Mt Barrow
MT BARROW STATE RES.

Railton
Merseylea
Sunnyside
Kimberley
Beulah
Lower Beulah
Moltema
Weegena
Dunorlan
Chudleigh
Parkham
Frankford
Birralee
Rosevale
Selbourne
Launceston
Westwood
Hadspen
Entally House
St Leonards
Relbia
White Hills
Burns Creek
Musselboro
Blessington

Mole Creek
Caveside
Western Creek
Meander
Deloraine
Red Hills
Needles
Montana
Elizabeth Town
Cheese Factory
Reedy Marsh
Weetah
Exton
Westbury
Hagley
Carrick
Quamby Brook
Golden Valley
Glenore
Whitemore
Bishopsbourne
Bracknell
Longford
Perth
Pateena
Breadalbane
Western Junction
Evandale
Deddington
Clarendon
Nile

Jackeys Marsh
Liffey
Liffey Falls
Blackwood Creek
Cressy
Epping Forest
Cleveland
Conara

Breona
Poatina
GREAT WESTERN TIERS AREA

Central Plateau Conservation Area
Lake Augusta
Rats Castle
Reynolds I.
Reynolds Neck
Cramps
Great Lake
CENTRAL PLATEAU CONS. AREA
Little Lake
Arthurs Lake
Millers Bluff
Campbell Town

Liawenee
Miena
Tods Corner
Flintstone
Brazendale I.
Neil I.
GREAT WESTERN TIERS CONS. AREA
Ross
Wool Centre
Female Factory Site
Ross Bridge (1836)
Mona Vale

Great Pine Tiers
Wilburville
Lagoon of Islands
Woods Lake
L. Sorell
Tunbridge

Bronte Park
Waddamana
Steppes
Alma Pass
Interlaken
Woodbury
Antil Ponds

Bronte
Lake Echo
Hermitage
Lake Crescent
York Plains
Pawtella

See page 236

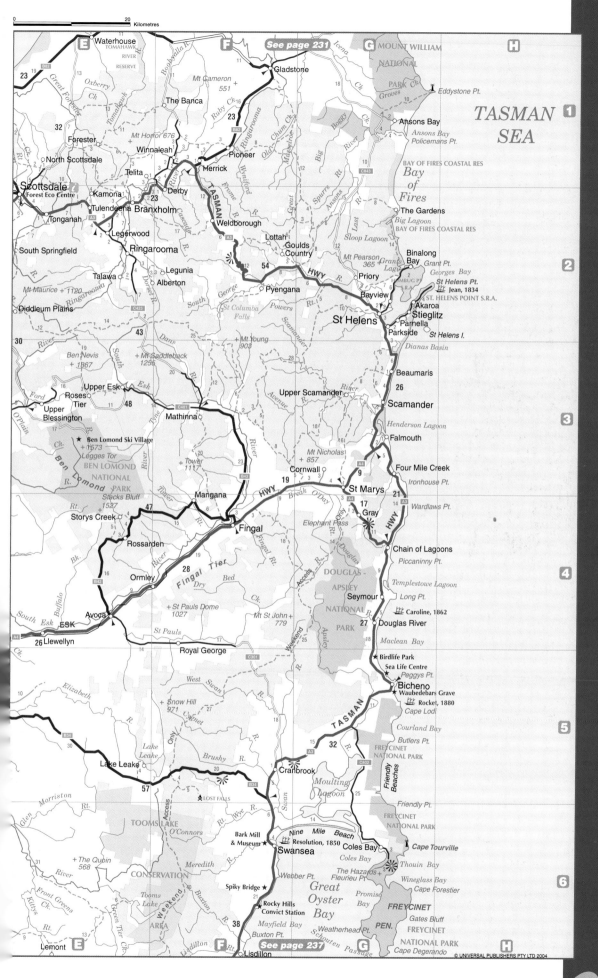

TASMAN SEA

1

TASMAN SEA

Waterhouse
TOMAHAWK RIVER RESERVE
Gladstone

23
B82
Oxberry Ck
Mt Cameron 551
The Banca
Eddystone Pt.
MOUNT WILLIAM NATIONAL PARK
Groves
Ansons Bay

32
Forester
Mt Horror 676
Winnaleah
Pioneer
Herrick
Ansons Bay Policemans Pt.

North Scottsdale
Telita
Derby
23
Frome R.
Weldborough
BAY OF FIRES COASTAL RES
Bay of Fires

Scottsdale
Forest Eco Centre
Kamona
Tulendeena Branxholm
Legerwood
Lottah
Goulds Country
The Gardens
Big Lagoon
BAY OF FIRES COASTAL RES

Tonganah
Ringarooma
Pyengana
Mt Pearson 365
Priory
Binalong Bay
Grant Pt.
Georges Bay

South Springfield
Legunia
Alberton
St Columba Falls
Sloop Lagoon
Bayview
St Helens Pt.
Jean, 1834
ST. HELENS POINT S.R.A.

Talawa
Mt Maurice 1120
Diddleum Plains
Scamander R.
St Helens
Akaroa
Stieglitz
Parnella
Parkside
St Helens I.

30
Ben Nevis 1867
Mt Saddleback 1256
Mt Young 903
Dianas Basin

43
Upper Esk
Roses Tier
Mathinna
Upper Scamander
Beaumaris
26
Scamander

Upper Blessington
48
Ben Lomond Ski Village 1573
Legges Tor
Henderson Lagoon
Falmouth

BEN LOMOND NATIONAL PARK
Stacks Bluff 1527
Tower 1117
Mt Nicholas 857
Cornwall
Four Mile Creek
Ironhouse Pt.

Storys Creek
47
Mangana
19
St Marys
21
Wardlaws Pt.

Rossarden
28
Fingal
17
Gray
Chain of Lagoons
Piccaninny Pt.

Ormley
St Pauls Dome 1027
Elephant Pass
DOUGLAS - APSLEY NATIONAL PARK
Templestowe Lagoon

Avoca
Mt St John 779
Seymour
Long Pt.
Caroline, 1862

ESK
Llewellyn
Royal George
27
Douglas River
Maclean Bay

Birdlife Park
Sea Life Centre
Peggys Pt.
Bicheno
Waubedebars Grave
Rocket, 1880
Cape Lodi

Snow Hill 971
West Swan R.
Courland Bay
Butlers Pt.

FREYCINET NATIONAL PARK

Lake Leake
57
Cranbrook
32
Friendly Beaches
Friendly Pt.

TOOMS LAKE
O'Connors
LOST FALLS
Moulting Lagoon
FREYCINET NATIONAL PARK

The Qubin 568
Bark Mill & Museum
Resolution, 1850
Nine Mile Beach
Swansea
Coles Bay
Cape Tourville
Thouin Bay

CONSERVATION AREA
Spiky Bridge
The Hazards
Fleurieu Pt.
Wineglass Bay
Cape Forestier

Rocky Hills Convict Station
Great Oyster Bay
Promise Bay
FREYCINET PEN.
Gates Bluff

Lemont
38
Lisdillon
Mayfield Bay
Buxton Pt.
Weatherhead Pt.
FREYCINET NATIONAL PARK
Cape Degerando

© UNIVERSAL PUBLISHERS PTY LTD 2004

Tasmania 235

Scale 1:625 000

See page 234

A **B** **C** **D**

Mt Hobhouse 1219
Mt King William II 1359
Mt King William III
Tarraleah
TYELL
Victoria Valley
Osterley
Bark Hut
Fordell
Golf Museum
Bothwell
Lower Marshes
Jericho
Strickland
Wayatinah
Liapootah
34
Wayatinah Lagoon
Wayatinah
Catagunya
L. Catagunya
Wylds Craig 1339
Ouse
Cluny
Lawrenny
Langloh
Hamilton
Hollow Tree
Pelham
Apsley
Black Tier 775
Melton Mowbray
Kempton
Quoin Mtn 899
Dysart
Bagdad
20
29
12
39
28
The Spires Range
Denison Range
The Pleiades
Clear Hill 1198
Lake Gordon
L. Repulse
Repulse
Meadowbank Lake
25
Meadowbank
Ellendale
MOUNT FIELD NATIONAL PARK
Mt Field West 1434
L. Seal
L. Fenton
Skiing
National Park
Marriotts Falls
Junee
Russell Falls
Fentonbury
Westerway
Karanja
Glenora
Bushy Park
Gretna
Rosegarland
Elderslie
Tanina
Broadmarsh
Mangalore
Pontville
Brighton
Bridgewater
Old Beach
Adamsfield
ROAD
Tyenna
Fitzgerald
Maydena
66
GORDON RIVER
Mt Wedge 1147
Frodshams Pass
McPartlan Pass
Creepy Crawly Walk
Snowy Ra.
Styx
20
16
Uxbridge
Moogara
Feilton
Plenty
Salmon Ponds
Lawitta
New Norfolk
Brookside
Molesworth
Collins Gap
Glenorchy
Collinsvale
Black Hills
Dromedary
Granton
Sorell Creek
Malbina
23
11
Glenfern
Lachlan
Mt Lloyd
Collins Bonnet 1260
Mt Montagu 1063
Wellington Falls
Mt Wellington 1270
Fern Tree
Neika
18
12
Lake Pedder
Mt Solitary
Mt Anne 1425
L. Skinner
L. Judd
Scotts Pk
Edgar Dam
Scotts Peak Dam
Lt Denison
Snowy Ranges Trout Fishery
Lonnanvale
Crabtree
Mountain River
Lucaston
Apple Museum
Grove
Lower Longley
Longley
Leslie Vale
Kingston
See page 238
Dodds R.
PEAK RD
SCOTTS
Gallagher Plateau
Mt Weld 1344
Lobster L.
Weld R.
Judbury
Ranelagh
14
16
Glen Huon
Huonville
Allens Rivulet
Kaoota
Nierinna
Morgan
Howden
WORLD HERITAGE AREA
Mt Hesperus 1098
PORT DAVEY TRACK
ARTHUR
Arthur Range
PLAINS
Mt Picton 1327
L. Riveaux
L. Picton
Cracroft R.
Tahune Forest AirWalk
Franklin
13
21
Woodstock
Upper Woodstock
Poverty Gully
Pelverata
Electrona
Snug
SOUTHWEST NATIONAL PARK
Mt Norold 978
Federation Pk 1284
L. Geeves
Mt Bobs 1109
Pine L.
Picton Ra.
HARTZ MTNS. NATIONAL PARK
Hartz
Hartz Pk 1254m
Arve Falls
22
17
24
Cradoc
South Franklin
Castle Forbes Bay
Port Huon
Glaziers Bay
Cygnet
Nicholas Rivulet
Woodbridge
Kettering
Roberts Point
Bay Range
Old River
Salisbury River
New River
Roberts River
Geeveston
Forest and Heritage Centre
Cairns Bay
Wattle Grove
Petcheys Bay
Waterloo
Surges Bay
Lymington
Glendevie
Police Point
Garden I.
Surveyors Bay
Glenbervie
Francistown
Walpole
Verona Sands
Gordon
Garden I. 49
Creek
Birchs Bay
Flowerpot
Gardners Bay
Talune Wildlife Pk
23
12
Mt La Perouse 1158
Swallows Nest Lakes
Catamaran
Cockle Creek
Adamsons Pk 1226
Creekton
Hastings Caves
Raminea
Strathblane
Harvey Town
Dover
Huon I.
Satellite I.
Ninepin Point
Simpsons Bay
Alonnah
Bruny Island
13
Port Esperance
Esperance Pt
Hope I.
Scott Pt
Ventenat Pt
Lunawanna
Partridge I.
Melaleuca Lagoon
Melaleuca Bird Observatory
Mt Counsel 800
Louisa Ck
Louisa R.
New River Lagoon
Thermal Springs
Lune River
Ida Bay
Hastings
Southport
Enchantress 1835
Great Taylors Bay
Cloudy Bay Lagoon
Mt Bruny 504
South Bruny Lighthouse
Tasman Head
The Friars
James Lucas 1829
17
COX BIGHT
Cox Bluff
Red Pt
Louisa I.
Havelock Bluff
Ile du Golfe
Prion Bay
Point Vivian
COAST
Mt La Perouse 1158
Catamaran R.
Oval L.
South Cape R.
D'Entrecasteaux
Historic Railway
Southport I. N.P.
George III, 1835
Courts I.
Eliza Pt
Maria Orr, 1846
Wallace, 1835
Actaeon I.
Recherche Bay
Fishers Pt
SOUTH BRUNY
Cloudy Bay
Cape Bruny
Abeona I. 1848
SOUTHWEST NATIONAL PARK
De Witt I.
Walker I.
Flat Witch I.
Maatsuyker I.
Maatsuyker Group
Shoemaker Pt
South Soldier Bluff
South Cape Bay
Whale Hd
South East Cape
Cape Bruny

© UNIVERSAL PUBLISHERS PTY LTD 2004

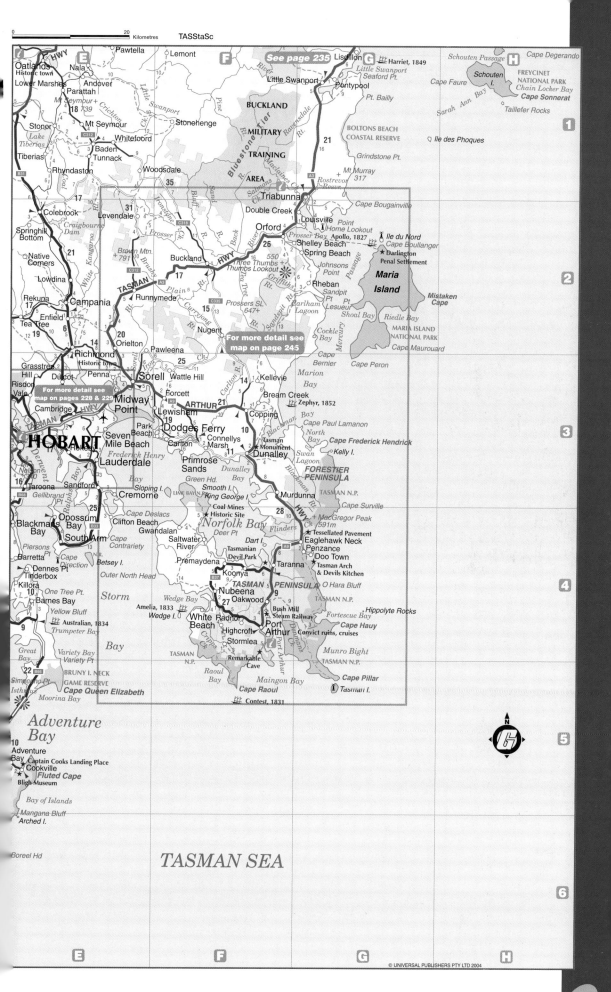

See page 235

For more detail see map on page 245

For more detail see map on pages 228 & 225

BUCKLAND
MILITARY
TRAINING
AREA

HOBART

FORESTIER
PENINSULA

Norfolk Bay

*Maria
Island*

MARIA ISLAND
NATIONAL PARK

FREYCINET
NATIONAL PARK

*Storm
Bay*

*Great
Bay*

*Adventure
Bay*

Bay of Islands

TASMAN SEA

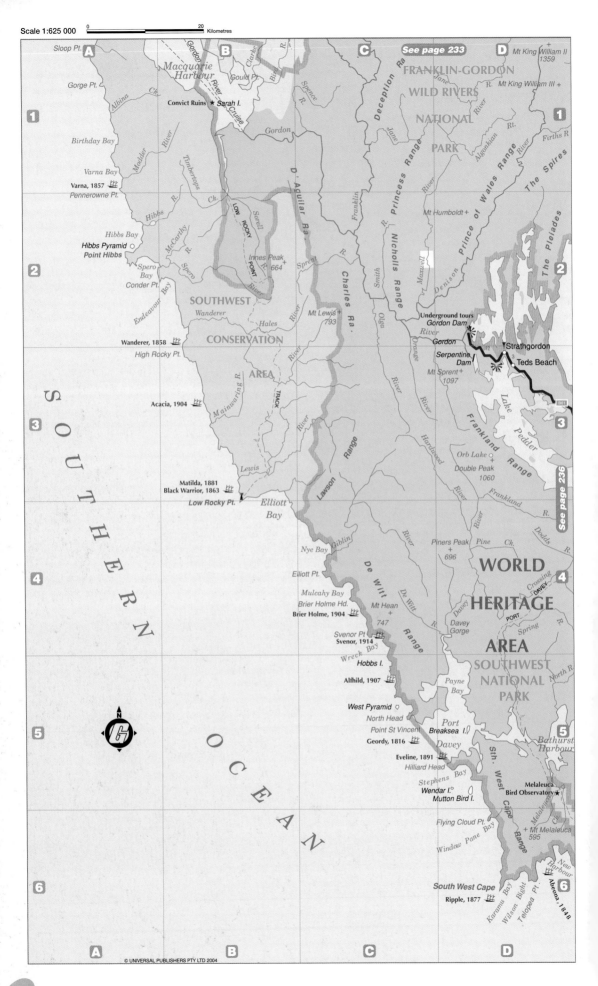

Scale 1:625 000

20 Kilometres

A · B · C · D

Sloop Pt.
Gorge Pt.

Macquarie
Harbour

Gould Pt.

Convict Ruins ★ Sarah I.

Birthday Bay

Varna Bay
Varna, 1857
Pennerowne Pt.

Hibbs R.

Hibbs Bay
Hibbs Pyramid ○
Point Hibbs

Spero
Bay
Conder Pt.

Endeavour Bay

SOUTHWEST

Wanderer

Wanderer, 1858

CONSERVATION

High Rocky Pt.

AREA

Acacia, 1904

TRACK

Matilda, 1881
Black Warrior, 1863
Low Rocky Pt.

Elliott
Bay

Lewis

Nye Bay

Elliott Pt.

Mulcahy Bay
Brier Holme Hd.
Brier Holme, 1904

Svenor Pt
Svenor, 1914

Hobbs I.

Alfhild, 1907

West Pyramid ○
North Head
Point St Vincent
Geordy, 1816

Eveline, 1891
Hilliard Head

Wendar I. ○
Mutton Bird I.

Flying Cloud Pt.

Window Pane Bay

South West Cape
Ripple, 1877

LOW ROCKY POINT

Innes Peak +
664

Mt Lewis +
793

Hales

Charles Ra.

Lawson
Range

De Witt

Mt Hean
+
747

Wreck
Bay

Port
Breaksea I.
Davey

Stephens Bay

FRANKLIN-GORDON

WILD RIVERS

NATIONAL

PARK

Mt King William II
1359
Mt King William III +

The Spires

The Pleiades

Deception Ra

Princess Range

Nicholls Range

Prince of Wales Range

Mt Humboldt +

Underground tours
Gordon Dam
Gordon
Serpentine
Dam

Mt Sprent +
1097

Frankland Range

Lake
Pedder

Strathgordon
Teds Beach

Orb Lake ○
Double Peak
1060

Frankland

Piners Peak
+
696

Pine Ck.

WORLD

HERITAGE

Davey
Gorge

PORT
DAVEY
Crossing

AREA

SOUTHWEST
NATIONAL
PARK

Payne
Bay

North R.

Bathurst
Harbour

Melaleuca
Bird Observatory ★

Sth West Cape Range

Mt Melaleuca
595

New
Harbour

Abeona, 1848

S O U T H E R N   O C E A N

N
G

World Heritage Cruises

Cradle Mountain–
Lake St Clair National Park

Cradle Mountain

Cradle Mountain-Lake St Clair National Park is part of the acclaimed Tasmanian Wilderness World Heritage Area that protects a diversity of environments waiting to be explored by the adventurous.

The founding father of the park, Austrian immigrant Gustav Weindorfer, was overwhelmed by the other-worldliness of this area, proclaiming that it "must be a national park for the people of all time".

The park's 1612 square kilometres boast stunning scenery, wild landscapes, buttongrass plains, primordial rainforests and alpine heathlands, interspersed with glacial lakes, icy rivers, and streams cascading from the mountains. The park is renowned for its excellent bushwalking tracks.

Cradle Mountain forms the northern end of the park and its jagged contours epitomise the feel of a wild landscape. Attractions include Pencil Pine Falls, a short stroll from the visitors centre; and Ballroom Forest, part of the Dove Lake Loop Track. Facilities include picnic shelters with BBQs, campgrounds, lodges and track huts, Cradle Mountain Lodge Store and Cradle Mountain Wilderness Centre.

Lake St Clair, 85 km away at the southern end of the park, was carved out by ice over the last two million years. Romantically named attractions in the area include Forgotten Lake, Travellers Rest Lake and the Acropolis.

Lake St Clair

This lake was formed by a glacier and is Australia's deepest natural freshwater lake, 17 km long and 200m deep. It is the source of the Derwent River, upon which Hobart is situated.

Tourist information

Cradle Mtn Visitor Centre

Park entrance, Cradle Mtn Rd, Cradle Mtn-Lake St Clair National Park Tas.
Ph: (03) 6492 1110
www.parks.tas.gov.au

Main Attractions

◈ **Cradle Valley Boardwalk** This new boardwalk runs from the Visitor Centre along the Dove River to Dove Lake.

◈ **Dove Lake Loop Track** The shores of this picturesque lake are ideal for observing wallabies and wombats in the late afternoon. A highlight of the walk is the majestic Ballroom Forest.

◈ **Overland Track** Considered one of Australia's premier wilderness walking tracks, this 5-8 day expedition covers 85km. Highlights can include a side trip to the ascent of Tasmania's highest peak, Mt Ossa.

◈ **Waldheim Chalet** Waldheim (meaning 'forest home') is located at the northern end of the Overland Track. Waldheim Cabins offer an authentic wilderness experience in this pristine area.

Trout fishing in Lake St Clair

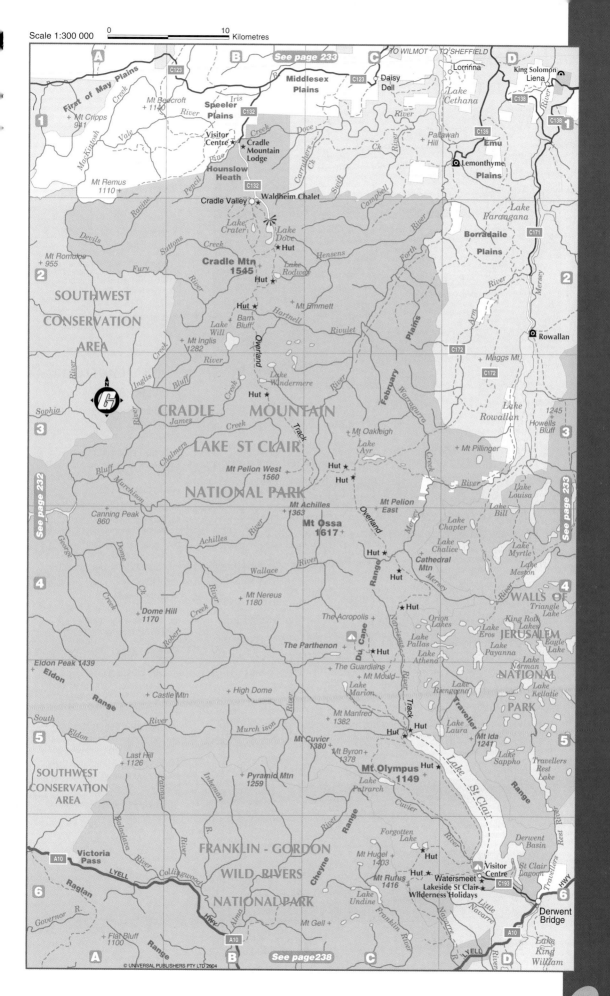

0   10 Kilometres

See page 233

TO WILMOT TO SHEFFIELD

A   **B**   **C**   **D**

Lorrinna

King Solomon
Liena

C123

First of May Plains

Middlesex
Plains

C123

Daisy
Dell

Lake
Cethana

C138

1

+ Mt Cripps
911

Mt Beecroft
+ 1140

Iris
River

Speeler
Plains

C132

Dove

River

C138

C139

Pattawah
Hill

Emu

Mt Remus
1110 +

Hounslow
Heath

C132

Visitor
Centre ★

Cradle
Mountain
Lodge

Creek

Campbell

Lemonthyme
Plains

Cradle Valley ○

Waldheim Chalet

Lake
Parangana

C171

Borradaile
Plains

Lake
Crater

Lake
Dove

Hensens

Forth

2

Mt Romulus
+ 955

★ Hut

Cradle Mtn
1545 +

Lake
Rodwoa

Hut ★

Plains

River

Mersey

Lake
Will

Hut ★

+ Mt Emmett

Barn
Bluff

Hartnell

Rivulet

C172

Rowallan ○

SOUTHWEST

CONSERVATION

AREA

+ Mt Inglis
1282

Overland

Lake
Windermere

C172

+ Maggs Mt

3

Sophia

N
G

CRADLE MOUNTAIN

LAKE ST CLAIR

Hut ★

Track

+ Mt Oakleigh

Lake
Ayr

Lake
Rowallan

Lake
Louisa

1245
+ Howells
Bluff

See page 232

NATIONAL PARK

Canning Peak
860

Bluff

Murchison

Mt Achilles
+ 1363

Mt Ossa
1617 +

Hut ★

Hut ★

Overland

Mt Pelion
East

Mt Pelion
West
1560

Mt Pillinger +

Lake
Bill

Lake
Chapter

Lake
Myrtle

Lake
Meston

See page 233

4

Dome Hill
1170

Achilles

River

Wallace

River

Range

Hut ★

Cathedral
Mtn

Mersey

WALLS OF

Triangle
Lake

+ Mt Nereus
1180

The Acropolis +

Du Cane

Hut ★

Orion
Lakes

King Roth
Lakes

JERUSALEM

Eagle
Lake

Eldon Peak 1439

Eldon

The Parthenon

Range

+ The Guardians

+ Mt Mould

Lake
Marion

Lake
Pallas

Lake
Athena

Lake
Eros

Lake
Payanna

Lake
Norman

NATIONAL

Lake
Kellatie

+ Castle Mtn

+ High Dome

Mt Manfred
+ 1382

River

Track

Hut ★

Lake
Reengeena

Lake
Laura

PARK

5

South

Eldon

Last Hill
+ 1126

Range

Murchison

River

Mt Cuvier
1380 +

Mt Byron +
1378

Hut ★

Traveller

Lake
Sappho

Mt Ida
1241

Travellers
Rest
Lake

SOUTHWEST

CONSERVATION

AREA

+ Pyramid Mtn
1259

Mt Olympus
1149 +

Hut ★

Lake
Patrarch

Cuvier

Lake
St Clair

Range

6

Victoria
Pass

LYELL

Raglan

Governor
R.

A10

FRANKLIN - GORDON

WILD RIVERS

NATIONAL PARK

+ Flat Bluff
1100

Range

A10

HWY

Cheyne

Range

Mt Hugel +
1403

Mt Rufus
1416

Mt Gell +

Forgotten
Lake

River

Lake
Undine

Franklin River

Hut ★

Hut ★

Watersmeet
Lakeside St Clair
Wilderness Holidays

Derwent
Basin

Visitor
Centre ★

St Clair
Lagoon

C193

Little
Navarre

LYELL

Navarre

River

Rest

River

HWY

Derwent
Bridge

A10

Lake
King
William

A   **B**   **C**   **D**

See page 238

Flinders Island and
King Island

Trouser Point, Flinders Island

Perched respectively above the east and west extremes of Tasmania's north coast, Flinders Island and King Island were once centres of the long-banned sealing industry, but now support celebrated agricultural industries of their own.

Flinders Island is the largest in the Furneaux Group, and is named after pioneer Matthew Flinders. Since its colonial settlement, the island has witnessed many changes: in the 1950s a Soldier/Farmer scheme was initiated, leading to 336 square kilometres being cleared and sown. The island is now an ideal place to escape the stresses of city life, offering many natural attractions such as bushwalking in Strzelecki National Park, scuba diving around 60 wrecks off the coastline, swimming and fishing.

King Island lies on the western edge of Bass Strait and covers 1260 square kilometres. Gold and tin mining were once the island's primary industries: this has shifted to making dairy products of exceptional quality, livestock farming, cray fishing, abalone harvesting, and even kelp drying.

With more than 145km of picturesque coastline and abundant natural attractions, King Island is a haven for those wishing to get away from it all.

History of King Island

The first European thought to have visited this island was Captain James Black. He named it after Philip King, the Governor of NSW in 1801. The island's once thriving seal and sea elephant colonies have suffered from extensive sealing and hunting in the past.

Tourist information

Tourism King Island
Freecall: 1800 645 014
www.kingisland.org.au

Flinders Island Area Marketing and Development Office

7 Lagoon Rd, Whitemark, Flinders Island Tas.7255
Ph: (03) 6359 2380
Freecall: 1800 994 477
www.flindersislandonline.com.au

Main Attractions

FLINDERS ISLAND

◈ **Emita Museum** This museum displays the history of various groups of pioneer settlers.

◈ **Logan Lagoon Wildlife Sanctuary** This sanctuary has been included on the list of Wetlands of International Importance.

◈ **Strzelecki National Park** This 422 sq km park offers many recreational opportunities including bushwalking, boating and swimming. The climb to Mt Strzelecki's 756m summit is a six-hour return journey.

◈ **Wybalenna** An historic, culturally significant and tragic site for Tasmanian Aborigines, who were exiled there in the 1830s.

KING ISLAND

◈ **Cape Wickham Lighthouse** Australia's tallest lighthouse was built in 1861 to guide travellers safely into Bass Strait.

◈ **King Island Dairies** Now producing prize-winning cheeses and delicacies, the dairy was established in 1902 because dairy products were easier to transport than livestock.

◈ **Grassy** This area is well known for its penguin rookery.

Strzelecki Peaks, Flinders Island

Tasman Peninsula

Port Arthur from Palmers Lookout

The Tasman Peninsula's landscape is rugged – like much of its history. The coastline features geological curiosities, fascinating seascapes and spectacular seaside walks, while the inland and the offshore islands are protected habitats for a rich variety of flora and fauna.

The coastline offers many opportunities for adventure, such as abseiling, rock climbing, scuba diving and sea kayaking. There is also a vast array of walking trails, horse riding trails, and mountain bike tracks, which allow visitors to view the stunning surroundings at close range.

The peninsula is scattered with the remains of Tasmania's oldest colonial and penal settlements, including the infamous convict sites at Port Arthur and Eaglehawk Neck. This harsh chapter of Australia's history is brought to life along the Convict Trail, which takes in seven historic sites, the nightly 'Historic Ghost Tour' at Port Arthur, and tours to the Isle of the Dead.

Eaglehawk Neck

Once guarded by vicious dogs in an attempt to turn the Peninsula into a virtual prison, infamous Eaglehawk Neck is a must to visit. It is the site of many natural wonders including the extraordinary Tessellated Pavement wave platform, the Blowhole, and Pirates Bay Lookout.

Tourist information

i Port Arthur Visitor Centre

Port Arthur Historic Site,
Port Arthur Tas. 7182
Freecall: 1800 659 101
www.portarthur-region.com.au

Main Attractions

◈ **Bush Mill Steam Railway and Settlement** A reconstructed timber-mill settlement near Oakwood, with a 4 km miniature railway.

◈ **Isle of the Dead** Cruises are available across the bay from Port Arthur to the historic cemetery.

◈ **Maria Island National Park** Originally a convict station, this National Park's isolation has preserved a rich variety of wildlife.

◈ **Port Arthur Historic Site** The site of Australia's longest established penal colony, operating between 1830 and 1877, the area is now filled with ruins. Lantern-lit 'ghost tours' are available in the evening.

◈ **Tasman National Park** This park boasts some of Australia's most dramatic coastal walks. Australian fur seals breed and rest along its rugged coastline.

◈ **Tasmanian Devil Park** This centre offers the chance to get close to Tasmania's famous devils, and other native animals.

Cape Raoul

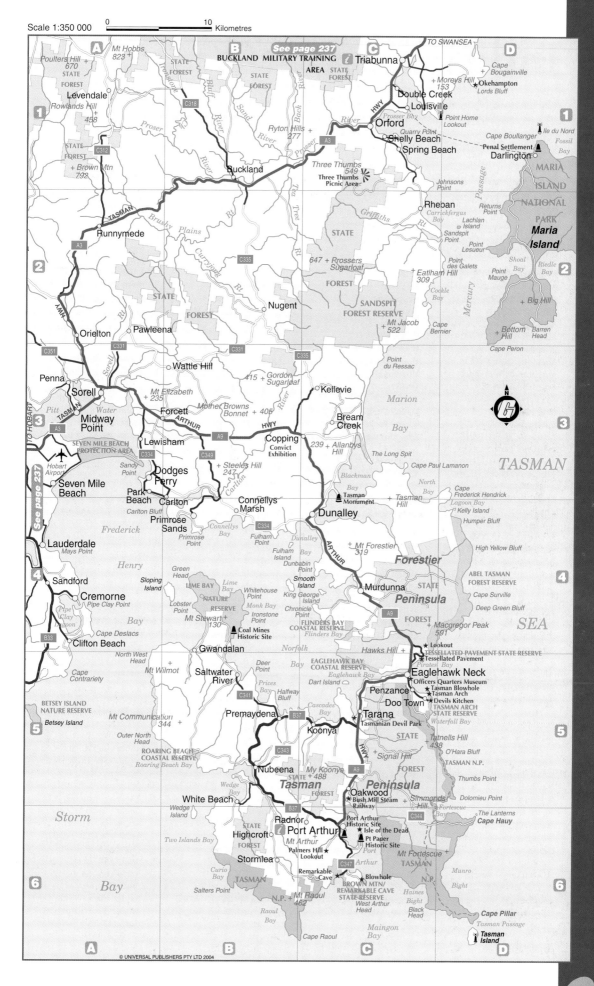

Scale 1:350 000

0 · · · 10 Kilometres

A B C D

Mt Hobbs
823
Poulters Hill
670
STATE
FOREST

Levendale
Rowlands Hill
458

STATE
FOREST

C312

Brown Mtn
792

C318

STATE
FOREST

BUCKLAND MILITARY TRAINING
AREA

See page 237

STATE
FOREST

Triabunna

TO SWANSEA

Cape
Bougainville

Moreys Hill
153
Okehampton
Lords Bluff

Double Creek
Louisville

Point Home
Lookout

Ile du Nord

Cape Boullanger
Fossil
Bay

Orford
Quarry Point
Shelly Beach
Spring Beach

Penal Settlement
Darlington

MARIA
ISLAND

Ryton Hills
277

Three Thumbs
549
Three Thumbs
Picnic Area

Johnsons
Bay

NATIONAL
PARK

Maria
Island

Buckland

Runnymede

A3

Brushy Plains

STATE

FOREST

Rheban
Carrickfergus
Bay
Lachlan
Island
Sandspit
Point

Returns
Point

Point
Lesueur

Point
des Galets

647 Prossers
Sugarloaf

Eatlham Hill
309

Point
Mauge

Shoal
Bay

Big Hill

Riedle
Bay

Orielton

Pawleena

C351 C331

Nugent

STATE

FOREST

SANDSPIT
FOREST RESERVE
Mt Jacob
522

Cape
Bernier

Cape Peron

Bottom
Hill

Barren
Head

Point
du Ressac

Penna

Sorell

Midway
Point

TASMAN A3

C331

Wattle Hill

C335

Mt Elizabeth
235

415 Gordon
Sugarloaf

Kellevie

Marion

Bay

TASMAN

Forcett
Mother Browns
Bonnet 405

Bream
Creek

SEVEN MILE BEACH
PROTECTION AREA

Lewisham

C334

ARTHUR A9

HWY

C349

Copping
Convict
Exhibition

239 Allanbys
Hill

The Long Spit

Cape Paul Lamanon

SEA

Hobart
Airport

Dodges
Ferry

Steeles Hill
247

Blackman
Bay

North
Bay

Cape
Frederick Hendrick

Seven Mile
Beach

Sandy
Point

Carlton

Park
Beach
Carlton Bluff

Primrose
Sands

Connellys
Marsh

C334

Tasman
Monument

Dunalley

Tasman
Hill

Lagoon Bay

Kelly Island

Humper Bluff

Lauderdale
Mays Point

Frederick

Henry

Primrose
Point

Connellys
Bay

Fulham
Point

Dunalley
Bay

Mt Forestier
319

High Yellow Bluff

Sandford

Green
Head

Fulham
Island

Dunbabin
Point

ARTHUR

Forestier

ABEL TASMAN
FOREST RESERVE

Cremorne
Pipe Clay Point

LIME BAY
NATURE
RESERVE

Whitehouse
Point

Smooth
Island

Monk Bay

King George
Island

Peninsula

STATE

Murdunna

Cape Surville

Deep Green Bluff

Pipe
Clay
Lagoon

Bay

Cape Deslacs

Sloping
Island

Lobster
Point

Mt Stewart
130

Ironstone
Point

Chronicle
Point

FLINDERS BAY
COASTAL RESERVE
Flinders Bay

A9

FOREST

Macgregor Peak
591

Clifton Beach

North West
Head

Coal Mines
Historic Site

Hawks Hill

Lookout

TESSELLATED PAVEMENT STATE RESERVE
Tessellated Pavement

Cape
Contrariety

Gwandalan

Mt Wilmot

Deer
Point

Norfolk

EAGLEHAWK BAY
COASTAL RESERVE
Eaglehawk Bay
Dart Island

Eaglehawk Neck
Officers Quarters Museum
Tasman Blowhole
Tasman Arch

BETSEY ISLAND
NATURE RESERVE

B33

Betsey Island

Saltwater
River

Prices
Bay

Halfway
Bluff

Penzance
Doo Town

Devils Kitchen

TASMAN ARCH
STATE RESERVE
Waterfall Bay

C341

Outer North
Head

Mt Communication
344

Premaydena

B37

Koonya

Cascades
Bay

Tarana
Tasmanian Devil Park

STATE

Signal Hill

Tatnells Hill
438

O'Hara Bluff

TASMAN N.P.

ROARING BEACH
COASTAL RESERVE
Roaring Beach Bay

C343

Nubeena

My Koonya
488

STATE

FOREST

A9

FOREST

Thumbs Point

Wedge
Bay

Tasman

Peninsula

Simmonds
Hill

Dolomieu Point

White Beach

Wedge
Island

B37

Oakwood
Bush Mill Steam
Railway

Fortescue

The Lanterns
Cape Hauy

Storm

Two Islands Bay

Radnor

Port Arthur
Historic Site
Highcroft
Mt Arthur

Port Arthur

Isle of the Dead
Pt Puer
Historic Site

Stormlea

Palmers Hill
Lookout

STATE
FOREST

Mt Fortescue

TASMAN

N.P.

Munro

Bight

Curio
Bay

Remarkable
Cave

C347

Blowhole

BROWN MTN/
REMARKABLE CAVE
STATE RESERVE
West Arthur
Head

Haines
Bight

Cape Pillar

Salters Point

N.P. Mt Raoul
462

Black
Head

Tasman Passage

Bay

Raoul
Bay

Maingon
Bay

Tasman
Island

Cape Raoul

© UNIVERSAL PUBLISHERS PTY LTD 2004

Index

This alphabetical index covers the cities, towns, localities and homesteads in the maps in this publication.

The index entries are followed by the state, the page number and grid reference. eg **Abbeys, WA** 189 A2

Entries under one word are grouped together. Where entries consist of two or more, the alphabetical sequence is governed by the first, then second word. eg Little Swanport, Little Toplar Roadhouse, Little Wobby, Littlemore, Littles Crossing.

Entries beginning with Mc are treated as though they are spelt Mac, similarly Mt is indexed as Mount and St is indexed as Saint.

The following state abbreviations are used in this index: ACT-Australian Capital Territory, NSW-New South Wales, NT-Northern Territory, QLD-Queensland, SA-South Australia, TAS-Tasmania, VIC-Victoria, WA-Western Australia.

Note: this index does not purport to include every city, suburb, town, locality or homestead in Australia.

Balnarring Beach, VIC 73 F6
Balook, QLD 116 D2
Balook, VIC 85 F4
Balranald, NSW 42 D1
Balwyn, VIC 71 E3
Balwyn North, VIC 71 E3
Bamaga, QLD 113 B1
Bamarang, NSW 61 A2
Bambaroo, QLD 112 A5
Bambill, VIC 74 B4
Bambilla, NSW 37 H3
Bamboo Creek Mine, WA
  180 B6, 183 E1
Bambra, VIC 83 H4, 89 F4
Ban Ban Springs, NT 201 E5
Ban Ban Springs, QLD
  117 G6, 121 G1
Banana, QLD 117 E5
Bancroft, QLD 117 F5
Banda, WA 183 G6
Bandiana, VIC 79 G3
Bang Bang, QLD 110 C5
Bangalee, QLD 129 C3
Bangalow, NSW 35 G3,
  46 D2
Bangerang, VIC 77 E3
Bangham, SA 155 G4, 163 D2
Bangholme, VIC 73 F1
Bangor, NSW 28 D4
Bangor, TAS 234 C2
Banjawarn, WA 183 F6
Banjeroop, VIC 77 H1
Banjoura, QLD 115 G2
Banjup, WA 170 D6, 172 D2
Banka Banka, NT 210 B1
Banks, ACT 20 B6
Banksia, NSW 29 E3
Banksia, QLD 129 A2
Banksia Beach, QLD 131 C6
Banksia Park, SA 143 E5
Banksmeadow, NSW 29 G3
Bankstown, NSW 28 D2
Bankstown Airport, NSW
  28 C2
Bannerton, VIC 75 F5
Bannister, WA 176 C3
Bannockburn, QLD 115 H2
Bannockburn, VIC 84 A3,
  89 G2
Banora Point, NSW 127 D6
Banyan, VIC 77 E2
Banyena, VIC 77 E4
Banyo, QLD 107 F6, 108 D1
Barabon, QLD 115 F1
Baradine, NSW 33 H6, 39 H1
Barakula, QLD 121 E1
Baralba, QLD 117 E5
Barataria, QLD 115 F3
Baratta, SA 153 F3
Barcaldine, QLD 115 H4
Barcaldine Downs, QLD
  115 H4
Barden Ridge, NSW 28 C4
Bardoc, WA 178 B4
Bardon, QLD 108 B2
Bardwell Park, NSW 29 E3
Bardwell Valley, NSW 29 E3
Barellan, NSW 38 D6
Barfold, VIC 78 A6
Barford, QLD 116 A6
Bargara, QLD 117 H6, 125 A1
Bargo, NSW 40 B6, 45 G1,
  55 B2

Barham, NSW 43 E3
Baring, VIC 76 C1
Baringhup, VIC 77 H6,
  95 D2
Barjarg, VIC 79 E5
Barkly, VIC 77 F5
Barkly Downs, QLD 114 A1
Barkly Homestead
  Roadhouse, NT 210 D3
Barmah, VIC 78 B3
Barmedman, NSW 39 E6
Barmera, SA 153 G6, 155 G1,
  165 B2
Barnadown, VIC 78 B5
Barnato, NSW 38 B2
Barnawartha, VIC 79 G3,
  99 B1
Barnawartha South, VIC
  79 G3, 99 B1
Barnes Bay, TAS 237 E4
Barnong, WA 174 C1
Barooga, NSW 43 H3
Barooga, VIC 78 D3
Baroondah, QLD 116 D6,
  120 D1
Baroota, SA 152 D4
Barossa Goldfields, SA
  143 G2
Barpinba, VIC 83 G3, 89 E2
Barraba, NSW 34 C5
Barradeen, QLD 120 A1
Barragup, WA 191 C2
Barramunga, VIC 83 H4,
  89 F4
Barraport, VIC 77 G3
Barraroo, NSW 37 F3
Barratta, QLD 112 B6
Barretta, TAS 236 D4
Barrington, NSW 41 E2
Barrington, QLD 112 A6,
  116 A1
Barrington, TAS 233 G2
Barringun, NSW 32 C3
Barrow Creek Roadhouse,
  NT 209 H5, 210 B5
Barry, NSW 40 D2
Barrys Reef, VIC 84 A1,
  95 E4
Bartle Frere, QLD 123 D5
Barton, ACT 19 C5, 20 B3
Barton, VIC 83 E1, 97 D4
Barunduda, VIC 79 G3
Barunga, NT 201 G6, 205 G1
Barwidgee, WA 183 F5
Barwon Downs, VIC 83 H4,
  89 F4
Barwon Heads, VIC 84 A4
Baryugil, NSW 35 F4
Basalt Creek, QLD 116 D5
Basin View, NSW 61 A4
Basket Range, SA 145 F1
Bass, VIC 84 D4
Bass Hill, NSW 28 C2
Bassendean, WA 171 E2
Batavia Downs, QLD 113 B3
Batchelor, NT 200 D4,
  221 C1
Batchica, VIC 76 D3
Bateau Bay, NSW 51 C4
Batehaven, NSW 45 F3
Bateman, WA 170 C5, 172 C1
Batemans Bay, NSW 45 F3
Bathurst, NSW 40 A5

Batlow, NSW 44 C3, 65 A1
Batten Pt, NT 207 E3
Battery, QLD 112 A6
Battery Point, TAS 227 D4,
  228 C3
Bauhinia Downs, NT 206 D3
Bauhinia Downs, QLD
  114 D1, 116 D5
Baulkamaugh Nth, VIC
  78 C3
Baulkham Hills, NSW
  26 C4
Bauple, QLD 125 A5
Bawley Point, NSW 45 G3,
  55 A6
Baxter, VIC 73 F3
Bayindeen, VIC 95 A3
Baykool, QLD 116 A6
Baynton, VIC 78 B6
Baynton, VIC 90 D1
Bayswater, VIC 71 G4
Bayswater, WA 170 D2
Bayswater North, VIC 71
  G3, 93 A2
Bayulu, WA 181 B5
Bayview, NSW 27 H3
Bayview, NT 198 B4
Bayview, TAS 235 G2
Beachmere, QLD 107 F2,
  131 C6
Beachport, SA 155 F5,
  163 B4
Beacon, WA 175 E4
Beacon Hill, NSW 27 G4
Beaconsfield, NSW 29 F2
Beaconsfield, TAS 234 B2
Beaconsfield, WA 170 B5,
  172 B1
Beaconsfield Upper, VIC
  84 D3
Beagle Bay, WA 180 D4
Bealiba, VIC 77 G5, 95 C1
Beallah, QLD 137 B6
Beardmore, VIC 85 F2
Bearii, VIC 78 C3
Bears Lagoon, VIC 77 H4
Beaudesert, QLD 114 D2,
  121 H3, 133 C2
Beaufort, VIC 83 G1, 95 B4
Beaumaris, TAS 235 G3
Beaumaris, VIC 70 D6
Beaumont, NSW 61 A1
Beaumont, SA 144 D1
Beauty Point, NSW 27 G5
Beauty Point, TAS 234 B2
Beazleys Br., VIC 77 F5
Beckenham, WA 171 E4
Beckom, NSW 39 E6, 44 B1
Bedford, NSW 40 C4
Bedford, WA 170 D2
Bedford Downs, WA 181 C4
Bedford Park, SA 144 C3
Bedfordale, WA 173 G3
Bedgerebong, NSW 39 F5
Bedourie, QLD 114 B5,
  116 D6
Bedunburru, WA 180 D4
Beeac, VIC 83 G3, 89 E3
Beebyn, WA 182 D5
Beech Forest, VIC 83 G5,
  89 E5
Beechboro, WA 171 E1
Beechford, TAS 234 C1

Beechmont, QLD 127 A5,
  133 D3
Beechworth, VIC 79 G4,
  99 B2
Beecroft, NSW 26 D4
Beelbangera, NSW 38 C6
Beeliar, WA 170 C6, 172 C2
Beenleigh, QLD 121 H3,
  127 A1, 133 D1
Beerburrum, QLD 131 B6
Beerwah, QLD 121 H2,
  131 C5
Beetaloo, NT 205 H5, 206 A5
Beete, WA 179 B3
Bega, NSW 45 F5
Beilpajah, NSW 37 G4
Belah, NSW 32 B6
Belair, SA 144 D2
Belarabon, NSW 38 B2
Belconnen, ACT 20 B2,
  21 C2
Belele, WA 182 D5
Belfield, NSW 29 E2
Belford, NSW 57 A1
Belgrave, VIC 71 H5, 84 C3,
  93 B5
Belgrave Heights, VIC
  71 H5, 93 B5
Belgrave South, VIC 71 H5,
  93 B5
Belingerable, NSW 38 B5
Belka, WA 175 F5, 177 F1
Bell, NSW 40 B5, 48 D1
Bell, QLD 135 B2
Bell Bay, TAS 234 B1
Bella Vista, NSW 26 C4
Bellalie, QLD 119 F2
Bellangry, NSW 41 F1
Bellara, QLD 107 G1, 131 C6
Bellarwi, NSW 39 E6
Bellata, NSW 34 A5
Bellbird, NSW 40 D4, 57 B6
Bellbird Park, QLD 108 A6
Bellbowrie, QLD 108 A4
Bellbridge, VIC 79 G3
Bellbrook, NSW 35 F6
Bellbuoy Beach, TAS 234 B1
Bellellen, VIC 77 E6, 83 E1,
  97 D3
Bellenden Ker, QLD 123 D5
Bellerive, TAS 228 D3
Bellevue, QLD 111 G3
Bellevue, WA 171 F2
Bellevue Heights, SA 144 C3
Bellevue Hill, NSW 29 G2
Bellfield, QLD 111 F6
Bellfield, VIC 70 D2
Belli Park, QLD 131 B4
Bellingen, NSW 35 F6, 53 B4
Bellingham, TAS 234 C1
Bellmere, QLD 106 C1
Belltrees, NSW 40 C2
Bellum Bellum, SA 163 D6
Belmont, NSW 40 D4, 51 D1
Belmont, QLD 109 E3
Belmont, WA 171 E3
Belmore, NSW 29 E2
Beloka, NSW 44 D4, 65 D6
Belrose, NSW 27 G4
Beltana, SA 153 E2
Beltana Roadhouse, SA
  153 E2
Belton, SA 153 E4

Blyth (Ruins), NT 221 A2
Blythdale, QLD 120 D1
Boallia, WA 189 C2
Boambee, NSW 35 G6, 53 C3
Boat Harbour, NSW 63 B4
Boat Harbour, TAS 230 D6
Boat Harbour Beach, TAS 230 D6
Boatman, QLD 120 B2
Boatswain Point, SA 163 A3
Bobadah, NSW 38 D3
Bobawba, QLD 112 C6
Bobbin Head, NSW 27 F3, 51 A6
Bobs Farm, NSW 63 A4
Bodalla, NSW 45 F4
Bodallin, WA 175 G5, 177 G1
Boddington, WA 176 C3
Bogan Gate, NSW 39 F4
Bogangar, NSW 35 G2
Bogantugan, QLD 116 B4
Bogee, NSW 40 B4
Bogewong, NSW 33 F5
Boggabilla, NSW 34 B2
Boggabri, NSW 34 B6
Bogolo, NSW 38 D4
Bogolong Creek, NSW 39 F5
Bogong, VIC 79 H5, 80 A3, 99 C3
Boho South, VIC 78 D5
Boigbeat, VIC 77 E2
Boinka, VIC 74 C6, 76 B1
Boisdale, VIC 85 G3
Bolgart, WA 174 C5 176 C1
Bolingbroke, QLD 116 D2
Bolivar, SA 142 C4
Bollards Lagoon, SA 149 H5
Bollon, QLD 120 B3
Bolong, NSW 61 B1
Bolton, VIC 75 F5
Bolwarra, QLD 111 G4
Bolwarra, VIC 82 C4
Bolwarrah, VIC 90 A4
Bomaderry, NSW 45 G1, 55 B4, 61 B1
Bombah Point, NSW 63 C2
Bombah Pt, NSW 41 E3
Bombala, NSW 45 E5
Bomera, NSW 40 A2
Bon Bon, SA 152 A1
Bonalbo, NSW 35 F3
Bonang, VIC 80 D4
Bonbeach, VIC 73 E1
Bond Springs, NT 213 H2, 214 B2
Bondi, NSW 29 G2
Bondi Beach, NSW 29 G2
Bondi Junction, NSW 29 G2
Bonegilla, VIC 79 G3, 99 C1
Bongaree, QLD 107 H1, 121 H2, 131 C6
Bonnet Bay, NSW 28 D4
Bonnet Hill, TAS 228 C6
Bonnie Doon, VIC 79 E6
Bonnie Downs, WA 183 E2
Bonnie Rock, WA 175 F4
Bonnie Vale, WA 178 B4
Bonny Hills, NSW 41 F2
Bonnyrigg, NSW 28 B2
Bonnyrigg Heights, NSW 28 A2
Bono, NSW 37 E3

Bonogin, QLD 127 B6
Bonrook, NT 201 F5
Bonrook Resort, NT 220 A1
Bonshaw, NSW 34 D3
Bonton, NSW 37 H4
Bonus Downs, QLD 120 B2
Bonview, NSW 37 H1
Bonville, NSW 35 F6, 53 C4
Bonython, ACT 20 B5
Booberoi, NSW 38 D4
Booborowie, SA 153 E5
Boobyalla, TAS 231 B6
Boodarie, WA 180 A6, 182 D1
Boodua, QLD 135 C3
Boogardie, WA 182 D6
Bookabie, SA 151 F3
Bookaloo, SA 152 C3
Bookar, VIC 83 F3, 88 C3
Bookham, NSW 44 D1
Bookin, QLD 114 D1
Boola Boolka, NSW 37 F3
Boolambayte, NSW 63 C1
Boolardy, WA 182 C5
Boolarra, VIC 85 F4
Boolarra South, VIC 85 F4
Boolba, QLD 120 C3
Boolbanna, QLD 119 G2
Boolcoomta, SA 153 G3
Booleroo Centre, SA 153 E4
Booligal, NSW 38 A6
Boolite, VIC 77 E4
Boologooro, WA 182 A4
Boomarra, QLD 110 C6
Boomi, NSW 34 A3
Boomley, NSW 39 H2
Boompa, QLD 117 G6, 121 G1
Boonah, QLD 121 G3, 133 B2
Boonarga, QLD 121 E2
Boondall, QLD 107 F6
Boondandilla, QLD 121 E3
Boondara, NSW 38 A5
Boonderoo, QLD 115 G1
Boondoola, QLD 129 B3
Boongoondoo, QLD 116 A3
Boonoo Boonoo, NSW 35 E3
Boonooroo, QLD 125 B4
Booraan, WA 175 F5, 177 F1
Boorabbin, WA 175 H5, 178 A5
Booragoon, WA 170 C4
Booral, NSW 41 E3, 63 A1
Boorara, QLD 119 G4
Boorhaman, VIC 79 F3, 99 A1
Booroobin, QLD 131 B5
Booroolite, VIC 79 E6
Boorooma, NSW 38 D1
Booroomba, ACT 21 B3
Booroopki, VIC 76 B5
Booroorban, NSW 43 F2
Boorowa, NSW 39 G6, 44 D1
Boort, VIC 77 G3
Boort East, VIC 77 H3
Boorungie, NSW 37 E2
Boosey, VIC 79 E3
Boothulla, QLD 119 H1
Booyal, QLD 117 G6
Booylgoo Spring, WA 183 E6
Booyong, NSW 46 C3
Boppy Mount, NSW 38 D2

Borambil, NSW 40 B2
Borden, WA 177 F5
Border Downs, NSW 30 C5
Border Village, SA 150 A3
Border Village, WA 185 D3
Bordertown, SA 155 G4, 163 D1
Boree, NSW 39 G4
Boree, QLD 115 G1
Boree Creek, NSW 44 A2
Boree Plains, NSW 37 G5
Boreen Point, QLD 131 C3
Borenore, NSW 39 H4
Boronia, VIC 71 G4, 93 A3
Boronia Park, NSW 27 E6, 29 E1
Bororen, QLD 117 G5
Borrika, SA 155 G2
Borroloola, NT 207 E3
Borung, VIC 77 H4
Bossley Park, NSW 26 A6, 28 A1
Bostocks Creek, VIC 88 C3
Bosworth, SA 152 D2
Botany, NSW 29 F3
Bothwell, TAS 236 C1
Bouldercombe, QLD 117 F4, 129 B5
Boulia, QLD 114 C4
Boundain, WA 177 E3
Boundary Bend, NSW 42 D1
Boundary Bend, VIC 75 F5
Bourbah, NSW 39 G1
Bourke, NSW 32 C5
Bouvard, WA 191 A4
Bow Bowing, NSW 28 A4
Bow Bridge, WA 176 D6
Bow Hill, SA 155 F2
Bow River, WA 181 D4
Bowden, SA 141 A2
Bowelling, WA 176 C4
Bowen, QLD 112 D6
Bowen Downs, QLD 115 H3
Bowen Hills, QLD 105 C1, 108 C2
Bowenfels, NSW 48 B1
Bowenville, QLD 121 F2, 135 B3
Bower, SA 153 F6
Boweya, VIC 79 E4
Bowgada, WA 174 C2
Bowie, QLD 116 A2
Bowna, NSW 44 B3
Bowning, NSW 44 D1
Bowral, NSW 45 G1, 55 B2
Bowraville, NSW 35 F6, 53 B6
Bowser, VIC 79 F4
Bowser, VIC 99 A1
Bowthorn, NT 207 H6
Bowthorn, QLD 110 A4
Box Hill, NSW 26 B3
Box Hill, VIC 71 E3
Box Hill North, VIC 71 E3
Box Hill South, VIC 71 E3
Box Tank, NSW 37 E3
Box Valley, NSW 37 H3
Boxgrove, QLD 117 E6
Boxwood Hill, WA 177 F5
Boya, WA 171 F2, 187 B6
Boyeo, VIC 76 B4
Boyer, TAS 236 D3
Boyne Island, QLD 129 D6

Boynedale, QLD 117 F5, 129 D6
Boyup Brook, WA 176 C4
Bracalba, QLD 131 B6
Brachina, SA 153 E2, 159 B2
Bracken Ridge, QLD 107 E6
Brackenburgh, QLD 114 D3
Brackendale, NSW 40 D1
Bracknell, TAS 234 B4
Bradbury, NSW 28 A5
Bradbury, SA 145 E4
Braddon, ACT 19 C1, 20 B3
Bradshaw, NT 204 C2
Bradvale, VIC 83 G2, 88 D1
Braemar, SA 153 F5
Braemar Bay, NSW 65 C4
Braeside, QLD 116 D2
Braeside, VIC 71 E6
Brahma Lodge, SA 142 D4
Braidwood, NSW 45 F2
Braidwood, QLD 115 F5
Bramfield, SA 151 H5, 152 A5
Brampton Vale, QLD 129 B2
Bramston Beach, QLD 112 A4, 123 D5
Bramwell, QLD 113 B3
Brandon, QLD 112 C6
Brandy Ck, VIC 85 E3
Bransby, QLD 119 E3
Branxholm, TAS 235 E2
Branxholme, VIC 82 C3
Branxton, NSW 40 D4, 57 C1
Brawlin, NSW 44 C1
Bray Park, QLD 106 D5
Braybrook, VIC 70 B3
Brayton, NSW 45 F1
Breadalbane, NSW 45 E1
Breadalbane, QLD 114 B4
Breadalbane, TAS 234 C3
Break O Day, VIC 84 C1
Breakfast Point, NSW 27 E6, 29 E1
Bream Creek, TAS 237 F3
Bream Creek, TAS 245 C3
Breamlea, VIC 84 A4, 89 H3
Bredbo, NSW 21 C6, 45 E3
Breeza, NSW 40 B1
Bremer Bay, WA 177 G5
Brenda Gate, QLD 120 B4
Brendale, QLD 106 D5
Brentwood, SA 154 C1
Brentwood, VIC 76 D3
Brentwood, WA 170 C4
Breona, TAS 233 H4, 234 B4
Bretti, NSW 41 E2
Brewarrina, NSW 32 D5
Briagolong, VIC 85 G2, 86 A3
Briar Hill, VIC 71 E1
Bribbaree, NSW 39 F6
Bridge Creek, VIC 79 E6
Bridgeman Downs, QLD 106 D6
Bridgenorth, TAS 234 C2
Bridgetown, WA 176 C4
Bridgewater, SA 145 F3, 153 E4
Bridgewater, TAS 236 D2
Bridgewater, VIC 77 H5
Bridport, TAS 234 D1
Brierfield, NSW 53 B5
Brigalow, QLD 121 F2

Burracoppin, WA 175 F5, 177 F1
Burraga, NSW 40 A6, 39 H6
Burragate, NSW 45 F5
Burragenup, WA 187 B4
Burramine, VIC 79 E3
Burrandana, NSW 44 B2
Burraneer, NSW 29 E5
Burrapine, NSW 35 F6
Burrawantie, NSW 32 B3
Burrell Creek, NSW 41 E2
Burren Junction, NSW 33 H5
Burrereo, VIC 77 E4
Burrill Lake, NSW 45 G2, 55 B6
Burringbar, NSW 35 G2
Burringurrah, WA 182 C4
Burrinjuck, NSW 44 D2
Burrum Heads, QLD 117 H6, 125 A3
Burrumbeet, VIC 83 G1, 95 C4
Burrumbuttock, NSW 44 A3
Burrundie, NT 201 E5
Burslem, QLD 115 G3
Burswood, WA 170 D3
Burta, NSW 36 C3
Burthong, NSW 38 D3
Burton, SA 14 C3
Burtundy, NSW 37 E, 37 G3
Burunga, QLD 121 E1
Burwood, NSW 29 E2
Burwood, VIC 71 E4
Burwood East, VIC 71 F4
Burwood Heights, NSW 29 E2
Busby, NSW 28 B2
Bush Grove, QLD 135 B1
Bushfield, VIC 83 E4, 88 A3
Bushy Park, NT 214 B2
Bushy Park, TAS 236 C2
Busselton, WA 176 B4, 189 C1
Busthinia, QLD 116 A4
Butchers Creek, QLD 123 C5
Butchers Ridge, VIC 80 C4
Bute, SA 152 D6
Butlerville, QLD 129 C5
Buxton, NSW 40 B6, 55 B1
Buxton, QLD 125 A3
Buxton, VIC 84 D1
Byabarra, NSW 41 F2
Byaduk, VIC 82 C3
Byaduk North, VIC 82 C3
Byfield, QLD 117 F3, 129 B3
Byford, WA 173 F3, 174 C6, 176 C2
Bylong, NSW 40 B3
Bylong, QLD 115 F1
Byrnedale, NSW 37 E3
Byrnestown, QLD 117 G6
Byrneville, VIC 76 D4
Byro, WA 182 C5
Byrock, NSW 32 D6
Byron Bay, NSW 35 H3, 46 E2
Bywong, NSW 21 D1

C Lake, NSW 37 G4
Cabanandra, VIC 80 D4
Cabarita, NSW 27 E6, 29 E1

Cabarup, WA 193 B2
Cabawin, QLD 121 E2
Cabbage Tree Creek, VIC 80 D5
Caboolture, QLD 106 D1, 121 H2, 131 B6
Cabramatta, NSW 28 B2
Cabramatta West, NSW 28 B2
Cabramurra, NSW 44 D3, 65 B3
Cacoory (Ruins), QLD 114 B6
Cadelga (Ruins), SA 149 H1
Cadell, SA 153 F6
Cadney Homestead (Roadhouse), SA 147 G3
Cadney Park, SA 147 G3
Cadoux, WA 174 D4
Caiguna, WA 185 B4
Cairns, QLD 112 A3, 119 H1, 123 C3
Cairns Bay, TAS 236 C4
Caiwarro, QLD 119 G4
Cal Lal, NSW 36 D6
Calamvale, QLD 108 D5
Calca, SA 151 H5
Calcium, QLD 112 B6
Calder, TAS 233 E1
Calder Park, VIC 70 A1
Caldervale, QLD 116 B6
Caldwell, NSW 43 F3
Caledonia, QLD 115 H3
Calen, QLD 116 D1, 137 B5
Calga, NSW 51 A4
Calingiri, WA 174 C5
Calista, WA 172 C4
Calivil, VIC 77 H4
Callabonna (Ruins), SA 149 G6
Callagiddy, WA 182 A4
Callala Bay, NSW 55 C4, 61 C3
Callala Beach, NSW 61 C3
Callandoon North, QLD 121 E3
Callanna, SA 148 D6
Callanna (Ruins), SA 148 E6
Callawa, WA 180 B6, 183 F1
Callawadda, VIC 77 E5, 97 D1
Callide, QLD 117 F5
Callide Mine, QLD 117 F5
Callindary, NSW 31 E5
Callington, SA 155 E2
Calliope, QLD 117 F5, 129 D6
Callytharra Springs, WA 182 B4
Caloundra, QLD 121 H2, 131 C5
Calrossie, VIC 85 G4
Calton Hills, QLD 114 B1
Caltowie, SA 153 E5
Calulu, VIC 80 A6, 86 C2
Calvert, VIC 97 D5
Calvert Hills, NT 207 F5
Calwell, ACT 20 B5
Camballin, WA 181 A4
Cambeela, QLD 115 E3
Camberville, VIC 85 E2
Camberwell, NSW 40 C3
Camberwell, VIC 71 E3
Cambewarra, NSW 55 B4, 61 A1

Cambooya, QLD 121 G3, 135 C4
Cambrai, SA 155 F1
Cambridge, TAS 229 G1, 237 E3
Cambroon, QLD 131 A4
Camdale, TAS 233 E1
Camden, NSW 40 C6, 55 C1
Camden Park, SA 144 B2
Camel Creek, QLD 111 H5, 112 A5
Camellia, NSW 26 D6, 28 D1
Camena, TAS 233 F2
Cameron Downs, QLD 115 G2
Camerons Pocket, QLD 137 A5
Camfield, NT 205 E4
Camira, QLD 108 A6
Cammeray, NSW 27 G6, 29 G1
Camooweal, QLD 110 A6, 114 A1
Camp Creek, NT 200 D4, 221 C2
Camp Hill, QLD 108 D3
Camp Mountain, QLD 108 A1
Campania, TAS 237 E2
Campbell, ACT 19 D3, 20 C3
Campbell Town, TAS 234 D5
Campbellfield, VIC 70 C1
Campbells Bridge, VIC 77 E5, 97 D1
Campbells Pocket, QLD 106 A1
Campbells River, NSW 40 A6
Campbelltown, NSW 28 A5, 40 C6, 55 C1
Campbelltown, SA 142 D6
Campbelltown, VIC 77 H6, 83 H1, 95 D3
Camperdown, NSW 29 F2
Camperdown, VIC 83 F4, 88 C3
Campsie, NSW 29 E2
Canada Bay, NSW 27 E6, 29 E1
Canal Creek, QLD 129 B3
Canary Island, VIC 77 H3
Canaway Downs, QLD 119 G1
Canbelego, NSW 38 D2
Canberra, ACT 19 C2, 20 B3, 21 C2, 45 E2
Canberra Airport, ACT 20 D3
Canberra Central, ACT 20 B3
Candelo, NSW 45 F5
Cane River, WA 182 B2
Canegrass, SA 153 G5
Caniaba, NSW 46 A4
Caniambo, VIC 78 D4
Canley Heights, NSW 28 B2
Canley Vale, NSW 28 B2
Cann River, VIC 81 E5
Canna, WA 174 C1
Cannawigara, SA 155 G3
Cannie, VIC 77 G2
Canning Mills, WA 171 G5, 173 G1

Canning Vale, WA 171 E5, 173 E1
Cannington, QLD 114 D2
Cannington, WA 171 E4
Cannon Hill, QLD 108 D2
Cannons Creek, VIC 73 H3
Cannonvale, QLD 137 A2
Canobie, QLD 110 D6
Canonba, NSW 39 E1
Canopus, SA 153 G5
Canowindra, NSW 39 G5
Canteen Creek, NT 210 D4
Canterbury, NSW 29 E2
Canterbury, QLD 115 E6
Canterbury, VIC 71 E3
Canungra, QLD 121 H3, 133 D2
Capalaba, QLD 109 F4
Capalaba West, QLD 109 F3
Cape Barren Island, TAS 231 B4
Cape Bridgewater, VIC 82 B4
Cape Clear, VIC 83 G2, 89 E1
Cape Crawford Roadhouse, NT 206 D4
Cape Jaffa, SA 155 F4, 163 A3
Cape Jervis, SA 154 D2, 158 A3, 161 E2
Cape Paterson, VIC 84 D4
Cape River, QLD 115 H1, 116 A1
Cape Woolamai, VIC 91 E3
Capel, WA 176 B4, 187 A6
Capella, QLD 116 C4
Capels Crossing, VIC 77 H2
Capertee, NSW 40 B4
Capital Hill, ACT 19 B5, 20 B3
Capon, NSW 37 G2
Capricorn Roadhouse, WA 183 E3
Capricorn Roadhouse Fuel Dump, WA 183 G2
Captain Billy Landing, QLD 113 B2
Captains Flat, NSW 45 E3
Carabost, NSW 44 C3
Caradoc, NSW 31 F6
Caragabal, NSW 39 F5
Caralue, SA 152 B5
Caralulup, VIC 77 G6, 83 G1, 95 C3
Caramut, VIC 83 E3, 88 A2
Carandotta, QLD 114 A3
Carapooee, VIC 77 G5
Carapook, VIC 82 B2
Caravan Head, NSW 29 E4
Carawa, SA 151 H4
Carbeen Park, NT 201 F6, 205 F1
Carbine, WA 178 A4
Carbla, WA 182 B5
Carboor, VIC 79 F4, 99 A2
Carboor Upper, VIC 79 F5
Carbrook, QLD 109 G6
Carbunup River, WA 176 B4, 189 B2
Carcoar, NSW 39 H5
Cardigan, QLD 116 B1
Cardigan Village, VIC 83 H2, 95 C4
Cardinia, VIC 84 D3

Claremont, WA 170 B3
Clarence, NSW 48 C1
Clarence Gardens, SA 144 C2
Clarence Park, SA 144 C2
Clarence Point, TAS 234 B1
Clarencetown, NSW 40 D3
Clarendon, SA 144 D4
Clarendon, TAS 234 D4
Clareville, NSW 27 H2
Clarina, QLD 110 D4
Clarinda, VIC 71 E5
Clarke River, QLD 111 H5, 112 A5
Clarkefield, VIC 84 B1, 90 E3
Claude Road, TAS 233 G3
Claverton, QLD 120 A2
Clay Wells, SA 163 B4
Clayfield, QLD 108 D1
Claymore, NSW 28 A5
Clayton, SA 149 E5
Clayton, VIC 71 E5
Clayton South, VIC 71 E5
Clear Lake, VIC 76 C5
Clear Mountain, QLD 106 C5
Clear Ridge, NSW 39 E5
Clearview, SA 142 C6
Cleary, WA 175 E4
Cleland, SA 145 E2
Clematis, VIC 93 D5
Clermont, QLD 116 C3
Cleve, SA 152 B6
Cleveland, QLD 109 H4, 133 D1
Cleveland, TAS 234 D4
Clifford Creek, VIC 182 C3
Clifton, QLD 115 F6, 119 F1, 121 G3, 135 C5
Clifton Beach, QLD 112 A3, 123 C2
Clifton Beach, TAS 237 E4
Clifton Beach, TAS 245 A4
Clifton Creek, VIC 86 C2
Clifton Gardens, NSW 27 G6, 29 E1
Clifton Hill, VIC 70 D3
Clifton Hills, SA 149 F2
Clifton Park, WA 187 A5
Clifton Springs, VIC 84B3
Clio, QLD 115 E2
Clonagh, QLD 114 C1
Cloncurry, QLD 114 C1
Clontarf, NSW 27 G5
Clontarf, QLD 107 F4
Closeburn, QLD 106 B5
Clouds Creek, NSW 35 F5
Clovelly, NSW 29 G2
Clovelly Park, SA 144 C3
Clover Hills, QLD 116 A4
Cloverdale, WA 171 E3
Cloyna, QLD 121 G1
Club Terrace, VIC 81 E5
Clunes, NSW 35 G3, 46 C3
Clunes, VIC 77 H6, 83 H1, 95 C3
Clybucca, NSW 41 F1
Clyde, VIC 73 H2
Clyde North, VIC 73 H1
Clydebank, VIC 80 A6, 85 H2, 86 A4
Coalbrook, QLD 111 G6, 115 F1
Coalcliff, NSW 55 D1

Coaldale, NSW 35 F4
Coasters Retreat, NSW 27 H2
Cobains, VIC 85 H3, 86 A4
Cobar, NSW 38 C1
Cobargo, NSW 45 F4
Cobaw, VIC 78 B6, 84 B1, 90 D2
Cobbadah, NSW 34 C5
Cobba-da-mana, QLD 121 F3
Cobbannah, VIC 80 A5, 85 H2, 86 A1
Cobbora, NSW 40 A2, 39 H2
Cobbrum, QLD 120 A3
Cobden, VIC 83 F4, 88 C3
Cobdogla, SA 165 B2
Cobera, SA 155 G1
Cobra, WA 182 C3
Cobram, VIC 78 D3
Cobrico, VIC 83 F4, 88 C3
Cobrilla, NSW 37G1
Cobungra, VIC 79 H6, 80 A4, 99 D4
Coburg, VIC 70 C2, 84 C2
Coburg East, VIC 70 C2
Coburg North, VIC 70 C2
Coburn, WA 182 B5
Cocamba, VIC 75 F6
Cochranes Ck, VIC 77 G5
Cockaleechie, SA 152 B6, 154 B1
Cockatoo, QLD 117 E6, 121 E1
Cockatoo, VIC 84 D3
Cockatoo Valley, SA 143 G1
Cockburn, SA 153 H3
Cockle Ck, TAS 236 C6
Cocklebiddy, WA 185 C4
Coconut Grove, NT 198 B2
Codrington, VIC 82 C4
Coen, QLD 113 C5
Coffee Camp, NSW 46 A2
Coffin Bay, SA 154 A1
Coffs Harbour, NSW 35 G5, 53 D3
Coghills Ck, VIC 83 H1
Cogla Downs, WA 183 E5
Cohuna, VIC 78 A2
Coimadai, VIC 90 C4
Cokum, VIC 77 F2
Colac, VIC 83 G4, 89 E3
Colac Colac, VIC 80 B1
Colbinabbin, VIC 78 B4
Coldstream, VIC 71 H1, 84 D2
Coleambally, NSW 43 H1
Colebee, NSW 26 A4
Colebrook, TAS 237 E2
Coledale, NSW 55 D2
Coleraine, QLD 115 F2
Coleraine, VIC 82 C2
Coles Bay, TAS 235 G6
Colignan, VIC 75 E4
Colinton, NSW 21 C6
Collarenebri, NSW 33 G4
Collaroy, NSW 27 H4
Collaroy Plateau, NSW 27 H4
Collector, NSW 45 E2
College Park, SA 141 D3
Collerina, NSW 32 D4
Colley, SA 151 H5

Collie, NSW 39 G2
Collie, WA 176 C4, 187 D5
Collingullie, NSW 44 B2
Collingwood, QLD 121 E1
Collingwood, VIC 70 D3
Collins Gap, TAS 236 D3
Collinsvale, TAS 236 D3
Collinsville, QLD 116 C1
Collinswood, SA 142 C6
Colly Blue, NSW 40 B1
Colo, NSW 40 C5
Colonel Light Gardens, SA 144 C2
Colton, QLD 117 H6, 125 A4
Colton, SA 151 H5
Columboola, QLD 121 E2
Comara, NSW 35 E6
Comarto, NSW 37 F2
Combaning, NSW 44 C1
Combanning, QLD 120 A1
Combara, NSW 39 G1
Combienbar, VIC 81 E5
Comboyne, NSW 41 E2
Come By Chance, NSW 33 G5
Comet, QLD 116 D4
Commodore, SA 153 E2, 159 B1
Commonwealth Hill, SA 147 G6
Como, NSW 28 D4
Como, WA 170 D4
Comobella, NSW 39 H3
Comongin, QLD 119 G1
Compton, SA 163 C5
Compton Downs, QLD 115 F1
Conara, TAS 234 D4
Conargo, NSW 43 G2
Concongella, VIC 77 E6
Concord, NSW 27 E6, 29 E1
Concord West, NSW 27 E6, 29 E1
Condah, VIC 82 C3
Condamine, QLD 121 E2
Condell Park, NSW 28 D2
Conder, ACT 20 B6
Condobolin, NSW 39 E4
Congelin, WA 176 D3
Congie, QLD 119 F2
Congupna, VIC 78 D4
Coningham, TAS 236 D4
Coniston, NT 209 G6
Conjola, NSW 55 B5
Conlea, NSW 31 H5, 32 A5
Conn, QLD 112 A5
Connells Point, NSW 29 E4
Connellys Marsh, TAS 237 F3
Connellys Marsh, TAS 245 B4
Connemarra, NSW 40 A2
Connemarra, QLD 115 E5
Conoble, NSW 38 A4
Conondale, QLD 131 A5
Consuelo, QLD 116 C5
Conway, QLD 116 D1, 137 A3
Conway Beach, QLD 137 A3
Coober Pedy, SA 147 H5
Cooberrie, QLD 129 B3
Coobowie, SA 154 D2
Coodanup, WA 191 C2

Coodardy, WA 182 D5
Cooee, TAS 233 F1
Coogee, NSW 29 G2
Coogee, WA 170 B6, 172 B2
Cooinda, QLD 115 F2
Coojar, VIC 82 C1
Cook, ACT 20 A2
Cook, SA 150 C1
Cookamidgera, NSW 39 G4
Cookardinia, NSW 44 B3
Cooke Plains, SA 155 F2
Cookernup, WA 187 C2
Cooktown, QLD 111 H2
Cookville, TAS 237 E5
Coolabah, NSW 32 D6, 38 D1
Coolabri, QLD 116 B6
Coolabunia, QLD 135 D1
Coolac, NSW 44 C2
Cooladdi, QLD 119 H1
Coolah, NSW 40 A2
Coolamine, NSW 65C1
Coolamon, NSW 44B1
Coolangatta, NSW 35 G2
Coolangatta, QLD 121 H3, 127 D6, 133 E3
Coolanie, SA 152 C5
Coolaroo, VIC 70 C1
Coolatai, NSW 34 C4
Coolawanyah, WA 182 D2
Coolbellup, WA 170 C5, 172 C1
Coolbinga, QLD 119 G1
Coolbinia, WA 170 C2
Coolcalalya, WA 182 B6
Coolcorra, QLD 129 B4
Coolgardie, WA 178 B4
Coolibah, NT 204 D2
Coolimba, WA 174 A3
Coolongolook, NSW 41 E3
Cooloola Village, QLD 121 H1, 125 C6, 131 C1
Cooloongup, WA 172 B5
Cooloothin, QLD 131 C3
Cooltong, SA 165 D1
Coolullah, QLD 110 C6
Coolum Beach, QLD 121 H2, 131 C4
Coolup, WA 176 C3, 187 C1
Cooma, NSW 45 E4
Coomaba, SA 152 A6
Coomandook, SA 155 F2
Coomba, NSW 41 E3
Coombabah, QLD 127 B3
Coomba Roadhouse, NSW 36 D4
Coombe, SA 155 G3
Coomberdale, WA 174 C4
Coombie, NSW 38 B4
Coomburrah, QLD 120 B4
Coomera, QLD 127 B3
Coomeratta, NSW 38 A2
Coomoora, VIC 78 A6, 84 A1, 90 A2, 95 E3
Coomrith, QLD 120 D2
Coomunga, SA 154 A1
Coonabarabran, NSW 40 A1, 39 H1
Coonalpyn, SA 155 F3
Coonamble, NSW 33 G6, 39 G1
Coonana, WA 178 D5, 185 A3
Coonarr, QLD 125 A2

Curra, QLD 125 A6, 131 A2
Currabubula, NSW 40 C1
Curragh Mine, QLD 116 D4
Curralong, WA 173 F6
Curramulka, SA 154 D1
Curraong, NSW 55 C4
Currarong, NSW 45 G2,
61 D3
Currawarna, NSW 44 B2
Currawilla, QLD 114 D6
Currawong Beach, NSW
27 H2
Currency Creek, SA 158 E2
Currie, TAS 230 A2
Currumbin, QLD 127 D6
Currumbin Waters, QLD
127 C6
Curtin, ACT 20 B3
Curtin Springs Roadhouse,
NT 213 F5, 223 B3
Curyo, VIC 77 E3
Custon, SA 163 D1
Cuthero, NSW 37 E4
Cygnet, TAS 236 D4
Cygnet River, SA 154 C3,
161 C2

D'Aguilar, QLD 131 B6
Daceyville, NSW 29 G3
Dadswells Bridge, VIC
77 E5, 97 C1
Daglish, WA 170 C3
Daguragu, NT 204 D5
Dagworth, QLD 111 G4,
115 E2
Dahwilly, NSW 43 F2
Daintree, QLD 111 H2
Daisy Dell, TAS 233 F3
Daisy Dell, TAS 241 C1
Daisy Hill, QLD 109 F6
Dajarra, QLD 114 B2
Dakabin, QLD 106 D4
Dalbeg, QLD 116 B1
Dalby, QLD 121 F2, 135 B3
Dalgaranga, WA 182 C6
Dalgety, NSW 44 D4, 65 D6
Dalgety Downs, WA 182 C4
Dalgonally, QLD 110 D6,
114 D1
Dalhousie (Ruins), SA 148 A1
Dalkeith, WA 170 C4
Dallas, VIC 70 C1
Dalma, QLD 129 A4
Dalmeny, NSW 45 F4
Dalmore, QLD 115 G4
Dalmorton, NSW 35F5
Dalton, NSW 45E1
Dalveen, QLD 121G4
Dalwallinu, WA 174D3
Daly River (Police Stn), NT
200 C5
Daly Waters, NT 205 H3,
206 A3
Dalyellup, WA 187 A5
Dalyston, VIC 84 D4
Dalyup, WA 179 B4
Damperwah, WA 174 D2
Dampier, WA 182 C1
Dampier Downs, WA
180 D5
Dandaloo, NSW 39 F3
Dandaraga, WA 183 E6
Dandaragan, WA 174 B4

Dandenong, VIC 71 F6,
84 C3
Dandenong North, VIC 71 G5
Dandenong South, VIC 71
F6
Dandongadale, VIC 79 F5,
99 B3
Dangar Island, NSW 27 G1
Dangin, WA 175 E6, 177 E2
Dapto, NSW 45 G1, 55 C2
Daradgee, QLD 123 D6
Dardanup, WA 187 B5
Dareton, NSW 37 E6
Dargo, VIC 80 A5, 85 H2,
86 B1
Darke Peak, SA 152 B5
Darkin, WA 176 D4
Darling Downs, WA 173 F3
Darling Harbour, NSW 25 B5,
27 F6, 29 F1
Darling Point, NSW 27 G6,
29 G1
Darlinghurst, NSW 29 G2
Darlington, NSW 29 F2
Darlington, SA 144 B3
Darlington, TAS 245 D1
Darlington, VIC 83 F3,
88 C2
Darlington, WA 171 G2
Darlington Point, NSW
43 H1
Darnick, NSW 37 G4
Darnum, VIC 85 E3
Daroobalgie, NSW 39 F5
Darr, QLD 115 G4
Darr Creek, QLD 135 A1
Darra, QLD 108 B4
Darraweit Guim, VIC 84 B1
Darriman, VIC 85 G4
Darrine, WA 175 H4
Dartmoor, VIC 82 B3
Dartmouth, QLD 115 H4
Dartmouth, VIC 79 H4,
80 A2, 99 D2
Darwin, NT 197 C5, 198 B5,
200 D3
Darwin International
Airport, NT 198 C3
Daubeny, NSW 37 F1
Davenport Downs, QLD
114 D5
Davidson, NSW 27 F4
Davoren Park, SA 142 D2
Davyhurst (Ruins), WA
178 A3
Daw Park, SA 144 C2
Dawes Point, NSW 25 B2,
27 F6, 29 F1
Dawesville, WA 176 B3,
191 A4
Dawson, SA 153 E4
Dawson Park, QLD 117 E6
Dayboro, QLD 106 A3,
121 H2
Daylesford, VIC 83 H1,
84 A1, 90 A2, 95 E3
Daymar, QLD 120 D4
Daysdale, NSW 44 A3
De Grey, WA 180 A6
Deagon, QLD 107 F6
Deakin, ACT 19 A6, 20 B3
Dean, VIC 83 H1, 95 D4

Dean Park, NSW 26 A4
Deans Marsh, VIC 83 H4,
89 F4
Deception Bay, QLD 107 E3
Deddington, TAS 234 D3
Dederang, VIC 79 G4, 99 C2
Dee, TAS 233 H6, 234 A6
Dee Why, NSW 27 H4
Dee Why Beach, NSW 27 H4
Deep Lead, VIC 77 E6
Deep Lead, VIC 97 D2
Deep Well, NT 214 B3,
223 E2
Deepdene, VIC 71 E3
Deepwater, NSW 35 E4
Deer Park, VIC 70 A3, 84 B2
Deeragun, QLD 112 B6
Deeral, QLD 112 A3, 123 D4
Delahey, VIC 70 A2
Delamere, NT 205 E3
Delamere, SA 158 A3
Delaney Creek, QLD 131 B6
Delburn, VIC 85 F4
Delegate, NSW 45 E5
Delegate River, VIC 80 D4
Delmore Downs, NT 210 C6,
214 C1
Delny, NT 214 C1
Deloraine, TAS 234 B3
Delta Downs, QLD 110 D3
Delungra, NSW 34 C4
Den Barm, QLD 135 B2
Denham, WA 182 A5
Denham Court, NSW 28 A3
Denial Bay, SA 151 G3
Denilcull Ck, VIC 83 F1
Deniliquin, NSW 43 G3
Denison, VIC 85 G3
Denistone, NSW 27 E5
Denistone East, NSW 27 E5
Denistone West, NSW
26 D5
Denman, NSW 40 C3, 59 C3
Denmark, WA 177 E6,
193 A4
Dennes Pt, TAS 237 E4
Dennington, VIC 83 E4,
88 A4
Denver, VIC 78 A6, 84 A1,
90 B2, 95 E3
Depot Springs, WA 183 E6
Derain, NSW 44 B1
Derby, TAS 235 F2
Derby, VIC 77 H5, 95 D1
Derby, WA 180 D4
Dereel, VIC 83 H2, 89 F1
Dergholm, VIC 82 B1
Deringulla, NSW 40 A1,
39 H1
Dernancourt, SA 142 D6
Deroora, QLD 115 H4
Derrimut, VIC 70 A3
Derrinal, VIC 78 B5
Derrinallum, VIC 83 F3,
88 B2
Derriwong, NSW 39 E4
Derry Downs, NT 210 C6
Derwent, NT 213 F2, 22 3C1
Derwent Bridge, TAS 233 G6
Derwent Bridge, TAS 241 D6
Derwent Park, TAS 228 B1
Devenish, VIC 79 E4
Deviot, TAS 234 B2

Devon Meadows, VIC 73 H3
Devon Park, SA 141 A1,
142 C6
Devonborough Downs, SA
153 G4
Devoncourt, QLD 114 C2
Devonport, TAS 233 G2,
234 A2
Devonshire, QLD 115 G4
Dewhurst, VIC 93 E6
Dharruk, NSW 26 A4
Dhuragoon, NSW 43 E2
Dhurringile, VIC 78 C4
Diamantina Lakes, QLD
114 D4
Diamond Bay, NSW 27 H6,
29 H1
Diamond Creek, VIC 71 F1
Diamond Well, WA 183 E5
Dianella, WA 170 D2
Diapur, VIC 76 B4
Dickson, ACT 20 C2
Dicky Beach, QLD 131 C5
Didcot, QLD 117 G6
Diddleum Plains, TAS
234 D2, 235 E2
Diemals, WA 175 G2
Digby, VIC 82 B3
Diggers Rest, VIC 84 B2,
90 D4
Diggora West, VIC 78 A4
Dillalah, QLD 120 A2
Dillcar, QLD 115 F3
Dilli Village, QLD 125 C4
Dilpurra, NSW 43 E2
Dilston, TAS 234 C2
Dimboola, VIC 76 C4
Dimbulah, QLD 111 H3
Dingee, VIC 78 A4
Dingley Village, VIC 71 F6
Dingo, QLD 116 D4
Dingo Beach, QLD 112 D6,
116 D1
Dingwall, VIC 77 H2
Dinner Plain, VIC 79 H6,
80 A4, 99 C4
Dinninup, WA 176 C4
Dinyarrak, VIC 76 A4
Diranbandi, QLD 120 C4
Direk, SA 142 C3
Dirk Hartog, WA 182 A5
Dirnaseer, NSW 44 C1
Dirrung, NSW 38 B5
Disney, QLD 116 B2
Dixie, QLD 111 F1, 113 C6
Dixie, VIC 83 F4, 88 C3
Dixons Ck, VIC 84 D2
Djuan, QLD 135 D3
Dneiper, NT 214 C1
Dobroyd Point, NSW 27 E6,
29 E2
Docker, VIC 79 F4, 99A 2
Docklands, VIC 70 C3
Doctors Flat, VIC 80 B4
Dodges Ferry, TAS 237 F3,
245 A3
Dolans Bay, NSW 29 E5
Dollar, VIC 85 E4
Dolls Point, NSW 29 F4
Dolomite, QLD 114 C1
Don, QLD 114 A1
Donald, VIC 77 F4
Doncaster, QLD 115 F1

Elaine, VIC 83 H2, 89 G1
Elalie, QLD 117 E3
Elanda Point, QLD 131 C2
Elands, NSW 41 E2
Elanora, QLD 127 C5
Elanora Heights, NSW 27 G3
Elbow Hill, SA 152 C6
Elderslie, NSW 40 D3
Elderslie, TAS 236 D2
Eldorado, VIC 79 F4, 99 A1
Electrona, TAS 236 D4
Elgin, WA 187 A6
Elgin Vale, QLD 121 G1
Elginbah, NSW 43 G1
Elimbah, QLD 131 B6
Elizabeth, SA 142 D3
Elizabeth Bay, NSW 27 G6, 29 G1
Elizabeth Beach, NSW 41 E3
Elizabeth Downs, NT 200 C5
Elizabeth Downs, SA 143 E3
Elizabeth East, SA 142 D3
Elizabeth Grove, SA 142 D3
Elizabeth North, SA 142 D3
Elizabeth Park, SA 143 E3
Elizabeth South, SA 142 D3
Elizabeth Town, TAS 233 H3, 234 A3
Elizabeth Vale, SA 142 D3
Elizabeth West, SA 142 D3
Elkedra, NT 210 D5
Ella Vale, NSW 32 B4
Ella Valla, WA 182 B4
Ellam, VIC 76 C3
Ellangowan, QLD 135 C5
Elleker, WA 193 B4
Ellen Grove, QLD 108 B5
Ellenborough, NSW 41 E2
Ellenbrae, WA 181 C3
Ellendale, TAS 236 B2
Ellendale, WA 181 A4
Ellerslie, VIC 83 E3, 88B 3
Ellerston, NSW 40 D2
Ellinbank, VIC 85 E4
Ellinminyt, VIC 83 G4, 89 E4
Ellinthorp, QLD 135 C6
Elliott, NT 205 H5, A5
Elliott, QLD 117 G6
Elliott, TAS 233 E1
Elliott Heads, QLD 117 H6, 125 A2
Elliston, SA 151 H5
Elmhurst, VIC 77 F6, 83 F1, 95 B3
Elmina, QLD 120 A2
Elmore, VIC 78 B4
Elong Elong, NSW 39 H3
Elphinstone, QLD 116 C2
Elphinstone, VIC 78 A6, 90 B1
Elsey, NT 205 H2, 206 A2
Elsmore, NSW 34 D4
Elsternwick, VIC 70 D4
Eltham, NSW 46 B3
Eltham, VIC 71 F2
Eltham North, VIC 71 F1
Elvina Bay, NSW 27 G2
Elvo, QLD 115 E4
Elwood, VIC 70 D4
Embleton, WA 170 D2
Emby, NSW 39 F1
Emerald, QLD 116 C4

Emerald, VIC 84 D3, 93 D5
Emerald Beach, NSW 35 G5, 53 D2
Emerald Hill, NSW 34 B6
Emerald Springs Roadhouse, NT 201 E5
Emita, TAS 231 B2
Emmaville, NSW 34 D4
Emmdale Roadhouse, NSW 37 H2
Emmet, QLD 115 G5
Empire Bay, NSW 51 B5
Emu, VIC 77 G5, 95 B1
Emu Bay, SA 154 C2, 161 C2
Emu Flat, VIC 78 B6, 90 E1
Emu Junction (Ruins), SA 147 E4
Emu Park, QLD 117 F4, 129 C4
Emu Vale, QLD 135 D6
Enarra, QLD 120 D3
Encounter Bay, SA 158 D3
Endeavour Hills, VIC 71 G6, 93 A6
Eneabba, WA 174 B3
Eneby, QLD 112 B6
Enfield, SA 142 C6
Enfield, TAS 237 E2
Enfield, VIC 83 H2, 89 F1
Enfield South, NSW 29 E2
Engadine, NSW 28 C5
Engineer Barracks, NSW 28 B3
Englefield, VIC 82 C1
Enmore, NSW 29 F2, 34 D6, 36 D3
Enngonia, NSW 32 C4
Ennuin, WA 175 G4
Enoch Point, VIC 85 E1
Enoggera, QLD 108 C2
Enoggera Reservoir, QLD 108 A2
Enryb Downs, QLD 115 F2
Ensay, VIC 80 B5
Epala, QLD 117 F4, 129 C5
Epenarra, NT 210 C4
Epping, NSW 26 D5
Epping, VIC 84 C2
Epping Forest, TAS 234 D4
Epsilon, QLD 118 D3
Epsom, VIC 78 A5, 95 E1
Eraring, NSW 51 C1
Eriaba, QLD 116 C1
Eribung, NSW 39 F3
Erica, VIC 85 F3
Erigolia, NSW 38 D5
Erina, NSW 51 B4
Erindale, SA 144 D1
Eringa (Ruins), SA 147 H1
Eringa Park, SA 153 G4
Erinundra, VIC 81 E5
Erldunda, NT 213 G5, 214 A5, 223 D3
Erldunda Roadhouse, NT 213 G5, 214 A5, 223 D3
Erlistoun, WA 178 C1, 183 G6
Ermington, NSW 26 D6, 28 D1
Ernest, QLD 127 B4
Eromanga, QLD 119 F2
Erong, WA 182 C4
Erowal Bay, NSW 61 B4

Errabiddy, WA 182 C4
Erriba, TAS 233 F3
Erskine, WA 191 B2
Erskinville, NSW 29 F2
Erudina, SA 153 F3
Esdai, NSW 59 C4
Esk, QLD 121 G2
Eskdale, QLD 115 G3
Eskdale, VIC 79 H4, 80 A2, 99 D2
Esmeralda, QLD 111 F5
Esperance, WA 179 C4
Essendon, VIC 70 C2
Essendon Airport, VIC 70 B2
Essendon North, VIC 70 B2
Essendon West, VIC 70 B2
Essex Downs, QLD 115 F2
Etadunna, SA 149 E5
Ethelton, SA 142 A5
Eton, QLD 116 D2
Ettalong Beach, NSW 51 B5
Euabalong, NSW 38 D4
Euabalong West, NSW 38 D4
Euchareena, NSW 39 H4
Eucla, WA 185 D3
Eucumbene, NSW 44 D4
Eucumbene Dam, NSW 65 C4
Eudamullah, WA 182 B3
Eudlo, QLD 131 B5
Eudunda, SA 153 E6, 155 E1
Eugowra, NSW 39 G5
Eulo, NSW 37 F5
Eulo, QLD 119 H3
Eulolo, QLD 114 D2
Eumemmerring, VIC 71 G6
Eumundi, QLD 121 H1, 131 B3
Eumungerie, NSW 39 G2
Eurabba, NSW 39 F6
Eurack, VIC 83 H3, 89 F2
Eurardy, WA 182 B6
Euratha, NSW 38 D6
Eurebia, TAS 230 B6, 232 C1
Eureka, NSW 46 C2
Eurelia, SA 153 E4
Euroa, VIC 78 D5
Eurobin, VIC 79 G5, 99 B3
Eurobodalla, NSW 45 F4
Euroka, NSW 48 C6
Eurolie, NSW 43 G1
Eurong, QLD 117 H6, 125 C4
Eurongilly, NSW 44 C2
Euston, NSW 42 C1
Eva Downs, NT 206 C6
Evandale, SA 144 D1
Evandale, TAS 234 D3
Evans Head, NSW 35 G4
Evansford, VIC 77 G6, 83 G1, 95 C3
Evanston, SA 143 E1
Evanston Gardens, SA 143 E1
Evanston Park, SA 143 E1
Evanston South, SA 143 E1
Evatt, ACT 20 A2
Eveleigh, NSW 29 F2
Evelyn Downs, SA 147 H4
Evengy, QLD 115 F5
Everard Park, SA 144 C2

Everton, VIC 79 F4, 99 A2
Everton Hills, QLD 108 B1
Everton Park, QLD 108 C1
Evesham, QLD 115 G4
Evora, QLD 115 H5, 116 A5
Ewan, QLD 112 A5
Ewingsdale, NSW 46 D2
Exeter, NSW 45 G1, 55 A3
Exeter, SA 142 A5
Exeter, TAS 234 C2
Exford, VIC 84 B2
Exmoor, QLD 115 F2
Exmouth, WA 182 A2
Exmouth Gulf, WA 182 A2
Exton, TAS 234 B3

Fadden, ACT 20 B5
Failford, NSW 41 E3
Fairfield, NSW 26 B6, 28 B2
Fairfield, QLD 108 C3
Fairfield, VIC 70 D2
Fairfield, WA 181 A4
Fairfield East, NSW 26 C6, 28 C2
Fairfield Heights, NSW 26 B6, 28 B1
Fairfield West, NSW 26 B6, 28 B1
Fairhill, QLD 116 D4
Fairholme, NSW 39 E4
Fairleigh, QLD 137 C6
Fairlight, NSW 27 G5
Fairlight, QLD 111 G2, 113 D6
Fairview, NSW 38 D4, 39 F3
Fairview, QLD 111 G2, 113 D6
Fairview Park, SA 143 E4
Fairyland, QLD 135 A1
Falcon, WA 191 A3
Falls Creek, NSW 45 G2, 55 B4, 61 A3
Falls Creek, VIC 79 H5, 80 A3, 99 D3
Falmouth, TAS 235 G3
Fannie Bay, NT 197 B1, 198 A3
Fanning River, QLD 112 B6
Faraday, VIC 78 A6, 95 E2
Faraway Hill, SA 153 F5
Farina (Ruins), SA 149 E6, 153 E1
Farrer, ACT 20 B4
Fassifern, NSW 51 D1
Fassifern, QLD 133 B2
Faulconbridge, NSW 49 H4
Fawcett, VIC 78 D6
Fawkner, VIC 70 C1
Federal, NSW 46 C2
Federal, QLD 131 B3
Federal (Ruins), SA 148 A1
Feilton, TAS 236 C3
Felixstow, SA 142 D6
Felton East, QLD 135 C5
Fentonbury, TAS 236 C2
Fentons Ck, VIC 77 G4
Ferguson, SA 151 H2
Ferguson, VIC 83 G5, 89 E5
Ferguson, WA 187 B5
Fermoy, QLD 115 F4
Fern Tree, TAS 228 A4, 236 D3

Gidgee, WA 183 E5
Gidgegannup, WA 171 H1
Gidginbung, NSW 39 E6,
44 B1
Giffard, VIC 85 G4
Gilbert River, QLD 111 F4
Gilberton, SA 141 C1
Gilberton, SA 142 C6,
144 C1
Gilgai, NSW 34 D5, 38 D2
Gilgandra, NSW 39 G2
Gilgooma, NSW 33 G6
Gilgunnia, NSW 38 C3
Giligulgul, QLD 121 E1
Gilles Plains, SA 142 D5
Gilliat, QLD 114 D1
Gillman, SA 142 B5
Gilmore, ACT 20 B5
Gilmore, NSW 44 C2
Gilmore, QLD 115 H6
Gilroyd, WA 182 B4
Gilston, QLD 127 B4
Gin Gin, NSW 39 F2
Gin Gin, QLD 117 G6
Gina, SA 147 H6
Gindalbie, WA 178 C3
Gindie, QLD 116 C4
Gingin, WA 174 C5, 176 C1
Gipsy Point, VIC 81 F5
Giralang, ACT 20 B2
Giralia, WA 182 A2
Girgarre, VIC 78 C4
Girilambone, NSW 39 E1
Girragulang, NSW 40 A2
Girral, NSW 39 E5
Girraween, NSW 26 B5
Girrawheen, WA 170 C1
Giru, QLD 112 B6
Girvan, NSW 41 E3, 63 A2
Gisborne, VIC 84 B1, 90 D3
Glacier Rock, SA 158 C2
Gladesville, NSW 27 E6,
29 E1
Gladfield, VIC 77 H3
Gladstone, NSW 41 F1
Gladstone, QLD 117 F5,
129 D5
Gladstone, SA 153 E5
Gladstone, TAS 231 B6,
235 F1
Gladstone Park, VIC 70 B1
Gladysdale, VIC 84 D2
Glan Devon, QLD 135 D1
Glandore, SA 144 C2
Glanville, SA 142 A5
Glass House Mountains,
QLD 131 B5
Glastonbury, QLD 125 A6,
131 A2
Glaziers Bay, TAS 236 C4
Glebe, NSW 29 F2
Glebe, TAS 227 C3, 228 C3
Gleeson, QLD 110 C6
Glen, WA 182 D5
Glen Albyn, NSW 37 G3
Glen Alice, NSW 40 B4
Glen Alpin, QLD 121 G4
Glen Avon, QLD 116 B5
Glen Boree, SA 151 E3
Glen Creek, VIC 79 G4
Glen Davis, NSW 40 B4
Glen Forrest, WA 171 G2
Glen Gailic, NSW 40 C3

Glen Gallic, NSW 59 C4
Glen Geddes, QLD 117 E4,
129 A3
Glen Helen, NT 213 F2,
223 C1
Glen Hill, WA 181 D3
Glen Huntly, VIC 70 D4
Glen Huon, TAS 236 C4
Glen Idol, NSW 37 E2
Glen Innes, NSW 34 D4
Glen Iris, VIC 71 E4
Glen Mervyn, WA 187 D6
Glen Ora, NSW 37 G3
Glen Osmond, SA 144 D2
Glen Ruth, QLD 111 H4
Glen Valley, VIC 79 H6,
80 A3, 99 D3
Glen Waverley, VIC 71 F4
Glenaire, VIC 83 G5, 89 E6
Glenaladale, VIC 80 A6,
85 H2, 86 B2
Glenalbyn, VIC 77 H4
Glenalta, SA 144 D3
Glenample, QLD 115 H3
Glenariff, NSW 32 D6
Glenaroua, VIC 78 C6
Glenayle, WA 183 G4
Glenbervie, QLD 115 E2
Glenbervie, TAS 236 D5
Glenbrook, NSW 40 B5
Glenbrook, WA 187 B5
Glenburgh, WA 182 C4
Glenburn, VIC 84 D1
Glencoe, NSW 34 D5
Glencoe, QLD 110 D4
Glencoe, SA 155 G5, 163 C5
Glendale Crossing, ACT 21 B4
Glendalough, WA 170 C2
Glendambo, SA 152 A2
Glendara, NSW 31 G5
Glenden, QLD 116 C2
Glendenning, NSW 26 A4
Glendevie, TAS 236 C5
Glendilla, QLD 119 H3
Glenelg, SA 144 B2
Glenelg East, SA 144 B2
Glenelg North, SA 144 B2
Glenelg South, SA 144 B2
Glenella, QLD 137 D6
Glenfern, TAS 236 C3
Glenferrie, VIC 70 D3
Glenfield, NSW 28 B3
Glengarland, QLD 111 F1,
113 C6
Glengarry, NSW 38 D2
Glengarry, TAS 234 B2
Glengarry, VIC 85 F3
Glengower, VIC 77 H6,
83 H1, 95 D3
Glengowrie, SA 144 B2
Glengyle, QLD 114 C6
Glenhaughton, QLD 116 D6
Glenhaven, NSW 26 C4
Glenhope, NSW 31 H3,
32 A3, 38 D1
Glenhope, VIC 78 B6
Gleniffer, NSW 53 B4
Glenisla, VIC 76 D6, 82 D1,
97 A3
Glenlee, VIC 76 C4
Glenlofty, VIC 77 F6, 95 A2
Glenloth, VIC 77 G3
Glenlyon, QLD 115 F2

Glenlyon, VIC 78 A6, 84 A1,
90 B2, 95 E3
Glenmaggie, VIC 85 G3
Glenmore, QLD 120 D2
Glenmorgan, QLD 120 D2
Glenoak, SA 159 C4
Glenora, NSW 32 A5
Glenora, QLD 111 F5
Glenora, TAS 236 C2
Glenorchy, TAS 228 A1,
236 D3
Glenorchy, VIC 77 E5, 97 D1
Glenore, QLD 110 D4
Glenore, TAS 234 B3
Glenorie, NSW 26 C2
Glenormiston, QLD 114 B4
Glenormiston, VIC 88 C3
Glenormiston North, VIC
88 C3
Glenormiston Nth, VIC
83 F3
Glenorn, WA 178 C2
Glenreagh, NSW 35 F5, 53 C1
Glenrowan, VIC 79 E4
Glenroy, QLD 117 E4
Glenroy, VIC 70 C1
Glenroy, WA 181 B4
Glenside, SA 144 D1
Glenstuart, QLD 115 H5
Glenthompson, VIC 83 E2,
97 C6
Glenunga, SA 144 D1
Glenusk, QLD 116 A5
Glenvale, VIC 84 C1
Glenwood, NSW 26 B4
Glenwood, QLD 125 A5,
131 A1
Globe Derby Park, SA
142 C4
Glossop, SA 153 G6, 155 G1,
165 C3
Gloucester, NSW 41 E3
Glynde, SA 142 D6
Gnaraloo, WA 182 A3
Gnarwarre, VIC 84 A3, 89 G3
Gnotuk, VIC 83 F3, 88 C3
Gnowangerup, WA 177 E4
Gobondery, NSW 39 F4
Gobur, VIC 78 D6
Gocup, NSW 44 C2
Godwin Beach, QLD 107 G1,
131 C6
Gogango, QLD 117 E4,
129 A5
Gol Gol, NSW 37 E6, 37 G5
Golconda, TAS 234 D2
Golden Bay, WA 174 B6,
176 B2
Golden Beach, QLD 131 C5
Golden Beach, VIC 85 H3,
86 B4
Golden Gate, QLD 111 E4
Golden Grove, SA 143 E4
Golden Valley, TAS 234 B4
Golembil, QLD 117 F5
Gollan, NSW 39 H3
Golspie, NSW 40 A6, 45 F1
Gomersal, SA 157 A4
Gongolon, NSW 33 E5
Goode, SA 147 H6, 151 H1
Goodger, QLD 135 C1
Goodna, QLD 108 A5,
133 C1

Goodooga, NSW 33 E3
Goodwood, SA 141 B6,
144 C1
Goodwood, TAS 228 B1
Goolgowi, NSW 38 C6
Goolma, NSW 40 A3, 39 H3
Goolmangar, NSW 46 A3
Gooloogong, NSW 39 G5
Goolwa, SA 155 E2, 158 E2
Goolwa South, SA 158 E2
Goomalibee, VIC 79 E4
Goomalling, WA 174 D5,
176 D1
Goomally, QLD 116 D5
Goombi, QLD 121 E2
Goomboorian, QLD 125 B6,
131 B2
Goombungee, QLD 121 G2,
135 C3
Goomburra, QLD 135 D6
Goomeri, QLD 121 G1
Goon Nure, VIC 80 A6, 86 C3
Goonalga, NSW 37 G2
Goondi, QLD 123 D6
Goondiwindi, QLD 121 E4,
34 B2
Goondooloo, NT 205 H1,
206 A1
Goondoon, QLD 117 G6
Goonellabah, NSW 46 B4
Goonengerry, NSW 46 C1
Goonery, NSW 32 B5
Goongarrie, WA 178 B3
Goongee, VIC 74 B6
Goongerah, VIC 80 D4
Goonoolchrach, NSW 37 G2
Goonumbla, NSW 39 F4
Goonwarra, QLD 117 E4
Goonyella Mine, QLD
116 C2
Gooralong, WA 173 F5
Gooram, VIC 78 D5
Goorambat, VIC 79 E4
Goorawin, NSW 38 C5
Gooray, QLD 121 E3
Goornong, VIC 78 A5
Gooroc, VIC 77 F4
Gooseberry Hill, WA 171 F3
Goovigen, QLD 129 A6
Gooyea, QLD 115 G6
Gorae, VIC 82 C4
Gorae West, VIC 82 B4
Goranba, QLD 121 E2
Gordon, ACT 20 B6
Gordon, NSW 27 F4
Gordon, TAS 236 D5
Gordon, VIC 83 H2, 84 A2,
90 A4, 95 D4
Gordon (Ruins), SA 153 E3
Gordon Downs, WA 181 D5
Gordon Park, QLD 108 C1
Gordonvale, QLD 112 A3,
123 C4
Gore, QLD 121 F3, 135 B6
Gore Hill, NSW 27 F5, 29 F1
Gorge Creek, QLD 111 G6
Gormandale, VIC 85 G4
Gorokan, NSW 51 C3
Goroke, VIC 76 B5
Gorrie, NT 205 G2
Goschen, VIC 77 G1
Gosford, NSW 40 D5, 51 B4
Gosnells, WA 171 E5, 173 E1

Hanson, SA 153 E6
Hanwood, NSW 38 C6, 43 H1
Happy Valley, QLD 115 F4, 117 H6, 125 C3
Happy Valley, SA 144 C4
Harbord, NSW 27 H5
Harcourt, NSW 37 E4
Harcourt, VIC 78 A6, 95 E2
Harden, NSW 44 D1
Hardington, QLD 115 H3
Hardwicke Bay, SA 154 C1
Harefield, NSW 44 C2
Harford, TAS 233 H2, 234 A2
Hargraves, NSW 40 A4
Harkaway, VIC 71 H6, 93 C6
Harman, ACT 20 C4
Harmans, WA 189 B2
Harrietville, VIC 79 G5, 99 C4
Harrington, NSW 41 F2
Harris Park, NSW 26 C6, 28 C1
Harrismith, WA 177 E3
Harrison, ACT 20 C1
Harrisville, QLD 133 B2
Harrow, VIC 76 B6, 82 B1
Hartley, NSW 40 B5
Hartley Vale, NSW 48 D2
Harts Range (Police Stn), NT 214 C2
Hartwood, NSW 38 D2
Harvest Home, QLD 116 B1
Harvey, WA 176 C3, 187 C3
Harvey Town, TAS 236 C5
Harwood, NSW 35 G4
Haslam, SA 151 H4
Hassall Grove, NSW 26 A4
Hastings, TAS 236 C5
Hastings, VIC 73 G5, 84 C4
Hastings Point, NSW 35 G2, 133 E4
Hat Head, NSW 41 F1
Hatfield, NSW 37 G6
Hatfield, QLD 116 D2
Hatherleigh, SA 155 G5
Hatherleigh, SA 163 B4
Hattah, VIC 74 D5
Hatton Vale, QLD 133 B1
Haughton Valley, QLD 112 B6
Havelock, VIC 77 H6, 95 C2
Havilah, VIC 79 G5, 99 C2
Havillah, QLD 116 C1
Hawker, ACT 20 A2
Hawker, SA 153 E3, 159 B4
Hawkesdale, VIC 82 D3
Hawks Nest, NSW 41 E4, 63 C3
Hawkston, QLD 120 C4
Hawley Beach, TAS 233 H1, 234 A1
Hawthorn, SA 144 C2
Hawthorn, VIC 70 D3
Hawthorn East, VIC 70 D3
Hawthorndene, SA 144 D3
Hawthorne, QLD 108 D2
Hay, NSW 43 F1
Hay Flat, SA 158 B2
Hay Point, QLD 116 D2
Hay River, WA 193 B3
Hayborough, SA 158 D3
Haydon, QLD 110 D4

Hayes, TAS 236 C3
Hayes Creek Roadhouse, NT 201 E5
Haymarket, NSW 25 B5, 29 F2
Haysdale, VIC 75 G5
Haythorpe, NSW 37 E3
Hazel Vale, NSW 37 E2
Hazelbrook, NSW 40 B5, 49 G5
Hazeldean, QLD 131 A6
Hazeldene, VIC 84 C1
Hazelmere, WA 171 F2
Hazelwood Park, SA 144 D1
Headingly, QLD 114 A2
Healesville, VIC 84 D2
Heathcote, NSW 28 C5, 40 C6, 55 D1
Heathcote, VIC 78 B5
Heathcote Junction, VIC 84 C1
Heatherton, VIC 71 E5
Heathfield, SA 145 E3
Heathmere, VIC 82 C4
Heathmont, VIC 71 G3
Heathpool, SA 144 D1
Heathwood, QLD 108 B6
Hebel, QLD 120 B4
Hebersham, NSW 26 A4
Heckenberg, NSW 28 B2
Hectorville, SA 142 D6
Hedley, VIC 85 F5
Heidelberg, QLD 116 C1
Heidelberg, VIC 71 E2, 84 C2
Heidelberg Heights, VIC 70 D2
Heidelberg West, VIC 70 D2
Heka, TAS 233 F2
Helen, QLD 117 F5
Helen Springs, NT 205 H6, 206 B6, 209 H1, 210 B1
Helena Valley, WA 171 F2
Helensburgh, NSW 55 D1
Helensvale, QLD 127 B3
Helenvale, QLD 111 H2
Helidon, QLD 121 G3, 133 A1, 135 D4
Hells Gate Roadhouse, QLD 110 A4, 207 H5
Hellyer, TAS 230 D6
Hemmant, QLD 109 E2
Henbury, NT 213 H4, 214 A4, 223 D2
Henderson, WA 170 B6, 172 B2
Hendon, QLD 121 G3
Hendon, SA 142 B6
Hendra, QLD 108 D1
Henley, NSW 27 E6, 29 E1
Henley Beach, SA 144 A1
Henley Beach South, SA 144 A1
Henlow, VIC 99 D2
Henrietta, TAS 233 E1
Henty, NSW 44 B3
Henty, VIC 82 B2
Hepburn Springs, VIC 77 H6, 78 A6, 83 H1, 84 A1, 90 A2, 95 D3
Herbert Downs, QLD 114 B4
Herberton, QLD 111 H4, 112 A4
Herberton, QLD 123 A5

Herbertvale, QLD 110 A6
Herdsman, WA 170 C2
Heritage Park, QLD 108 D6
Hermannsburg, NT 213 G3, 223 D2
Hermidale, NSW 38 D2
Hermitage, TAS 234 B6
Herne Hill, WA 171 F1
Herons Ck, NSW 41 F2
Herrick, TAS 235 F1
Herston, QLD 105 B1, 108 C2
Hervey Bay, QLD 117 H6, 125 B3
Hesket, VIC 90 D2
Hesso, SA 152 D3
Hexham, NSW 40 D4
Hexham, VIC 83 E3, 88 B2
Heybridge, TAS 233 F1
Heyfield, VIC 85 G3
Heywood, VIC 82 C3
Hiamdale, VIC 85 G4
Hidden Valley, NT 198 D4, 205 G4
Hidden Valley, QLD 112 A5
Hideaway Bay, QLD 112 D6, 116 D1
Higgins, ACT 20 A2
Higginsville, WA 178 B6, 179 B1
High Camp, VIC 90 E1
High Wycombe, WA 171 F3
Highbury, QLD 111 F3
Highbury, SA 143 E5
Highbury, WA 176 D3
Highclere, TAS 233 E2
Highcroft, TAS 237 F4, 245 B6
Highett, VIC 70 D5
Highfields, QLD 135 D4
Highgate, SA 144 C2
Highgate, WA 169 C2
Highgate, WA 170 D3
Highgate Hill, QLD 105 A, 108 C3
Highland Plains, QLD 135 C3
Highlands, QLD 115 G6
Highlands, VIC 78 D6
Highvale, QLD 106 A6
Hill End, NSW 40 A4, 39 H4
Hill End, VIC 85 E3
Hill Springs, WA 182 B3
Hill Top, NSW 55 B2
Hillarys, WA 170 B1
Hillbank, SA 142 D3
Hillcrest, QLD 108 C6
Hillcrest, SA 142 D6
Hillgrove, NSW 35 E6
Hillgrove, QLD 112 A6
Hillier, SA 143 E1
Hillman, WA 172 B4
Hillsdale, NSW 29 G3
Hillside, NSW 26 C2
Hillside, QLD 114 C1, 116 C6
Hillside, VIC 86 C2
Hillside, WA 183 E1
Hillston, NSW 38 B5
Hilltown, SA 153 E6
Hillview, NSW 38 C2
Hillwood, TAS 234 C2
Hiltaba, SA 152 A3

Hilton, SA 144 C1
Hilton, WA 172 B1
Hinchinbrook, NSW 28 A2
Hindmarsh, SA 144 C1
Hindmarsh Tiers, SA 158 D2
Hindmarsh Valley, SA 158 D2
Hines Hill, WA 175 E5, 177 E1
Hinnomunjie, VIC 80 B3
Hinnomunjie, VIC 99 E4
Hirstglen, QLD 133 A2, 135 D5
Hivesville, QLD 121 F1
Hi-Way Inn Roadhouse, NT 205 H3, 206 A3
HMAS Cerberus, VIC 73 F6
Hobart, TAS 227 C4, 228 C3, 237 E3
Hobartville, QLD 116 B4
Hobbys Yards, NSW 40 A5, 39 H5
Hodgson, QLD 120 C1
Hodgson River, NT 206 B2
Holbrook, NSW 40 B3, 44 B3
Holden Hill, SA 142 D5
Holder, ACT 20 A4
Holgate, NSW 51 B4
Holland Park, QLD 108 D3
Holland Park West , QLD 108 D3
Hollands Landing, VIC 80 A6, 85 H2, 86 B4
Hollow Tree, TAS 236 C2
Hollydeen, NSW 59 B2
Hollywell, QLD 127 C3
Holmesglen, VIC 71 E4
Holowilena, SA 153 E3, 159 D4
Holroyd, NSW 26 C6, 28 C1
Holroyd, QLD 113 B5
Holsworthy, NSW 28 B4
Holsworthy Barracks, NSW 28 C3
Holt, ACT 20 A2
Holtze, NT 199 H5
Holwell, TAS 234 B2
Home Hill, QLD 112 C6
Home Valley, WA 181 C3
Homeboin, QLD 120 B3
Homebush, NSW 27 E6, 28 D1
Homebush Bay, NSW 26 D6, 28 D1
Homebush West, NSW 26 D6, 28 D1
Homerton, VIC 82 C3
Homestead, QLD 116 A1
Homewood, VIC 78 C6, 84 C1
Hookhams Corner, NSW 27 E3
Hookina (Ruins), SA 153 E3
Hookina (Ruins), SA 159 B4
Hooley, WA 182 D2
Hope Island, QLD 127 B3
Hope Valley, SA 143 E5
Hope Valley, WA 172 C3
Hopefield, NSW 44 A3
Hopeland, WA 172 D6
Hopelands, NSW 32 A5
Hopetoun, VIC 76 D2
Hopetoun, WA 177 H4

Jung, VIC 76 D5
Jurema, QLD 116 C4
Jurien, WA 174 A3

Kaarimba, VIC 78 C3
Kaban, QLD 123 A6
Kabelbarra, QLD 116 C4
Kabininge, SA 157 C4
Kabra, QLD 117 E4, 129 B4
Kadina, SA 152 D6
Kadji Kadji, WA 174 C2
Kadnook, VIC 76 B6, 82 B1
Kadungle, NSW 39 F4
Kaimkillenbun, QLD
121 F2, 135 B2
Kairi, QLD 123 B4
Kajabbi, QLD 110 C6,
114 C1
Kajuligah, NSW 38 A3
Kalabity, SA 153 G3
Kalala, NT 205 H3, 206 A3
Kalamia, QLD 112 C6
Kalamunda, WA 171 F3
Kalamurina, SA 149 E3
Kalanbi, SA 151 G3
Kalang, NSW 35 F6, 53 A5
Kalangadoo, SA 155 G5,
163 D5
Kalannie, WA 174 D3
Kalarka, QLD 117 E3
Kalbar, QLD 121 G3, 133 B2
Kalbarri, WA 182 B6
Kalbeeba, SA 143 F1
Kaldow, SA 152 A6
Kaleen, ACT 20 B2
Kaleentha Loop, NSW 37 F3
Kaleno, NSW 38 B2
Kalgan, WA 177 E6, 193 C3
Kalgoorlie-Boulder, WA
178 B4
Kalimna, VIC 80 B6, 86 D3
Kalinga, QLD 111 G1,
113 C6
Kalinjarri, NT 210 B4
Kalkadoon, QLD 115 E3
Kalkallo, VIC 84 B2
Kalkarindji (Police Stn), NT
204 D5
Kalkaroo, NSW 37 H1
Kalkaroo, SA 153 G3
Kalkee, VIC 76 D4
Kalkite, NSW 65 C5
Kallala, QLD 114 B2
Kallangur, QLD 107 E4
Kalli, WA 182C5
Kallista, VIC 93C4
Kalorama, VIC 93C2
Kalpienung, VIC 77F2
Kalpowar, QLD 111 G1,
113 D6, 117 F5
Kaltukatjara (Docker River),
NT 212 B4
Kalumburu, WA 181 B2
Kaluwiri, WA 183 E6
Kalyeeda, WA 181 A5
Kamarah, NSW 38 D6, 44 A1
Kamarooka East, VIC 78 A4
Kambah, ACT 20 A4
Kambalda, WA 178 B5
Kambalda West, WA 178 B5,
179 B1
Kamballup, WA 177 E5,
193 C2

Kameruka, NSW 45 F5
Kamileroi, QLD 110 C6
Kamma, QLD 123 C4
Kammel, QLD 116 C4
Kamona, TAS 235 E2
Kanagulk, VIC 76 C6, 82 C1
Kanandah, WA 185 B3
Kanawarrji, WA 183 H2,
184 A2
Kancoona, VIC 79 G4, 99 C2
Kandanga, QLD 121 G1,
131 A3
Kandanga Upper, QLD 131 A3
Kandos, NSW 40 B4
Kangan, WA 182 D1
Kangarilla, SA 144 D5
Kangaroo Flat, NSW 41 E1
Kangaroo Flat, VIC 78 A5,
95 E1
Kangaroo Ground, VIC
71 F1
Kangaroo Inn, SA 163 B4
Kangaroo Point, NSW 29 E4
Kangaroo Point, QLD
105 D3, 108 D2
Kangaroo Valley, NSW
45 G1, 55 B3
Kangaroo Well, SA 152 A3
Kangawall, VIC 76 B5
Kangiara, NSW 44 D1
Kaniva, VIC 76 B4
Kanowna, WA 178 B4
Kantappa, NSW 36C1
Kanumbra, VIC 78 D6
Kanunnah Bridge, TAS
232 B1
Kanwal, NSW 51 C3
Kanya, VIC 77 F5, 95 A1
Kanyaka (Ruins), SA 153 E3
Kaoota, TAS 236 D4
Kapaldo, QLD 117 F6
Kapinnie, SA 152 A6
Kapooka, NSW 44 B2
Kapunda, SA 153 E6, 155 E1
Karabeal, VIC 82 D2, 97 A6
Karadoc, VIC 74 D4
Karalundi, WA 182 D5
Karama, NT 198 D2
Karangi, NSW 53 C3
Karanja, TAS 236 C2
Karara, QLD 121 F3, 135 B6
Karara, WA 174 D2
Karatta, SA 161 B3
Karawara, WA 170 D4
Karawatha, QLD 108 D5
Karbar, WA 182 D5
Karcultaby, SA 151 H4,
152 A4
Kardinya, WA 170 C5,
172 C1
Kareela, NSW 29 E4
Kareela, QLD 116 C5
Kariah, VIC 83 F3, 88 D3
Karin, QLD 116 C3
Kariong, NSW 51 B4
Karkoo, SA 152 A6
Karlgarin, WA 177 F2
Karmona, QLD 119 E2
Karnak, VIC 76 B5
Karonie, WA 178 D4
Karoo, NSW 32 B6
Karoola, NSW 37 E4
Karoola, TAS 234 C2

Karoonda, SA 155 F2
Karpa Kora, NSW 37 F4
Karragullen, WA 171 G5,
173 G1
Karrakatta, WA 170 C3
Karrakup, WA 173 F4
Karratha, WA 182 C1
Karratha Roadhouse, WA
182 C1
Karridale, WA 176 B5
Karridale, WA 189 B5
Karrinyup, WA 170 B2
Karrup, WA 173 F4
Kars, NSW 37 E3
Kars Springs, NSW 40 C2
Karte, SA 155 G2
Karuah, NSW 41 E4, 63 A3
Karumba, QLD 110 D4
Karunjie, WA 181 C3
Karwarn, NSW 38 B3
Karween, VIC 74 B4
Katamatite, VIC 78 D3
Katandra, QLD 115 G2
Katanning, WA 177 E4
Katherine, NT 201 F6,
205 F1, 220 C4
Katoomba, NSW 40 B5,
48 D5
Katunga, VIC 78 D3
Katyil, VIC 76 D4
Kawana, QLD 129 B4
Kawana, WA 175 G3
Kawarren, VIC 83 G4, 89 E4
Kayrunnera, NSW 31 E6
Kayuga, NSW 59 E1
Kealba, VIC 70 A2
Kearsley, NSW 57 D6
Kedron, QLD 108 C1
Keeroongooloo, QLD 119 E1
Keewong, NSW 38 B3
Keilor, VIC 70 A1
Keilor Downs, VIC 70 A2
Keilor East, VIC 70 B2
Keilor Lodge, VIC 70 A1
Keilor North, VIC 70 A1
Keilor Park, VIC 70 B2
Keith, SA 155 G3
Keith Hall, NSW 46 D4
Kellalac, VIC 76 D4
Kellatier, TAS 233 E1
Kellerberrin, WA 175 E5,
177 E1
Kellevie, TAS 237 F3, 245 C3
Kellys Beach, QLD 125 A1
Kellyville, NSW 26 C4
Kellyville Ridge, NSW 26 B4
Kelmscott, WA 171 F6,
173 F1
Kelpum, QLD 116 B5
Kelso, TAS 234 B1
Kelvin, NSW 34 B6
Kelvin Grove, QLD 108 C2
Kelvin View, VIC 78 D5
Kempsey, NSW 41 F1
Kempton, TAS 236 D2
Kendall, NSW 41 F2
Kendenup, WA 177 E5,
193 B1
Kendenup West, WA 193 B1
Kenebri, NSW 33 H6
Kenilworth, QLD 121 G2,
131 A4
Kenley, VIC 75 G5

Kenmare, VIC 76 D3
Kenmore, QLD 108 B3
Kenmore Hills, QLD 108 B3
Kennedy, QLD 112 A4
Kennedys Ck, VIC 83 G5
Kennedys Creek, VIC 88 D5
Kennett River, VIC 83 H5,
89 F5
Kenny, ACT 20 C2
Kensington, NSW 29 G2
Kensington, SA 144 D1
Kensington, VIC 70 C3
Kensington, WA 170 D3
Kensington Downs, QLD
115 G3
Kensington Gardens, SA
144 D1
Kensington Park, SA 144 D1
Kent Town, SA 141 D3,
144 D1
Kentbruck, VIC 82 B3
Kenthurst, NSW 26 C3
Kentlyn, NSW 28 A5
Kenton Valley, SA 143 H5
Kentucky, NSW 34 D6
Kenwick, WA 171 E4
Keperra, QLD 108 B1
Keppel Sands, QLD 117 F4,
129 C4
Keppoch, SA 155 G4
Kerang, VIC 77 H2
Kerang Sth, VIC 77 H2
Kerein Hills, NSW 39 E3
Kergunyah, VIC 79 G4,
99 C1
Kergunyah South, VIC
99 C2
Kergunyah Sth, VIC 79 G4
Kerrabee, NSW 40 B3
Kerrie, VIC 90 D3
Kerrisdale, VIC 78 C6
Kerriwah, NSW 39 E3
Kerrs Creek, NSW 39 H4
Kerry, QLD 133 C3
Kersbrook, SA 143 G4,
155 E1
Keswick, SA 141 A6, 144 C1
Keswick Terminal, SA
141 A5, 144 C1
Ketchowla, SA 153 F5
Kettering, TAS 236 D4
Kevington, VIC 85 E1
Kew, NSW 41 F2
Kew, VIC 70 D3
Kew East, VIC 70 D3
Kewdale, WA 171 E3
Kewell, VIC 76 D4
Kewell East, NSW 37 H2
Keysborough, VIC 71 F6
Keysbrook, WA 174 C6,
176 C2
Khancoban, NSW 44 C4,
65 A4
Ki Ki, SA 155 F2
Kia Ora, NSW 33 E5
Kia Ora, QLD 125 B6, 131 B1
Kia Ora, SA 153 F5
Kia Ora, VIC 97 D5
Kiacatoo, NSW 38 D4
Kiama, NSW 38 B3, 45 G1
Kiama, NSW 55 C3
Kiamal, VIC 75 E5
Kiamba, QLD 131 B4

Kybong, QLD 131 A3
Kybybolite, SA 155 G4,
163 D3
Kyeamba, NSW 44 C2
Kyeemagh, NSW 29 F3
Kyena, QLD 120 B4
Kyle Bay, NSW 29 E4
Kyneton, VIC 78 A6, 84 A1,
90 C2
Kynuna, QLD 115 E2
Kyogle, NSW 35 G3, 133 C4
Kyong, QLD 116 A2
Kyvalley, VIC 78 C4
Kywong, NSW 44 A2
Kywong, QLD 115 F3

La Perouse, NSW 29 G4, 40 C6
Laanecoorie, VIC 77 H5,
95 D1
Laang, VIC 83 E4, 88 B4
Labrador, QLD 127 C4
Laceby, VIC 79 F4, 99 A2
Laceys Creek, QLD 106 A3
Lachlan, TAS 236 D3
Lachlan Downs, NSW 38 C3
Lady Barron, TAS 231 C3
Lady Bay, SA 158 B2
Lady's Pass, VIC 78 B5
Ladysmith, NSW 44 B2
Laen East, VIC 77 E4
Lagaven, QLD 114 D2
Laggan, NSW 40 A6, 45 E1,
39 H6
Laglan, QLD 116 B3
Laguna, NSW 40 C4
Laguna Quays, QLD 137 A4
Lah, VIC 76 D3
Laharum, VIC 76 D6, 97 B1
Laidley, QLD 121 G3, 133 B1
Lajamanu (Police Stn), NT
204 D6, 208 D1
Lake Argyle Village, WA
181 D3
Lake Barlee, WA 175 G2
Lake Bathurst, NSW 45 F2
Lake Boga, VIC 77 G1
Lake Bolac, VIC 83 E2, 88 B1
Lake Cargelligo, NSW 38 D5
Lake Cathie, NSW 41 F2
Lake Charm, VIC 77 H2
Lake Clifton, WA 187 A1
Lake Conjola, NSW 45 G2,
55 B5
Lake Cowal, NSW 39 E5
Lake Dunn, QLD 116 A3
Lake Everard, SA 152 A3
Lake Goldsmith, VIC 83 G2
Lake Grace, WA 177 F3
Lake Harry (Ruins), SA
149 E5
Lake Illawarra, NSW 45 G1,
55 C3
Lake Julia, WA 175 G4
Lake King, WA 177 H3
Lake Leake, TAS 235 E5
Lake Marmal, VIC 77 G3
Lake Mundi, VIC 82 A2
Lake Munmorah, NSW
51 D2
Lake Nash, NT 211 G4
Lake Nerramyne, WA 182 B6
Lake Rowan, VIC 79 E4
Lake Stewart, NSW 30 C4

Lake Tabourie, NSW 45 G2,
55 A6
Lake Torrens, SA 152 D3,
159 A3
Lake Tyers, VIC 80 C6, 86 E3
Lake Victoria, NSW 36 D6
Lake Violet, WA 183 F5
Lake Wallace, NSW 30 D5
Lake Way, WA 183 F5
Lake Wells, WA 183 G5
Lakeland, QLD 111 H2
Lakemba, NSW 28 D2
Lakes Entrance, VIC 80 B6,
86 E3
Lal Lal, VIC 83 H2
Lalbert, VIC 77 G2
Lalbert Rd, VIC 77 G2
Lalguli, QLD 120 D3
Lalla, TAS 234 C2
Lalla Rookh, WA 180 A6,
183 E1
Lalor, VIC 70 D1
Lalor Park, NSW 26 B5
Lambina, SA 147 G2
Lamboo, WA 181 C5
Lameroo, SA 155 G2
Lamington, QLD 133 C3
Lammermoor, QLD 115 H2
Lana, QLD 115 F3
Lancefield, VIC 78 B6, 84
B1, 90 E2
Lancelin, WA 174 B4
Lancevale, QLD 116 A4
Landor, WA 182 C4
Landridge, QLD 120 C3
Landrigans, NSW 53 C3
Landsborough, QLD
121 H2, 131 C5
Landsborough, VIC 77 F6,
95 A2
Landwreath, QLD 120 C1
Lane Cove, NSW 27 F5,
29 F1
Lane Cove West, NSW 27 F5
Lanena, TAS 234 C2
Lang Lang, VIC 84 D4
Langawirra, NSW 37 E2
Langford, WA 171 E4
Langhorne Creek, SA 155 E2
Langi Logan, VIC 83 F1,
95 A3
Langidoon, NSW 37 E2
Langkoop, VIC 76 A6, 82 A1
Langley, VIC 78 A6, 84 A1,
90 C1
Langleydale, NSW 37 G6
Langloh, TAS 236 C2
Langshaw, QLD 131 A3
Langton, QLD 116 C3
Langtree, NSW 38 C5
Langville, VIC 77 H2
Langwarrin, VIC 73 F3
Langwarrin South, VIC
73 F3
Langwell, NSW 36 D3
Lansdale, NSW 39 E3
Lansdown, NSW 32 B5
Lansdowne, NSW 28 C2,
41 F2
Lansdowne, QLD 116 A5
Lansdowne, WA 181 C4
Lansvale, NSW 28 C2
Lanyon, ACT 21 B3

Lapoinya, TAS 233 E1
Lappa, QLD 111 H4
Lara, QLD 111 E5, 114 D1
Lara, VIC 84 A3, 89 H2
Lara Lake, VIC 84 A3, 89 H2
Laramba, NT 213 G1
Larapinta, QLD 108 C6
Laravale, QLD 133 C3
Largs Bay, SA 142 A5
Largs North, SA 142 A5
Larloona, NSW 37 E3
Larnook, NSW 35 G3
Larpent, VIC 83 G4
Larrakeyah, NT 197 A5,
198 A5
Larras Lee, NSW 39 G4
Larrimah, NT 205 G2,
206 A2
Lascelles, VIC 77 E2
Latham, ACT 20 A2
Latham, WA 174 C3
Lathlain, WA 170 D3
Latrobe, TAS 233 G2, 234 A2
Lauderdale, TAS 229 G4,
237 E3, 245 A4
Launceston, TAS 234 C3
Launching Place, VIC 84 D2
Laura, QLD 111 G2, 113 D6
Laura, SA 153 E5
Laura Bay, SA 151 G4
Lauradale, NSW 32 C4
Laurel Hill, NSW 44 C3,
65 A1
Laureldale, NSW 46 C3
Laurelvale, NSW 31 G6
Laurieton, NSW 41 F2
Lauriston, VIC 90 B2
Lavers Hill, VIC 83 G5, 88 D5
Laverton, VIC 70 A4, 84 B2
Laverton, WA 178 D1,
183 G6
Laverton Downs, WA
178 D1, 183 G6
Laverton North, VIC 70 A3
Lavington, NSW 44 B3
Lawitta, TAS 236 D3
Lawler, VIC 77 E4
Lawloit, VIC 76 B4
Lawn Hill, QLD 110 A5
Lawnton, QLD 106 D5
Lawrence, NSW 35 G4
Lawrenny, TAS 236 C2
Lawson, ACT 20 B2
Lawson, NSW 40 B5, 49 F5
Leabrook, SA 144 D1
Leadville, NSW 40 A2
Leaghur, VIC 77 H3
Leam, TAS 234 C2
Leanyer, NT 198 D2
Learmonth, VIC 83 H1 95 C4
Learmonth, WA 182 A2
Leawood Gardens, SA
144 D2
Lebrina, TAS 234 C2
Leda, WA 172 C4
Ledcourt, VIC 97 C2
Ledge Point, WA 174 B5
Leederville, WA 170 C2
Leeka, TAS 231 B2
Leeman, WA 174 A3
Leeming, WA 170 D5,
172 D1
Leesville, TAS 230 B6

Leeton, NSW 44 A1
Lefroy, TAS 234 C1
Legana, TAS 234 C2
Legerwood, TAS 235 E2
Legume, NSW 35 F2, 133 A4
Legune, NT 204 B2
Legunia, TAS 235 F2
Leichhardt, NSW 29 F2
Leigh, NSW 53 A3
Leigh Creek, SA 153 E1
Leinster, WA 183 F6
Leinster Downs, WA 183 F6
Leitchville, VIC 78 A3
Leith, TAS 233 G1
Lemon Tree, NSW 51 B2
Lemon Tree Passage, NSW
41 E4, 63 A4
Lemont, TAS 235 E6, 237 F1
Lenah Valley, TAS 228 B2
Leneva, VIC 79 G3, 99 B1
Lennox Head, NSW 35 G3,
46 D3
Lenswood, SA 145 G1
Leongatha, VIC 85 E4
Leongatha Sth, VIC 85 E4
Leonora, WA 178 B1, 183 F6
Leonora Downs, NSW 37 E3
Leopold, VIC 84 A3
Leopold Downs, WA 181 B4
Lerida, NSW 38 C2
Lesley, WA 171 H6, 173 H2
Leslie Vale, TAS 228 A6,
236 D3
Lesmurdie, WA 171 F4
Lethbridge, VIC 84 A3,
89 G2
Lethebrook, QLD 137 A3
Lethere, NSW 37 E5
Letts Beach, VIC 86 B4
Letts Beach (Paradise
Beach), VIC 85 H3
Leumeah, NSW 28 A5
Leura, NSW 49 E5
Levendale, TAS 237 E2,
245 A1
Lewisham, NSW 29 E2
Lewisham, TAS 237 F3,
245 A3
Lewiston, SA 142 C1
Lexton, VIC 77 G6, 83 G1,
95 B3
Leyburn, QLD 121 F3,
135 B5
Liawenee, TAS 233 H5,
234 B5
Liberty Grove, NSW 27 E6,
29 E1
Licola, VIC 85 F2
Lidcombe, NSW 26 D6,
28 D1
Liena, TAS 233 G3, 241 D1
Lietinna, TAS 234 D2
Liffey, TAS 234 B4
Lightning Ridge, NSW 33 F4
Likkaparta, NT 210 B2
Lileah, TAS 232 C1
Lilla Creek, NT 214 B5,
223 E4
Lilli Pilli, NSW 29 E5
Lillimur, VIC 76 A4
Lillimur South, VIC 76 A4
Lilliput, VIC 79 F3
Lilydale, SA 153 G5

Maggea, SA 155 G1
Maggieville, QLD 110 D4
Magill, SA 143 E6, 145 E1
Magowra, QLD 110 D4
Magrath Flat, SA 155 F3
Mahanewo, SA 152 B3
Mahogany Creek, WA
    171 G2
Maianbar, NSW 29 E5
Maida Vale, WA 171 F3
Maidenwell, QLD 121 G2,
    135 C2
Maidstone, VIC 70 B3
Mailapunyah, NT 206 D4
Mailer Flat, VIC 83 E4, 88 A3
Maimuru, NSW 39 G6
Main Beach, QLD 127 C4
Maindample, VIC 79 E6
Mainoru, NT 202 B6
Maitland, NSW 40 D4
Maitland, SA 152 D6, 154 D1
Maitland Downs, QLD
    111 H2
Majors Creek, NSW 45 F3
Majura, ACT 20 D2
Makowata, QLD 117 G5
Malabar, NSW 29 G3, 33 F4
Malacura, QLD 111 F5
Malaga, WA 170 D1
Malagarga, QLD 119 E1
Malak, NT 198 D2
Malanda, QLD 112 A4,
    123 B5
Malbina, TAS 236 D3
Malbon, QLD 114 C2
Malbooma, SA 151 G1
Malcolm (abandoned), WA
    178 B, 183 F6
Maldon, VIC 77 H6, 95 D2
Maldorkey, SA 153 G4
Malebo, NSW 44 B2
Maleny, QLD 121 H2, 131 B5
Malinns, VIC 80 D5
Mallacoota, VIC 81 G5
Mallala, SA 155 E1
Mallanganee, NSW 35 F3
Mallawillup, WA 193 A1
Mallina, WA 182 D1
Malmsbury, VIC 78 A6,
    84 A1, 90 B1, 95 E3
Malta, QLD 116 B6
Maltee, SA 151 G3
Malvern, SA 144 C2
Malvern, VIC 70 D4
Malvern East, VIC 71 E4
Malverton, QLD 115 H5
Mamboo, QLD 116 B4
Mambray Creek, SA 152 D4
Manangatang, VIC 75 F6
Manangoora, NT 207 F3
Manara, NSW 37 G4
Manara Mine, NSW 37 G4
Manberry, WA 182 A3
Mandagery, NSW 39 G4
Mandalong, NSW 51 C2
Mandelman, NSW 37 G5
Mandogalup, WA 172 C3
Mandora, WA 180 B6
Mandorah, NT 200 D3
Mandurah, WA 176 B2,
    191 B2
Mandurama, NSW 39 H5
Mandurang, VIC 78 A5

Maneroo, QLD 115 G4
Manfred, NSW 37 G5
Mangalo, SA 152 B5
Mangalore, QLD 120 A2
Mangalore, TAS 236 D2
Mangalore, VIC 78 C5
Mangana, TAS 235 F4
Mangaroon, WA 182 B3
Mango Hill, QLD 107 E4
Mangoola, NSW 59 C2
Mangoplah, NSW 44 B2
Mangrove Mountain, NSW
    51 A3
Manguri, SA 147 H5
Manifold, QLD 129 B2
Manildra, NSW 39 G4
Manilla, NSW 34 C6, 37 E5
Maningrida (Police Stn.), NT
    202 B3
Manjimup, WA 176 C5
Manly, NSW 27 H5, 40 C5
Manly, QLD 109 F2
Manly Vale, NSW 27 G5
Manly West, QLD 109 F2
Manmanning, WA 174 D4
Mannahill, SA 153 G4
Mannanarie, SA 153 E5
Mannering Park, NSW
    51 C2
Manners Creek, NT 211 G6
Manning, WA 170 D4
Manning Point, NSW 41 F2
Manningham, SA 142 C6
Manns Beach, VIC 85 G5
Mannuem Creek, QLD
    135 C1
Mannum, SA 155 F2
Mannus, NSW 44 C3
Manoora, SA 153 E6
Mansfield, QLD 109 E4
Mansfield, VIC 79 E6
Mansfield Park, SA 142 B6
Mantamaru, WA 184 C4
Mantuan Downs, QLD
    116 B5
Mantung, SA 155 G1
Manuka, NSW 38 C3
Manunda, SA 153 F4
Many Peaks, QLD 117 F5
Manyallaluk, NT 201 G6,
    205 G1, 220 E3
Manyana, NSW 61 A6
Manypeaks, WA 177 F6,
    193 D3
Mapleton, QLD 131 B4
Mapoon, QLD 113 A3
Maragle, NSW 65 A3
Maralinga, SA 146 D6,
    150 D1
Marama, SA 155 G2
Maranalgo, WA 175 E2
Marananga, SA 157 B3
Maranboy, NT 220 E4
Maranboy (Police Stn), NT
    201 G6, 205 G1
Marandoo, WA 182 D2
Marangaroo, WA 170 C1
Marathon, QLD 115 F1
Maraylya, NSW 26 B2
Marayong, NSW 26 B4
Marble Bar, WA 183 E1
Marble Hill, SA 145 F1
Marburg, QLD 133 B1

March, NSW 39 H4
Marchagee, WA 174 C3
Marcoola, QLD 131 C4
Marcorna, VIC 77 H3
Marcus Beach, QLD 131 C3
Marcus Hill, VIC 84 B4
Mardan, VIC 85 E4
Mardathuna, WA 182 B4
Mardella, WA 173 E5
Marden, SA 142 D6
Mardie, WA 182 B1
Mareeba, QLD 111 H3,
    112 A3, 123 A3
Marengo, VIC 89 E5
Marfield, NSW 37 H3
Margaret River, WA 176 B4,
    181 C5, 189 B3
Margate, QLD 107 F4
Margate, TAS 236 D4
Marian, QLD 116 D2, 137 B6
Maribyrnong, VIC 70 B2
Marillana, WA 183 E2
Marimo, QLD 114 C1
Marino, SA 144 B3
Marion, SA 144 B2
Marion Bay, SA 154 C2
Marion Downs, QLD 114 B4
Marita Downs, QLD 115 G3
Markwood, VIC 79 F4
Marla, SA 147 G3
Marlborough, QLD 117 E3
Marleston, SA 144 C1
Marlo, VIC 80 D6
Marlow Lagoon, NT 199 F6
Marma, VIC 77 E5
Marmion, WA 170 B1
Marmor, QLD 117 F4,
    129 B5
Marnhull, QLD 135 A2
Marnoo, VIC 77 E5
Marnoo East, VIC 77 F5,
    95 A1
Marona, NSW 37 G5
Maronan, QLD 114 D2
Marong, NSW 38 C5
Marong, VIC 77 H5, 78 A5,
    95 D1
Maroochydore, QLD
    121 H2, 131 C4
Maroomba, QLD 115 G3
Maroon, QLD 133 B3
Maroona, VIC 83 F1
Maroonah, WA 182 B3
Maroubra, NSW 29 G3
Maroubra Junction, NSW
    29 G3
Marqua, NT 215 F1
Marrabel, SA 153 E6
Marradong, WA 176 C3
Marrar, NSW 44 B1
Marrara, NT 198 C3
Marrawah, TAS 230 A6
Marraweeny, VIC 78 D5
Marree, SA 148 D6
Marrickville, NSW 29 F2
Marrickville South, NSW
    29 F2
Marrilla, WA 182 B3
Marron, WA 182 B4
Marryat, SA 147 F1
Marsden, NSW 39 E5
Marsden, QLD 109 E6
Marsfield, NSW 27 E5

Marshall, VIC 89 H3
Martin, WA 171 F5, 173 F1
Martindale, NSW 59 C4
Martins Well, SA 153 F3,
    159 E2
Martinsdale, NSW 51 B1
Marulan, NSW 45 F1
Marungi, VIC 78 D3
Marvell Loch, WA 175 G5,
    177 G1
Mary River, NT 201 F5
Mary River Roadhouse, NT
    201 F5
Mary Springs, WA 182 B6
Mary Valley, QLD 111 G1,
    113 C6
Maryborough, QLD 117 H6,
    125 B4
Maryborough, VIC 77 H6,
    95 C2
Maryborough West, QLD
    125 A4
Marybrook, WA 189 B2
Maryfield, NT 205 H3,
    206 A3
Marymia, WA 183 E4
    184 D1
Maryvale, NSW 39 H3
Maryvale, QLD 111 H6,
    114 C3, 129 B3
Mascot, NSW 29 F2
Maslin Beach, SA 158 C1
Massey, VIC 77 E4
Massie, QLD 135 C6
Matakana, NSW 38 C4
Mataranka, NT 205 G2
Mathiesons, VIC 78 B4
Mathinna, TAS 235 F3
Mathoura, NSW 43 G3
Matlock, VIC 85 F2
Matong, NSW 44 B1
Matraville, NSW 29 G3
Maude, NSW 43 F1
Maude, VIC 84 A3, 89 G2
Maudsland, QLD 127 A4
Maules Creek, NSW 34 B6
Mawbanna, TAS 232 D1
Mawson, ACT 20 B4
Mawson, WA 174 D6, 176 D2
Mawson Lakes, SA 142 C5
Maxwellton, QLD 115 F1
May Downs, QLD 116 D3
Maya, WA 174 C3
Mayberry, TAS 233 G3
Maydena, TAS 236 B3
Maylands, WA 170 D3
Mayneside, QLD 115 E4
Mayrung, NSW 43 G2
Mays Hill, NSW 26 C6, 28 C1
Maytown (Ruins), QLD
    111 G2
Mazar, NSW 36 C4
Mead, VIC 77 H2, 78 A2
Meadow, WA 182 B5
Meadow Glen, NSW 38 B2
Meadow Heights, VIC 70 C1
Meadow Springs, WA 191 B5
Meadowbank, NSW 27 E5,
    29 E1
Meadowbank, QLD 111 H4
Meadowbrook, QLD 109 E6
Meadows, SA 145 F6
Meandarra, QLD 121 E2

Mission Beach, QLD 112 A4
Mistake Creek, NT 204 B5
Mitakoodi, QLD 114 C1
Mitcham, SA 144 D2
Mitcham, VIC 71 F3
Mitchell, ACT 20 C2
Mitchell, NT 199 H5
Mitchell, QLD 120 C1
Mitchell Park, SA 144 C2
Mitchellstown, VIC 78 C5
Mitchellville, SA 152 C5
Mitchelton, QLD 108 C1
Mitiamo, VIC 78A3
Mitre, VIC 76C5
Mitta Mitta, VIC 79 H4,
  80 A2, 99 D2
Mittagong, NSW 45 G1,
  55 B2
Mittagong, QLD 111 E5
Mittebah, NT 211 F2
Mittyack, VIC 75 E6, 77 E1,
  125 A6
Moama, NSW 43 F4
Moana, SA 144 A6
Mobbs Hill, NSW 26 D5
Moble, QLD 119 G2
Mockinya, VIC 97 A2
Mockinyah, VIC 76 D6
Modanville, NSW 46 A3
Modbury, SA 143 E5
Modbury Heights, SA 143 E5
Modbury North, SA 143 E5
Moe, VIC 85 F3
Mogal Plain, NSW 39 E3
Moggill, QLD 108 A4
Moglonemby, VIC 78 D5
Mogo, NSW 45 F3
Mogongong, NSW 39 G6
Mogriguy, NSW 39 G2
Mogumber, WA 174 C4
Moil, NT 198 C2
Moina, TAS 233 F3
Mokepilly, VIC 77 E6, 97 D2
Mole Creek, TAS 233 G3,
  234 A3
Molesworth, TAS 236 D3
Molesworth, VIC 78 D6,
  84 D1
Moliagul, VIC 77 G5, 95 C1
Molka, VIC 78 D5
Mollerin, WA 175 E4
Mollongghip, VIC 83 H1,
  95 D4
Mollymook, NSW 55 B6
Molong, NSW 39 G4
Moltema, TAS 233 H3,
  234 A3
Momba, NSW 3 1G6, 37 E1
Mona Vale, NSW 27 H3,
  40 C5, 51 B6
Mona Vale, QLD 119 G1
Mona Vale, TAS 234 D6
Monak, NSW 37 E6, 42 B1
Monash, ACT 20 B5
Monash, SA 165 C2
Monbulk, VIC 93 D4
Moncrieff, ACT 20 B1
Monegeetta, VIC 84 B1,
  90 E3
Monia Gap, NSW 38 C5
Monivea, NSW 37 H4
Monkey Mia, WA 182 A5
Monkira, QLD 114 C5

Monomie, NSW 39 F4
Monstraven, QLD 110 D6
Mont Albert, VIC 71 E3
Mont Albert North, VIC
  71 E3
Montacute, SA 143 F6
Montagu, TAS 230 B6
Montagu Bay, TAS 228 D2
Montana, TAS 233 H3,
  234 A3
Monteagle, NSW 39 G6
Montejinni, NT 205 F4
Monterey, NSW 29 F3
Montgomery, VIC 85 G3,
  86 A3
Montmorency, VIC 71 E2
Monto, QLD 117 F6
Montrose, TAS 228 A1
Montrose, VIC 71 H3, 93 B2
Montumana, TAS 232 D1
Montville, QLD 131 B4
Mooball, NSW 133 E4
Moockra, SA 153 E4
Moodiarrup, WA 176 D4
Moogara, TAS 236 C3
Moojeeba, QLD 113 C5
Mooka, WA 182 B4
Mookarra, QLD 112 D6,
  116 C1
Moola, QLD 135 B3
Moolah, NSW 38 B3
Moolap, VIC 89 H3
Moolawatana, SA 149 F6
Moolbong, NSW 38 B5
Mooleulooloo, SA 153 G3
Mooloo, QLD 131 A3
Mooloo Downs, WA 182 C4
Mooloogool, WA 183 E5
Mooloolaba, QLD 131 C4
Mooloolah, QLD 131 C5
Mooloolerie, NSW 37 F4
Moolooloo O.S., NT 205 E3
Moolort, VIC 77 H6, 95 D2
Moomba (Private), SA
  149 G4
Moona Plains, NSW 41 E1
Moonah, TAS 228 B2
Moonambel, VIC 77 G6,
  95 B2
Moonan Flat, NSW 40 D2
Moonaree, SA 152 B3
Moonbah, NSW 65 C6
Moonbi, NSW 40 C1
Moonbria, NSW 43 G2
Moondarra, VIC 85 F3
Moondene, NSW 37 H4,
  38 A4
Moonee Beach, NSW 35 G5,
  53 D2
Moonee Ponds, VIC 70 C2
Moonera, WA 185 C3
Mooney Mooney, NSW
  51 A5
Moonie, QLD 121 E3
Moonijin, WA 174 D4
Moonta, SA 152 D6
Moonya, QLD 115 H4
Moonyoonooka, WA 174 A1
Moora, WA 174 C4
Moorabbin, VIC 70 D5,
  84 C3
Moorabbin Airport, VIC
  71 E6

Mooraberree, QLD 114 D6
Moorak, QLD 116 B6, 120 B1
Mooralla, VIC 97 A5
Mooramanna, QLD 120 C3
Moorara, NSW 37 E5
Moorarie, WA 182 D4
Moore, NSW 40 C1, 34 C6
Moore, QLD 121 G2
Moore Park, NSW 29 G2
Moore Park, QLD 117 G5
Moorebank, NSW 28 B3
Moorebank Village, NSW
  28 B3
Mooren, NSW 40 A2, 39 H2
Mooreville, TAS 233 F1
Moorina, QLD 106 B2
Moorine Rock, WA 175 G5,
  177 G1
Moorland, NSW 41 F2
Moorleah, TAS 233 E1
Moorna, NSW 36 D6
Moorngag, VIC 79 E5
Moorooduc, VIC 73 E4
Moorook, SA 153 G6,
  155 G1, 165 B2
Moorook South, SA 165 B3
Moorooka, QLD 108 C4
Mooroolbark, VIC 71 H3,
  93 B2
Mooroopna, VIC 78 C4
Mooroopna Nth, VIC 78 C4
Moorooroo, SA 157 B5
Moppa, SA 157 C1
Moppin, NSW 34 A3
Morago, NSW 43 F2
Moralana, SA 153 E3, 159 B3
Moralla, VIC 82 D1
Moranbah, QLD 116 C3
Morangarell, NSW 39 F6
Morapoi, WA 178 B2
Morawa, WA 174 C2
Moray Downs, QLD 116 B2
Morayfield, QLD 106 D1,
  131 B6
Morchard, SA 153 E4
Mordialloc, VIC 71 E6
Morea, VIC 76 B5
Moree, NSW 34 B4
Morella, QLD 115 G4
Morgan, SA 153 F6
Morgan Vale, SA 153 G5
Moriac, VIC 84 A4, 89 G3
Morialpa, SA 153 G4
Moriarty, TAS 233 H2, 234 A2
Morisset, NSW 40 D4, 51 C2
Morkalla, VIC 74 B4
Morley, WA 170 D2
Morney, QLD 114 D6
Morning Bay, NSW 27 G2
Morning Side, NSW 37 H4,
  38 A4
Morningside, QLD 108 D2
Mornington, TAS 229 E2
Mornington, VIC 73 E3,
  84 C3
Mornington, WA 181 B4
Moroak, NT 205 H1, 206 A1
Moroco, NSW 43 G3
Morongla Creek, NSW 39 G6
Morphett Vale, SA 144 B5
Morphettville, SA 144 B2
Morri Morri, VIC 77 F5
Morrisons, VIC 84 A2, 89 G1

Morstone Downs, QLD
  110 A6
Mortdale, NSW 29 E3
Mortlake, NSW 27 E6, 29 E1
Mortlake, VIC 83 E3, 88 B2
Morton Plains, VIC 77 E3
Morundah, NSW 44 A2
Moruya, NSW 45 F3
Moruya Head, NSW 45 F3
Morven, QLD 120 B1
Morwell, VIC 85 F4
Moselle, QLD 115 F1
Mosman, NSW 27 G6, 29 G1
Mosman Park, WA 170 B4
Moss Vale, NSW 45 G1, 55 A3
Mossgiel, NSW 38 A4
Mossman, QLD 111 H3,
  123 A1
Mossy Point, NSW 45 F3
Motajup, VIC 97A6
Mothar Mountain, QLD
  131B2
Motpena, SA 159 B1
Moulamein, NSW 43 E2
Moulden, NT 199 G6
Moulyinning, WA 177 E3
Mt Aberdeen, QLD 116 C1
Mount Alford, QLD 133 B2
Mount Amhurst, WA 181 C5
Mount Arrowsmith, NSW
  30 D5
Mt Barker, SA 145 H4,
  155 E2
Mount Barker, WA 177 E5,
  193 B2
Mount Barnett Roadhouse,
  WA 181 B3
Mount Barry, SA 147 H4,
  148 A4
Mt Baw Baw Alpine Village,
  VIC 85 F2
Mount Beauty, VIC 79 H5,
  80 A3, 99 C3
Mt Beckworth, VIC 77 G6,
  83 G1
Mount Benson, SA 163 A3
Mount Brockman Mine, WA
  182 C2
Mount Bryan, SA 153 E5
Mt Buffalo, VIC 79 G5, 99 B3
Mt Buller Alpine Village, VIC
  79 F6, 85 F1, 99 A4
Mt Bundy, NT 201 E4,
  221 E2
Mount Burges, WA 178 B4
Mount Burr, SA 155 G5,
  163 C5
Mount Carbine, QLD
  111 H3
Mount Carnage, WA 178 B3
Mount Cavenagh, NT
  213 G5, 214 A6, 223 D4
Mount Celia, WA 178 D2
Mount Charlton, QLD
  137 A6
Mt Claremont, WA 170 B3
Mount Clarence, SA 147 H5
Mount Clere, WA 182 D4
Mt Colah, NSW 27 E3
Mount Compass, SA 158 D1
Mt Coolon, QLD 116 B2
Mount Coolum, QLD 131 C4
Mount Cooper, QLD 116 B1

Mungo, NSW 37 F5
Mungo Brush, NSW 63 D2
Mungunburra, QLD 116 A1
Mungungo, QLD 117 F5
Munna, NSW 40 A3
Munno Para Downs, SA 142 D2
Munno Para West, SA 142 D2
Munro, VIC 80 A6, 85 H2, 86 A3
Munster, WA 170 B6, 172 B2
Muntadgin, WA 175 F5, 177 F1
Muradup, WA 176 D4
Muralgarra, WA 174 D1, 182 D6
Murarrie, QLD 109 E2
Murchison, VIC 78 C5
Murchison Downs, WA 183 E5
Murchison East, VIC 78 C5
Murchison Roadhouse, WA 182 C5
Murdinga, SA 152 A6
Murdoch, WA 170 C5, 172 C1
Murdong, WA 177 E4
Murdunna, TAS 237 F3, 245 C4
Murgenella (Ranger Stn.), NT 201G 2
Murgheboluc, VIC 83 H3, 84 A3, 89 G2
Murgon, QLD 121 G1
Murgoo, WA 182 C6
Muriel, NSW 38 D2
Murkaby, SA 153 F5
Murmungee, VIC 79 G4, 99 B2
Murnpeowie, SA 149 F6
Murphys Ck, VIC 77 H5
Murphys Creek, QLD 135 D4
Murphys Creek, VIC 95 C1
Murra Murra, QLD 120 B3
Murra Warra, VIC 76 D4
Murrabit, VIC 77 H2
Murrami, NSW 38 D6, 44 A1
Murranji, NT 205 G4
Murrawal, NSW 40 A1, 39 H1
Murray Bend, WA 191 D3
Murray Bridge, SA 155 F2
Murray Downs, NT 210 B4
Murray Lakes, WA 191 D3
Murray Town, SA 152 D5
Murrays Run, NSW 51 A1
Murrayville, VIC 74 B6, 76 A1
Murrindal, VIC 80 C5
Murrindindi, VIC 84 D1
Murringo, NSW 39 G6
Murroon, VIC 83 H4, 89 F4
Murrumba Downs, QLD 107 E4
Murrumbateman, NSW 45 E2
Murrumbeena, VIC 71 E4
Murrumburrah, NSW 44 D1
Murrungowar, VIC 80 D5
Murrurundi, NSW 40 C2
Murtoa, VIC 77 E5
Murweh, QLD 120 A2

Murwillumbah, NSW 35 G2, 133 D4
Museum, NSW 25 C5
Musgrave, QLD 111 F1, 113 C5
Musk, VIC 90 A2
Musselboro, TAS 234 D3
Muswellbrook, NSW 40 C3, 59 E1
Mutarnee, QLD 112 A5
Mutawintji, NSW 37 E1
Mutchilba, QLD 111 H3
Mutijulu, NT 213 E5, 223 B3
Mutooroo, SA 153 H4
Muttaburra, QLD 115 G3
Muttama, NSW 44 C1
Mutton Hole, QLD 110 D4
Myall, VIC 77 H2
Myall Creek, SA 152 C4
Myalla, TAS 232 D1
Myally, QLD 110 C6
Myalup, WA 176 B3
Myalup Beach, WA 187 A3
Myambat, NSW 59 B3
Myamyn, VIC 82 C3
Myaree, WA 170 C4
Myendett, QLD 120 A1
Mylor, SA 145 F3
Mylsetom, NSW 53 C4
Myocum, NSW 46 D1
Myola, NSW 61 B3
Myola, QLD 110 D6, 123 B2
Myola, VIC 78 B5
Mypolonga, SA 155 F2
Myponga, SA 155 E2, 158 C1
Myponga Beach, SA 158 C1
Myria, SA 155 G1, 165 A4
Myrniong, VIC 84 A2, 90 B4
Myrrhee, VIC 79 F5, 99 A3
Myrtle Bank, SA 144 D2
Myrtle Bank, TAS 234 D2
Myrtle Scrub, NSW 41 E1
Myrtle Springs, SA 153 E1
Myrtleford, VIC 79 G4, 99 B2
Myrtletown, QLD 109 E1
Mysia, VIC 77 H3
Mystic Park, VIC 77 G2
Myuna, NSW 32 D4

Naas, ACT 21 B4
Nabageena, TAS 232 C1
Nabawa, WA 174 A1, 182 B6
Nabiac, NSW 41 E3
Nabowla, TAS 234 D2
Nackara, SA 153 F4
Nagaela, NSW 36 D4
Nagambie, VIC 78 C5
Nagari, SA 165 E4
Nagoorin, QLD 117 F5
Nailsworth, SA 142 C6
Nain, SA 157 A2
Nairne, SA 145 H3
Nairns, WA 191 C2
Nakara, NT 198 C1
Nala, TAS 237 E1
Nalbarra, WA 175 E1
Nalinga, VIC 78 D4
Nallan, WA 182 D5
Nambeelup, WA 191 D2
Nambi, WA 178 C1, 183 G6
Nambour, QLD 121 H2, 131 B4

Nambrok, VIC 85 G3
Nambucca Heads, NSW 35 F6, 53 C6
Nana Glen, NSW 35 F5, 53 C2
Nanambinia, WA 185 A4
Nanami, NSW 39 G5
Nanango, QLD 121 G2, 135 D1
Nanarup, WA 193 D4
Nandaly, VIC 75 E6, 77 E1
Nandi, QLD 121 F2, 135 A3
Nanga, WA 187 D1
Nanga Bay, WA 182 A5
Nangerybone, NSW 38 D3
Nangiloc, VIC 75 E4
Nangkita, SA 158 E1
Nangus, NSW 44 C2
Nangwarry, SA 155 G5, 163 D5
Nankin, QLD 129 B4
Nanneella, VIC 78 B4
Nannup, WA 176 C4
Nantawarra, SA 152 D6
Nantawarrina, SA 153 F2
Nanutarra, WA 182 B2
Nanutarra Roadhouse, WA 182 B2
Nanya, QLD 116 C4
Nap Nap, NSW 43 E1
Napier, WA 193 C3
Napier Downs, WA 181 A4
Napoleon, QLD 119 G2
Napoleons, VIC 83 H2
Nappa Merrie, QLD 118 D3
Napperby, NT 209 G6, 213 G1
Napperby, SA 152 D5
Napranum, QLD 113 A3
Napunyah, NSW 31 H6
Naracoopa, TAS 230 B2
Naracoorte, SA 155 G4, 163 D3
Naradhan, NSW 38 D5
Naragamba, QLD 106 D3
Narara, NSW 51 B4
Narbethong, VIC 84 D2
Nardoo, NSW 31 H4
Nardoo, QLD 110 B5, 120 A3
Nareen, VIC 82 B1
Narembeen, WA 175 F6, 177 F2
Naremburn, NSW 27 F5, 29 F1
Nariel, QLD 120 D3
Nariel, VIC 80 B2, 99 E2
Nariel Creek, VIC 80 B2, 99 E2
Naringal, VIC 83 E4, 88 B4
Narndee, WA 175 F1
Narooma, NSW 45 F4
Narrabeen, NSW 27 H4, 51 B6
Narrabeen Peninsula, NSW 27 H4
Narrabri, NSW 34 A5
Narrabundah, ACT 20 C4
Narrandera, NSW 44 A1
Narraport, VIC 77 F3
Narrapumelap, VIC 97 D6
Narrawa, TAS 233 F2
Narrawallee, NSW 55 B6
Narraway, NSW 33 F6
Narraweena, NSW 27 G4

Narrawong, VIC 82 C4
Narre Warren, VIC 71 H6
Narre Warren East, VIC 71 H5, 93 B6
Narre Warren North, VIC 71 H6, 93 A6
Narre Warren South, VIC 73H1
Narrewillock, VIC 77 G3
Narriah, NSW 38 D6
Narridy, SA 153 E5
Narrikup, WA 177 E6, 193 B3
Narrina, SA 153 E2
Narrogin, WA 176 D3
Narromine, NSW 39 G3
Narwee, NSW 28 D3
Narwietooma, NT 213 G2, 223 C1
Narwonah, NSW 39 F3
Naryilco, QLD 119 E4
Nashdale, NSW 39 H5
Nashua, NSW 46 C3
Nathalia, VIC 78 C3
Nathan, QLD 108 D4
Nathan River, NT 206 D2
Natimuk, VIC 76 C5
National Park, TAS 236 B2
Native Corners, TAS 237 E2
Natone, TAS 233 F1
Nattai, NSW 55 B1
Natte Yallock, VIC 77 G, 95 B2
Natya, VIC 75 G5
Naval Base, WA 172 B3
Navarre, VIC 77 F5, 95 A2
Nea, NSW 40 B1
Nebo, QLD 116 D2
Nectar Brook, SA 152 D4
Nedlands, WA 170 C3
Neds Creek, WA 183 E4
Needles, TAS 233 H3, 234 A3
Neerdie, QLD 125 B6
Neerim, VIC 85 E3
Neerim Junct., VIC 85 E3
Neerim South, VIC 85 E3
Neeworra, NSW 33 H3
Neika, TAS 228 A5, 236 D3
Neilrex, NSW 40 A2, 39 H2
Nelia, QLD 115 E1
Nelia Gaan, NSW 37 F3
Nelia Outstation, NSW 37 F4
Nelligen, NSW 45 F3
Nelson, NSW 26 B3
Nelson, VIC 82 A3
Nelson Bay, NSW 41 E4, 63 B4
Nelson Springs, NT 204 B5
Nelungaloo, NSW 39 F4
Nembudding, WA 175 E5
Nemingha, NSW 40 C1
Nene Valley, SA 163 C6
Nepabunna, SA 153 F1
Nerang, QLD 121 H3, 127 B4, 133 D2
Nerangwood, QLD 127 B5
Nereena, QLD 115 G4
Nerren Nerren, WA 182 B5
Nerrena, VIC 85 E4
Nerriga, NSW 45 F2
Nerrigundah, NSW 45 F4
Nerrima, WA 181 A5

Pingelly, WA 176 D2
Pingine, QLD 119 H1
Pingrup, WA 177 F4
Pinjarra, WA 176 C3, 191 E4
Pinjarra Hills, QLD 108 A4
Pinjin, WA 178 D3
Pinkenba, QLD 109 E1
Pinkilla, QLD 119 F1
Pinnacle, QLD 137 A6
Pinnacles, WA 183 F6
Pinnaroo, SA 155 H2
Pintharuka, WA 174 C2
Pioneer, QLD 112 C6
Pioneer, TAS 235 F1
Pioneer, WA 178 B6, 179 B2
Piora, NSW 35 F3
Pipalyatjara, SA 146 A1
Pipers Brook, TAS 234 C1
Pipers River, TAS 234 C1
Piries, NSW 79 E6
Pirita, VIC 74 C4
Pirron Yallock, VIC 83 G4, 88 D4
Pitfield, VIC 83 G2, 89 E1
Pithara, WA 174 D4
Pitt Town, NSW 26 A2
Pitt Town Bottoms, NSW 26 A2
Pittong, VIC 83 G2
Pittsworth, QLD 121 F3, 135 C4
Planet Downs, QLD 110 B5, 116 D5, 119 E2
Planet Downs O.S., QLD 118 D1
Platina, NSW 39 E4
Playstowe, QLD 137 C6
Pleasant Hills, NSW 44 A2
Pleasure Point, NSW 28 C3
Plenty, TAS 236 C2
Plenty, VIC 71 E1
Plumbago, SA 153 G3
Plumpton, NSW 26 A4
Plushs Corner, SA 157 D2
Plympton, SA 144 B2
Plympton Park, SA 144 B2
Pmara Jutunta, NT 209 H6, 210 A6, 213 H1, 214 A1
Poatina, TAS 234 C4
Point Cook, VIC 70 A5, 84 B3
Point Frederick, NSW 51 B4
Point Grey, WA 191 B4
Point Piper, NSW 27 G6, 29 G1
Point Samson, WA 182 C1
Point Talburpin, QLD 109 H6
Pokolbin, NSW 57 B4
Poldinna, SA 152 A4
Polelle, WA 183 E5
Police Point, TAS 236 D5
Policemans Point, SA 155 F3
Pollygammon, QLD 114 C3
Polocara, NSW 31 H6
Pomborneit, VIC 83 G4, 88 D3
Pomborneit North, VIC 88 D4
Pomborneit Nth, VIC 83 G4
Pomona, QLD 121 H1, 131 B3
Pomonal, VIC 77 E6, 83 E1, 97 C3

Pondana, WA 185 B3
Pontville, TAS 236 D2
Pontypool, TAS 237 G1
Pony Hills, QLD 120 D1
Poochera, SA 151 H4
Poolaigelo, VIC 76 A6, 82 A1
Poole, TAS 231 C6
Poona, QLD 125 B5
Pooncarie, NSW 37 F5
Poonindie, SA 154 B1
Pooraka, SA 142 C5
Pootilla, VIC 83 H2, 95 D4
Pootnoura, SA 147 G4
Poowong, VIC 84 D4
Popanyinning, WA 176 D3
Popiltah, NSW 36 D5
Poplar Grove, NSW 39 E2
Porepunkah, VIC 79 G5, 99 B3
Pormpuraaw, QLD 110 D1, 113 A6
Porongurup, WA 177 E5
Porongurup, WA 193 C2
Port Adelaide, SA 142 B5
Port Albert, VIC 85 G5
Port Alma, QLD 117 F4, 129 C5
Port Augusta, SA 152 D4
Port Bonython, SA 152 D5
Port Botany, NSW 29 G3
Port Broughton, SA 152 D5
Port Campbell, VIC 83 F5, 88 C5
Port Clinton, SA 152 D6, 154 D1
Port Davis, SA 152 D5
Port Denison, WA 174 A2
Port Douglas, QLD 112 A3, 123 B1
Port Elliot, SA 155 E2, 158 E3
Port Fairy, VIC 82 D4
Port Franklin, VIC 85 F5
Port Gawler, SA 142 A2
Port Germein, SA 152 D5
Port Gibbon, SA 152 C6
Port Hacking, NSW 29 E5
Port Hedland, WA 180 A6, 182 D1
Port Huon, TAS 236 C4
Port Julia, SA 154 D1
Port Kembla, NSW 45 H1, 55 C2
Port Kennedy, WA 172 B6
Port Kenny, SA 151 H5
Port Latta, TAS 230 C6
Port Lincoln, SA 154 B1
Port MacDonnell, SA 155 G6, 163 D6
Port Macquarie, NSW 41 F2
Port Melbourne, VIC 70 C4
Port Neill, SA 152 B6
Port Newry, QLD 137 B5
Port Noarlunga, SA 144 A5
Port Noarlunga South, SA 144 A6
Port Pirie, SA 152 D5
Port Rickaby, SA 154 C1
Port Roper, NT 206 D1
Port Sorell, TAS 233 H2, 234 A2

Port Victoria, SA 154 C1
Port Vincent, SA 154 D1
Port Wakefield, SA 152 D6, 154 D1
Port Welshpool, VIC 85 F5
Portarlington, VIC 84 B3
Porters Retreat, NSW 40 A6
Portland, NSW 40 B5
Portland, VIC 82 C4
Portland Downs, QLD 115 H5
Portland Roads, QLD 113 C3
Portsea, VIC 84 B4
Possum Creek, NSW 46 C2
Postans, WA 172 C3
Potato Point, NSW 45 F4
Potts Hill, NSW 28 D2
Potts Point, NSW 27 G6, 29 G1
Pottsville, NSW 133 E4
Pottsville Beach, NSW 35 G2
Poverty Gully, TAS 236 D4
Powell Creek, NT 205 H6, 206 A6
Powelltown, VIC 84 D2
Powers Creek, VIC 76 B6, 82 B1
Prague, NT 221 E1
Prahran, VIC 70 D4
Prairie, QLD 115 G1, 119 G2
Prairie, VIC 78 A4
Prairie Downs, WA 183 A3
Prairiewood, NSW 26 B6, 28 B1
Pratten, QLD 135 C6
Premaydena, TAS 237 F4, 245 B5
Premer, NSW 40 B1
Premier Downs, WA 185 B3
Prenti Downs, WA 183 G5
Preolenna, TAS 232 D1
Preston, TAS 233 F2
Preston, VIC 70 D2
Preston, WA 187 C6
Preston Beach, WA 176 B3, 187 A2
Prestons, NSW 28 A3
Pretty Beach, NSW 51 B5
Prevelly, WA 176 B5, 189 A4
Price, SA 152 D6, 154 D1
Priestdale, QLD 109 F5
Primrose Sands, TAS 237 F3, 245 B4
Princes Hill, VIC 70 C3
Princetown, VIC 83 F5, 88 C5
Princhester, QLD 117 E3, 129 A3
Prior Vale, QLD 129 B5
Priory, TAS 235 G2
Promised Land, TAS 233 G3
Prooinga, VIC 75 F5
Proserpine, QLD 116 D1, 137 A3
Prospect, NSW 26 B5, 28 B1
Prospect, QLD 111 E5
Prospect, SA 141 B1, 142 C6
Proston, QLD 121 F1
Providence Portal, NSW 65 C3
Prubi, QLD 115 F3
Prungle, NSW 37 F6
Pt Lonsdale, VIC 84 B4

Pt Lookout, QLD 121 H3
Pucawan, NSW 39 E6, 4 4B1
Puckapunyal, VIC 78 C6
Puggoon, NSW 40 A3, 39 H3
Pukatja (Ernabella), SA 147 E1
Pularumpi, NT 200 C2
Pulgamurtie, NSW 31 E5
Pull Pulla, NSW 38 B1
Pullabooka, NSW 39 F5
Pullagaroo, WA 175 E2
Pullenvale, QLD 108 A3
Pullut, VIC 76 C3
Punchbowl, NSW 28 D2
Pungalina, NT 207 F4
Punjaub, QLD 110 B5
Punmu, WA 183 G2
Puntabie, SA 151 G3
Pura Pura, VIC 83 F2, 88 C1
Puralka, VIC 82 A3
Purbrook, QLD 116 D5
Purfleet, NSW 41 E2
Purlewaugh, NSW 40 A1
Purnamoota, NSW 36 D2
Purnango, NSW 31 G6
Purnawilla, NSW 37 G1
Purnim, VIC 83 E4, 88 A3
Purnong, SA 155 F1
Purple Downs, SA 152 C2
Purrawunda, QLD 135 C4
Purrumbete, VIC 88 D4
Putney, NSW 27 E6, 29 E1
Puttapa, SA 153 E1
Pyalong, VIC 78 B6, 90 E1
Pyap, SA 165 C4
Pyengana, TAS 235 F2
Pygery, SA 152 A5
Pymble, NSW 27 E4
Pymurra, QLD 114 C1
Pyramid, WA 182 C1
Pyramid Hill, VIC 77 H3, 78 A3
Pyree, NSW 61 B2
Pyrmont, NSW 25 A3, 27 F6, 29 F1

Quaama, NSW 45 F4
Quairading, WA 175 E6, 177 E2
Quakers Hill, NSW 26 B4
Quambatook, VIC 77 G2
Quambetook, QLD 115 E2
Quambone, NSW 33 F6
Quamby, QLD 114 C1
Quamby Brook, TAS 234 B3
Quandary, NSW 39 E6, 44 B1
Quandialla, NSW 39 F6
Quandong Vale, SA 153 G5
Quantong, VIC 76 C5
Quarrells, QLD 115 E1
Quarry Hill, NSW 37 E3
Quartz Hill, NT 214 C2
Queanbeyan, NSW 20 D4, 21 D2, 45 E2
Queens Park, NSW 29 G2
Queenscliff, NSW 27 H5
Queenscliff, VIC 84 B4
Queenstown, SA 142 B6
Queenstown, TAS 232 D5
Queenwood, WA 187 C6
Questa Park, NSW 31 F5
Quilberry, QLD 120 A2
Quilpie, QLD 119 G1

Rose Park, SA 144 D1
Rosebank, NSW 46 B2
Roseberth, QLD 118 B1
Rosebery, NSW 29 F2
Rosebery, NT 199 G6
Rosebery, TAS 232 D4
Rosebery, VIC 76 D2
Rosebery East, VIC 77 E2
Rosebrook, VIC 82 D4
Rosebud, VIC 72 C6, 84 B4
Rosebud West, VIC 72 B6
Rosedale, NSW 65 D3
Rosedale, QLD 117 G5
Rosedale, VIC 85 G3
Rosegarland, TAS 236 C2
Rosehill, NSW 26 D6, 28 D1
Roselands, NSW 29 E3
Rosella Plains, QLD 111 H5
Rosemount, QLD 115 H4
Roses Tear, TAS 235 E3
Rosetta, TAS 228 A1
Rosevale, QLD 115 E2,
133 B2
Rosevale, TAS 234 B3
Rosevears, TAS 234 C2
Roseville, NSW 27 F5
Roseville Chase, NSW 27 F5
Rosewater, SA 142 B5
Rosewhite, VIC 79 G4, 99 B2
Rosewood, NSW 44 C3
Rosewood, NT 204 B4
Rosewood, QLD 121 G3,
133 B1
Roslyn, NSW 45 F1
Roslynmead, VIC 78 A3
Rosny, TAS 228 D3
Ross, TAS 234 D5
Ross Ck, VIC 83 H2
Rossarden, TAS 235 E4
Rossbridge, VIC 83 E2
Rosscommon, NSW 33 E4
Rosslyn, QLD 117 F6
Rosslyn Park, SA 144 D1
Rossmount, QLD 125 B6,
131 B2
Rossmoya, QLD 129 B3
Rossmoyne, WA 170 D4
Rossville, QLD 111 H2
Rostrevor, SA 143 E6
Rostron, VIC 95 A1
Rothbury, NSW 57 C3
Rothwell, QLD 107 F3
Roto, NSW 38 B4
Round Corner, NSW 26 C3
Rouse Hill, NSW 26 B3
Rowella, TAS 234 B2
Rowena, NSW 33 H4
Rowland Flat, SA 157 B5
Rowsley, VIC 84 A2, 89 H1
Rowville, VIC 71 G5
Roxborough Downs, QLD
114 B3
Roxburgh, NSW 40 C3,
59 D2
Roxby Downs, SA 152 C1
Roy Hill, WA 183 E2
Royal George, TAS 235 F4
Royal Park, SA 142 B6
Royalla, ACT 20 B6, 21 C3
Royles, QLD 116 D4
Royston Park, SA 142 D6
Rozelle, NSW 27 F6, 29 F1
Rubicon, VIC 79 E6, 85 E1

Ruby Plains, WA 181 C5
Rubyvale, QLD 116 C4
Rudall, SA 152 B5
Ruffy, VIC 78 D6
Rufus River, NSW 36 D6
Rugby, NSW 45 E1, 39 H6
Rules Point, NSW 65 C2
Rum Jungle, NT 200 D4
Runaway Bay, QLD 127 C3
Runcorn, QLD 108 D5
Running Creek, VIC 79 G4,
99 C2
Running Stream, NSW
40 A4
Runnymede, QLD 115 E1,
120 B3
Runnymede, TAS 237 E2,
245 A2
Runnymede, VIC 78 B4
Rupanyup, VIC 77 E5
Rupanyup North, VIC 77 E4
Rupanyup South, VIC 77 E5
Ruse, NSW 28 A5
Rush Creek, QLD 106 B3
Rushcutters Bay, NSW
27 G6, 29 G2
Rushworth, VIC 78 C4
Rushy Lagoon, TAS 231 B6
Russell, ACT 19 D4, 20 C3
Russell Lea, NSW 27 E6, 29 E1
Russell River, QLD 123 D6
Russells, NSW 37 H1, 38 A1
Rutchillo, QLD 114 D1
Rutherglen, VIC 79 F3
Ruthven, QLD 115 G5
Rydalmere, NSW 26 D5
Ryde, NSW 27 E5, 29 E1
Rye, VIC 72 A6, 84 B4
Rye Park, NSW 45 E1
Rylstone, NSW 40 B4
Ryton, VIC 85 F4
Rywung, QLD 121 E2

Saddleworth, SA 153 E6
Sadleir, NSW 28 B2
Safety Bay, WA 172 A5
Safety Beach, NSW 53 D2
Safety Beach, VIC 72 D5
St Agnes, SA 143 E5
St Albans, NSW 40 C5
St Albans, VIC 70 A2
St Albans East, VIC 70 A2
St Andrews, NSW 28 A4
St Andrews, VIC 84 C2
St Arnaud, VIC 77 F5
St Arnaud East, VIC 77 G5
St Clair, NSW 40 D3
St Evins, VIC 76 C6
St Fillans, VIC 84 D2
St George, QLD 120 C3
St Georges, SA 144 D2
St Georges Basin, NSW 61 A4
St Germains, VIC 78 C3
St Helena, VIC 71 E1
St Helens, TAS 235 G2
St Helens Park, NSW 28 A6
St Helens Plains, VIC 76 D5
St Ives, NSW 27 F4
St Ives Chase, NSW 27 F4
St James, VIC 79 E4
St James, WA 170 D4
St Johns Park, NSW 28 B2
St Kilda, SA 142 B3

St Kilda, VIC 70 C4, 84 C2
St Kilda East, VIC 70 D4
St Kilda West, VIC 70 C4
St Lawrence, QLD 117 E3
St Leonards, NSW 27 F6,
29 F1
St Leonards, TAS 234 C3
St Leonards, VIC 84 B3
St Lucia, QLD 108 C3
St Marys, SA 144 C2
St Marys, TAS 235 G3
St Morris, SA 144 D1
St Patricks River, TAS 234 D2
St Pauls, QLD 113 A1
St Peters, NSW 29 F2
St Peters, SA 141 D2, 142 C6,
144 C1
Sale, VIC 85 G3, 86 A4
Salisbury, NSW 40 D3
Salisbury, QLD 108 C4
Salisbury, SA 142 D4
Salisbury, VIC 76 C4
Salisbury Downs, NSW
31 F5
Salisbury Downs, SA 142 C4
Salisbury East, SA 142 D4
Salisbury Heights, SA
142 D4
Salisbury North, SA 142 C3
Salisbury Park, SA 142 D4
Salisbury Plain, SA 142 D4
Salisbury South, SA 142 D4
Salisbury West, VIC 77 H4
Salmon Gums, WA 179 B3
Salt Ash, NSW 63 A4
Salt Creek, SA 155 F3
Salter Point, WA 170 D4
Saltern, QLD 115 H4
Saltwater River, TAS 237 F4,
245 B5
Samaria, VIC 79 E5
Samford, QLD 121 H2
Samford Valley, QLD 106 B6
Samford Village, QLD 106 C6
Sampson Flat, SA 143 F4
Samson, WA 170 C5, 172 C1
Samsonvale, QLD 106 B4
San Marino, SA 147 H3
San Remo, VIC 84 C4
San Remo, WA 191 C1
Sanctuary Lakes, VIC 70 A4
Sanctuary Point, NSW
55 B5, 61 B4
Sandalwood, SA 155 G2
Sandbar, NSW 63 E1
Sandfire Roadhouse, WA
180 C6
Sandfly, TAS 236 D4
Sandford, TAS 229 H5,
237 E3, 245 A4
Sandford, VIC 82 B2
Sandgate, QLD 107 F5
Sandhill Lake, VIC 77 G2
Sandigo, NSW 44 A2
Sandilands, SA 154 D1
Sandon, NSW 35 G4
Sandon, VIC 77 H6, 83 H1,
95 D3
Sandown Park, VIC 71 F5
Sandringham, NSW 29 E4
Sandringham, QLD 114 B5
Sandringham, VIC 70 D5,
84 C3

Sandsmere, VIC 76 B4
Sandstone, WA 183 E6
Sandstone Point, QLD
107 G1, 131 C6
Sandy Bay, TAS 227 D5,
228 C3
Sandy Beach, NSW 53 D2
Sandy Camp, NSW 33 F6
Sandy Ck, VIC 79 H4
Sandy Creek, SA 143 G1
Sandy Flat, NSW 35 E4
Sandy Hollow, NSW 40 B3,
59 B2
Sandy Point, NSW 28 C3
Sandy Point, VIC 85 E5
Sangar, NSW 43 H3, 44 A3
Sanpah, NSW 30 C6
Sans Souci, NSW 29 E4
Santa Teresa, NT 214 B3
Santos, QLD 118 D3
Sapphire, QLD 116 C4
Sapphire Beach, NSW 35 G5
Saraji Mine, QLD 116 C3
Sarina, QLD 116 D2
Sarina Beach, QLD 116 D2
Sarsfield, VIC 80 B6, 86 C2
Sassafras, NSW 55 A5
Sassafras, TAS 233 H2,
234 A2
Sassafras, VIC 71 H4, 93 C3
Sassafras Flat, VIC 99 E2
Sassafras Gap, VIC 80 B2
Sassafrass, NSW 45 G2
Saunders Beach, QLD
112 B5
Savage River, TAS 232 C3
Savannah Downs, QLD
111 E5
Savernake, NSW 43 H3
Sawpit Creek, NSW 65 C5
Sawtell, NSW 35 G6, 53 C4
Sawyers Valley, WA 171 H2
Saxby Downs, QLD 111 E6
Sayers Lake, NSW 37 G4
Scaddan, WA 179 B4
Scamander, TAS 235 G3
Scarborough, QLD 107 G3
Scarborough, WA 170 B2
Scarsdale, VIC 83 G2
Scartwater, QLD 116 B2
Sceale Bay, SA 151 G5
Scheyville, NSW 26 A2
Schofields, NSW 26 A3
Scone, NSW 40 C3
Scoresby, VIC 71 G4
Scotchtown, TAS 230 B6
Scotland Island, NSW 27 H2
Scotsburn, VIC 83 H2
Scott Creek, NT 205 F1
Scott Creek, SA 145 E3
Scotts Ck, VIC 83 F4
Scotts Creek, VIC 88 C4
Scotts Head, NSW 35 F6,
53 C6
Scottsdale, TAS 235 E2
Scullin, ACT 20 A2
Sea Elephant, TAS 230 B2
Sea Lake, VIC 77 E2
Seabird, WA 174 B5, 176 B1
Seabrook, TAS 233 E1
Seabrook, VIC 70 A4
Seacliff, SA 144 B3
Seacliff Park, SA 144 B3

Spring Ridge, NSW 40 B1
Springbrook, QLD 133 D3
Springdale, NSW 44 C1
Springfield, QLD 108 A6,
111 G4, 120 C2
Springfield, SA 144 D2
Springfield, TAS 234 D2
Springfield, VIC 90 E2
Springhill Bottom, TAS
237 E2
Springhurst, VIC 79 F3,
99 A1
Springsure, QLD 116 C5
Springton, SA 155 E1
Springvale, NT 220 C4
Springvale, QLD 111 H2,
113 D6, 114 D4, 116 A4,
116 B3
Springvale, VIC 71 F5
Springvale, WA 181 C4
Springvale South, VIC
71 F6
Springwood, NSW 40 B5,
49 H4
Springwood, QLD 109 E5,
116 C5
Squeaking Point, TAS
233 H2, 234 A2
Squirrel Hills, QLD 114 D2
Stafford, QLD 108 C1
Stafford Heights, QLD
108 C1
Staghorn Flat, VIC 79 G4,
99 C1
Stake Hill, WA 191 D1
Stamford, QLD 115 G2
Stanage, QLD 117 E3, 129 A1
Stanbroke, QLD 114 B2
Stanhope, VIC 78 C4
Stanhope Gardens, NSW
26 B4
Stanifords, NSW 38 C3
Stanley, TAS 230 C6
Stanley, VIC 79 G4, 99 B2
Stanmore, NSW 29 F2
Stanmore, QLD 131 B5
Stannifer, NSW 34 D5
Stannum, NSW 35 E4
Stansbury, SA 154 D1
Stanthorpe, QLD 121 G4
Stanwell, QLD 117 E4, 129
A4
Stanwell Park, NSW 40 C6,
55 D1
Stapylton, QLD 127 A1
Starke, QLD 111 H1
Staughton Vale, VIC 84 A2,
89 H1
Staverton, TAS 233 G3
Stavley, VIC 97 D6
Stawell, VIC 77 E6, 97 D2
Steiglitz, QLD 127 B1
Steiglitz, VIC 84 A3, 89 G1
Stenhouse Bay, SA 154 C2
Stephens Creek, NSW 36 D2
Stepney, SA 144 D1
Steppes, TAS 234 B6
Stewart, WA 178 A4
Stieglitz, TAS 235 G2
Stirling, ACT 20 A4
Stirling, NT 209 H5, 210 A5
Stirling, QLD 111 E3,
115 H4, 116 A4, 120 C1

Stirling, SA 145 E2
Stirling, WA 170 C2
Stirling North, SA 152 D4
Stirrat, QLD 129 C6
Stockdale, VIC 86 A2
Stockinbingal, NSW 44 C1
Stockmans Reward, VIC
85 E2
Stockwell, SA 157 D2
Stokes Bay, SA 154 C2,
161 C2
Stonehenge, QLD 115 F5
Stonehenge, TAS 237 F1
Stoneville, WA 171 H1
Stoneyford, VIC 83 G4,
88 D3
Stonor, TAS 237 E1
Stony Crossing, NSW 43 E2
Stony Point, VIC 73 G6
Stonyfell, SA 144 D1
Stormlea, TAS 237 F4,
245 B6
Storys Creek, TAS 235 E4
Stowport, TAS 233 F1
Stradbroke, VIC 85 G4
Strahan, TAS 232 D6
Strangways Bore (Ruins), SA
148 C5
Stratford, NSW 41 E3
Stratford, VIC 85 G3, 86 A3
Strath Creek, VIC 78 C6,
84 C1
Strathalbyn, SA 155 E2
Stratham, WA 176 B4,
187 A6
Strathaven, QLD 111 F1,
113 B6
Strathblane, TAS 236 C5
Strathbogie, NSW 34 D4
Strathbogie, VIC 78 D5
Strathburn, QLD 111 F1,
113 B5
Strathdickie, QLD 137 A2
Strathdownie, VIC 82 A2
Strathearn, SA 153 G3
Strathelbiss, QLD 114 C3
Strathfield, NSW 26 D6,
29 E2
Strathfield, QLD 114 D2
Strathfield South, NSW
28 D2
Strathfieldsaye, VIC 78 A5,
95 E1
Strathgordon, QLD 111 E1,
113 B5
Strathgordon, TAS 238 D3
Strathkellar, VIC 82 D2
Strathleven, QLD 111 F2
Strathmay, QLD 111 F1,
113 B6
Strathmerton, VIC 78 D3
Strathmore, QLD 111 E4,
116 C4
Strathmore, VIC 70 C2
Strathmore Hts, VIC 70 B2
Strathpark, QLD 111 F6
Strathpine, QLD 106 D5,
121 H2
Stratton, VIC 77 E1
Stratton, WA 171 F1
Straun, SA 163 D3
Streaky Bay, SA 151 H4
Streatham, VIC 83 F2

Strelley, WA 180 A6, 183 E1
Strenton Elbow, WA 187 C5
Stretton, QLD 108 D5
Strickland, TAS 236 B1
Stromlo, ACT 20 A3
Stroud, NSW 41 E3, 63 A1
Stroud Road, NSW 41 E3
Struan, SA 155 G5
Strzelecki, VIC 85 E4
Stuart Creek, SA 148 C6
Stuart Mill, VIC 77 F5, 95 B1
Stuart Park, NT 197 C4,
198 B4
Stuart Town, NSW 39 H4
Stuarts Point, NSW 35 F6
Stuarts Well Roadhouse, NT
213 H3, 214 A, 223 D2
Sturt, SA 144 B3
Sturt Creek, WA 181 D5
Sturt Meadows, WA 178 B1,
183 F6
Sturt Vale, SA 153 G5
Subiaco, WA 170 C3
Success, WA 170 C6, 172 C2
Sudley, QLD 113 B3
Suffolk Park, NSW 35 G3,
46 E2
Sugarloaf, QLD 137 A2
Suggan Buggan, VIC 80 C3
Sujeewong, QLD 117 F6,
121 E1
Sullivan, WA 174 B1
Sulphur Creek, TAS 233 F1
Summer Hill, NSW 29 E2
Summerfield, VIC 78 A4
Summerlands, VIC 91 A3
Summertown, SA 145 E2
Summervale, QLD 115 H6,
116 A6
Sumner, QLD 108 B4
Sunbury, VIC 84 B2, 90 E4
Sunday Creek, NT 205 G3
Sunderland Bay, VIC 91 D3
Sunnybank, QLD 108 D4
Sunnybank Hills, QLD 108 D5
Sunnyside, TAS 233 H2,
234 A2
Sunnyside, VIC 79 H5,
80 A3, 99 D3
Sunset Strip, NSW 37 E3
Sunshine, VIC 70 B3, 84 B2
Sunshine Beach, QLD
131 C3
Sunshine North, VIC 70 B2
Sunshine West, VIC 70 A3
Supplejack, NT 208 C2
Surat, QLD 120 D2
Surfers Paradise, QLD
121 H3, 127 C4, 133 E2
Surges Bay, TAS 236 C5
Surrey Downs, SA 143 E4
Surrey Hills, VIC 71 E3
Surry Hills, NSW 25 C6,
29 F2
Surveyors Bay, TAS 236 D5
Surveyors Lake, NSW 37 G3
Sussex, NSW 38 D1
Sussex Inlet, NSW 45 G2,
55 B5, 61A 5
Sutherland, NSW 28 D4,
40 C6, 55 D1
Sutherland, VIC 77 F4
Sutherlands, SA 153 F6

Sutton, NSW 20 D1, 21 D1,
45 E2
Sutton, VIC 77 F2
Sutton Forest, NSW 45 G1,
55 A3
Sutton Grange, VIC 78 A6,
95 E2
Swan Bay, NSW 63 A3
Swan Haven, NSW 61 A5
Swan Hill, VIC 75 G6, 77 G1
Swan Marsh, VIC 83 G4,
88 D4
Swan Reach, VIC 80 B6,
86 D2, 155 F1
Swan View, WA 171 F2
Swanbourne, WA 170 B3
Swanpool, VIC 79 E5
Swansea, NSW 40 D4, 51 D1
Swansea, TAS 235 F6
Swanwater, VIC 77 F4
Swifts Creek, VIC 80 B4
Swim Creek, NT 201 E3
Sydenham, NSW 29 F2
Sydenham, VIC 70 A1, 84 B2
Sydney, NSW 25 C3, 27 G6,
29 G1, 40 C6
Sylvania, NSW 29 E4
Sylvania, WA 183 E3
Sylvania Heights, NSW 29 E4
Sylvania Waters, NSW 29 E4
Symonston, ACT 20 C4

Taabinga, QLD 135 C1
Tabacum, QLD 123A4
Tabba Tabba, WA 180 A6,
182 D1
Tabberabbera, VIC 80 A5,
85 H2, 86 B1
Tabbita, NSW 38 C6
Tableland, WA 181 C4
Tabletop, QLD 111 E4
Tabratong, NSW 39 E3
Tabulum, NSW 35 F3
Taggerty, VIC 78 D6, 84 D1
Tahara, VIC 82 C2
Taigum, QLD 107 F6
Tailem Bend, SA 155 F2
Takalarup, WA 193 D2
Takenup, WA 193 D3
Takone, TAS 233 E2
Takone West, TAS 232 D2
Takura, QLD 117 H6, 125 B3
Talarm, NSW 53 B6
Talawa, TAS 235 E2
Talawanta, QLD 110 C5
Talbingo, NSW 44 D3, 65 B1
Talbot, VIC 77 G6, 83 G1,
95 C3
Taldora, QLD 110 D6
Taldra, SA 155 G1, 165 E3
Taleeban, NSW 38 D6
Talgarno, VIC 79 H3, 80 A1
Talia, SA 151 H5
Talisker, WA 182 B5
Tallai, QLD 127 B5
Tallalara, NSW 31 H6, 37 E1
Tallanalla, WA 187 D3
Tallandoon, VIC 79 H4,
80 A2, 99 C2
Tallangatta, VIC 79 H3,
80 A1, 99 C1
Tallangatta Valley, VIC
79 H4, 80 A1

Thornton, QLD 133 A2
Thornton, VIC 78 D6, 85 E1
Thorntonia, QLD 110 B6
Thorpdale, VIC 85 E4
Thowgla, VIC 80 B1
Thowgla Upper, VIC 80 B2
Thredbo, NSW 44 D4, 65 B6
Three Rivers, WA 183 A4
Three Springs, WA 174 B2
Three Ways Roadhouse,
  NT 210 B2
Throsby, ACT 20 C1
Thrungli, QLD 116 A5
Thuddungra, NSW 39 F6
Thulloo, NSW 38 D5
Thundelarra, WA 174 D1
Thurlga, SA 152 A4
Thurloo Downs, NSW 31 G4
Thurrulgoona, QLD 120 A4
Thursday Island, QLD
  113 A1
Thylungra, QLD 119 F1
Thyra, NSW 43 F3
Ti Tree Roadhouse, NT
  209 H6, 210 A6
Tiaro, QLD 117 H6, 121 G1,
  125 A5
Tiarra, NSW 38 B4
Tibarri, QLD 114 D1
Tiberias, TAS 237 E1
Tibooburra, NSW 30 D4
Tichborne, NSW 39 F4
Tickera, SA 152 D6
Ticklara, QLD 119 E4
Tidal River, VIC 85 F6,
  101 B5
Tielta, NSW 30 C6, 36 C1
Tieri, QLD 116 C4
Tieyon, SA 147 G1
Tilba Tilba, NSW 45 F4
Tilcha, SA 149 H6
Tilmouth Roadhouse, NT
  213 G1
Tilpa, NSW 31 H6, 32 A6,
  37 E1, 38 A1
Tilpal, QLD 129 A2
Tiltagara, NSW 38 A2
Tiltagoonah, NSW 38 A1
Timbarra, VIC 80 C4
Timber Creek (Police Stn),
  NT 204 D3
Timberfield, WA 175 H4
Timberoo South, VIC 74 D6,
  76 D1
Timbertop, VIC 79 F6
Timboon, VIC 83 F4, 88 C4
Timmering, VIC 78 B4
Timmsvale, NSW 53 B2
Timor, NSW 40 C2
Timor, VIC 77 G6, 95 C2
Timora, QLD 110 D4
Tin Can Bay, QLD 121 H1,
  125 C5, 131 C1
Tinaburra, QLD 123 B5
Tinamba, VIC 85 G3
Tinana, QLD 125 A4
Tinaroo, QLD 123 B4
Tincurrin, WA 177 E3
Tindarey, NSW 38 C1
Tinderbox, TAS 237 E4
Tinderry, QLD 119 G2
Tindo, QLD 115 G1
Tingalpa, QLD 109 E3

Tingha, NSW 34 D5
Tingoora, QLD 121 G1
Tinnanbar, QLD 125 C5
Tinnenburra, QLD 119 H4
Tintaldra, VIC 80 B1
Tintenbar, NSW 46 D3
Tintinara, SA 155 F3
Tipperary, NT 200 C5
Tiranna, QLD 119 H1
Tirlta, NSW 37 E1
Tirranna Roadhouse, QLD
  110 B4
Titjikala (Maryvale), NT
  214 B4, 223 E3
Tittybong, VIC 77 G2
Tiverton, SA 153 F4
Tiwi, NT 198 C1
Tjarramba, WA 180 D4
Tjirrkarli, WA 184 B4
Tjukayirla Roadhouse, WA
  183 H5, 184 A5
Tjukurla, WA 184 D3
Tobermory, NT 215 G1
Tobermory, QLD 119 F2
Tocal, QLD 115 F5
Tocumwal, NSW 43 G3
Todd River, NT 214 B3
Todmorden, SA 147 H2
Togari, TAS 230 A6, 232 B1
Tolga, QLD 112 A3, 123 B4
Tolmie, VIC 79 E5
Tom Price, WA 182 D2
Tomahawk, TAS 231 A6
Tomerong, NSW 45 G2,
  55 B5, 61 A4
Tomingley, NSW 39 G3
Tomingley West, NSW 39 F3
Tomoo, QLD 120 B2
Tongala, VIC 78 B4
Tonganah, TAS 235 E2
Tongio, VIC 80 B4
Tongio West, VIC 80 B4
Tongy, QLD 120 B2
Tonimbuk, VIC 84 D3
Tonkoro, QLD 115 E5
Toobanna, QLD 112 A5
Toobeah, QLD 121 E3
Tooborac, VIC 78 B6
Toodyay, WA 174 C5, 176 C1
Toogong, NSW 39 G5
Toogoolawah, QLD 121 G2
Toogoom, QLD 125 B3
Toolakea, QLD 112 B5
Toolamba, VIC 78 C4
Toolangi, VIC 84 D2
Toolara, QLD 125 C5, 131 C1
Toolara Forest, QLD 125 B6,
  131 B1
Toolebuc, QLD 114 D3
Toolern Vale, VIC 84 B2,
  90 D4
Tooleybuc, NSW 42 D2
Toolibin, WA 177 E3
Tooligie, SA 152 A6
Toolleen, VIC 78 B5
Toolondo, VIC 76 C6
Tooloom, NSW 35 F3
Tooloombilla, QLD 120 C1
Tooma, NSW 44C 3
Toombullup, VIC 79 F5,
  99 A4
Toompine Hotel, QLD
  119 G2

Toongabbie, NSW 26 C5
Toongabbie, VIC 85 F3
Tooperang, SA 158 E1
Toora, VIC 85 F5
Tooradin, VIC 84 C3
Toorak, VIC 70 D4
Toorak Gardens, SA 144 D1
Toorale, NSW 32 B5
Tooraweenah, NSW 39 H1
Toorbul, QLD 131 C6
Toormina, NSW 53 C3
Tooronga, VIC 85 E2
Tootgarook, VIC 72 B6
Toowong, QLD 108 B3
Toowoomba, QLD 121 G3,
  135 D4
Toowoon Bay, NSW 51 C4
Top Hut, NSW 37F 5
Top Springs Roadhouse, NT
  205 F4
Topar, NSW 37 E2
Topaz, QLD 123 C5
Torbanlea, QLD 117 H6,
  125 A3
Torbay, WA 177 E6, 193 B4
Torilla Plains, QLD 129 A2
Toronto, NSW 40 D4, 51 D1
Torquay, VIC 84 A4, 89 H3
Torrens, ACT 20 B4
Torrens Creek, QLD 115 H1
Torrens Park, SA 144 C2,
  158 C2
Torrensville, SA 144 B1
Torrington, NSW 34 D4
Torrita, VIC 74 D6, 76 C1
Torrumbarry, VIC 78 A3
Torwood, QLD 111 G4
Tostaree, VIC 86 E2
Tottenham, NSW 39 E3
Tottenham, VIC 70 B3
Tottington, VIC 77 F5, 95 A1
Toukley, NSW 40 D5, 51 C3
Tourello, VIC 95 C3
Towaninny, VIC 77 G2
Towaninny South, VIC
  77 G3
Towera, WA 182 B3
Town Hall, NSW 25 C4
Townson, QLD 121 G3,
  133 A2
Townsville, QLD 112 B6
Towong, VIC 80 C1
Trafalgar, VIC 85 E3
Tragowel, VIC 77 H2
Trajere, NSW 39 G5
Trangie, NSW 39 F2
Tranmere, SA 142 D6, 144 D1
Tranmere, TAS 229 E3
Traralgon, VIC 85 F3
Traralgon Sth, VIC 85 F4
Travancore, VIC 70 C3
Traveston, QLD 131 B3
Trawalla, VIC 83 G1, 95 B4
Trawool, VIC 78 C6
Trayning, WA 175 E5
Traynors Lagoon, VIC 77 F4
Trebonne, QLD 112 A5
Tregeagle, NSW 46 B4
Tregony, QLD 133 A2
Trelega, NSW 37 E5
Tremont, VIC 71 H4, 93 B4
Trentham, VIC 84 A1, 90 B3,
  95 E3

Tresco, VIC 77 G1
Trevallyn, NSW 37 H1
Trewalla, VIC 82B4
Trewilga, NSW 39G4
Triabunna, TAS 237 G1,
  245 C1
Trial Harbour, TAS 232 C5
Trida, NSW 38 B4
Trigg, WA 170 B2
Trillbar, WA 182 D4
Trinidad, QLD 115 G6
Trinity Beach, QLD 123 C2
Trinity Gardens, SA 144 D1
Trott Park, SA 144 B4
Trowutta, TAS 232 C1
Trundle, NSW 39 F4
Trunkey Creek, NSW 40 A5,
  39 H5
Truro, SA 155 E1
Tryphinia, QLD 117 E4
Tuan, QLD 117 H6, 121 H1,
  125 B4
Tuart Hill, WA 170 C2
Tubbut, VIC 80 D4
Tucabia, NSW 35 G4
Tuckanarra, WA 182 D5
Tudor, WA 193 A4
Tuena, NSW 40 A6, 39 H6
Tuerong, VIC 73 E5
Tuggerah, NSW 51 C3
Tuggeranong, ACT 20 A5,
  21 B3
Tugun, QLD 127 D6
Tulendeena, TAS 235 E2
Tullagrie, QLD 121 E2
Tullah, TAS 233 E4
Tullamarine, VIC 70 B2
Tullamore, NSW 39 F3
Tullera, NSW 46 A3
Tullibigeal, NSW 38 D5
Tully, QLD 112 A4
Tully Heads, QLD 112 A4
Tulmur, QLD 115 E3
Tumbar, QLD 116 A5
Tumbarumba, NSW 44 C3
Tumblong, NSW 44 C2
Tumby Bay, SA 152 B6,
  154 B1
Tummaville, QLD 135 B5
Tumorrama, NSW 44 D2
Tumoulin, QLD 123 B6
Tumut, NSW 44 C2
Tunart, VIC 74 B4
Tunbridge, TAS 234 D6
Tuncester, NSW 46 A3
Tuncurry, NSW 41 E3
Tundulya, NSW 32 B6
Tungamah, VIC 79 E3
Tungamull, QLD 129 B4
Tunnack, TAS 237 E1
Tunnel, TAS 234 C2
Tunney, WA 177 E5
Tuntable Creek, NSW 46 A2
Tuntable Falls, NSW 46 A1
Turallin, QLD 135 A5
Turee Creek, WA 182 D3
Turill, NSW 40 A3
Turlee, NSW 37 F6
Turlinjah, NSW 45 F3
Turner, ACT 19 B1, 20 B3
Turners Beach, TAS 233 G1
Turners Marsh, TAS 234 C2
Turnip Fields, TAS 228 B4

Walkley Heights, SA 142 D5
Walla Walla, NSW 44 B3
Wallabadah, NSW 40 C2
Wallace, VIC 83 H2, 95 D4
Wallace Rockhole, NT
    213 G3, 214 A3, 223 D2
Wallacia, NSW 40 B6
Wallal, QLD 120 A2
Wallal Downs, WA 180 B6
Wallaloo, VIC 77 F5
Wallan, VIC 84 C1
Wallan East, VIC 84 C1
Wallangarra, QLD 121 G4
Wallangra, NSW 34 C4
Wallareenya, WA 180 A6,
    182 D1
Wallaroo, QLD 117 E4
Wallaroo, SA 152 D6
Wallatinna, SA 147 F3
Wallerawang, NSW 40 B5,
    44 C1
Wallerberdina, SA 152 D3,
    159 A4
Wallerobba, NSW 40 D3
Walleroo, WA 178 A4
Walligan, QLD 125 B3
Wallinduc, VIC 83 G3, 89 E1
Walling Rock, WA 178 A2
Wallington, VIC 84 A3
Walliston, WA 171 G4
Walloway (Ruins), SA 153 E4
Wallumbilla, QLD 120 D1
Wallundry, NSW 39 F6,
    44 C1
Wallup, VIC 76 D4
Walmer, NSW 39 G3
Walpa, VIC 86 B2
Walpeup, VIC 74 D6, 76 C1
Walpole, TAS 236 C5
Walpole, WA 176 D6
Walsall, WA 189 C2
Walton, QLD 116 D4
Walwa, VIC 80 B1
Wamberal, NSW 51 C4
Wamberra, NSW 37 E6
Wamboin, NSW 21 D2
Wamboyne, NSW 39 E5
Wammadoo, QLD 115 F4
Wammutta, QLD 114 C2
Wamuran, QLD 106 B1,
    131 B6
Wanaaring, NSW 31 H4
Wanalta, VIC 78 B4
Wanbi, SA 155 G1
Wandagee, WA 182 B3
Wandana, SA 151 G3
Wandanian, NSW 55 B5,
    61 A4
Wandering, WA 176 D3
Wandi, WA 172 D3
Wandiligong, VIC 79 G5
Wandilo, SA 155 G5, 163 D5
Wandin North, VIC 93 D1
Wando Bridge, VIC 82 B2
Wandoan, QLD 121 E1
Wandong, VIC 84 C1
Wandovale, QLD 111 H6
Wandsworth, NSW 34 D5
Wandsworth, QLD 115 G6
Wanertown, SA 152 D5
Wangan, QLD 123 D6
Wanganella, NSW 43 F2
Wangangong, NSW 38 D4

Wangarabell, VIC 81 F5
Wangaratta, VIC 79 F4,
    99 A2
Wangary, SA 154 A1
Wangi, NT 200 D4, 221 A2
Wangi Wangi, NSW 51 D1
Wangkatjungka, WA 181 B5
Wanguri, NT 198 C1
Wanilla, SA 154 A1
Wanko, QLD 120 A1
Wanna, WA 182 C3
Wannanup, WA 191 A3
Wannarra, WA 174 D2
Wanneroo, WA 174 C6,
    176 C1
Wanniassa, ACT 20 B5
Wannon, VIC 82 C2
Wannoo Billabong
    Roadhouse, WA 182 B5
Wansey Downs, QLD
    116 A6, 120 A1
Wantirna, VIC 71 G4
Wantirna South, VIC 71 G4
Wapet Camp, WA 182 B1
Wappilka, SA 165 A4
Warakurna, WA 184 C4
Warakurna Roadhouse, WA
    184 C4
Waramanga, ACT 20 A4
Warana, QLD 131 C5
Waratah, NSW 33 E5
Waratah, QLD 129 A1
Waratah, TAS 232 D3
Waratah Bay, VIC 85 E5
Waratah Nth, VIC 85 E5
Warawaralong, NSW 49 G1
Warbreccan, QLD 115 F5
Warburn, NSW 38 C6
Warburton, VIC 84 D2
Warburton, WA 184 B4
Warcowie, SA 153 E3,
    159 C4
Wards River, NSW 41 E3
Wareek, VIC 77 G6
Wareemba, NSW 27 E6,
    29 E1
Wareo, QLD 119 G2
Wargambegal, NSW 38 D5
Warialda, NSW 34 C4
Warianna, QLD 115 G2
Warkton, NSW 40 A1, 39 H1
Warkworth, NSW 40 C3
Warmun (Turkey Creek), WA
    181 D4
Warnambool Downs, QLD
    115 F3
Warnbro, WA 172 B5
Warncoort, VIC 83 H4, 89 F3
Warne, VIC 77 F2
Warneet, VIC 73 H4
Warner, QLD 106 D5
Warner Glen, WA 189 B5
Warnervale, NSW 51 C3
Warooka, SA 154 C2
Waroona, WA 176 C3, 187 C1
Waroula, QLD 129 A4
Warra, QLD 114 C4, 121 F2
Warrachie, SA 152 A5
Warracknabeal, VIC 76 D4
Warradale, SA 144 B3
Warraderry, NSW 39 F5
Warragoon, NSW 43 H3
Warragul, VIC 85 E3

Warrak, VIC 77 F6, 83 F1,
    95 A3
Warrakimbo, SA 152 D3
Warral, NSW 40 C1
Warralakin, WA 175 F4
Warrambine, VIC 83 H3,
    89 F2
Warramboo, SA 152 A5
Warranangra, NSW 36 D6
Warrandyte, VIC 71 G2
Warrandyte South, VIC
    71 G2
Warrane, TAS 228 D2
Warranwood, VIC 71 G2
Warrawagine, WA 180 B6,
    183 F1
Warrawee, NSW 27 E4
Warraweena, SA 153 E2
Warreah, QLD 115 H1
Warrell Ck, NSW 35 F6
Warren, NSW 39 F2
Warren, QLD 129 A4
Warren, SA 143 H3
Warren Vale, QLD 110 D5
Warrenbayne, VIC 79 E5
Warriedar, WA 174 D2
Warriewood, NSW 27 H3
Warrigal, NSW 39 E2
Warrigal, QLD 115 H1
Warrina (Ruins), SA 148 B4
Warringa, TAS 233 F2
Warrion, VIC 83 G4, 89 E3
Warrnambool, VIC 83 E4,
    88 A4
Warrobil, NSW 40 A3
Warrong, QLD 116 C6
Warrong, VIC 82 D4
Warroo, NSW 39 F5
Warroora, WA 182 A3
Warrow, SA 152 A6, 154 A1
Warrumbungle, NSW 39 G1
Warruwi, NT 201 H2,
    202 A2
Wartaka, SA 152 C4
Wartook, VIC 76 D6, 97 B2
Warumbul, NSW 29 E5
Warwick, QLD 121 G3,
    135 D6
Warwick, WA 170 C1
Warwick Farm, NSW 28 B2
Watalgan, QLD 117 G5
Watchem, VIC 77 E3
Watchupga, VIC 77 E2
Waterbag, NSW 37 E2
Waterbank, WA 180 C4
Waterfall, NSW 28 C6, 55 D1
Waterfall Gully, SA 144 D2
Waterford, VIC 80 A5, 85 H2,
    86 A1
Waterford, WA 170 D4
Waterhouse, TAS 231 A6,
    235 E1
Waterloo, NSW 29 F2
Waterloo, NT 204 B4
Waterloo, SA 153 E6
Waterloo, TAS 236 C4
Waterloo, VIC 83 G1, 95 B3
Waterloo Corner, SA 142 B3
Waterman, WA 170 B1
Watersmeet, TAS 241 D6
Watervale, SA 153 E6
Watgania, VIC 97 C5
Wathana, QLD 112 C6

Watheroo, WA 174 C3
Wathumba Creek, QLD
    125 D2
Watson, ACT 20 C2
Watsonia, VIC 71 E1
Watsonia North, VIC 71 E1
Watsons Bay, NSW 27 H6,
    29 H1
Watsons Ck, NSW 34 C6
Wattamolla, NSW 29 E6
Watten, QLD 115 G1
Wattle Creek, VIC 77 F6
Wattle Flat, NSW 40 A4
Wattle Flat, SA 158 C2
Wattle Glen, VIC 71 F1
Wattle Grove, NSW 28 B3
Wattle Grove, TAS 236 C4
Wattle Grove, WA 171 F4
Wattle Hill, TAS 237 F3,
    245 B3
Wattle Hill, VIC 83 G5,
    88 D5
Wattle Park, SA 144 D1
Wattle Vale, NSW 31 F5
Wattleup, WA 172 C2
Waubra, VIC 83 G1, 95 C3
Wauchope, NSW 41 F2
Wauchope Roadhouse, NT
    210 B4
Waukaringa (Ruins), SA
    153 F4
Wave Hill, NSW 37 G2
Wave Hill, NT 205 E5
Wavell Heights, QLD 108 D1
Waverley, NSW 29 G2
Waverley, QLD 116 B6
Waverley Downs, NSW
    31 G3
Waverney, QLD 115 E6
Waverton, NSW 27 F6, 29 F1
Wayatinah, TAS 236 B1
Wayville, SA 141 B6
Wayville, SA 144 C1
Weabonga, NSW 40 D1
Wearne, NSW 34 B3
Webbs, NSW 39 G3
Wedderburn, NSW 28 A6
Wedderburn, VIC 77 G4
Wedderburn Junction, VIC
    77 G4
Wee Elwah, NSW 38 B4
Wee Jasper, NSW 44 D2
Wee Waa, NSW 33 H5,
    34 A5
Weebo, WA 183 F6
Weedallion, NSW 39 F6
Weegena, TAS 233 H3,
    234 A3
Weelamurra, QLD 120 A3
Weelarrana, WA 183 E3
Weemelah, NSW 33 H3,
    34 A3
Weeragua, VIC 81 E5
Weerangourt, VIC 82 C3
Weerite, VIC 83 F4, 88 D3
Weetah, TAS 233 H3, 234 A3
Weetaliba, NSW 40 A2
Weetangera, ACT 20 A2
Weethalle, NSW 38 D6
Weetulta, SA 152 D6,
    154 D1
Wee-Wee-Rup, VIC 78 A2
Wehla, VIC 77 G5

Wirraminna, SA 152 B2
Wirrappa, SA 152 C2
Wirrealpa, SA 153 E2, 159 E1
Wirrega, SA 155 G3
Wirrida, SA 147 H6
Wirrilyerna, QLD 114 B4
Wirring, WA 189 B3
Wirrinya, NSW 39 F5
Wirrulla, SA 151 H4
Wiseleigh, VIC 80 B5, 86 D2
Wisemans Ferry, NSW 40 C5
Wishart, QLD 109 E4
Wistow, SA 145 H4
Witchcliffe, WA 176 B5, 189 B4
Witchelina, SA 148 D6, 152 D1
Witchitie, SA 153 E3
Withcott, QLD 135 D4
Withers, WA 187 A5
Withersfield, QLD 116 C4
Withywine, QLD 115 F4
Witta, QLD 131B5
Wittenburra, QLD 119 G3
Wittenoom, WA 182D2
Wivenhoe, TAS 233F1
Woden Valley, ACT 20 B4, 21 C2
Wodonga, VIC 79 G3, 99 B1
Wogamia, NSW 61 A2
Wogarl, WA 175 F6, 177 F1
Wogarno, WA 175 E1, 182 D6
Wokalup, WA 187 C3
Wollar, NSW 40 B3
Wolli Creek, NSW 29 F3
Wollombi, NSW 40 C4
Wollomombi, NSW 35 E6
Wollongbar, NSW 46 C4
Wollongong, NSW 45 G1, 55 C2
Wollstonecraft, NSW 27 F6, 29 F1
Wollun, NSW 34 D6
Wolseley, SA 155 G4, 163 D1
Wolumia, NSW 45 F5
Wolverton, QLD 113 B4
Wolvi, QLD 125 B6, 131 B2
Womalilla, QLD 120 C1
Wombat, NSW 39 G6, 44 D1
Wombelano, VIC 76 B6
Womboota, NSW 43 F3
Wombungi, NT 204 D1
Won Wron, VIC 85 G4
Wonboyn, NSW 45 F6
Wondai, QLD 121 G1
Wondalga, NSW 44 C2
Wondecla, QLD 123 A5
Wondinong, WA 182 D6
Wondoola, QLD 110 D5
Wonga, NSW 31 F4 36 D3
Wonga Lilli, NSW 31 G5
Wonga Lower, QLD 125 A6
Wonga Park, VIC 71 G2
Wonga Upper, QLD 125 A6
Wongabinda, NSW 34 B4
Wongalara, NSW 37 H2
Wongalee, QLD 115 G1
Wongan Hills, WA 174 D4
Wonganoo, WA 183 F5
Wongarbon, NSW 39 G3
Wongarra, VIC 83 H5, 89 F5
Wongatoa, NSW 38 B6
Wongawallan, QLD 127 A3

Wongawol, WA 183 G4
Wongianna (Ruins), SA 148 D6
Wongulla, SA 155 F1
Wonnerup, WA 189 D1
Wonthaggi, VIC 84 D4
Wonwondah East, VIC 76 D5, 97 A1
Wonwondah North, VIC 76 D5, 97 A1
Wonyip, VIC 85 F4
Woodanilling, WA 177 E4
Woodbine, NSW 28 A5
Woodbine, QLD 135 D5
Woodbourne, VIC 83 H2, 84 D1, 89 G1
Woodbridge, TAS 236 D4
Woodbridge, WA 171 F2
Woodburn, NSW 35 G3
Woodburn, WA 193 C3
Woodbury, TAS 234 D6
Woodcroft, NSW 26 A4
Woodcroft, SA 144 C5
Woodenbong, NSW 35 F2, 133 B4
Woodend, NSW 44 B2
Woodend, VIC 84 B1, 90 C2
Woodfield, VIC 79 E6
Woodford, NSW 49 G5
Woodford, QLD 121 G2, 131 B6
Woodforde, SA 143 E6,145 E1
Woodgate, QLD 117 H6, 125 A2
Woodglen, VIC 86 B2
Woodie Woodie Mine, WA 183 F1
Woodlands, QLD 120 C2
Woodlands, WA 170 B2, 182 D4
Woodlawn, NSW 46 B3
Woodlawn, QLD 135 B2
Woodleigh, WA 182 B5
Woodpark, NSW 26 C6, 28 C1
Woodridge, QLD 109 E5
Woodroffe, NT 199 G6
Woods Point, VIC 85 F2
Woods Well, SA 155 F3
Woodsdale, TAS 237 E1
Woodside, SA 145 H1, 155 E2
Woodside, VIC 85 G4
Woodside Beach, VIC 85 G4
Woodstock, NSW 39 G5
Woodstock, QLD 111 F6, 112 B6, 115 E3
Woodstock, TAS 236 D4
Woodstock, VIC 77 H5, 84 C2, 95 D1
Woodstock, WA 183 E1
Woodvale, VIC 78 A5
Woodville, SA 142 B6
Woodville Gardens, SA 142 B6
Woodville North, SA 142 B6
Woodville Park, SA 142 B6
Woodville South, SA 142 B6
Woody Point, QLD 107 G4
Woogenellup, WA 193 C2
Woohlpooer, VIC 82 D1, 97 A4
Woolah, WA 181 D3
Woolamai, VIC 84 D4

Woolamia, NSW 61 B3
Woolbrook, NSW 40 D1, 34 D6
Wooleen, WA 182 C5
Woolerina, QLD 120 B3
Woolgoolga, NSW 35 G5, 53 D2
Woolgorong, WA 182 C6
Wooli, NSW 35 G5
Woolibar, WA 178 B5
Woolla Downs, NT 209 H6, 210 A6, 213 H1, 214 A1
Woollahra, NSW 29 G2
Woolloomooloo, NSW 27 G6, 29 G1
Woolloongabba, QLD 105 C6, 108 D3
Woolner, NT 197 D3, 198 B4, 201 E3
Woolomin, NSW 40 C1
Woolooga, QLD 121 G1
Woolooma, NSW 40 C2
Woolooware, NSW 29 F5
Wooloowin, QLD 108 C1
Woolshed Flat, SA 152 D4
Woolsthorpe, VIC 83 E3, 88 A3
Wooltana, SA 153 F1
Woolwich, NSW 27 F6, 29 F1
Woomargama, NSW 44 B3
Woomelang, VIC 77 E2
Woomera, SA 152 C2
Woondum, QLD 131 B2
Woongoolba, QLD 127 B1
Woonigan, QLD 114 B2
Woorabinda, QLD 117 E5
Wooragee, VIC 79 G4, 99 B1
Woorak, VIC 76 C4
Wooramel Roadhouse, WA 182 B4
Woorarra, VIC 85 F5
Woori Yallock, VIC 84 D2
Woorim, QLD 107 H1, 131 D6
Woorinen, VIC 75 G6, 77 G1
Woorlba, WA 185 A4
Woorndoo, VIC 83 E3, 88 B1
Wooroloo, WA 174 C6, 176 C1
Wooroona, QLD 114 A1
Wooroonook, VIC 77 F4
Woosang, VIC 77 G4
Wootaroo (St Helens), QLD 137 B5
Wootha, QLD 131 B5
Wootton, NSW 41 E3
Woronora, NSW 28 D4
Woronora Heights, NSW 28 D4
Worrigee, NSW 61 B2
Worsley, WA 187 C4
Worsley Refinery, WA 176 C3
Wotonga, QLD 116 C2
Wowan, QLD 117 E5, 129 A5
Woy Woy, NSW 40 D5, 51 B5
Wrattonbully, SA 155 G5, 163 D3
Wreck Bay, NSW 61 B5
Wright Bay, SA 163 A3
Wrightley, VIC 79 E5
Wrotham Park, QLD 111 G3
Wubin, WA 174 D3
Wudinna, SA 152 A5

Wujal Wujal, QLD 111 H2
Wuk Wuk, VIC 80 A6, 85 H2, 86 B2
Wulagi, NT 198 D2
Wulgulmerang, VIC 80 C4
Wumalgi, QLD 117 E3
Wundowie, WA 174 C6, 176 C1
Wunghnu, VIC 78 D3
Wungong, WA 173 F3
Wunkar, SA 155 G11, 65 A4
Wurankuwu, NT 200 C2
Wurruk, VIC 85 G3, 86 A4
Wurtulla, QLD 131 C5
Wuttagoona, NSW 38 B1
Wutul, QLD 121 G2
Wyaga, QLD 121 E3
Wyalkatchem, WA 175 E5
Wyalong, NSW 39 E6
Wyan, NSW 35 F3
Wyandotte, QLD 111 H5
Wyandra, QLD 120 A2
Wyanga, NSW 39 F3
Wyangala, NSW 39 H6
Wybong, NSW 59 C1
Wycarbah, QLD 117 E4, 129 A4
Wycheproof, VIC 77 F3
Wychitella, VIC 77 G4
Wycliffe Well Roadhouse, NT 210 B4
Wydgee, WA 175 E1
Wye River, VIC 83 H5, 89 F5
Wyee, NSW 40 D4, 51 C2
Wyeebo, VIC 79 H4, 80 A2, 99 D1
Wyelangta, VIC 83 G5, 89 E5
Wyena, TAS 234 D2
Wyerba, QLD 121 G4
Wyloo, WA 182 C2
Wyloona, NSW 37 H1
Wymah, NSW 44 B3
Wyndham, NSW 45 F5
Wyndham, WA 181 D3
Wynn Vale, SA 142 D4
Wynnum, QLD 109 F2
Wynnum West, QLD 109 F2
Wynyangoo, WA 182 D6
Wynyard, NSW 25 C3
Wynyard, TAS 233 E1
Wyomi, SA 163 A2
Wyoming, NSW 38 B6
Wyong, NSW 40 D5, 51 C3
Wyong Creek, NSW 51 B3
Wyreema, QLD 135 C4
Wyrra, NSW 39 E5
Wyseby, QLD 116 D6
Wyuna, VIC 78 C3

Yaamba, QLD 117 F4, 129 A3
Yaapeet, VIC 76 C2
Yabba Nth, VIC 78 D3
Yabba Vale, QLD 131 A3
Yaboroo, QLD 116 D1
Yabulu, QLD 112 B5
Yacka, SA 153 E5
Yackandandah, VIC 79 G4, 99 B1
Yadlamulka, SA 152 D3
Yagoona, NSW 28 D2
Yahl, SA 163 D6
Yakabindie, WA 183 F6
Yakara, QLD 119 G3

A Guide to First Aid

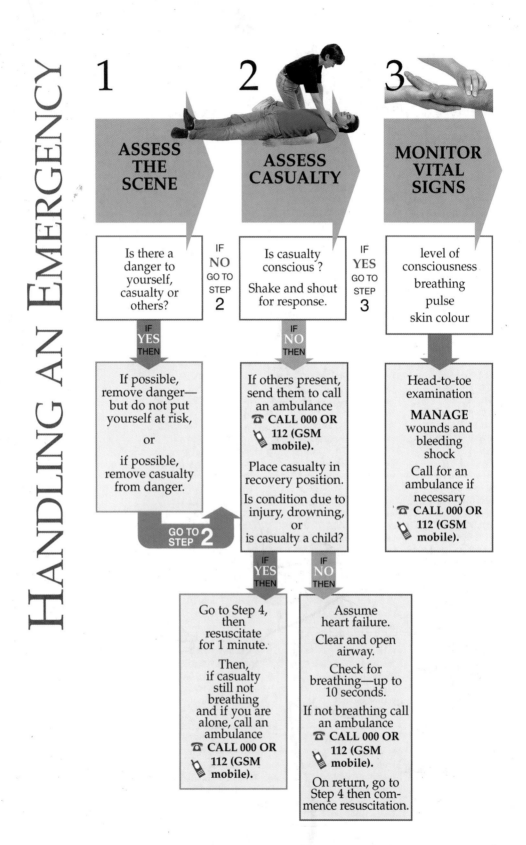

HANDLING AN EMERGENCY

1

ASSESS THE SCENE

2

ASSESS CASUALTY

3

MONITOR VITAL SIGNS

Is there a danger to yourself, casualty or others?

IF NO GO TO STEP 2

Is casualty conscious? Shake and shout for response.

IF YES GO TO STEP 3

level of consciousness
breathing
pulse
skin colour

IF YES THEN

If possible, remove danger— but do not put yourself at risk,

or

if possible, remove casualty from danger.

GO TO STEP 2

IF NO THEN

If others present, send them to call an ambulance
☎ **CALL 000 OR** 📱 **112 (GSM mobile).**

Place casualty in recovery position.

Is condition due to injury, drowning, or is casualty a child?

Head-to-toe examination

MANAGE wounds and bleeding shock

Call for an ambulance if necessary
☎ **CALL 000 OR** 📱 **112 (GSM mobile).**

IF YES THEN

Go to Step 4, then resuscitate for 1 minute.

Then, if casualty still not breathing and if you are alone, call an ambulance
☎ **CALL 000 OR** 📱 **112 (GSM mobile).**

IF NO THEN

Assume heart failure.

Clear and open airway.

Check for breathing—up to 10 seconds.

If not breathing call an ambulance
☎ **CALL 000 OR** 📱 **112 (GSM mobile).**

On return, go to Step 4 then commence resuscitation.